Catholicism FOR DUMMIES®

2ND EDITION

by Rev. John Trigilio, Jr., PhD, ThD and Rev. Kenneth Brighenti, PhD

Nihil Obstat: Rev. Msgr. James Cafone, STD, Censor Librorum
Imprimatur: Most Rev. John J. Myers, DD, JCD, Archbishop of Newark
August 30, 2011 — Newark, New Jersey

*The Nihil Obstat and Imprimatur are official declarations that a book or pamphlet is free
of doctrinal or moral error. No implication is contained therein that those who granted the
Nihil Obstat and the Imprimatur agree with the contents, opinions, or statements expressed.*

WILEY

John Wiley & Sons, Inc.

Catholicism For Dummies®, 2nd Edition

Published by
John Wiley & Sons, Inc.
111 River St.
Hoboken, NJ 07030-5774
www.wiley.com

Published by John Wiley & Sons, Inc., Hoboken, New Jersey

Published simultaneously in Canada

For general information on our other products and services, please contact our Customer Care Department within the U.S. at 877-762-2974, outside the U.S. at 317-572-3993, or fax 317-572-4002.

For technical support, please visit www.wiley.com/techsupport.

Wiley publishes in a variety of print and electronic formats and by print-on-demand. Some material included with standard print versions of this book may not be included in e-books or in print-on-demand. If this book refers to media such as a CD or DVD that is not included in the version you purchased, you may download this material at http://booksupport.wiley.com. For more information about Wiley products, visit www.wiley.com.

Library of Congress Control Number: 2011939647

ISBN 978-1-118-07778-8 (pbk); ISBN 978-1-118-17042-7 (ebk); ISBN 978-1-118-17043-4 (ebk); ISBN 978-1-118-17044-1 (ebk)

Manufactured in the United States of America

WILEY

About the Authors

Rev. John Trigilio, Jr., PhD, ThD, serves as pastor of Our Lady of Good Counsel (Marysville, Pennsylvania) and St. Bernadette (Duncannon, Pennsylvania). He is President of the Confraternity of Catholic Clergy. Father Trigilio co-hosts with Fr. Brighenti several weekly programs on the Eternal Word Television Network (EWTN): *Web of Faith, Council of Faith, Crash Course in Catholicism, Crash Course on Pope John Paul II,* and *Crash Course on the Saints.* He is a member of the Fellowship of Catholic Scholars and was ordained a priest for the Diocese of Harrisburg (Pennsylvania) in 1988. Father Trigilio can also be found on *Catholic Answers Radio.* He preaches retreats, gives parish missions, and speaks at Catholic conferences across the U.S. and Canada. His personal website is www.trigilio.com.

Rev. Kenneth Brighenti, PhD, is Vice Rector for Pastoral Formation and Assistant Professor at Mount St. Mary Seminary and University (Emmitsburg, Maryland). He is a member of the Board of Directors for the Confraternity of Catholic Clergy. Father Brighenti also served as a U.S. Naval Reserve Chaplain for ten years and in 1988 was ordained a priest for the Diocese of Metuchen (New Jersey), where he served as pastor of St. Ann's Parish (Raritan, New Jersey) for more than eight years. Fr. Brighenti has coauthored the following books with Fr. Trigilio: *Women in the Bible For Dummies, John Paul II For Dummies, Saints For Dummies, Catholic Mass For Dummies, Everything Bible,* and *Catholic Answer Book: 300 of the Most Frequently Asked Questions.*

Dedication

This book is dedicated to Our Lady, Queen of the Clergy, and Saint Joseph, Patron of the Universal Church.

To Blessed Pope John Paul II, of happy memory, who inspired us to work on this project by his life and pontificate.

To His Holiness Pope Benedict XVI, the Bishop of Rome, Vicar of Christ, Supreme Head of the Catholic Church, and the Servant of the Servants of God.

To His Eminence, Raymond Cardinal Burke, Prefect of the Apostolic Signatura; Most Rev. Kevin Rhoades, Bishop of Fort Wayne-South Bend, Indiana; Most Rev. David O'Connell, CM, Bishop of Trenton, New Jersey; Rev. Msgr. Roger Roensch, Director of the Bishops' Office for U.S. Visitors to the Vatican; and Rev. Msgr. Walter Rossi, Rector of the Basilica of the National Shrine of the Immaculate Conception, Washington, DC.

And to Reverend Mother Angelica, PCPA, founder of EWTN, who despite her many sufferings (both physical and by persecution) has never stopped loving, hoping, and serving the Lord Jesus in His Holy Catholic Church by spreading the Word and teaching and defending the faith through electronic modern media and telecommunications.

We also dedicate this book to our loving parents, who gave us life and love and shared their Catholic faith:

Percy and Norma Brighenti

John and Elizabeth Trigilio

Finally, in loving memory of the following faithful departed:

John Trigilio, Sr. (1927–1998), father

Joseph P. Trigilio (1964–1997), brother

Michael S. Trigilio (1966–1992), brother

Mary Jo Trigilio (1960), sister

Rev. Fr. Stefan Katarzynski, cousin

Authors' Acknowledgments

Father Brighenti and Father Trigilio are indebted to the following for their assistance, encouragement, opinions, guidance, advice, and input throughout this project:

Rev. Msgr. James Cafone (Seton Hall University); Rev. Msgr. Steven P. Rohlfs, S.T.D. (Rector, Mt. St. Mary Seminary); Rev. Fr. Robert J. Levis, PhD; Rev. Fred Miller; Rev. Fr. Thomas Nicastro, Jr.; Rev. Fr. Dennis G. Dalessandro; Louis and Sandy Falconeri & family; Doctors Keith and Christina Burkhart & family; Thomas & Bridgette McKenna; Michael Drake; Dr. Elizabeth Frauenhoffer; and a special note of thanks and gratitude to the parishioners at Our Lady of Good Counsel (Marysville, Pennsylvania) and Saint Bernadette (Duncannon, Pennsylvania), and the faculty, staff, and students of Mt. Saint Mary Seminary (Emmitsburg, Maryland), and the priests and deacons of the Confraternity of Catholic Clergy.

We are also grateful to the Poor Clare Nuns of Perpetual Adoration (Hanceville, Alabama), the Religious Teachers Filippini (New Jersey), the Discalced Carmelite Nuns (Erie, Pennsylvania), and the Dominican Nuns of the Perpetual Rosary (Lancaster, Pennsylvania) for their prayers and support throughout our seminary formation and sacred priesthood.

Publisher's Acknowledgments

We're proud of this book; please send us your comments at http://dummies.custhelp.com. For other comments, please contact our Customer Care Department within the U.S. at 877-762-2974, outside the U.S. at 317-572-3993, or fax 317-572-4002.

Some of the people who helped bring this book to market include the following:

Acquisitions, Editorial, and Vertical Websites

Project Editor: Heike Baird

   (Previous Edition: Tim Gallan)

Acquisitions Editor: Tracy Boggier

Copy Editor: Christine Pingleton

   (Previous Edition: Esmeralda St. Clair)

Assistant Editor: David Lutton

Editorial Program Coordinator: Joe Niesen

Technical Editor: Rev. Eric Augenstein

Senior Editorial Manager: Jennifer Ehrlich

Editorial Assistants: Rachelle S. Amick, Alexa Koschier

Art Coordinator: Alicia B. South

Cover Photos: © iStockphoto.com / kryczka

Cartoons: Rich Tennant (www.the5thwave.com)

Composition Services

Project Coordinator: Sheree Montgomery

Layout and Graphics: Claudia Bell, Joyce Haughey, Corrie Socolovitch

Proofreaders: Rebecca Denoncour, Toni Settle

Indexer: Dakota Indexing

Special Help: Joan Friedman, Maureen Sweeney

Publishing and Editorial for Consumer Dummies

   Kathleen Nebenhaus, Vice President and Executive Publisher

   Kristin Ferguson-Wagstaffe, Product Development Director

   Ensley Eikenburg, Associate Publisher, Travel

   Kelly Regan, Editorial Director, Travel

Publishing for Technology Dummies

   Andy Cummings, Vice President and Publisher

Composition Services

   Debbie Stailey, Director of Composition Services

Contents at a Glance

Introduction 1

Part 1: What Do Catholics Believe? 7
Chapter 1: What It Means to Be Catholic................................9
Chapter 2: Having Faith in God's Revealed Word.....................21
Chapter 3: In the Beginning: Catholic Teachings on Creation and Original Sin.......37
Chapter 4: Believing in Jesus...........................47
Chapter 5: Defining "The Church" and What Membership Means 65
Chapter 6: Who's Who in the Catholic Church 73

Part 11: Celebrating the Mysteries of Faith.............. 95
Chapter 7: Body and Soul: Worshipping Catholic Style.................97
Chapter 8: Entering the Church: Baptism, Communion, and Confirmation 107
Chapter 9: The Sacraments of Service and Healing 125
Chapter 10: Celebrating the Catholic Mass 145

Part 111: Living a Saintly Life 173
Chapter 11: Obeying the Rules: Catholic Law 175
Chapter 12: Loving and Honoring: The Ten Commandments...............187
Chapter 13: Being Good When Sinning Is So Easy 203
Chapter 14: Standing Firm: The Church's Stance on Some Sticky Issues..............219

Part 1V: Praying and Using Devotions 245
Chapter 15: Growing in the Faith.........................247
Chapter 16: Showing Your Love for God.......................261
Chapter 17: Expressing Affection for Mary 275
Chapter 18: Honoring the Catholic Saints 291
Chapter 19: Practicing Catholic Traditions 311

Part V: The Part of Tens 329
Chapter 20: Ten Famous Catholics....................331
Chapter 21: Ten (Plus One) Popular Catholic Saints 341
Chapter 22: Ten Popular Catholic Places 351

Part VI: Appendixes *361*
Appendix A: A Brief History of Catholicism 363
Appendix B: Popular Catholic Prayers................................... 391
Index *399*

Table of Contents

Introduction 1

About This Book 1
Conventions Used in This Book 2
Foolish Assumptions...3
How This Book Is Organized 3
    Part I: What Do Catholics Believe? 4
    Part II: Celebrating the Mysteries of Faith 4
    Part III: Living a Saintly Life 4
    Part IV: Praying and Using Devotions 5
    Part V: The Part of Tens 5
    Part VI: Appendixes 5
Icons Used in This Book 5
Where to Go from Here...6

Part 1: What Do Catholics Believe? 7

Chapter 1: What It Means to Be Catholic. 9

What Exactly Is Catholicism Anyway? 9
Knowing What the Catholic Church Teaches 11
    Grasping the basic beliefs.......................................11
    Respecting the role of the Church and its leaders 13
Worshipping as a Catholic: The Holy Mass........................15
    Bringing body and soul into the mix 16
    Participating inside and out 16
Behaving Like a Catholic 17
    Following the general ground rules.........................17
    Avoiding sin 18
    Heeding the Church's stance on tough issues 19
Praying as a Catholic: Showing Your Devotion 19
    Praying and using devotions 19
    Realizing the importance of Mary and the saints 20
    Following traditions..20

Chapter 2: Having Faith in God's Revealed Word. 21

How Do You Know If You Have Faith? 21
Having Faith in Revelation..22
    Faith in the written word: The Bible.......................23
    Faith in the spoken word: Sacred Tradition 27

Backing Up Your Faith with Reason: Summa Theologica.......................33
Through motion 34
Through causality..35
Through necessity 35
Through gradation...35
Through governance 36

**Chapter 3: In the Beginning: Catholic Teachings
on Creation and Original Sin 37**

Making Something out of Nothing...38
Breathing Life into the World: Creationism or Evolution?......................38
Angels and Devils: Following God or Lucifer 40
Infused knowledge, eternal decisions 40
The angels' test and the devil's choice.............................40
Witnessing the Original Sin 41
Tempting our first parents 41
Losing gifts...42
Wounding our nature 43
Being redeemed by God's grace 43
Facing the four last things 44
Anticipating What's to Come: Moving toward the End of Creation 44
The Second Coming..45
Resurrection of the dead 46
General judgment...46
The end of the world 46

Chapter 4: Believing in Jesus 47

Understanding Jesus, the God-Man...47
The human nature of Jesus 48
The divine nature of Jesus..51
The Savior of our sins; the Redeemer of the world.......................52
The obedient Son of God 53
The Gospel Truth: Examining Four Written Records of Jesus................54
Catholic beliefs about the Gospel.......................................54
How the Gospels came to be 55
Comparing Gospels...56
Dealing with Heresy and Some Other $10 Words....................60
Gnosticism and Docetism 61
Arianism..62
Nestorianism 63
Monophysitism 63

Chapter 5: Defining "The Church" and What Membership Means . . .65

Establishing a Foundation: Built on Rock.....................................65
Seeing the Church as the Body of Christ and Communion of Saints......66
Understanding the Four Marks of the Church................................67

Fulfilling Its Mission...69
  The priestly office: Sanctifying through the sacraments...............70
  The prophetic office: Teaching through the Magisterium 70
  The kingly office: Shepherding and governing
    through the hierarchy 71
Membership Has Its Benefits 72

Chapter 6: Who's Who in the Catholic Church **73**
Getting to Know the Pope...74
  How the pope gets his job 74
  Is he really infallible?...77
  Now that's job security 82
  Where the pope hangs his hat 83
Who's Next in the Ecclesiastical Scheme of Things........................84
  Cardinals...84
  Bishops and archbishops 86
  The vicar general 88
  The parish priest..89
  Deacons..92
  Monks and nuns, brothers and sisters.....................................92

Part II: Celebrating the Mysteries of Faith **95**

Chapter 7: Body and Soul: Worshipping Catholic Style **97**
Getting Your Body and Soul into the Act 97
Understanding Some Symbols and Gestures 98
  The sign of the cross 98
  The genuflection 99
  The crucifix...99
  Holy water..99
Sensing God...101
  Through sight...101
  Through touch 103
  Through smell 104
  Through sound...105
  Through taste 106

**Chapter 8: Entering the Church: Baptism,
Communion, and Confirmation**. **107**
Come On In — The Water's Fine...107
  Becoming Christ's kith and kin 108
  Washing away original sin 109
  Baptizing with water...110
  Receiving the sacrament of Baptism in other ways..................115

The Holy Eucharist..118
Understanding the consecrated host.................................118
Discovering who can receive Holy Communion 119
Partaking of First Holy Communion 121
Coming of Age: Confirmation 121

Chapter 9: The Sacraments of Service and Healing **125**
The Sacraments of Service and Community 125
Marriage — Catholic style 126
Holy Orders 132
The Sacraments of Mercy and Healing 135
Penance..135
Anointing of the Sick...142

Chapter 10: Celebrating the Catholic Mass.....................**145**
What Exactly Is the Mass?...145
Honoring the Sabbath publicly 147
Participating fully...147
Uniting past, present, and future 148
The Two Parts of the Mass...148
Beginning the Mass...149
Acknowledging sin (Penitential Act) 150
Gloria 151
Opening Prayer (Collect) 152
The Liturgy of the Word..152
The Liturgy of the Eucharist..157
Vatican II and the Celebration of Mass 165
Allowing worship in vernacular languages.....................166
Other changes resulting from Vatican II 166
Checking out the Roman Missal, Third Edition 167
Understanding the Latin roots..167
Seeing why change was necessary 168
Knowing what it means for you in the pew 168
Adjusting the Mass for the Occasion 169
Weekday and Sunday 169
Holy days of obligation 169
Simple and solemn celebrations..170
Spiritual Seasons of the Year 171
Christ Our Light: The first half of the liturgical year....171
Christ Our Life: The second half of the liturgical year....172

Part III: Living a Saintly Life **173**

Chapter 11: Obeying the Rules: Catholic Law....................**175**
Following the Eternal Law of God..175
The divine positive law 176
The natural moral law 177
The human positive law...179

Playing by the Church's Rules 183
   Attending Mass on all Sundays and holy days of obligation 183
   Receiving the Holy Eucharist during Easter season 184
   Confessing your sins at least once a year 184
   Fasting and abstaining on appointed days 185
   Contributing to the support of the Church 185
   Observing Church marriage laws 186
   Supporting Missionary Work of the Church 186

Chapter 12: Loving and Honoring: The Ten Commandments **187**
Demonstrating Love for God 188
   I: Honor God 188
   II: Honor God's name 190
   III: Honor God's day 191
Loving Your Neighbor 193
   IV: Honor your parents 193
   V: Honor human life 194
   VI and IX: Honor human sexuality 196
   VII and X: Honor the property of others 199
   VIII: Honor the truth 199
Coming Out Even Steven 201

Chapter 13: Being Good When Sinning Is So Easy **203**
Cultivating Good Habits 204
   Prudence: Knowing what, when, and how 204
   Justice: Treating others fairly 206
   Temperance: Moderating pleasure 208
   Fortitude: Doing what's right come hell or high water 209
The Seven Deadly Sins 210
   Pride goeth before the fall 212
   Envying what others have or enjoy 213
   Lusting after fruit that's forbidden 214
   Anger to the point of seeking revenge 215
   Gluttony: Too much food or firewater 216
   Greed: The desire for more and more 217
   Sloth: Lazy as a lotus-eater 217

**Chapter 14: Standing Firm: The Church's
Stance on Some Sticky Issues** **219**
Celibacy and the Male Priesthood 220
   Flying solo for life 220
   No-woman's-land 226
Matters of Life and Death 228
   Abortion 228
   Euthanasia 231
   The death penalty 233
   The Just War Doctrine 234

Planning Your Family Naturally...237
    The moral argument against artificial contraception 238
    The natural alternative to contraception 239
    What if you can't conceive naturally?.........................241
Defending Traditional Family Life 242

Part IV: Praying and Using Devotions 245

Chapter 15: Growing in the Faith 247

Having a Personal Relationship with God through Prayer 247
    Practicing the four types of prayer 248
    Getting to know spontaneous and formal prayer................249
Praying in Private and in a Community 251
    Taking personal time with God: Private prayer................251
    Joining others for communal prayer...........................253
    Saying the Lord's Prayer.....................................254
Taking It to the Next Level: The Stages of Spiritual Growth 256
    Purgative: Practicing self-denial and sacrifice 256
    Illuminative: Distinguishing good from evil..................258
    Unitive: Connecting with God.................................259

Chapter 16: Showing Your Love for God. 261

Going Beyond Your Basic Duty...261
    Knowing when and where to pray devotions....................262
    Separating devotions from Mass 262
Running the Gamut of Devotions......................................263
    Praying novenas to the saints 263
    Loving litanies 264
    Looking at statues and icons.................................265
    Making pilgrimages...266
    Going on a retreat 267
    Wearing sacred gear 267
    Praying the Rosary 268
    Saying the Divine Mercy Chaplet 272
    The Way of the Cross 273

Chapter 17: Expressing Affection for Mary 275

No, Catholics Don't Worship Mary.....................................275
What Catholics Believe about Mary....................................278
    She's the Mother of God 278
    She's the Mother of the Church...............................279
    She's the Mother of the Mystical Body of Christ 280
    She was conceived through Immaculate Conception 280
    She went to heaven, body and soul...........................283
    Her never-ending virginity 284

Up Close and Personal with Mary 285
    May crowning...285
    First Saturdays 286
    Marian shrines and apparitions...............................287

Chapter 18: Honoring the Catholic Saints **291**
    Having a Place in the Hearts of Catholics.....................291
    Honoring God's Good Friends....................................293
    It's All about Intercession.......................................294
    Recognizing a Saint...296
        Looking at the process to becoming a saint..............297
        Going through the investigations for sainthood.........298
        Experiencing the beatification and canonization Mass 302
    A Saint for Every Day of the Year 303
    Discovering the Communion of Saints..........................304
        Saints in heaven 305
        Believers on earth..306
        Souls in purgatory..307

Chapter 19: Practicing Catholic Traditions **311**
    Adoring the Blessed Sacrament................................311
        Participating in Benediction.................................312
        Adoring at church during Perpetual Adoration
          or the 40-hour devotion...................................313
    Representing Life's Journey: Other Religious Processions.........316
    Meatless Fridays 317
        The tradition of abstaining 318
        Substituting Corporal and Spiritual
          Works of Mercy for abstinence 319
    Using Sacramentals 319
        Signifying death with ashes 320
        Commemorating with blessed palms.....................321
        Receiving the blessing of throats..........................321
        Exorcising demons 321
        Tolling bells..322
    Celebrating Year-Round..323
        Feast of the Epiphany.......................................325
        Feast of Candlemas...326
        St. Patrick's Day 326
        St. Joseph's Day 326
        Marian Feasts in May.......................................327
        Feast of St. Anthony of Padua 327
        Feast of St. Thérèse of Lisieux.............................327
        Feast of Our Lady of Guadalupe............................328

Part V: The Part of Tens **329**

Chapter 20: Ten Famous Catholics **331**
Blessed Mother Teresa of Calcutta (1910–1997) 331
Blessed Pope John Paul II (1920–2005) 333
Archbishop Fulton J. Sheen (1895–1979) 335
Mother Angelica (1923) 336
John F. Kennedy (1917–1963) 337
Alfred E. Smith (1873–1944) 338
Father Edward Flanagan (1886–1948) 338
John Ronald Reuel Tolkien (1892–1973) 339
Gilbert Keith Chesterton (1874–1936) 339
Christopher Columbus (1451–1506) 339

Chapter 21: Ten (Plus One) Popular Catholic Saints **341**
St. Peter (Died around A.D. 64) 341
St. Jude (Died during the first century A.D.) 342
St. Benedict (480–circa 543) 343
St. Dominic de Guzman (1170–1221) 344
St. Francis of Assisi (1181–1226) 344
St. Anthony of Padua (1195-1231) 345
St. Thomas Aquinas (1225–1274) 346
St. Ignatius of Loyola (1491–1556) 347
St. Bernadette Soubirous (1844–1879) 348
St. Thérèse of Lisieux (1873–1897) 349
St. Pio of Pietrelcina (1887–1968) 350

Chapter 22: Ten Popular Catholic Places **351**
Rome 351
The Basilica de Guadalupe 353
San Giovanni Rotondo, Italy 354
The Basilica of Czestochowa, Poland 354
The Basilica of Lourdes, France 355
Fatima, Portugal 356
The Cathedral of Notre Dame 357
The National Shrine of the Immaculate Conception 358
The Minor Basilica of Saint Anne de Beaupré 359
The Shrine of the Most Blessed Sacrament 359

Part VI: Appendixes **361**

Appendix A: A Brief History of Catholicism **363**
Ancient Times (A.D. 33–741) 363
Non-Christian Rome (A.D. 33–312) 363
Christian Rome (A.D. 313–475) 365

Barbarian invasions and the fall of Rome (A.D. 476–570)............366
Pope St. Gregory the Great to Charles Martel (590–741)..............367
The Middle Ages (A.D. 800–1500) 368
Christendom: One big, mighty kingdom 368
The Golden Age..371
The downward spiral 372
The Reformation to the Modern Era (1517–Today)...............................375
The growing need for reform 375
The reformers..377
The Catholic Church's response: The Counter Reformation.......380
The Age of Reason 381
The Age of Revolution 382
The Modern Era 385

Appendix B: Popular Catholic Prayers..........................391

Latin Rite (Western Catholic) Prayers 391
Our Father (Pater Noster)...391
Hail Mary (Ave Maria) 392
Glory Be..392
Salve Regina..392
Memorare..393
Act of Contrition 393
Prayer to Guardian Angel..394
Grace Before/After Meals...394
Prayer to St. Michael the Archangel..395
Act of Faith...395
Act of Hope 396
Act of Love (Charity)..396
Byzantine and Eastern Catholic Prayers 396
Prayer before meals...396
Prayer after meals..396
Prayer of the Publican...397
Prayer of St. Ephraim of Syria 397
Prayer to St. Maron...397

Index.. *399*

Introduction

. . . .

*T*hree great religions trace their roots to the prophet Abraham: Judaism, Christianity, and Islam. And one of those religions, Christianity, is expressed in three different traditions: Catholicism, Protestantism, and Eastern Orthodoxy. You may already know that. You may also already know that, currently, more than 1 billion Catholics occupy the earth. That's approximately one-fifth of the world's population.

Whether you're Catholic or not, you may be totally clueless about or just unaware of some aspects of Catholic tradition, history, doctrine, worship, devotion, or culture. No sweat. Regardless of whether you're engaged, married, or related to a Catholic; your neighbor or co-worker is a Catholic; or you're just curious about what Catholics really do believe, this book is for you.

Catholicism For Dummies, 2nd Edition, realizes that you're smart and intelligent, but maybe you didn't attend Blessed Sacrament Grade School, St. Thomas Aquinas High School, or Catholic University of America. This book's goal is to give you a taste of Catholicism. It's not a Catechism or religion textbook but a casual, down-to-earth introduction for non-Catholics and a reintroduction for Catholics. It gives common-sense explanations about what Catholics believe and do in plain English, with just enough why and how thrown in to make solid sense.

Although *Catholicism For Dummies,* 2nd Edition, is no substitute for the official *Catechism of the Catholic Church,* our hope is that it'll wet your whistle. We don't cover everything about Catholicism, but we do discuss the basic stuff so that the next time you're invited to a Catholic wedding, baptism, funeral, confirmation, or First Communion, you won't be totally confused. And you may have an edge on other people in your life who are less informed about Catholicism than you.

About This Book

This book covers plenty of material on Catholicism — from doctrine to morality and from worship and liturgy to devotions — but you don't need a degree in theology to comprehend it. Everything is presented in an informal, easy-to-understand way.

This book is also a reference, unlike the schoolbooks you had as a kid. You don't have to read the chapters in order, one after the other, from front cover to back cover. You can just pick the topic that interests you or find the page that addresses the specific question you have. Or you can indiscriminately open the book and pick a place to begin reading.

Conventions Used in This Book

The Catholic Church is known to be among the top ten when it comes to keeping good records. In fact, the monks were the first to print the Bible, by hand, long before Gutenberg was able to mass-produce it on his printing press in 1450. And if you were baptized or married in a Catholic church, you can always find a record of your baptism in the parish where the baptism or marriage took place — even if it was more than say, 60 years ago. So naturally, after 2,000 years of baptisms, weddings, funerals, tribunals, annulments, Church councils, papal documents of one kind or another, *hagiographies* (biographies of the saints), investigations for canonization, and so on, the Church has its share of records and printed text, for sure. What's more, Latin is still the official language of the Church, so official documents are first written in Latin before being translated into English or some other language.

The upshot of the Church's penchant for carefully written and well-kept texts is that we couldn't avoid using Catholic-specific terms and some Latin in this book. However, we italicize difficult terms and then do our utmost to offer complete but easy-to-understand definitions and translations alongside those terms. If you'd like some help with the Latin, we suggest that you start with a copy of *Latin For Dummies* by Clifford A. Hull, Steven R. Perkins, and Tracy Barr (John Wiley & Sons, Inc.).

Throughout this book, if you see the word *orthodox* with a small letter *o*, it means correct or right believer. However, if you see the capital letter *O*, then *Orthodox* refers to the Eastern Orthodox Churches, such as the Greek, Russian, and Serbian Orthodox Churches.

Also, if you see the word *church* with a small letter *c*, it refers to a church building or parish, but *Church* with a capital *C* refers to the universal Catholic Church.

Bible references in this book use the traditional chapter and verse designation of a chapter number followed by a colon and the verse number(s). For example, Deuteronomy 6:4–6 refers to the sixth chapter of Deuteronomy from verse 4 all the way to and including verse 6. Unless we tell you otherwise, our Scripture references are from the Revised Standard Version (RSV).

Foolish Assumptions

While writing this book, we made some assumptions about you:

- ✔ You have Catholic friends, neighbors, or relatives, and you're curious about Catholicism and want to know a little more about it.

- ✔ You've heard or read something about Catholics or Catholicism, and you have questions about Catholic beliefs or practices.

- ✔ You may or may not be Catholic. Perhaps you were baptized Catholic but not raised Catholic. Maybe you're committed to a different faith, still searching, or have no faith to speak of. Regardless, you do want to know something about Catholics.

How This Book Is Organized

Two thousand years of history, theology, spirituality, prayer, devotion, worship, and morality can't be put into one small book. We've obviously left some stuff out. We've summarized plenty, too. Our goal is to give you the bottom line — the essential guts of Catholicism.

To make it easy for you to find the particular innards that you're interested in, we've divided this book into parts, each covering a particular topic. Each part contains chapters relating to that topic.

Rather than reinventing the wheel, we decided to take advantage of the wisdom of the Church, which uses four pillars of faith to divide the material contained in the *Catechism of the Catholic Church.* The *Catechism* is the formal collection of dogmas and doctrines of the *Magisterium:* the official teaching authority of Catholicism as exercised through the pope and the bishops in union with him around the world. (The word Magisterium comes from the Latin *magister,* meaning teacher.)

The pillars upon which the Catholic religion stands are these:

- ✔ **The Creed:** What is believed
- ✔ **The Sacraments:** Liturgically celebrating what is believed
- ✔ **The Commandments:** Living the faith
- ✔ **The Lord's Prayer:** Making the faith personal

The first four parts of this book correspond with these four pillars.

Part 1: What Do Catholics Believe?

This part deals with fundamentals of the Catholic faith; it zeroes in on the Creed, the first pillar. Church doctrines are rooted in divine revelation, which is communicated through Sacred Scripture and Sacred Tradition: the subjects of Chapter 2. We then walk through Catholic beliefs related to creation, Jesus, and the Church itself (including — in Chapter 6 — an introduction to the hierarchy and organization of the Catholic Church).

In Part I, we look at the principal tenets of this 2,000-year-old religion and connect the individual pieces (doctrines) like a jigsaw puzzle to show how they support the Catholic view (perspective) of the world.

Part 11: Celebrating the Mysteries of Faith

This part deals with the *liturgical* celebration of faith — the public worship of God. The second pillar of faith covered here consists of the Seven Sacraments (baptism, penance, confirmation, Holy Eucharist, matrimony, holy orders, and the Anointing of the Sick), which are not private but rather communal rituals that unite members and reinforce their beliefs.

Before we launch into discussion of the sacraments, we first look (in Chapter 7) at the essence of Catholic worship, which is both physical and spiritual in order to address the needs of body and soul. And after the sacraments, in Chapter 10, we detail the most common public celebration of the Catholic faith: the Mass.

Part 111: Living a Saintly Life

This part deals with the third pillar of faith as found in the Ten Commandments. The commandments are the basis for Catholic behavior — Catholic morality — which basically answers this question: How do Catholics put their Christian faith into practice? In other words, how do they live their faith from day to day through what they say and do?

We cover the moral laws of Catholicism as a natural extension of laws in general — rules or codes of conduct meant to protect members by promoting good behavior and discouraging bad. From the natural moral law to the Ten Commandments to the moral virtues and the seven deadly sins, we examine various boundaries of behavior. We also get specific in Chapter 14 about the Church's stand on some very controversial issues.

Part IV: Praying and Using Devotions

This part of the book deals with the fourth pillar of faith, the Our Father (or Lord's Prayer) Catholic devotions: special prayers and activities that Catholics say and do outside of the Mass and sacraments that continue and cultivate a personal relationship with God.

The Church believes that the ultimate goal of all true devotion is promoting, supporting, enhancing, and encouraging a strong, healthy, and total love of God. So this part begins with devotions centering on God alone and then covers devotions to those whom Catholics believe are God's faithful servants and friends: the saints. This part also explains that showing devotion to the Virgin Mary and other saints isn't considered worship; it's merely *honoring* special people.

Part V: The Part of Tens

Every *For Dummies* book has a Part of Tens. In this part, we give you ten famous Catholics, ten popular saints, and ten popular Catholic places. These people and places put faces and scenic backgrounds on the doctrines, morals, and rituals discussed throughout the book.

Part VI: Appendixes

In the back of this book, you can find a couple of very useful appendixes.

Appendix A contains a *very* condensed history of the Catholic Church from the ancient and medieval period, through the time of the Reformation and Counter-Reformation, through the Renaissance and Enlightenment, to the modern era.

Some of the most well-known and beloved Catholic prayers are presented in Appendix B.

Icons Used in This Book

This book uses icons to point out various types of information:

The From the Bible icon helps you make the connection between Catholicism and Sacred Scripture. If you read the text that's next to this icon, you'll see how Catholicism — the Mass, the Rosary, the hierarchy of the Church, and so on — is rooted in Scripture.

Ummm, well, we can't remember what this icon's supposed to point out. Just kidding. This icon draws your attention to information that's worth remembering because it's basic to Catholicism.

This icon alerts you to technical or historical background stuff that's not essential to know. Feel free to divert thine eyes whenever you see this icon.

This icon points out useful tidbits to help you make more sense out of something Catholic.

This icon points out cautionary areas of Catholicism, such as the obligation to attend Mass on Sunday or Saturday evening. (Not doing so without a legitimate excuse, such as illness or severe weather, is a grave sin.)

Where to Go from Here

Catholicism For Dummies, 2nd Edition, is sort of like Sunday dinner at an Italian grandmother's home. Nonna brings everything to the table: bread, antipasto, cheese, olives, prosciutto and melon, tomatoes and mozzarella; then comes the pasta or macaroni in marinara or meat sauce with sausage and peppers, meatballs, and veal; then comes the chicken, the pork, or the beef; followed by salad; and topped off with fruit and cheese, spumoni, gelato, ricotta pie, zabaglione, and an espresso with a splash of sambucca.

Likewise, in this book, we've brought out a little bit of everything on Catholicism: doctrine, morality, history, theology, canon law, spirituality, and liturgy. You can go to any section to discover Catholicism. You can pick and choose what interests you the most, get answers to specific questions on your mind, or just randomly open this book anywhere and begin reading. On the other hand, you may want to start at the beginning and work your way to the end, going through each chapter one by one. We don't guarantee that you'll be full when you're finished, but we hope that you'll get a good taste of what Catholicism is really about.

Part I
What Do Catholics Believe?

"This is our family bible. It's truly a lamp to my feet, a light for my path, and a balance unto our bookshelf."

In this part . . .

Here, you find out what Catholics learn in religion class and what their Church teaches all its members. This part looks at the doctrines and beliefs every Catholic is expected to know and accept. Chapter 2 focuses on the revealed Word of God, including the Bible. In Chapter 3, we explain Catholic beliefs about God as the Creator of everything. Catholicism is a Christian faith, so in Chapter 4 we examine fundamental teachings such as the divinity of Christ and Jesus as Lord and Savior.

Catholics believe that Jesus established the Church, and Chapter 5 is devoted to defining the Church, its mission, and the means by which it fulfills that mission. The Church cannot function without an organization of many, many people, and Chapter 6 gives you the rundown of the key figures in the Catholic hierarchy.

Chapter 1

What It Means to Be Catholic

In This Chapter

▶ Getting a sense of the Catholic perspective

▶ Introducing Church teachings

▶ Participating in Catholic worship

▶ Behaving and praying like a Catholic

*B*eing Catholic means more than attending parochial school or going to religion class once a week, owning some rosary beads, and going to Mass every Saturday night or Sunday morning. It means more than getting ashes smeared on your forehead once a year, eating fish on Fridays, and giving up chocolate for Lent. Being Catholic means living a totally Christian life and having a Catholic perspective.

What is the Catholic perspective? In this chapter, you get a peek at what Catholicism is all about — the common buzzwords and beliefs — a big picture of the whole shebang. (The rest of this book gets into the nitty-gritty details.)

What Exactly Is Catholicism Anyway?

The cut-to-the-chase answer is that *Catholicism* is a Christian religion (just as are Protestantism and Eastern Orthodoxy). *Catholics* are members of the Roman Catholic Church (which means they follow the authority of the bishop of Rome, otherwise known as the pope), and they share various beliefs and ways of worship, as well as a distinct outlook on life. Catholics can be either Latin (Western) or Eastern Catholic; both are equally in union with the bishop of Rome (the pope), but they retain their respective customs and traditions.

Catholics believe that all people are basically good, but sin is a spiritual disease that wounded humankind initially and can kill humankind spiritually if left unchecked. Divine grace is the only remedy for sin, and the best source of divine grace is from the *sacraments,* which are various rites that Catholics believe have been created by Jesus and entrusted by Him to His Church.

From the Catholic perspective, here are some of the bottom-line beliefs:

- ✔ More than an intellectual assent to an idea, Catholicism involves a daily commitment to embrace the will of God — whatever it is and wherever it leads.

- ✔ Catholicism means cooperation with God on the part of the believer. God offers His divine grace (His gift of unconditional love), and the Catholic must accept it and then cooperate with it.

- ✔ Free will is sacred. God never forces you to do anything against your free will. Yet doing evil not only hurts you but also hurts others because a Catholic is never alone. Catholics are always part of a spiritual family called the *Church.*

- ✔ More than a place to go on the weekend to worship, the Church is a mother who feeds spiritually, shares doctrine, heals and comforts, and disciplines when needed. Catholicism considers the Church as important to salvation as the sacraments because both were instituted by Christ.

The Catholic perspective sees everything as being intrinsically created good but with the potential of turning to darkness. It honors the individual intellect and well-formed conscience and encourages members to use their minds to think things through. In other words, instead of just giving a list of do's and don'ts, the Catholic Church educates its members to use their ability to reason and to apply laws of ethics and a natural moral law in many situations.

Catholicism doesn't see science or reason as enemies of faith but as cooperators in seeking the truth. Although Catholicism has an elaborate hierarchy to provide leadership in the Church (see Chapter 6), Catholicism also teaches individual responsibility and accountability. Education and the secular and sacred sciences are high priorities. Using logical and coherent arguments to explain and defend the Catholic faith is important.

Catholicism isn't a one-day-a-week enterprise. It doesn't segregate religious and moral dimensions of life from political, economic, personal, and familial dimensions. Catholicism tries to integrate faith into everything.

The general Catholic perspective is that because God created everything, *nothing* is outside God's jurisdiction, including your every thought, word, and deed — morning, noon, and night, 24/7.

Knowing What the Catholic Church Teaches

The Catholic religion is built (by Christ) on four pillars of faith: the creed (teachings), the sacraments (liturgical worship), the Ten Commandments (moral code), and the Lord's Prayer or Our Father (prayer and spirituality).

Church doctrine and dogma can be very sophisticated, which may intimidate some people. But the fundamentals are rooted in the Church's creed: the first pillar of faith. Either the Nicene Creed or the Apostles' Creed (which we introduce in Chapter 2) is said every Sunday and holy day to reaffirm what the Church actually teaches and expects her members to believe and profess. Catholics read the Bible and the *Catechism of the Catholic Church,* the definitive book explaining the official teachings of the Catholic Church on faith and morals.

In this section, we briefly overview the fundamental tenets of the Church, including what the Church is and who leads it.

Grasping the basic beliefs

Catholics are first and foremost *Christians.* Like Jews and Muslims, Catholics are *monotheistic,* which means that they believe in one God. But Catholics believe that Jesus Christ is the Son of God, which is unique to Christianity. Catholics also believe the following:

- **The Bible is the inspired, error-free, and revealed word of God.** See Chapter 2 for an introduction to the Bible.

- **Baptism, the rite of becoming a Christian, is necessary for salvation.** This is true whether the Baptism occurs by water, blood, or desire (see Chapter 8).

- **God's Ten Commandments provide a moral compass — an ethical standard to live by.** We discuss the Ten Commandments in detail in Chapter 12.

- **There is one God in three persons: the Holy Trinity.** In other words, Catholics embrace the belief that God, the one Supreme Being, is made up of three persons: God the Father, God the Son, and God the Holy Spirit (see Chapter 2).

Why is the Catholic Church's home in Rome?

Saint Peter, the first pope, began his ministry in Jerusalem. Eventually, he ended up in Rome, where he was its first bishop and was then crucified and buried on Vatican Hill. That spot was imperial property, but in the fourth century, the Roman emperor donated the land and buildings to the pope in compensation for property and funds that were seized from Christians during years of Christian persecutions (a topic we discuss in Appendix A). It's important that the Church continues to have its home in the place where Saint Peter spent his final years and was bishop and pope.

Catholics recognize the unity of body and soul for each human being. So the whole religion centers on the truth that humankind stands between the two worlds of matter and spirit. The physical world is considered part of God's creation and is, therefore, inherently good until an individual misuses it.

The *seven sacraments* — Baptism, Penance, Holy Eucharist, Confirmation, Matrimony, Holy Orders, and the Anointing of the Sick — are outward signs that Christ instituted to give grace. These Catholic rites marking the seven major stages of spiritual development are based on this same premise of the union of body and soul, matter and spirit, physical and spiritual. You find out more about the sacraments in this chapter's section "Worshipping as a Catholic: The Holy Mass," as well as in Chapters 8 and 9.

Grace is a totally free, unmerited gift from God necessary for our salvation. Grace is a sharing in the divine; it's God's help — the inspiration that's needed to do His will. Grace inspired martyrs in the early days of Christianity to suffer death rather than deny Christ. Grace bolstered St. Bernadette Soubirous (see Chapter 21) to sustain the derision of the locals who didn't believe she'd seen the Virgin Mary. You can't see, hear, feel, smell, or taste grace because it's invisible. Catholic belief, however, maintains that grace is the life force of the soul. Like a spiritual megavitamin, grace inspires a person to selflessly conform to God's will, and like the battery in the mechanical bunny, grace keeps the soul going, going, going, and going. Because grace is a gift, you can accept or reject it; if you reject it, you won't be saved, and if you accept it, you have to put it into action.

Respecting the role of the Church and its leaders

Catholics firmly believe that Jesus Christ personally founded the Church and He entrusted it to the authority and administration of Saint Peter (the first pope) and his successors. In this section, we explain what Catholics believe the Church really is, as well as how its leadership is structured.

What "the Church" really is

The word *church* has many meanings. Most obviously, it can signify a building where sacred worship takes place. The Catholic Church is not one particular building even though the head of the Church (the pope) lives next to Saint Peter's Basilica (the largest church in the world) in Rome.

People who use the church building — the body or assembly of believers — are also known as the *church.* When that body is united under one tradition of worship, it is called a *liturgical church,* such as the Eastern Catholic Church, the Melkite Church, the Ruthenian Church, or the Latin or Roman Rite Church.

Catholic Churches may differ liturgically, but they're still Catholic. The two main lungs of the Church are the Latin (Western) Church and the Eastern Catholic Church. The *Latin (Western) Church* follows the ancient traditions of the Christian community in Rome since the time of St. Peter and St. Paul; most parishes in the United States, Canada, Central America, and South America celebrate this type of Mass, said in either the location's common tongue or Latin. The *Eastern Catholic Church,* which includes the Byzantine Rite, celebrates its Mass like Greek or Russian Eastern Orthodox Churches. Both Masses are cool by the pope, though.

At an even more profound level, the entire *universal* church (meaning the Catholic Church around the world) is theologically considered the Mystical Body of Christ. In other words, the Church sees herself as the living, unifying, sanctifying, governing presence of Jesus Christ on earth today. Not just an organization with members or an institution with departments, the Church is an organic entity; it is alive. Its members, as Saint Paul says in his epistle (1 Corinthians 12:12–31), are like parts in a body. Just as your body has feet, hands, arms, legs, and so on, the Church has many members (parts) but is also one complete and whole *body.* (See Chapter 5 for a complete discussion of this topic.)

Unlike a club or association you belong to, the church is more than an informal gathering of like-minded people with similar goals and interests. The church was founded by Christ for a specific purpose: to save us. The church is an extension of Jesus and continues the work begun by Him. He came to teach, sanctify, and govern God's people as the Anointed One (called *Messiah* in Hebrew and *Christ* in Greek).

The Church is necessary for salvation because she is the Mystical Body of Christ, and Christ (being the Savior and Redeemer of the World) is necessary for salvation because He is the One Mediator between God and man. People who do not formally belong to the Church are not *de facto* lost, however, because the church believes in the universal salvific will of God. In other words, God offers salvation to all men and women, yet it is up to them to accept, believe in, and cooperate with that divine grace.

Anyone who has not consciously and deliberately rejected Christ and the Catholic Church can still be saved. In other words, besides the formal members (baptized, registered parishioners), there are many anonymous and unofficial members of the Church who act in good faith and follow their conscience, living virtuous lives. Someone may be innocently ignorant of the necessity of Christ and His Church and still achieve salvation from both.

One body with many members: That is how the Church sees herself. Her mission is to provide everything her members need — spiritually, that is. From the seven sacraments that give us grace to the Magisterium that teaches essential truths to the hierarchy that brings order through laws and governance, the church is there to give the soul what it needs on its journey to heaven. More than a convenient option, the church is a necessary and essential society (community) where members help each other, motivated by the same love.

The Catholic chain of command

Every group of human beings needs a chain of command (authority) and a set of rules (laws), which enable the group to maintain security, provide identity, and promote unity. Families depend on parental authority over the children. Nations have constitutions that delineate and define powers.

The church has authority that she believes comes directly from God. For example, the Lord gave Moses not only the Ten Commandments (see Chapter 12) but also many other laws and rules to help govern God's people to keep them safe.

Canon law is the set of rules and regulations the Church enacted to protect the rights of persons and the common good of all the members. The word *hierarchy* means "leveled tier." Like the Roman army of old, the Church adopted a chain of command. The highest authority resides in the person of the pope, who is always simultaneously the Bishop of Rome. He is the Successor of Saint Peter, the man to whom Christ entrusted the keys of the kingdom.

The pope is the Church's supreme lawmaker, judge, and visible leader. He is also called the Vicar of Christ on earth. As the Church's ambassador to the world, he possesses full, supreme, and universal power the moment he takes office. He is elected pope by the *college of cardinals,* which exists to elect a pope after the current one dies (or freely resigns) and also to advise, counsel, and assist the reigning pope (see Chapter 6).

The terms *Vatican* and *Holy See* refer to the various departments, commissions, congregations, and so on that help the pope govern the church, evangelize and teach the faith, and maintain and promote justice.

Jesus not only entrusted the church to Saint Peter and his successors (the popes), but He also had Twelve Apostles whose successors are called *bishops.* A bishop shepherds a local church called a *diocese,* whereas the pope shepherds the universal, global church around the world.

Bishops are helped in each parish church by a pastor who is a priest, and often they are helped by a deacon and/or a parochial vicar (assistant pastor). The bishops of a nation or geographical region form Episcopal conferences, which provide the benefit of pooled resources. For the complete scoop on the church hierarchy, be sure to check out Chapter 6.

Worshipping as a Catholic: The Holy Mass

The second pillar of faith in the Catholic religion is the seven sacraments — or in more general terms, divine worship of God as celebrated in the sacred liturgy (the topic of Part II of this book). The ceremonies, rituals, and rites performed for the past 2,000+ years were developed by the Church to render worship of the Almighty, to teach the faith to the believers, and to give moral guidance on how to live that faith. The seven sacraments are the most sacred and ancient Catholic rites; they mark the seven major stages of spiritual development:

- **Baptism:** You are born.
- **Holy Eucharist:** You are fed.
- **Confirmation:** You grow.
- **Penance:** You need healing.
- **Anointing of the Sick:** You recover.
- **Matrimony:** You need family.
- **Holy Orders:** You need leaders.

Because humans have five senses and can't physically see what's happening in the spiritual realm, the seven sacraments involve physical, tangible *symbols* (such as the water used in Baptism, the oil for anointing, and unleavened bread and wine). Symbols help connect us to the invisible spiritual reality, the *divine grace* (God's gift of unconditional love) given in each sacrament. (For more on the seven sacraments, see Chapters 8 and 9.) Catholics belong to their own churches, called *parishes,* which are local places of worship. The *Holy Mass,* the Catholic daily and weekly church service, is a reenactment of *Holy Thursday* (when Jesus celebrated the Last Supper) and *Good Friday* (when He died to purchase the rewards of eternal life in heaven for humankind). In Chapter 10, we explain the Mass in detail.

Sunday attendance at a parish isn't just expected; it's a moral obligation. Not going to Sunday Mass without a worthy excuse, such as illness or bad weather, is considered a grave sin. (Note that many Christians attend church services on Sunday, but Catholics can also attend Mass on Saturday evening instead to fulfill the Sunday requirement, as we explain in Chapter 10.)

Bringing body and soul into the mix

As we detail in Chapter 7, human beings are created as an essential union of body and soul. Material and spiritual worlds are bridged in each and every human person. Because God made us this way, it only makes sense that both body and soul are incorporated in worship.

Attending Mass requires more than just being physically present in Church. That's why Catholics use different postures, such as standing, sitting, kneeling, and bowing, and do plenty of listening, singing, and responding to phrases. For example, if the priest says, "The Lord be with you," Catholics respond, "And with your spirit."

During Mass, the inspired Word of God (see Chapter 2) is read, proclaimed, and heard through people's eyes, lips, and ears. Holy Communion, food for the soul, is given to believers.

Sacred art adorns the worship space (such as stained glass, statues, icons, paintings, mosaics, tapestries, and frescoes), sacred music is played and sung, bells are rung, incense is burned . . . the senses are stimulated as body and soul are united and nourished in the House of God.

Participating inside and out

Catholics are not spectators while at public worship. Yes, there is a distinction between the *clergy* (ordained ministers who perform the sacred rites and rituals in the name of the Church) and the congregants, but the people in the pews are crucial because they represent the entire human race.

Everyone in the church is asked to get involved in sacred liturgy. Divine worship is the adoration of God by man, and *interior* participation is the most important element. Every person at Mass should be open to God's grace to accept and cooperate with it. Interior participation means going to church not for what you get out of it but for what you can give to God.

Of all the sacraments and all the sacred liturgies, the Mass is par excellence, the source and summit of Christian worship. It is more than a mere reenactment of the Last Supper; it is the unbloody re-presentation of Christ's sacrifice on Calvary (Good Friday).

Mass is first and foremost sacred worship, but it also teaches and supports what Catholics believe in terms of the doctrines and dogmas that form the creed of the religion. Mass communicates religious truths and encourages parishioners to respond morally and spiritually by living holy lives.

Behaving Like a Catholic

The third pillar of the Catholic faith is the Ten Commandments, which represent the moral life of the believer. Behaving as Jesus would want us to is the basic premise. The concept is not puritanical; fun and enjoyment aren't frowned upon. All legitimate pleasures are allowed in moderation — and only if they aren't an end in themselves. The individual's goal is to maintain a happy balance of work and leisure.

As we explain in this section, there are certain activities the church recommends and encourages, and some she requires and demands. In all places and at all times, being docile to the will of God is paramount. For much more detail about how to behave like a Catholic, be sure to check out Part III of this book.

Following the general ground rules

The minimum requirements for being a Catholic are called the *precepts* of the Church:

- Attending Mass every Sunday (or Saturday evening) and holy day of obligation.
- Going to confession annually or more often (or when needed).
- Receiving Holy Communion during Easter. (Receiving weekly or daily Holy Communion is encouraged, though.)
- Observing laws on fasting and abstinence: one full meal on Ash Wednesday and Good Friday; not eating meat on Fridays during Lent.
- Supporting the Church financially and otherwise.

And, in the United States, the American bishops added two more precepts:

✔ Obeying the marriage laws of the Church.

✔ Supporting missionary activity of the Church.

You can find out more about the precepts of the Church in Chapter 11.

Catholics are also required to pray daily, participate in the sacraments, obey the moral law, and accept the teachings of Christ and His Church. If you haven't grown up knowing and accepting the faith, then you need to make sure you know and agree with all that the Catholic Church teaches before you can truly practice the faith.

Practicing the faith is the most difficult part of being Catholic. Obeying the rules isn't just mindless compliance. It involves appreciating the wisdom and value of the various Catholic rules and laws. Believers are asked to put that belief into action, to practice what they believe. Catholics are taught that all men and women are made in the image and likeness of God and that all men and women have been saved by Christ and are adopted children of God. That belief, if truly believed, requires that the person act as if she really means it.

Every organization, society, association, and group has rules. Even individual families and homes have their own rules, which exist for one purpose: the common good of all the members. Just like directions on a bottle of medicine tell you the proper use of something, church laws are signs that warn you of danger and give you the proper directions to your destination. The laws of God — be they the Ten Commandments, the Natural Moral Law, or the moral teachings of the Church — exist to protect us and to ensure our spiritual safety.

Avoiding sin

Sinning is not only breaking the law of God but also much more. Sin is a disease, a germ, an infection of the soul. Just as tumors can be either benign or malignant, sins can be either venial or mortal, either slightly wounding or actually killing the life of grace in the soul.

The best prevention is to avoid sin just as doctors advise us to avoid disease. Good spiritual health requires more than being free of infection, however. Living a virtuous moral life and maintaining a healthy spirituality, when combined with an aggressive program to avoid sin at all cost, is the best plan to live a holy life worthy of a true follower of Christ. In Chapter 13, we discuss this subject in detail.

Heeding the Church's stance on tough issues

Certain topics get much more media attention than the substance of Catholic religion (like doctrine, worship, prayer, and spirituality). These topics include the Church's stance on abortion, euthanasia, contraception, homosexuality, and more.

Many of the tough issues that distinguish Catholicism from other faiths are based on the Church's foundational beliefs. Issues such as priestly celibacy are matters of discipline, whereas the ordination of women contradicts a doctrine of the faith. Abortion, euthanasia, contraception, and homosexuality are moral issues that require the application of biblical and doctrinal principals in order to see clearly the spiritual dangers often overlooked by well-meaning people. War and capital punishment are examples where legitimate differences of opinions still exist, yet basic fundamentals must always be respected and upheld. We devote Chapter 14 to a discussion of all these tough issues.

Praying as a Catholic: Showing Your Devotion

Part IV of this book is devoted to a discussion of prayer and devotions. While public worship (such as the Holy Mass) is governed by the official church, private prayer is more a matter of personal taste and preference. Each person needs to cultivate his own spirituality just as he needs to develop a healthy lifestyle for his body.

When it comes to prayer, what works for one person may not work for another, but certain fundamentals almost always apply. Think of it this way: Your choices with regard to diet and exercise may differ from those of your friends and neighbors, but chances are your choices have a lot in common with those made by people of similar physical health. Likewise, your devotional choices (such as how and when to pray) can be tailored to meet your needs, but many similarities exist among people who share a certain faith.

Praying and using devotions

As we discuss in detail in Chapter 15, Catholicism promotes both public and private prayer. In Chapter 16, we explain that *devotions* are prayers or actions devoted to God, which can be private or public as well. Devotions are minor ways that believers cultivate a love and familiarity with theological truths and revealed mysteries of faith and (most importantly) develop a personal relationship with the Lord. The devotions mentioned in Chapter 16, such as praying the Rosary, are some of the more popular and effective ones around.

Realizing the importance of Mary and the saints

The Virgin Mary is the mother of Jesus, and she is also considered one of His most faithful disciples in her own way. While not an Apostle and never holding any authority in the early church, the Mother of Christ nonetheless has always been a model of humility, virtue, and obedience to the will of God.

As we explain in Chapters 17 and 18, Mary and the canonized saints of the Church are not objects of worship (which would be idolatry — something condemned by the First Commandment). Instead, they are living examples and models of holiness and sanctity. They are role models and heroes of faith who, in their own way, tried and succeeded in following Jesus as best they could.

Following traditions

The most visible aspects of Catholicism are not usually the most fundamental theological, doctrinal, or moral teachings. In other words, they aren't necessarily the meat-and-potatoes substance of what it means to be Catholic. But some traditions are so public or well known that people associate them with Catholicism much like people associate Judaism with a man wearing a yarmulke or Islam with the use of a prayer rug.

Some such Catholic traditions include meatless Fridays, ashes on the forehead to begin Lent, palms on Passion Sunday, and blessings (of throats, persons, homes, cars, and so on). Such pious practices are not the core of Catholicism, but they do connect and point in that direction, as we explain in Chapter 19.

Chapter 2

Having Faith in God's Revealed Word

In This Chapter

▶ Defining the real, practical meaning of faith

▶ Discovering the ways God reveals truth

▶ Believing in the written and spoken Word of God

▶ Using reason to defend what you believe

*Y*ou may think that having faith is similar to believing in fantasies or fairy tales, or accepting the existence of UFOs, ghosts, abominable snowmen, the Loch Ness monster, or Bigfoot. But faith is something entirely different. In this chapter, we tell you what faith really is and explain all the divine truths that Catholics believe in. We also sum up some proofs for God's existence that will make your faith stronger.

How Do You Know If You Have Faith?

St. Thomas Aquinas (theologian of the 13th century) said faith was the assent given by the mind (intellect) to what cannot be seen or proven but is taken on the word and authority of another. The ascertainment of faith is plain and simple: You have *faith* if you trust the word of someone else. When you take what someone says on faith, you believe in what the other person is telling you even though you haven't personally witnessed it, may not understand it, or may find it difficult to believe. In other words, faith means agreeing with, believing in, *trusting* something — without cold, hard evidence — that you can't know or comprehend on your own.

So far, faith doesn't sound all that different from believing in Santa Claus or the Easter Bunny, but having faith is a bit more complicated. Having faith means being able to live with unanswered questions — sometimes, tough ones. For example, why does evil exist in the world? Why do people still go to war? And what about the existence of terrorism, disease, and crime?

Faith doesn't answer these questions. (Some people think that the answer "It's God's will" suffices, but it doesn't.) Faith, however, gives you the courage to endure and survive without having the answers. Instead of providing a set of answers to painful and complicated enigmas, faith provides the means to persevere.

The *Catechism of the Catholic Church,* a book defining the official teachings of the Catholic Church, has this to say about faith:

- ✔ "Faith is first of all a personal adherence of man to God. At the same time, and inseparably, it is a *free assent to the whole truth that God has revealed.*" (150)

- ✔ "Faith is a personal act — the free response of the human person to the initiative of God who reveals himself. But faith isn't an isolated act. No one can believe alone, just as no one can live alone." (166)

To Catholics, faith is a supernatural virtue given to human beings from God. What we do or don't do with that faith is totally up to us. God offers it freely to anyone and everyone, but it must be freely received as well. No one can be forced to have or accept faith. And when it's presented, each individual responds differently — at different levels, at different times, and in different ways. Some reject it, some ignore it, and some treat it casually. Others cherish their faith deeply. As the adage goes: For those who believe, no explanation is necessary, and for those who do not believe, no explanation is possible.

Having Faith in Revelation

Catholic faith involves more than just believing that God exists. It's about believing *in* God as well as *whatever* God has revealed. Objectively, you can look at faith as the sum total of the truths God reveals, which form the basis for the doctrines of the Church and are often called the *deposit of faith* — the doctrines of the Church. Subjectively, you can consider faith as your personal response *(assent)* to those revealed truths.

We hear ya: "But what do you mean by revealed truths? And, for that matter, just what *are* God's revealed truths?" By *revealed truths,* we mean *revelations,* God's unveiling of supernatural truths necessary for human salvation. (The word *revelation* comes from the Latin *revelare,* meaning to *unveil.*) Some of these are truths that you could never know by science or philosophy; the human mind is incapable of knowing them without divine intervention, so God revealed them to mere mortals. For example, the revealed truth of the Holy Trinity is that there is only one God but three persons (not three gods, mind you). This truth is something that the human intellect could never discover on its own; God had to tell that one himself.

Other revelations, such as the existence of God, can be known by using human reason alone (see the section "Backing Up Your Faith with Reason: Summa Theologica" in this chapter), but God reveals these truths directly anyway because not everyone understands them at the same time and in the same way. The essence of these revelations can be — and is presumed to be — knowable to anyone with the use of reason; so, for example, someone can't claim he didn't know it was wrong to commit murder. But because of original sin (see Chapter 8), some of the applications and distinctions of these basic truths require more reasoning and thinking. To even out the playing field, God revealed some important truths so that even those people who aren't intelligent or quick-minded won't be caught off guard.

As for what God's revealed truths are, the most concise answer is *His word*. *The Word of God* is the revelation of God to His people. What is the Word of God? Catholics believe that the Word of God comes in two forms:

- ✔ **The written word:** Known also as *Scripture* or the *Bible*
- ✔ **The spoken word:** Also called the *unwritten word or Sacred Tradition*

Both the spoken and the written word come from the same source and communicate the same message — the truth. The written word and the spoken word of God are not in competition with one another, nor do Catholics believe one at the expense of the other. Rather, the written word and the spoken word have a mutual partnership. Whenever and wherever the Bible is silent on an issue or its meaning is ambiguous or disputed, the spoken word (Sacred Tradition) steps in to clarify the matter. Catholics believe that God's word reflects what's in His mind, and because God is all truth and all good, His word conveys truth and goodness. Catholics have deep respect for and devotion to the Word of God.

Faith in the written word: The Bible

Catholicism is a biblical religion. Like all Christian religions, it cherishes the Bible as the inspired, infallible, inerrant, and revealed Word of God.

Having faith in the following aspects of the Bible is crucial to being Catholic:

- ✔ The belief in the Bible as one of the two channels of revelation
- ✔ The literal and figurative interpretation of the biblical text
- ✔ The belief in the Catholic Bible as the most authoritative text

Bible trivia

Want a few interesting Bible tidbits? You got it:

The word *bible* isn't even in the Bible. Do a word search on your computer, and you'll see that nowhere from Genesis to the Apocalypse (Revelation) is the word *bible* ever mentioned. But the word *Scripture* appears 53 times in the King James Version of the Bible, and the phrase *Word of God* appears 55 times. So if the word itself isn't in the Bible, why call it the Bible? The word comes from the Greek *biblia,* meaning a collection of books, and the origin goes back even farther to the word *biblos,* meaning papyrus. In ancient times, the paper from trees to write on didn't exist — only stone or papyrus. Imagine — stone books.

The Catholic Church gave the name *Bible* to the Bible — to the collection of inspired books known as the Old and New Testaments. The Church also decided which books belonged in the Bible and which were left out, because nowhere from Genesis to Apocalypse (Revelation) can you find a list of which documents belong and which don't. Modern-day Bible publishers and editors have added the table of contents, but the contents weren't disclosed in the sacred text itself. Why does the Bible contain four Gospels? Who decided that Matthew should come before Mark? Why isn't the Gospel of Thomas or the Gospel of Peter in the Bible? Who says that the New Testament contains only 27 books? What happened to the Apocalypse of Moses and the Apocalypse of Adam? The Bible doesn't tell you what books belong in it, so the Church had to use her authority to make that decision. You can read more on this subject in the nearby section "Trusting the authority of the Catholic Bible."

Believing in two forms of revelation

Catholic Christianity and Eastern Orthodox Christianity believe in one common source of divine revelation (God himself), but they believe the revelation is transmitted to us through two equal and distinct modes: the written word (the Bible) and the spoken word (the *unwritten word*). Protestant Christianity regards the Bible as the only source of divine revelation. Another way of looking at it is to think of some Christians as seeing only one channel of revelation — *sola scriptura,* which is Latin for *Scripture alone* — and Catholic Christians as seeing two channels of revelation — both the written word and the unwritten word of God. (Just divert thine eyes to the "Faith in the spoken word: Sacred Tradition" section, later in this chapter, for an explanation of what the unwritten word is.)

Interpreting sacred literature both literally and figuratively

Catholics regard the Bible as the inspired and revealed word of God, but it's also seen as a collection of sacred literature. Rather than just looking at the Bible as one big book, Catholicism treats the Bible as a collection of smaller books under one cover: the word of God written by men yet inspired by God. Since the time of the Reformation, opinion on the interpretation of the sacred text has differed significantly. Some Christians hold for a literal interpretation of every word and phrase of Scripture; other Christians hold for a faithful interpretation, which is sometimes literal and sometimes not. (In other words, some text is meant to be interpreted figuratively.) Catholics belong to the second camp.

The Bible tells the history of salvation, but it's much more than a history book. It contains the Psalms of David — songs that the King wrote in honor of God — yet the Bible is much more than a hymnal. It contains poetry, prose, history, theology, imagery, metaphor, analogy, irony, hyperbole, and so on. Because it's not exclusively one form of literature, as you would have in a science textbook, one needs to know and appreciate the various literary forms in the Bible in order to interpret it as the author intended. For example, when Jesus says in the Gospel (Mark 9:43), "And if your hand causes you to sin, cut it off," the Catholic Church has interpreted that to be a *figure of speech* rather than something to be taken *literally*. At the same time, Catholicism interprets literally the passage of John 6:55 — "For my flesh is food indeed and my blood is drink indeed." Because individuals can disagree on what should be interpreted literally and what shouldn't, Catholicism resorts to one final authority to definitively interpret for all Catholics what the biblical text means for the Catholic faith. That ultimate authority is called the *Magisterium* (from the Latin word *magister* meaning *teacher*), which is the authority of the pope and the bishops around the world in union with him to instruct the faithful. (For more on the Magisterium, see Chapter 6.) Catholics believe that Christ founded the Church ("I will build my Church" [Matthew 16:18]), a necessary institution, to safeguard and protect revelation by authentically interpreting the biblical texts. The Church is not superior to Scripture, but she's the steward and guardian as well as interpreter of the inspired and revealed Word of God. The Church assumes the role of authentic interpreter not on her own but by the authority given her by Christ: "He who hears you, hears me" (Luke 10:16). The Church makes an authentic interpretation and an authoritative decision regarding those issues that aren't explicitly addressed in Sacred Scripture, but only because Christ has entrusted her to do so. To find out how the Church views tough modern-day issues that aren't addressed in the Bible, flip to Chapter 14.

Trusting the authority of the Catholic Bible

What follows is a snapshot of how the Bible was created and how different versions evolved — the Catholic versions and the Protestant versions. If you're eager for more information on the Bible, however, check out *The Bible For Dummies* by Jeffrey Geoghegan and Michael Homan (Wiley).

To understand the history of the Bible, you really have to go back to around 1800 B.C. when the oral tradition of the Hebrew people started, because Abraham and his tribes were nomadic people and didn't have a written language of their own. Mothers and fathers verbally (*orally*) handed down the stories of the Old Testament about Adam and Eve, Cain and Abel, and so on. (The Latin word *traditio* means to hand down, and it's the root of the English word for *tradition*.) The stories of the Old Testament were all told by word of mouth, which we call *oral tradition*.

Moses appeared sometime around 1250 B.C., when God delivered the Hebrew people from the bondage of slavery in Egypt and they entered the Promised Land. The era of Moses opened the road to some of the written word because Moses was raised in the court of Pharaoh, where he learned how to read and write. But the predominant bulk of revelation was still the oral tradition, handed down from generation to generation, because the rest of the Hebrews were slaves and most were unable to read or write at that time. Substantial writings weren't saved until 950 B.C., during the reign of King Solomon. But after his death, King Solomon's kingdom was divided between the northern and southern kingdoms of Israel and Judah, respectively.

The Assyrians conquered Israel in 721 B.C., and the Babylonians conquered Judah in 587 B.C. During the time of the Babylonian captivity and exile, the Jews of the *Diaspora* (forced exile of Jews) were spread all over the known world. Some retained their Hebrew language, but most lost it and adopted the common language: Greek. (If you could read and write at this time in history, most likely you were reading and writing Greek.)

Consequently, in the year 250 B.C., an effort was underway to translate all Jewish Scripture into the Greek language. The thing is, more Jews lived outside of Palestine than within it. In the third century B.C., nearly two-fifths of the population in Egypt alone, especially in Alexandria, was Jewish and yet unable to read and write in Hebrew. These Greek-speaking Jews were known as *Hellenistic Jews.* Seven books of Scripture were written in Greek by these Hellenistic Jews and were considered as inspired as the 39 Scriptural books written in Hebrew before the Diaspora.

The Greek version of the Old Testament was called the *Septuagint* (symbolized by the Roman numeral LXX for the number 70) because it took 70 scholars allegedly 70 years to complete the task. They met in Alexandria, Egypt, and translated 39 Hebrew Scriptures into Greek and included 7 other books originally written by Jews in the Greek language.

These seven books — the Books of Baruch, Maccabees I and II, Tobit, Judith, Ecclesiasticus (also known as *Sirach*), and Wisdom — were known and used by Jews even in the Holy Land, including Jesus and His disciples. The early Christians likewise accepted the inspired status of these seven books because no one had refuted them during the time of Christ. Because they were later additions to the more ancient Hebrew writings, however, these seven books were called the *Deuterocanonical Books* (meaning *second canon*); the 39 Hebrew books were known as the *Canonical Books.*

Jewish authorities in Jerusalem had no explicit objection to these seven books until the year A.D. 100, well after the Christians had split from formal Judaism and formed their own separate religion. The Temple of Jerusalem was destroyed in A.D. 70, and in the year A.D. 100, Jewish leaders at the Council of Jamnia sought to purify Judaism of all foreign and Gentile influence, which meant removing anything not purely Hebrew. Because the seven Deuterocanonical Books were never written in Hebrew, they got pitched.

By now, though, Christianity was totally separate from Judaism and didn't doubt the authenticity of the seven books, because these books were always considered equal to the other 39. (Much later, Martin Luther would initiate the Protestant Reformation in 1517 and choose to adopt the Hebrew canon [39 books] rather than the Greek canon [46 books], also called the Septuagint.)

So, in the listing of the Old Testament, a discrepancy exists between the Catholic and the Protestant Bibles. Catholic Bibles list 46 books and Protestant Bibles list 39. Recently, many publishers have reintroduced the seven books in Protestant Bibles, such as the King James Version, but they're carefully placed in the back (after the end of the canonical texts) and are identified as being part of the *Apocrypha,* which is from the Greek word *apokryphos* meaning *hidden*.

So what the Catholic Church considers Deuterocanonical, Protestant theologians consider Apocrypha. And what the Catholic Church considers Apocrypha, Protestants call *Pseudepigrapha* (meaning *false writings*), which are the alleged and so-called Lost Books of the Bible. These Lost Books were never considered as being inspired by the Church, so they were never included as part of any Bible, Catholic or Protestant. Such books as the Assumption of Moses, the Apocalypse of Abraham, the Ascension of Isaiah, the Gospel of Thomas, the Gospel of Peter, the Acts of St. John, and others were all considered uninspired and therefore never made it into the Bible.

Interestingly enough, Catholics and Protestants have never seriously disputed the list of the New Testament books, and both the Catholic and the Protestant Bibles have the exact same names and number (27) of books in the New Testament. (For more info about the New Testament, see Chapter 4.)

Faith in the spoken word: Sacred Tradition

God's word is more than letters on a page or sounds to the ear. His word is *creative*. When God speaks the word, it happens. For example, the book of Genesis in the Bible tells us that God created merely by saying the word: "And God said, 'Let there be light,' and there was light." (Genesis 1:3)

Catholics believe that the Word of God is found not only in the Bible but also in the unwritten or spoken word — *Sacred Tradition*. In this section, we show you what Sacred Tradition is and introduce you to the single most important part of that tradition, the Creed.

Filling in the gaps of the written word

Before the word was written, it was first spoken. God first said, "Let there be light," and later on, the sacred author wrote those words on paper. Jesus first spoke the word when He preached His Sermon on the Mount. He didn't dictate to Matthew as He was preaching. Instead, Matthew wrote things down much later, well after Jesus died, rose, and ascended into heaven. None of the Gospels were written during Jesus's life on earth. He died in A.D. 33, and the earliest Gospel manuscript, which is the Aramaic version of Matthew (alluded to by ancient sources), was written between A.D. 40 and 50. The other three Gospels — Mark, Luke, and John — were written between A.D. 53 and 100. Matthew and John, who wrote the first and the last Gospels, were 2 of the original 12 apostles, so they personally heard what Jesus said and saw with their own eyes what He did. Mark and Luke weren't apostles but disciples, and most of their information on what Jesus said and did wasn't a first-hand eyewitness account; rather, their information was handed down to them by others who were witnesses. (Remember that the word *tradition* means *to hand down.*) The unwritten or spoken Gospel was told by word of mouth by the apostles well before the *evangelists,* the Gospel writers, ever wrote one word. Luke received much of his data from Jesus's mother, the Virgin Mary, and Mark received plenty of info from Peter, the apostle Jesus left in charge.

If some time passed between what Jesus actually said and did and when the Gospel writers put His words and actions on paper (actually on parchment), what took place during that period? Before the written word was the unwritten, or spoken, word. In the Old Testament, things happened and were said long before they were written down. So, too, in the New Testament, Jesus preached His sermons and worked His miracles, died on the Cross, rose from the dead, and ascended into heaven long before anyone wrote it down. No one took notes while He preached. No letters were written between Jesus and the apostles. Sacred Tradition predates and precedes Sacred Scripture, but both come from the same source: God.

The New Testament is totally silent on whether Jesus ever married or had children. The Bible says nothing about His marital status, yet Christians believe He had neither a wife nor kids. Sacred Tradition tells that He never married, just as Sacred Tradition says that the Gospels number only four. Without a written list, who decides (and how) if the Old Testament contains 39 books in Protestant Bibles or 46 books in Catholic Bibles and the New Testament has 27? If Catholics were to believe only in the written word, then no answer would exist. But another avenue exists, the unwritten word, and we can go by that.

Existing separately from human tradition

Catholicism carefully distinguishes between mere human tradition and divinely inspired Sacred Tradition:

- ✔ **Human traditions** are man-made laws that can be changed. An example of a human tradition is Catholics not eating meat on Fridays during Lent. Celibacy for priests of the Western (Latin) Church is another human tradition, which any pope can dispense, modify, or continue.

- ✔ **Sacred Tradition** is considered part of the unwritten Word of God because it has been believed for centuries, since the time of the Apostolic Church, which refers to that period of time in Church history from the first (while the Apostles were still alive) to the second century A.D. (before the second-generation Christians died). It's called *Apostolic* because the apostles lived at that time.

An example of a Sacred Tradition is the dogma of the Assumption of Mary. A *dogma* is a revealed truth that's solemnly defined by the Church — a formal doctrine that the faithful are obligated to believe. Although it's not explicit in Sacred Scripture, the Assumption of Mary means that Mary was *assumed* (physically taken up), body and soul, into heaven by her divine Son. Even though it wasn't solemnly defined until 1950 by Pope Pius XII, this doctrine has been believed (and never doubted) by Catholic Christians since the time of the apostles. Other examples of Sacred Tradition can be found in the doctrines defined by the 21 General or Ecumenical Councils of the Church, from Nicea (A.D. 325) to Vatican II (1962–1965). (See Chapter 6 for more on the councils.)

The Creed

The most crucial and influential part of Sacred Tradition is the Creed. The word comes from the Latin *credo,* meaning "I believe." A Creed is a statement or profession of what members of a particular church or religion believe as being essential and necessary. The two most ancient and most important creeds are the *Apostles' Creed* and the *Nicene Creed;* the latter is recited or sung every Sunday and on holy days of obligation at Catholic Masses all over the world. (Like Sundays, *holy days of obligation* are specific days in the calendar year on which Catholics are required to go to Mass. See Chapter 10 for more on holy days.) The *Nicene Creed* was the fruit of the Council of Nicea, which convened in A.D. 325 to condemn the heresy of Arianism (see Chapter 4) and to affirm the doctrine of the divinity of Christ. The oldest creed, however, is the Apostles' Creed. Although it's doubtful that the 12 apostles themselves wrote it, the origin of this creed comes from the first century A.D.

A sophisticated development of the *Apostles' Creed,* which is a Christian statement of belief attributed to the 12 apostles, the Nicene Creed reflects one's loyalty and allegiance to the truths contained in it. The *Catechism of the Catholic Church* explains that the Creed is one of the four pillars of faith, along with the Ten Commandments, the seven sacraments, and the Our Father. The text of the Apostles' Creed and the Nicene Creed, which follows, succinctly summarizes all that Catholicism regards as divinely revealed truth:

> **The Apostles' Creed:** I believe in God, the Father Almighty, the Creator of heaven and earth, and in Jesus Christ, His only Son, our Lord: Who was conceived by the Holy Spirit, born of the Virgin Mary, suffered under Pontius Pilate, was crucified, died, and was buried. He descended into hell. On the third day He arose again from the dead. He ascended into heaven and is seated at the right hand of God the Father Almighty, from there He will come to judge the living and the dead. I believe in the Holy Spirit, the holy Catholic Church, the communion of saints, the forgiveness of sins, the resurrection of the body, and life everlasting. Amen.

If you're Catholic, you gotta go public

When you profess the faith, that is. At the Baptism of an infant, the parents and godparents are asked, "Do you renounce Satan, and all his works and all his empty promises?" (If the person being baptized is at the age of reason, 7 or older, he is asked the question directly.) If the answer is yes, then the priest or deacon proceeds with, "Do you believe in God, the Father Almighty, Creator of Heaven and Earth?" And so on.

After Baptism, Christians — when they're at the age of reason — are expected to publicly profess the faith by reciting or singing the Nicene Creed at Mass with the entire congregation. Want to know more about what happens at Baptism? Head over to Chapter 8.

The following list explains the Apostles' Creed in detail, so you can get a better understanding of this Sacred Tradition and the Catholic belief system. (It's divided into 12 articles for easier digestion.)

- ✓ **Article 1: I believe in God, the Father Almighty, the Creator of heaven and earth.** This affirms that God exists, that He's one God in three persons, known as the Holy Trinity, and that He created the known universe.

  Creation is understood as making something from nothing. The created world includes all inanimate matter, as well as plant, animal, human, and angelic life.

- ✓ **Article 2: And in Jesus Christ, His only Son, our Lord.** This attests that Jesus is the Son of God and that He's most certainly divine. The word *Lord* implies divinity, because the Greek word *Kyrios* and the Hebrew word *Adonai* both mean *Lord* and are only ascribed to God. So the use of *Lord* with *Jesus* is meant to profess His divinity. The name *Jesus* comes from the Hebrew word *Jeshua,* meaning *God saves.* So Catholics believe that Jesus is Savior.

- ✓ **Article 3: Who was conceived by the Holy Spirit [and] born of the Virgin Mary.** This affirms the human nature of Christ, meaning that He had a real, true human mother, and it also affirms His divine nature, meaning that He had no human father, but by the power of the Holy Spirit He was conceived in the womb of the Virgin Mary. Therefore, He's considered both God and man by Christians — fully divine and fully human.

  The union of the two natures in the one divine person of Christ is called the *Incarnation* from the Latin word *caro* meaning *flesh.* The Latin word *Incarnatio* or *Incarnation* in English translates to *becoming flesh.*

- ✓ **Article 4: [He] suffered under Pontius Pilate, was crucified, died, and was buried.** The human nature of Christ could feel pain and actually die, and He did on Good Friday. The mention of Pontius Pilate by name wasn't meant so much to vilify him forever in history but to place the Crucifixion within human history. So reference is made to an actual historical person, the Roman governor of Judea appointed by Caesar, to put the life and death of Jesus within a chronological and histori- cal context. It also reminds the faithful that one can't blame all Jews for the death of Jesus, as some have erroneously done over the ages. Certain Jewish leaders conspired against Jesus, but a Roman gave the actual death sentence, and Roman soldiers carried it out. So both Jew and Gentile alike shared in the spilling of innocent blood. Anti-Semitism based on the Crucifixion of Jesus is inaccurate, unjust, and erroneous.

✔ **Article 5: He descended into hell. The third day He arose again from the dead.** The *hell* Jesus descended into wasn't the hell of the damned, where Christians believe that the devil and his demons reside. *Hell* was also a word that Jews and ancient Christians used to describe the place of the dead, both the good and the bad. Before salvation and redemp- tion, the souls of Adam and Eve, Abraham, Isaac, Jacob, David, Solomon, Esther, Ruth, and so on, all had to wait in the abode of the dead, until the Redeemer could open the gates of heaven once more. They weren't paroled from hell for good behavior.

This passage affirms that on the third day He rose, meaning Jesus came back from the dead of His own divine power. He wasn't just clinically dead for a few minutes, He was *dead* dead; then He rose from the dead. More than a resuscitated corpse, Jesus possessed a glorified and risen *body*.

✔ **Article 6: He ascended into heaven and is seated at the right hand of God the Father Almighty.** The Ascension reminds the faithful that after the human and divine natures of Christ were united in the Incarnation, they could never be separated. In other words, after the saving death and Resurrection, Jesus didn't dump His human body as if He didn't need it anymore. Catholicism teaches that His human body will exist forever. Where Jesus went, body and soul, into heaven, the faithful hope one day to follow.

✔ **Article 7: From there He will come to judge the living and the dead.** This article affirms the Second Coming of Christ at the end of the world to be its judge. Judgment Day, Day of Reckoning, Doomsday — they're all metaphors for the end of time when what's known as the General Judgment will occur. Catholics believe that after the death of any human person, immediate private judgment occurs, and the person goes directly to heaven, hell, or *purgatory* — an intermediate place in prepara- tion for heaven. (For more on purgatory, see Chapter 18.) At the end of time, when General Judgment happens, all the private judgments will be revealed, so everyone knows who's in heaven or hell and why. Private judgment is the one that Catholics are concerned about most, because immediately after death, people are judged by their faith or lack of it and how they practiced that faith — how they acted and behaved as believ- ers. General Judgment is merely God's disclosure of everyone's private judgment. It's *not* an appeal of prior judgment, nor is it a second chance.

What's in a last name?

Jesus's last name wasn't Christ. So even if mailboxes existed back in His time, a mailbox wouldn't have listed the names Jesus, Mary, and Joseph Christ. *Christ* is a title meaning *anointed* from the Greek word *christos*. The Hebrew word *Messiah* also means *anointed*.

✔ **Article 8: I believe in the Holy Spirit.** This part reminds the believer that God exists in three persons: the Holy Trinity — God the Father, God the Son, and God the Holy Spirit. What's referred to as *the Force* in the movie *Star Wars* isn't the same as the Holy Spirit, who is a distinct person equal to the other two — God the Father and God the Son.

✔ **Article 9: [I believe in] the holy Catholic Church, the communion of saints.** Catholics believe that the Church is more than a mere institution and certainly not a necessary evil. It's an essential dimension and aspect of spiritual life. Christ explicitly uses the word *church* (*ekklesia* in Greek) in Matthew 16 when He says, "I will build My Church."

The role of the Church is seen as a continuation of the three-fold mission Christ had while He walked the earth — to *teach, sanctify,* and *govern* — just as He was simultaneously *prophet, priest,* and *king.* The Catholic Church continues His *prophetic* mission of *teaching* through the *Magisterium* (see Chapter 6), the teaching authority of the Church. She continues His *priestly* mission of *sanctification* through the celebration of the seven sacraments. And the Church continues His *kingly* mission of being shepherd and pastor through the *hierarchy.* The phrase *communion of saints* means that the Church includes not just all the living baptized persons on earth but also the saints in heaven and the souls in purgatory as well. (See Chapters 8 and 9 for an overview of the seven sacraments; see Chapter 6 for more on Church hierarchy; for more on the communion of saints, see Chapter 18.)

✔ **Article 10: [I believe in] the forgiveness of sins.** Christ came to save the world from sin. Belief in the forgiveness of sins is essential to Christianity. Catholicism believes sins are forgiven in Baptism and in the Sacrament of Penance, which is also known as the Sacrament of Reconciliation or Confession. (For more on the Sacrament of Penance, see Chapter 9.) Mother Teresa of Calcutta said, "It is not that God is calling us to be successful, rather He is calling us to be faithful." In other words, Catholicism acknowledges that all are sinners and all men and women are in need of God's mercy and forgiveness. Religion and the Church are not for perfect people who never sin (perfect people don't exist anyway), but they're for sinners who need the help that religion and the Church provide.

✔ **Article 11: [I believe in] the resurrection of the body.** From the Catholic perspective, a human being is a union of body and soul, so death is just the momentary separation of body and soul until the world ends and all the dead are resurrected. The just will go, body and soul, into heaven, and the damned will go, body and soul, into hell.

Belief in the Resurrection leaves no room for reincarnation or past-life experiences. Catholics believe that you're unique, body and soul, and neither part of you can or will be duplicated even if human cloning is perfected someday. This tenet is why Christians believe that death isn't the last chapter in anyone's life. For the believer, death is a doorway for the soul. The body and soul will eventually get back together again because the body participated in the good that the soul performed or the evil it committed. So the body as well as the soul must be rewarded or punished for all eternity.

✔ **Article 12: [I believe in] life everlasting.** As Christ died, so, too, must mere mortals. As He rose, so shall all human beings.

Death is the only way to cross from this life into the next. At the very moment of death, private judgment occurs; Christ judges the soul. If a person was particularly holy and virtuous on earth, the soul goes directly to heaven. If an individual was evil and wicked and dies in the state of mortal sin, that soul is damned for eternity in hell.

But what if a person lived a life not bad enough to warrant hell but not holy enough to go right to heaven? Catholics believe that *purgatory* is a middle ground between heaven and earth. It's a place of *purgation,* hence the name *purgatory.* Everyone in purgatory eventually gets into heaven. (For more on purgatory, see Chapter 18.)

Backing Up Your Faith with Reason: Summa Theologica

So are having faith and hoping to be saved the same as believing in the Tooth Fairy and hoping for a dollar bill under your pillow? Of course not. The First Vatican Council (1869–1879; also known as *Vatican I*) taught that you need the intervention of supernatural revelation to be saved, but certain truths, like the existence of God, are attainable on your own power by using human reason.

In the 13th century, St. Thomas Aquinas (see Chapter 21), a philosopher, explained how the human mind seeks different kinds of truth. He said that

✔ **Scientific truth** (also known as *empirical truth*) is known by observation and experimentation. So, for example, you know that fire is hot by burning your finger with a lit match.

✔ **Philosophical truth** is known by using human reason. You know that two plus two equals four, for example. So if two chairs are in a room and someone says, "I'll get two more," you know by using reason that the total will be four chairs. You don't need to count the chairs after they arrive.

✔ **Theological truth,** known only by faith, is the final and highest level of truth. It can't be observed, and it can't be reasoned; it must be believed by faith — taken on God's word, because He revealed it.

St. Thomas Aquinas also delineated five philosophical proofs for the existence of God in a monumental work called the *Summa Theologica.* Because Vatican I taught that the human mind can know some things of religion on its own without having to depend on divine revelation, it's good to see the example given by St. Thomas. Aquinas reasoned that humans can prove the existence of God through motion, causality, necessity, gradation, and governance. Granted, you may not be able to persuade an atheist to become a missionary priest this way, but these proofs are still pretty compelling.

Through motion

Before you were conceived in your mother's womb, you were merely a *potential* being. You didn't become real, or actual, until the occurrence of the act that created a new human life.

Likewise, at one time, everything now in existence was merely potential, because everything has a beginning. In other words, to get to the actual here and now, you first must have an actual beginning — a start. So at some point, all human beings — and all things — never were.

Some force had to start the motion from potential existence to actual existence. And that force could never have been potential itself; it always was, is, and shall be. Otherwise, that force would've had to be started by some other force, which would've had to be started by some other force, and so on. This chain of forces means that an actual beginning would never have been. And, again, the here and now must have an actual beginning.

Before the Big Bang, when the universe was only potential, what force started the motion for it to become actual and real? St. Thomas said that the force is God, the Prime Mover — moving the potential universe into becoming the actual one.

Through causality

Our parents caused us to be born, just as yours did. Our grandparents caused our parents to be born. And so on. So every cause was first an effect of a previous cause. So if you go all the way back to the beginning of everything, something or someone had to be the cause of all causes. Just as the force that started the motion from potential existence to actual existence could never have been potential itself, the cause of all causes could never have been the effect of a previous cause. In other words, the cause of all causes was never an effect but always a cause — or, as philosophers put it, an uncaused cause. St. Thomas said that uncaused cause is God. He caused everything to be by starting creation in the first place.

Through necessity

The universe would not blow up or crash to a screeching halt if you had never been born. This fact is a real ego-popper.

No one individual is necessary. Everything in the universe is basically contingent on — dependent on — something else to exist. Think of it this way: If you turn off a light switch, the flow of electricity to the light bulb is cut off. Without the electricity, you don't have light. If God removed His Being from sustaining you, you'd be like a turned-off light bulb.

One being must be necessary in order to keep the contingent (unnecessary) beings in existence. Otherwise, nothing would exist at all. St. Thomas said the necessary being is God.

Through gradation

Existence and being have different levels. Following is a gradation, or hierarchy, from the lowest level of existence to the highest level of being:

- ✔ **Inanimate matter:** Look at inanimate matter, such as rocks. They represent a basic level of existence. They're just there.

- ✔ **Plant life:** The next level is plant or vegetative life — simple but able to reproduce.

- ✔ **Animal life:** Farther up is animal life. Not only can it reproduce and grow like plant life, but it also has *sense* knowledge. Animals can detect information from their eyes, ears, nose, mouth, and so on.

✔ **Human life:** Next is human life, which can do all the stuff animal life can, as well as reason. Plus, human life has free will.

✔ **Angelic life or pure beings:** Angelic life consists of pure spirits without bodies. Angels are superior to men and women in that their minds have all the knowledge they will ever have all at one time. Their minds are much more powerful than the minds of mere mortals, too, because they're not distracted by having a body. Without bodies, they never get sick, feel pain, or need food or sleep or shelter. They're immortal and, as pure spirits, have power over the material world.

✔ **The Supreme Pure Being:** The final and ultimate level of existence is a Supreme Pure Being who has no beginning and no end. St. Thomas said that this Supreme Being is God. Like angels, God has no mortal body but is pure spirit. Unlike angels, He has no beginning, whereas He created the angels. Unlike angels, who have limited knowledge and power, God has infinite power, which means that He's *omnipotent;* He has infinite knowledge, which means that He's *omniscient;* and He's everywhere — He's *omnipresent.*

Through governance

Ever wonder why the earth is just the right distance from the sun and has just the right balance of gases to maintain an atmosphere that supports life? The balance is delicate, much like the ecosystem in which plants produce oxygen and animals produce carbon dioxide to keep one another alive.

The planets rotate and orbit at fixed rates instead of crashing into one another. The fundamental laws of physics, chemistry, and biology must be followed; otherwise, life wouldn't exist. These facts point to a higher intelligence — a being that made these physical laws, because they didn't just happen on their own.

Nature tends to go from order to chaos. Who put things in order to begin with? A higher intelligence is indicated when you study how human DNA is so intricate, orderly, and consistent. Rather than being mere chance, life on earth is no mistake, and it follows a plan. St. Thomas said that the Great Governor is God.

These five proofs alone can't convince atheists or agnostics, but they may get their minds clicking. The bottom line is that the existence of God is reasonable and that faith doesn't contradict or oppose reason. Rather, faith complements reason.

Chapter 3

In the Beginning: Catholic Teachings on Creation and Original Sin

- -

In This Chapter

▶ Acknowledging that creation has a Creator

▶ Seeing where the devil and hell came from

▶ Experiencing the fallout of Adam and Eve's sin

▶ Expecting the world to end

- -

Since the dawn of civilization, humankind has sought to discover the origins of the world and of the universe itself. Where did we come from? How did we get here? These questions inevitably lead to others, such as who are we? And where are we going?

Catholics believe that God is the Creator of heaven and earth because that's what Divine Revelation (as found in Sacred Scripture and Sacred Tradition — see Chapter 2) tells us. This belief is supported by our human logic and science, which tell us that time and space had a beginning, whether we call that moment *creation* or the *Big Bang*. Catholics also believe that because of Adam and Eve's Original Sin, all of us have a wounded sinful nature. We all face judgment at the end of the world, and Catholicism has certain beliefs about what the end of the world will look like.

In this chapter, we explore what Catholicism teaches about the moment when the material world came into existence, the moment when the devil and sin were introduced, and what we know about the end of creation.

Making Something out of Nothing

Technically speaking, *creation* is the act of making something out of nothing, or *creatio ex nihilo* in Latin. (Changing something into something else is called *transmutation* and is a different subject entirely.) Catholics believe that God created the earth and the heavens, meaning that He made them out of nothing.

To grasp how profound this concept is, consider what scientists do in a laboratory. They mix elements to come up with new compounds, and they combine compounds to make all sorts of materials. And when they produce something that has widespread applications, such as plastic, their efforts revolutionize how people live. Their efforts can seem truly miraculous at times.

But who made the elements themselves? Who created the stuff out of which all other stuff is made? To literally make something out of thin air is something no scientist can do (not even the Professor on *Gilligan's Island*). Moving a potential thing into actuality is what a creator does, and Catholics believe that the Creator of heaven and earth is God.

The first chapter of Genesis, the first book of the Bible, tells us that in the beginning nothing existed but God. His first act of creation was to make light: "and God said, 'Let there be light' and there was light." (Genesis 1:3) If plastic has revolutionized the way we live, how much more revolutionary was the creation of light?! (Keep in mind that scientists tell us the beginning of the physical universe took place after what they call the Big Bang. That super-stellar explosion just happened to cause an enormous amount of — you guessed it — *light*.)

Breathing Life into the World: Creationism or Evolution?

A great battle has waged for centuries between those who call themselves pure creationists and those who call themselves pure evolutionists. The Catholic Church has solemnly defined that God is the Creator of the universe. At the same time, the Church has never condemned any modified version of evolution that allows for a Creator and for the spiritual creation of the immortal soul.

Intelligent design is one way Catholics approach creation from a standpoint that accommodates both faith and reason (religion and science). Are not the laws of physics and chemistry part of the divine plan of God? Because God made the universe, didn't He also make the laws that govern the planets and all the beings that exist on them?

But what about the apes?

Did human beings come from apes? If God could create something out of nothing, He could create man out of apes or He could create man from the dust of the earth. Whether using an ape or dust, at one point God breathed into man and woman an immortal soul that made them in the image and likeness of God.

During the 1960s and 1970s, many textbooks told our children that we evolved from apes. Homo Sapiens are a unique class of beings, distinct from apes just as dogs are distinct from cats. Neanderthals and Cro-Magnon beings may have resembled humans and apes, but they were not of our species. Some may have initially co-existed with our first ancestors, but they died out (just as some species do today). Human beings survived and are distinctively different from apes. British scientists working in genetics discovered that all human beings can be genetically traced to one human female via mitochondrial DNA. The newspapers nicknamed her "Eve" after the first woman and the mother of all the living in the Book of Genesis. The bottom line: However long it took and whatever process was used, it was God who designed and directed the creation of human beings.

A purely atheistic theory of evolution is incompatible with Christianity. Life did not create itself, nor is pure chance or randomness the master of the universe. All of creation works according to a design and plan — so much so that scientists can discern and ascertain that design. The planets rotate around the sun and follow orbits in such a way that we can determine every day when sunrise and sunset will occur, when the seasons will take place, and when a whole calendar year will elapse. The planetary movement is orderly; it is not chaotic or spontaneous. Otherwise, we would have crashed into Mars or Venus or the sun long ago.

Order does not happen by itself. If you throw marbles in the air, they do not land spelling words. Chaos is what happens when order is removed, and without a guiding design and plan, all of creation would be in chaos. Intelligent design and order are obvious everywhere we look. Consider these examples:

- Every human being has human DNA, which is distinct from animal DNA. We can use DNA to determine paternity or who committed a crime.
- Seasons are predictable enough that farmers know when to plant and when to harvest.
- Chemists know what elements combine with other ones to form stable and safe compounds.

Studying the order of our universe got a man to the moon and offers medical science the ability to treat deadly diseases, but Catholics trace it all back to the Creator. Evolution is still a theory and not a proven law of science. But as long as room is made in that theory for the intelligent design of a Creator, nothing is intrinsically wrong with evolution. Only when evolution kicks God out of the equation is it an offense to religion (as well as illogical).

Angels and Devils: Following God or Lucifer

The Catholic Church teaches that before the first human beings (Adam and Eve) were created in the Garden of Eden, God created beings known as *angels:* beings with no bodies. Angels are pure spirit. An angelic nature consists of an angelic intellect (mind) and an angelic will (heart). In this section, we explain Catholic beliefs about God's creation of angels — and how some of them decided to become devils.

Infused knowledge, eternal decisions

You and I are a union of body and soul. Our souls are where our rational intellect and free will reside, but our souls depend on our bodies to retrieve all necessary data. Like the memory in a brand-new computer, a soul begins life on earth totally clean and needs input from your keyboard (your body). As the body transmits that data to the soul, humans gain what is called *acquired* knowledge.

Angels have no bodies, so they cannot acquire knowledge; they need *infused* knowledge. Whereas you and I learn each day and extrapolate more from that knowledge, angels know everything at the moment of their creation. Their knowledge is gained all at once, and their will makes one choice that lasts for all eternity. In other words, angels cannot change their minds after they have made a decision. Unfortunately, some of the angels in heaven made the decision to turn away from God.

The angels' test and the devil's choice

After the angels were created but before they were in heaven, God put them to a test. To explain the point of this test, we first need to clarify what Catholics believe about heaven.

The Catholic Church teaches that once you are in heaven, you can never leave. (That's a good thing!) You can never be tempted, either — whether you're a saint (a human soul) or an angel. Heaven is being in the immediate, direct presence of God (called the *Beatific Vision*). Your intellect, which seeks truth, and your will, which seeks the good, are both perfectly fulfilled and satisfied in heaven. The same is true for angels. So, no one in heaven can sin or be tempted to sin.

Outside of heaven is a different story. Man and angel alike can be tested and tempted. Angels were created first, so their test was different than ours. We don't know the exact nature of the angels' test, but some theologians over the ages have speculated. Here are two such speculations:

✔ The angels were given a glimpse of the creation of human beings, and then God disclosed to them that out of pure love, He was going to invite the human race into heaven.

✔ God disclosed that men and women would sin, but God would forgive them and actually redeem them by becoming one of us.

No matter what the exact nature of the test, the end result is that one-third of the angels were unhappy with what God disclosed to them. Perhaps their pride resented that humans would be invited to heaven, or they were disdainful of the possibility that God would lower Himself to become a man and then raise human nature above angelic nature. Humans can look at Jesus as both King and as brother, but the angels in heaven see Christ only as Lord and King, surely another source of irritation to the rebellious angels.

Lucifer was the most intelligent of all the angels. He and one-third of the angels rebelled against God and refused to submit to His dominion. Saint Michael and the other two-thirds decided to remain loyal to God and fought against the angels who rebelled. Hell was created by God as a place of eternal punishment for Lucifer (who was thereafter known as the *devil*) and all the fallen angels who accompanied him.

It is not accurate to say that God created the devil. God created the angel Lucifer, who was intrinsically good and who freely chose to become bad. His evil decision cast him into hell.

Witnessing the Original Sin

The Book of Genesis begins with the story of creation in general and then focuses on Adam and Eve and their fall from God's grace. In this section, we explain the choice they made, God's punishment for it, and the everlasting effect of that choice on human nature.

Tempting our first parents

Just as God tested the angels (see the preceding section), He also tested the first human beings: Adam and Eve. He told them not to eat of the forbidden fruit, which was found on only one tree in the entire, bountiful Garden of Eden: the Tree of Knowledge of Good and Evil. All they had to do was overlook one tree! A serpent, who was the devil in disguise, told Eve that she and Adam wouldn't die if they ate the fruit of the tree forbidden by God. Eve ate from the tree and got her husband to do likewise. Adam and Eve chose to defy God and disobey His command. God punished them both — and one of the penalties was death. They didn't die on the spot, but had they not disobeyed the Lord, mankind would have remained immortal.

Of course, we must place some blame on the serpent. But he never coerced the free will of Eve or Adam. Another name for the devil is the Author of All Lies, which is evident in his distortion and perversion of the truth.

Temptation comes from the world, the flesh, or the devil. It is a proposition in our mind to choose an inferior good over a superior one. No rational person chooses evil for the sake of evil; such a person is a sociopath. Nonetheless, rational people do sometimes choose evil: They choose lower goods, ignore higher goods, and often employ immoral means to fulfill (supposedly) morally good ends.

The devil takes a lesser good — like pleasure, convenience, or comfort — and tempts us to raise it above higher goods like life, honor, duty, commitment, family, friendship, and faith. Adam and Eve succumbed to the temptation, and there were consequences.

Losing gifts

When Adam and Eve sinned by disobeying God, they felt ashamed and hid from God. But immediate consequences occurred. After all, sin is not just breaking the law of God; it's also engaging in activity that's dangerous (sometimes lethal) to the soul. Sin causes separation from the Lord.

Here is how Genesis 3:16–19 describes God's punishment:

> To the woman He said, "I will greatly multiply your pain in childbearing; in pain you shall bring forth children, yet your desire will be for your husband, and he shall rule over you."

> And to Adam He said, "Because you have listened to the voice of your wife and have eaten of the tree of which I commanded you, 'You shall not eat of it,' cursed is the ground because of you; in toil you shall eat of it all the days of your life; thorns and thistles it shall bring forth to you, and you shall eat the plants of the field. In the sweat of your face you shall eat bread until you return to the ground, for out of it you were taken; you are dust and to dust you shall return."

The main gifts Adam and Eve lost were *sanctifying grace* (that which makes a person holy and allows him to be in the presence of God), *immortality* (freedom from death), and *impassibility* (freedom from all pain). Without sanctifying grace, heaven was not possible, ever. Adam and Eve were subjected to disease, illness, pain, misery, suffering, toil, labor, and death itself.

As if all this weren't enough, Original Sin had another effect, which we explain next.

Wounding our nature

Concupiscence is the inclination of the human soul toward evil. It's a consequence of the wounds created by the sin of Adam and Eve, which every human being inherits, and is called *Original Sin.* The wound in human nature that took place immediately was the darkening of the intellect, the weakening of the will, and the disordering of the lower passions and emotions:

- **Darkening of the intellect:** This wound is the reason many times we can't see clearly the right path to take even though it's right under our nose, so to speak. Sometimes, our wounded human nature clouds our intellect's ability to see with precision the proper course to take. Often, we need good advice, counsel, and perhaps even fraternal correction to compensate when our minds are unable to digest the situation or we find it difficult to figure out the proper solution to our problem.

- **Weakening of the will:** Even if our mind knows what to do, we lack the patience or courage to see it through. An addict needs to quit and knows the drugs he takes are killing him, but his will is so weak that he can't just say no. Ask anyone who's on a diet or trying to quit smoking how hard it is. The intellect *knows* the body can do better, but the will is too weak to hang in there and do what needs to be done.

- **The disordering of the senses:** This phenomenon occurs when our emotions override or overcome our reason. Anger, lust, envy, and so on can become so strong and powerful that our minds are blinded to the evil within them. How many sins and crimes have been committed in the heat of anger or lust? Man was not made of stone with no emotions. Jesus had emotions in His human nature. But Original Sin wounded our human nature so that sometimes our emotions are no longer under the immediate control of our intellect.

Being redeemed by God's grace

If the wound resulting from Original Sin was the end of the human story, it would be bleak and pathetic, for sure. But God's mercy and love are without limit. God's justice condemned and punished humankind for disobeying, and God's mercy promised that a Messiah would redeem and save the human race. Salvation would then be possible for everyone, past, present and future. The Book of Genesis tells of punishment but also of promise.

Speaking to the serpent, God said:

> Upon your belly you shall go and dust you shall eat all the days of your life. I will put enmity between you and the woman, and between your seed and her seed; he shall bruise your head, and you shall bruise his heel (Genesis 3:14-15).

The Catholic Church sees a prophecy in this verse, which is fulfilled in the person of the Virgin Mary. She is considered the woman whose offspring (Jesus) will crush the head of the serpent (the devil). By His grace, God devised a plan to save and redeem man by sending the Son. When Jesus died on the cross (on Good Friday) and rose from the dead (on Easter), He opened the gates of Paradise and made heaven possible once again (see Chapter 4).

Facing the four last things

The Catholic Church teaches that when a person experiences *death,* she also experiences *particular judgment, heaven,* or *hell.* These are called the *four last things.* Why do we discuss this subject in a chapter about creation? Because without the Original Sin of Adam and Eve, humankind wouldn't experience the four last things. So at the beginning of the human experience, the seeds were sown for what occurs at the end of each human life.

When a person dies, there is immediate judgment on his soul, or *particular judgment.* If a person has lived an evil, immoral, sinful life and is unrepentant at the moment of death, he condemns himself to eternal damnation in hell. On the other hand, a holy person who has lived a virtuous and saintly life and dies in the state of grace is rewarded with eternal happiness in heaven. Most people are not bad enough to go to hell yet not good enough to go directly to heaven. These are people who die with some attachments to their former sins. In this case, the person is cleansed (purged) of his attachments in a state of being called *purgatory.* Purgatory is not hell with parole. Purgatory is the state of purification from sins. As we explain in Chapter 13, sin leaves a scar on the soul, and if the scar is deep, more treatment is needed to heal it and restore the former beauty.

Hell is pure punishment for evil — divine retribution. Purgatory is medicinal and therapeutic. Like gold that is purified in fire, purgatory cleanses our attachments to sin so when we do go through the pearly gates, we do so wearing the proper wedding garment. We talk even more about purgatory in Chapter 18.

Anticipating What's to Come: Moving toward the End of Creation

For Catholics (and most other Christians), inherent in the story of creation is the belief that God will create a new heaven and a new earth at the end of time. No one knows when the end of this present creation will occur, but the faithful believe in the Second Coming of Christ, the resurrection of the dead, the general judgment, and the end of the world: the four last things of the entire universe (for the four last things that each individual person encounters, check out the preceding section).

TECHNICAL STUFF

Researching the word "rapture"

The Latin Vulgate Bible of Saint Jerome (A.D. 400) uses the word *rapiemur* in 1 Thessalonians 4:17. Many Bible translators translate this as "being taken up." But no one coined the word *rapture* until the 17th century, and the belief that some people would be removed from earth and taken to heaven prior to the Second Coming was not well-known until the late 1950s when it was popularized in evangelical Christian magazines. These days, popular Christian books and movies have spread the idea of the rapture far and wide, as have so-called "prophets" who claim to know the precise date and time it will occur. Catholics don't ascribe to belief in the rapture, and they also don't claim to have any inside scoop on when the Second Coming will occur.

The Second Coming

Catholics believe that Jesus died on Good Friday, rose from the dead on Easter Sunday, and 40 days later ascended into heaven. They also believe there will be a Second Coming of Christ to mark the end times. He will not be born as a baby again. Instead, He will return to earth as a full-grown man, the same as He was when He ascended into heaven. The first time around, He entered the world in abject poverty and humility. He will return as the victorious conqueror of sin, death, and the devil.

Before the Second Coming of Christ, which will usher in the end times, these things will happen:

- ✔ All Gentiles will be united in the Church.
- ✔ All Jews will be one in the Messiah's salvation.
- ✔ The Church will be assailed one last time by the Antichrist, who will try to sway many people by deception.
- ✔ Christ will be victorious over this final unleashing of evil through a cosmic battle (Armageddon).

Notice that this list does not mention the *rapture* (a belief that certain "chosen" people will be taken up to heaven before the Second Coming of Christ) nor a reign of a thousand years of the Evil One (the Antichrist). That's because the Catholic Church does not ascribe to these beliefs, which tend to be held more frequently by evangelical Christians.

The tribulation of the church by the Antichrist may last a short or long period of time; the jury is out on that one. There will be a test of faith and a battle for souls. The end will happen when the Second Coming of Christ takes place and the Antichrist and the *Whore of Babylon* (the Antichrist's accomplice, who is mentioned in the Book of Revelation, or the Apocalypse) are defeated and vanquished.

Resurrection of the dead

Catholics believe that after Jesus returns, the dead will be raised. Bodies and souls will be reunited, but not like in any horror movie or thriller video you've seen. The dead bodies of the souls in heaven will be resurrected and then be *glorified* (meaning they will be like Jesus's resurrected body, which was immortal, was impervious to pain and injury, never aged, and never got sick) and taken into heaven. The damned will get their bodies back, but they'll not be glorified. The souls in purgatory will be released and get glorified bodies, which will enter heaven.

General judgment

Immediately after the resurrection of the dead, the general judgment will take place. The general judgment is not an appeal or second chance; it's merely the public disclosure of all the private judgments that took place earlier. The general judgment will manifest both divine justice (in rewarding good and punishing evil) and divine mercy (in the forgiveness of sinners). This way, nobody in heaven is going to ask, "How did *he* get in here?"

The end of the world

The Catholic Church teaches that after general judgment, the risen bodies go back to heaven or hell, and the world ends. The material universe ceases to exist, and reality consists only of heaven and hell — nothing else. Theologians and scientists are in agreement that the universe will end someday. *When* the world ends is irrelevant because your eternal destiny of heaven or hell is already decided well before that happens. Better to be worried and prepared for your *particular* judgment (see the earlier section "Facing the four last things") because you don't know the day or hour for that one, either. The Catechism also talks about the creation of a new heaven and new earth for the glorified, resurrected bodies, since the old earth will be destroyed at the end of the world. But no one knows what that'll be like except God alone.

You don't have to be worried about hell or the end of the world if you live a moral life by obeying the Ten Commandments (see Chapter 12), seeking God's forgiveness for your sins, and trying to live a saintly life. Thanks to Jesus, Original Sin doesn't prevent us from getting to heaven. Read more about Jesus's sacrifice in Chapter 4.

Chapter 4

Believing in Jesus

In This Chapter

▶ Understanding the human nature and the divine nature of Jesus

▶ Examining the Gospels from the Catholic perspective

▶ Looking at some nasty rumors about Jesus that ran wild

. . . .

*L*ike all Christians, Catholics share the core belief that Jesus of Nazareth is Lord and Savior. The term *Lord* is used because Christians believe Jesus is *divine* — the Son of God. The term *Savior* is used because Christians believe that Jesus saved all humankind by dying for our sins.

Some people may think that Catholicism considers Jesus a hybrid — half human and half divine. That's not the case at all. Catholicism doesn't see Jesus as having a split personality or as a spiritual Frankenstein, partly human and partly divine. He's regarded as fully human and fully divine — true man and true God. He's considered one divine person with two equal natures, human and divine. This premise is the cornerstone of all Christian mysteries. It can't be explained completely but must be believed on faith. (See Chapter 2 for the scoop on what faith really means.)

The Nicene Creed, a highly theological profession of faith, says volumes about what Christianity in general (and the Catholic Church in particular) believes about the person called Jesus. (You can read the Nicene Creed in Chapter 10 and the Apostles' Creed in Chapter 2.) This chapter doesn't say volumes, but it does tell you the need-to-know points for understanding Catholicism's perspective on Jesus.

Understanding Jesus, the God-Man

Jesus, the God-Man, having a fully divine nature and a fully human nature in one divine person, is the core and center of Christian belief.

"True God" and "became man" are key phrases in the Nicene Creed, which highlights the fundamental doctrine of Jesus as the God-Man:

- ✔ As God, Jesus possessed a fully divine nature, so He was able to perform miracles, such as changing water into wine; curing sickness, disease, and disability; and raising the dead. His greatest act of divinity was to rise from the dead Himself.

- ✔ As man, Jesus had a human mother, Mary, who gave birth to Him and nursed Him. He lived and grew up like any other man. He taught, preached, suffered, and died. So Jesus had a fully human nature as well.

You can read the complete Nicene Creed in Chapter 10.

The Old Testament usually uses the word *Lord* (*Adonai* in Hebrew) in connection with the word *God* (*Elohim* in Hebrew). An example is the phrase "Hear, O Israel, the Lord our God is one Lord" in Deuteronomy 6:4. But the New Testament asserts through the Epistle of St. Paul to the Philippians (2:11) "that Jesus Christ is Lord."

The human nature of Jesus

Jesus had a physical body with all the usual parts: two eyes, two ears, two legs, a heart, a brain, a stomach, and so on. He also possessed a human intellect (mind) and will (heart) and experienced human emotions, such as joy and sorrow. The Gospel According to John, for example, says that Jesus cried at the death of his friend Lazarus. Jesus wasn't born with the ability to speak. He had to learn how to walk and talk — how to be, act, and think as a human. These things are called *acquired* knowledge. Other things were directly revealed to His human mind by the divine intellect; these are called *infused* knowledge.

Jesus did *not* share sin with human beings. As a Divine Person, He could not sin because it would mean negating Himself (sin is going against the will of God). Being human doesn't mean being capable of sinning, nor does it mean that you've sinned somewhere along the line. Being human means having a free will and rational intellect joined to a physical body. Humans can choose to do good or choose to do evil.

Catholics believe that human beings don't determine what's good or evil because that's intrinsic to the thing itself. Whether something is good or evil is independent of personal opinion. Murder is evil in and of itself. Someone may personally think an action is okay, but if it's intrinsically evil, that person is only fooling himself and will eventually regret it. Jesus in His humanity always chose to do good, but that didn't make Him any less human. Even though He never got drunk, swore, or told a dirty joke, He was still human.

FROM THE BIBLE

Even Jesus got some downtime

Jesus wasn't a workaholic. He got some rest and recreation while visiting His friends Martha, Mary, and Lazarus (John 12:2), and He attended the wedding feast of Cana with His mother (John 2:1–2). Jesus took a nap in a boat while the apostles stayed awake on deck (Luke 8:22–23) and went to an out-of-the-way place to pray (Matthew 14:23). So, too, God the Father rested after creating the whole world (Genesis 2:1–3).

REMEMBER

It's important to keep in mind that Catholicism doesn't depend *exclusively* on the Bible for what's known about Jesus. *Sacred Tradition* (see Chapter 2) fills in some of the gaps when the Bible is silent or ambiguous on certain points, such as whether Jesus ever married or had any siblings.

Did Jesus have a wife and kids?

The last verse of the Gospel According to John (21:25) says, "There are also many other things which Jesus did; were every one of them to be written, I suppose that the world itself could not contain the books that would be written." The Bible is silent in some areas. Was Jesus ever married? Did He have a wife and children? The Bible doesn't say either way. You could presume He was unmarried, because a wife is never mentioned. (The Bible does mention Peter's *mother-in-law* being cured, but the Bible never classifies the other disciples and apostles as married or single.)

No Christian denomination or religion has ever believed that Jesus was married, even though the Bible never categorically states that He remained unmarried. The reason? Tradition. Christianity has maintained the tradition that Jesus was celibate and never married, even though the Bible at best implies it by never mentioning a wife or children.

WARNING!

Despite what you may read in some modern novels, Jesus and Mary Magdalene were never a couple, legally or romantically. Counterfeit Gospels were written a few hundred years after the legitimate ones that alleged such a relationship with the intent to undermine the Church. No one ever took them seriously, and no accredited scholar today gives them any credibility.

Medieval literature is filled with stories on the *Holy Grail,* which was the alleged chalice Jesus used at the Last Supper. Folklore and legend imply that the Knights Templar may have found it while on Crusade, but there has never been any evidence whatsoever to establish or even suggest that the Grail symbolizes a bloodline running through European monarchies going back to the supposed offspring of Christ and Mary Magdalene. These stories are all fiction; there is no historical or biblical evidence to suggest otherwise.

Whenever the Bible is silent or ambiguous, Sacred Tradition fills in the gaps. So to Catholics, a written record in the Bible is that He was a man, His name was Jesus, and His mother was Mary, and a revealed truth of Sacred Tradition is that He never married.

Did Jesus have any brothers or sisters?

Some Christians believe Mary had other children after she had Jesus, but the Catholic Church officially teaches that Mary always remained a virgin — before, during, and after the birth of Jesus. She had one son, and that son was Jesus.

Another belief among some Christians is that Joseph had children from a prior marriage, and after he became a widower and married the mother of Jesus, those children became stepbrothers and stepsisters of Jesus. Those who believe that Jesus had siblings invoke Mark 6:3: "Is not this the carpenter, the son of Mary and brother of James and Joses and Judas and Simon and are not his sisters here with us?" And Matthew 12:46 says, "His mother and his brothers stood outside."

So who were these brothers and sisters mentioned in the Gospel, if they weren't actual siblings of Jesus? The Catholic Church reminds its members that the original four Gospels were written in the Greek language, not English. The Greek word used in all three occasions is *adelphoi* (plural of *adelphos*), which can be translated as *brothers*. But that same Greek word can also mean *cousins* or *relatives*, as in an uncle or a nephew.

An example is shown in the Old Testament. Genesis 11:27 says that Abram and Haran were brothers, sons of Terah. Lot was the son of Haran and thus the nephew of Abram, who was later called Abraham by God. Ironically, Genesis 14:14 and 14:16 in the King James Version of the Bible refer to Lot as the *brother* of Abraham. The Greek word used in the Septuagint version of the Old Testament, the version used at the time of Jesus, is again *adelphos*. Obviously, a word that denoted a nephew-uncle relationship was unavailable in ancient Hebrew or Greek. So an alternative use of *brother* (*adelphos* in Greek) is used in those passages, because Lot was actually Abraham's nephew.

The Catholic Church reasons that if the Bible uses *brother* to refer to a nephew in one instance, then why not another? Why can't the *adelphoi* (brothers) of Jesus be his relatives — cousins or other family members? Why must that word be used in a restrictive way in the Gospel when it's used broadly in the Old Testament?

The Church uses other reasoning as well. If these *brothers* were siblings, where were they during the Crucifixion and death of their brother? Mary and a few other women were there, but the only man mentioned in the Gospel at the event was the Apostle John, and he was in no way related to Jesus, by blood or marriage. And before Jesus died on the cross, He told John, "Behold your mother" (John 19:27). Why entrust His mother to John if other adult children could've taken care of her? Only if Mary were alone would Jesus worry about her enough to say what He did to John.

And the Church asks this: If Jesus had blood brothers, or even half-brothers or stepbrothers, why didn't they assume roles of leadership after His death? Why allow Peter and the other apostles to run the Church and make decisions if immediate family members were around? Yet if the only living relatives were distant cousins, nieces, nephews, and such, it all makes sense.

The debate will continue for centuries to come. The bottom line is the authoritative decision of the Church. Catholicism doesn't place the Church above Scripture but sees her as the one and only authentic guardian and interpreter of the written word and the unwritten or spoken word, or Sacred Tradition.

The divine nature of Jesus

Catholics believe that Jesus performed miracles, such as walking on water; expelling demons; rising from the dead himself and raising the dead, such as Lazarus in Chapter 11 of the Gospel According to St. John; and saving all humankind, becoming the Redeemer, Savior, and Messiah. He founded the Catholic Church and instituted, explicitly or implicitly, all seven sacraments. (The *seven sacraments* are Catholic rituals marking seven stages of spiritual development. See Chapters 8 and 9 for more on the seven sacraments.)

Jesus is the second person of the Holy Trinity — God the Son. And God the Son (Jesus) is as much God as God the Father and God the Holy Spirit.

Although Christians, Jews, and Muslims all believe in one God, Christians believe in a *Triune God,* one God in three persons — God the Father, God the Son, and God the Holy Spirit — also known as the *Holy Trinity.* The mystery of the Holy Trinity is how you can have three divine persons but not three gods. Catholics don't perceive the Holy Trinity as three gods but as three distinct — but not separate — persons in one God.

The divine mind of Jesus was infinite, because He had the mind of God; the human mind of Jesus was, like the human mind, limited. The human mind could only know so much and only what God the Father wanted it to know. When asked about the time and date of the end of the world, Jesus's apparent ignorance in Mark 13:32 "of that day or that hour, no one knows, not even the angels in heaven, nor the Son, but only the Father," is proof that the human intellect of Christ was not privy to all that the divine intellect of Christ knew.

To the Catholic Church, overemphasizing Jesus's humanity to the exclusion of His divinity is as bad as ignoring or downplaying His humanity to exalt His divinity. To understand the Catholic Church's stance on Jesus's divinity even better, check out the doctrine of the Hypostatic Union in the section "Monophystism."

The Savior of our sins; the Redeemer of the world

The study of Christ evokes two key questions. The first is "Who is Jesus Christ?" So far in this chapter, we've been addressing this question like this: Jesus is the son of God, and He is both God and man, divine and human. The second question is "Why did Jesus become man?" This question is answered by the Cross.

Catholics firmly believe that Jesus is the Savior of the world and the Redeemer of the human race. Jesus died for our sins and ransomed us from sin and death. As we explain in Chapter 3, the first (original) sin of Adam and Eve incurred guilt and punishment on all human beings. Their act of disobedience resulted in a serious wound to human nature. Because of original sin, humans lost God's sanctifying grace; were expelled from paradise; and faced lives full of sickness and death, toil and labor. No one could enter heaven until a Savior was born.

Messiah is the Hebrew word for Savior, and in Greek the word is *Christos.* Both words also mean "Anointed One." The Old Testament prophesied that a Savior would be sent to save the human race from sin and death, and Christians believe that God sent His son, Jesus, to be that Savior.

As the Son of God, Jesus offered his life on the Cross as a supreme sacrifice to atone for sin. His blood redeemed us and freed us from the grip death had on us. Before Christ, no one could go to heaven after death. But because Jesus opened the gates by dying for our sins, everyone has the chance to enter Paradise forever. Appropriately, the word *redeemer* means someone who rescues others from danger.

The Catholic Church graphically reminds her members of the human nature of Jesus by conspicuously placing a crucifix in every church. A *crucifix* is a cross with the crucified figure of Jesus attached to it. It's a reminder to Catholics that Jesus didn't pretend to be human. The nails in His hands and feet, the crown of thorns on His head, and the wound in His side where a soldier thrust a lance into His heart all poignantly remind the faithful that Jesus's suffering, which is known as his *Passion,* was real. He felt real pain, and He really died. He was really human. If He had been only a god pretending to be human, His pain and death would have been faked.

Deep thoughts about Father and Son

To the Church, the relationship between God the Father and God the Son (Jesus) isn't the same as the relationship between human parents and children. Human fathers aren't fathers before their sons or daughters are born. If you were an only child, for example, could your dad ever have been called a father before you existed? No. Until a son or daughter is born, no man is a father.

So if you think in those terms, you may think that God the Father didn't exist before the Son

(Jesus) was born. But the Church says that God the Father has always been the Father. So if the Father has always been the Father, then the Son (Jesus) has always been, too. Jesus is the eternal Son of the Father. The Father didn't exist without the Son for even one instant, one second or microsecond, because the Father was always Father and the Son was always Son.

If you look closely at a crucifix, you may see the letters INRI on it. Those letters are an abbreviation for the Latin words *Iesus Nazarenus Rex Iudaeorum*, which mean "Jesus of Nazareth, King of the Jews." These words were written on the cross above Jesus's head by order of Pontius Pilate, the Roman governor who condemned Jesus to death.

In addition to reminding believers of Jesus's human nature and His painful sacrifice, the crucifix reminds them that Jesus commanded us to take up our cross daily and follow Him. (For this reason, many Catholics have a crucifix at home.) The concept of *dying to self* is something spiritual writers speak of often. The process of dying to self involves enduring unavoidable suffering with dignity and faith. Seeing Jesus depicted on His cross is meant to encourage the devout to do likewise and offer up their sufferings as did Jesus.

The obedient Son of God

Catholicism regards Jesus as the eternal Son of the Father and teaches that the relationship between Father and Son is one of profound love. To understand this dynamic even better, see the nearby sidebar "Deep thoughts about Father and Son."

The belief that the relationship between Father and Son is so close, intense, and perfect led St. Thomas Aquinas (see Chapter 21) to say that the third person of the Holy Trinity — the Holy Spirit — is the living, personified fruit of that mutual love.

Obedience is a sign of love and respect, and Catholics believe that Jesus obeyed the will of the Father. To Catholics, "Thy will be done" is more than just a phrase of the Our Father. It's the motto of Jesus Christ, Son of God.

And Catholic belief maintains that God the Father's will was for Jesus to

- ✔ Reveal God as a community of three persons (Father, Son, and Holy Spirit) united in divine love
- ✔ Show God's love for all humankind
- ✔ Be humankind's Redeemer and Savior

The Gospel Truth: Examining Four Written Records of Jesus

The New Testament contains four *Gospels,* books of the Bible that tell the life and words of Jesus. The four evangelists, Matthew, Mark, Luke, and John, each wrote one of the four Gospels, considered by Christians to be the most important of all biblical text, because these four books contain the words and deeds of Jesus when He walked this earth.

Even though a different man wrote each of the four Gospels, the same Holy Spirit inspired each man. *Inspiration* is a special gift of the Holy Spirit given to the *sacred authors* (those who wrote the Bible) so that only the words that God wanted written down *were* written down.

Catholic beliefs about the Gospel

The Catholic Church emphasizes that it's imperative to consider the four Gospels as actually forming one whole unit. The four Gospels aren't four *separate* Gospels but four *versions* of one Gospel. That's why each one is called *The Gospel According to Matthew* or *The Gospel According to Mark,* for example, and not *Matthew's Gospel* or *Mark's Gospel.* No one single account gives the entire picture, but like facets on a diamond, all sides form to make one beautiful reality. The faithful need all four versions to appreciate the full depth and impact of Jesus.

Catholicism cherishes each different perspective but stresses that all four together, in conjunction with the other inspired writings of the New and Old Testaments, give a better portrait of Jesus.

Both the Holy Spirit and the author, inspired by the Holy Spirit, intended to use or not use the same words and to present or not present the same ideas and images based on the particular author's distinct audience. For more on how the Gospels are both inspired and audience-savvy, see the section "Comparing Gospels."

Figure 4-1 shows how Matthew, Mark, Luke, and John are often depicted in art from Revelation (Apocalypse) 4:7. According to St. Ambrose (339-397), a Father of the Church (learned scholar), a man with wings symbolizes Matthew because he begins his Gospel account with the human origins and birth of Christ. Mark starts his account with the regal power of Christ, the reign of God, and is therefore symbolized by a lion with wings, which was held in high esteem by the Romans. Luke begins his account with the father of John the Baptist, Zachary, the priest, and is symbolized by an ox with wings because the priests of the temple often sacrificed oxen on the altar. John is shown as an eagle because he soars to heaven in his introduction to the Gospel with the preexistence of Christ as the Word (*logos* in Greek).

Figure 4-1:
The writers of the four Gospels are often depicted like this from Revelation (Apocalypse) 4:7.

Matthew, The Man

Mark, The Lion

Luke, The Ox

John, The Eagle

How the Gospels came to be

Were Matthew, Mark, Luke, and John standing on the sidelines taking notes as Jesus preached or performed miracles? No. In fact, only two of the four, Matthew and John, were actual apostles and eyewitnesses, so you can't think of Matthew, Mark, Luke, and John as, say, reporters covering a story for the media.

Before the Gospels were written, the words and deeds of Jesus were told by word of mouth. In other words, the Gospels were preached before they were written. The spoken word preceded the written word. And after it was written, because the papyrus on which the scrolls were written was so fragile, expensive, and rare, most people didn't read the Word but heard it as it was spoken in church during Mass. The Church calls it the three-level development of the Gospel: first, the actual sayings and teachings of Christ; second, the oral tradition where the apostles preached to the people what they saw and heard; and third, the writing by the sacred authors to ensure that the message wouldn't be altered.

The Gospel truth, literally

The Catholic Church firmly believes that every word of the Bible has a literal meaning in both the original language of the sacred author and in the language of the translator. However, the Church does not believe that every word is meant to have a literal interpretation. What's the difference?

Consider an example: Jesus says in John 15:5, "I am the vine, you are the branches." The literal meanings of the words *vine* and *branches* (*ampelos* and *klemata* in Greek) are essential to understanding the passage. You know what a vine is and the difference between a vine and a branch — you know the literal meaning of each word. But the intention of the original author (John) as well as the speaker (Jesus) in this passage requires you to go a step further. You are not a plant, so this passage must be a figure of speech.

Sometimes, Bible passages require a literal interpretation. For instance, in John 1:63, "his

name is John" literally means that the son of Elizabeth and Zecchariah is called John (who would later be known as John the Baptist). But the Bible is also rich with metaphors and other figures of speech, such as Jesus calling himself the Lamb of God (see John 1:29). Obviously, Jesus is not literally a four-legged sheep, but you still need to know what a lamb is in order to appreciate the analogy.

How do you know which biblical passages to interpret literally and which to approach as figures of speech? Well, we know of an ancient axiom regarding scripture: "If you take a text out of context, you get a pretext." In other words, the context of the word, phrase, or passage can be properly interpreted by the context. This means considering the previous and following words and phrases, verses, and chapters.

The New Testament was written between A.D. 35 and 100. St. Irenaeus (c. 130-200) in A.D. 188 was the first person to mention the four Gospels. But it wasn't until the Council of Carthage in A.D. 397 that the final and official judgment of the Church came out and explicitly listed the 27 books in the New Testament, including the four Gospels. St. Jerome (c. 341-420) was the first one to combine both the Old and New Testaments into one volume and to translate all the books from Hebrew, Aramaic, and Greek into Latin, which was the common tongue of his time. This Latin version of the Bible is the *Vulgate*. It took him from A.D. 382 to 405 to finish this monumental task, but he was the first person to coordinate the complete and whole Christian Bible.

Comparing Gospels

The Catholic Church regards the entire Bible as the inspired and inerrant (error-free) Word of God, so the Gospels in particular are crucial because they accurately relate what Jesus said and did while on earth. As we discuss in Chapter 2, the Catholic Church believes that the Bible is sacred literature, but as literature, some parts of it should be interpreted literally, and other parts are intended to be read figuratively. The Gospels are among the books that are primarily interpreted literally insofar as what Jesus said and did.

Matthew and Luke

Matthew opens his Gospel with a long genealogy of Jesus, beginning with Abraham and tracing it all the way down to Joseph, the husband of Mary, "of whom Jesus was born, who is called the Messiah."

Matthew was addressing potential converts from Judaism. A Jewish audience was probably interested in hearing this family tree because the Hebrew people are often called the Children of Abraham. That's why Matthew began with Abraham and connected him to Jesus to open his Gospel.

Luke offers a similar genealogy to Matthew's, but he works backward from Jesus to Adam, 20 generations before Abraham. Luke was a Gentile physician, and his audience was Gentile, not Jewish. Neither Matthew nor Luke used editorial fiction, but each carefully selected what to say to his respective audience through the inspiration of the Holy Spirit. A Gentile audience wasn't as concerned with a connection to Abraham as a Jewish audience. Gentiles were interested in a connection between Jesus and the first man, Adam, because Gentiles were big into Greek philosophy. Plato, Socrates, and Aristotle — just to mention a few famous Greek thinkers who lived before Christ — philosophized about the origins of humanity and, thus, making a link between Jesus and the first man would have greatly appealed to them. In the Sermon on the Mount, Matthew mentions that prior to giving the sermon, Jesus "went up on the mountain" (Matthew 5:1), but Luke describes Jesus giving a Sermon on the Plain, "a level place" (Luke 6:17). Both men quote the teachings from these sermons, called the *Beatitudes*. See the following version from Matthew 5:

> Seeing the crowds, he went up on the mountain, and when he sat down his disciples came to him. And he opened his mouth and taught them, saying:
>
> "Blessed are the poor in spirit, for theirs is the kingdom of heaven.
>
> "Blessed are those who mourn, for they shall be comforted.
>
> "Blessed are the meek, for they shall inherit the earth.
>
> "Blessed are those who hunger and thirst for righteousness, for they shall be satisfied.
>
> "Blessed are the merciful, for they shall obtain mercy.
>
> "Blessed are the pure in heart, for they shall see God.
>
> "Blessed are the peacemakers, for they shall be called sons of God.
>
> "Blessed are those who are persecuted for righteousness' sake, for theirs is the kingdom of heaven.

"Blessed are you when men revile you and persecute you and utter all kinds of evil against you falsely on my account. Rejoice and be glad, for your reward is great in heaven, for so men persecuted the prophets who were before you."

Now contrast the Sermon on the Mount in the Gospel of Matthew with Luke 6:17–26, which follows:

And he came down with them and stood on a level place, with a great crowd of his disciples and a great multitude of people from all Judea and Jerusalem and the seacoast of Tyre and Sidon, who came to hear him and to be healed of their diseases; and those who were troubled with unclean spirits were cured. And all the crowd sought to touch him, for power came forth from him and healed them all. And he lifted up his eyes on his disciples, and said:

"Blessed are you poor, for yours is the kingdom of God.

"Blessed are you that hunger now, for you shall be satisfied.

"Blessed are you that weep now, for you shall laugh.

"Blessed are you when men hate you, and when they exclude you and revile you, and cast out your name as evil, on account of the Son of man! Rejoice in that day, and leap for joy, for behold, your reward is great in heaven; for so their fathers did to the prophets.

"But woe to you that are rich, for you have received your consolation.

"Woe to you that are well fed now, for you shall hunger.

"Woe to you that laugh now, for you shall mourn and weep.

"Woe to you when all men speak well of you, for so their fathers did to the false prophets."

So why the difference in location for these sermons — mount and plain?

Any good preacher knows that when you have a good sermon, you can use it more than once, especially if you're preaching in another place to a different crowd. It's not unreasonable to presume that Jesus preached His Beatitudes more than once, because He moved around quite a bit and, aside from the apostles, no one in the crowd would have heard the message before.

Matthew mentions the occasion of the Sermon on the Mount because his Jewish audience would have been keen on such a detail. The reason? Moses was given the Law, the Ten Commandments, on Mount Sinai. So Jesus was giving the law of blessedness, also known as the Beatitudes, also from a mount. Matthew also makes sure to quote Jesus, saying that He had "come not to abolish them [the law and the prophets], but to fulfill them," (Matthew 5:17) also appealing to a Jewish listener. Moses gave the Ten Commandments that came from God to the Hebrew people, and now Jesus was going to fulfill that Law.

Luke, on the other hand, mentions the time that the sermon was given on a plain. Why mention the obscure detail of a level ground? Luke was writing for a Gentile audience. Unlike the Jewish audience of Matthew, which was used to the Law being given from God to Moses on Mount Sinai, the Gentiles were accustomed to giving and listening to philosophical debates in the Greek tradition. Philosophers such as Plato, Socrates, and Aristotle debated one another on level ground, standing shoulder-to-shoulder, eye-to-eye, instead of lecturing from an elevated podium, in order to give a sense of fairness and equality to the discussion. Because a Gentile audience would have been more interested in a speech given by Jesus in similar fashion, Luke retold such an occurrence.

A slight difference can be detected in some of the wording of Luke's account versus that of Matthew, as well as an addition of "woe to you" given by Jesus to correspond with each "blessed are you," which isn't found in Matthew. Again, a preacher often adapts an older sermon by adding to, subtracting from, or modifying his original work, depending on his second audience. The Catholic Church maintains that the discrepancy comes from a change Jesus made because neither sacred author would feel free to alter anything Jesus said or did on his own human authority.

Mark

Mark is the shortest of the four Gospels, due to the fact that his audience was mainly Roman. When you belong to an imperial police state, you're not as concerned about making intricate connections to a Hebrew past, and you're not interested in lengthy philosophical dialogues. You want action. That's why the Gospel According to Mark has fewer sermons and more movement. It's fast-paced, nonstop, continuous narrative, like an excited person telling the events "a mile a minute." Romans would have been far more attentive to the Gospel According to Mark than to the Gospels of Matthew, Luke, or John.

Mark explicitly describes the Roman Centurion, a military commander of a hundred soldiers, at the Crucifixion as making the proclamation, "Truly, this man was the Son of God" (Mark 15:39). His Roman audience would've certainly perked up when that was said because it was an act of faith from one of their own kind.

Like Luke, Mark wasn't one of the original 12 apostles. Matthew and John were apostles, but Luke and Mark were 2 of the 72 disciples. The *apostles* were there in person to witness all that Jesus said and did. The *disciples* often had to resort to secondhand information, told to them by other sources. Luke most likely received much of his information from Mary, the mother of Jesus, and Mark undoubtedly used his friend Peter, the chief apostle, as his source.

John

John was the last one to write a Gospel, and his is the most theological of the four. The other three are so similar in content, style, and sequence that they're often called the *Synoptic Gospels,* from the Greek word *sunoptikos,* meaning *summary* or *general view.*

John, who wrote his Gospel much later than the others, was writing for a Christian audience. He presumed that people had already heard the basic facts, and he provided advanced information to complement the Jesus 101 material covered in Matthew, Mark, and Luke. In other words, The Gospel According to John is like college calculus, whereas the Synoptic Gospels are like advanced high-school algebra.

John sets the tone by opening his Gospel with a philosophical concept of preexistence: Before Jesus became man by being conceived and born of the Virgin Mary, He existed from all eternity in His divinity because He's the second person of the Holy Trinity. Take a look at the first line from the Gospel According to John: "In the beginning was the Word, and the Word was with God and the Word was God."

This is a very philosophical and theological concept. John wanted his audience to see Jesus as being the living Word of God: As he says, "The Word became flesh and dwelt among us" (John 1:14). He was saying that Jesus was the incarnate Word — the Word taking on flesh. The first book of the Bible, Genesis, starts with the same phrase John uses in the opening of his Gospel: "In the beginning." According to Genesis 1:3, God said, "Let there be light; and there was light." In other words, by merely speaking the word, God *created.* John built on that in his Gospel, saying that Jesus *was* the Word. The Word of God wasn't a thing but a person. The Word was creative and powerful. Just as God said the word and light were created, Jesus spoke the word and the blind received their sight, the lame walked, and the dead came back to life.

Dealing with Heresy and Some Other $10 Words

Christians were violently and lethally persecuted for the first 300 years after the death of Jesus — from the time of Emperor Nero and the burning of Rome, which he blamed on the Christians. So for the first 300 years, Christianity remained underground. Through word of mouth, Christians learned about Jesus of Nazareth and his preaching, suffering, death, Resurrection, and Ascension.

It wasn't until A.D. 313, when Roman Emperor Constantine legalized Christianity in his Edict of Milan, that Christians were even allowed to publicly admit their religious affiliation. But once Christianity became legal, it soon became predominant and even became the state religion.

Leaving the *catacombs* (underground cemeteries sometimes used by Christians to hide from the Romans and as places of worship during times of persecution) and entering the public arena, Christians began devoting themselves to theological questions that the Bible didn't specifically address. For example, Scripture teaches that Jesus was God and man, human and divine. Yet *how* was He both? How were the human and divine natures of Jesus connected? So the second 300 years after Jesus's death, the fourth to seventh centuries, became a Pandora's box of theological debate.

To the Catholic Church, *heresy* is the denial of a revealed truth or the distortion of one so that others are deceived into believing a theological error. After Christianity was legalized, the *Christological heresies* that referred to the nature of Christ became rampant. Debates often degenerated into violent arguments, and the civil authorities, such as the Roman Emperor, often intervened, urging or even demanding that the religious leaders, such as the pope, patriarchs, and bishops, cease the unrest by settling the issues once and for all. This section explains some of the heresies, or false rumors, that plagued the Church during early Christianity.

Gnosticism and Docetism

Gnosticism comes from the Greek work *gnosis,* for *knowledge.* From the first century B.C. to the fifth century A.D., Gnostics believed in secret knowledge, whereas the Judeo-Christians were free and public about disclosing the truth divinely revealed by God. Gnostics believed that the material world was evil and the only way to salvation was through discovering the "secrets" of the universe. This belief flew in the face of Judaism and Christianity, both of which believed that God created the world (Genesis) and that it was good, not evil. Keeping revelation secret wasn't meant to be; rather, it should be shared openly with others.

Docetism, a spin-off from Gnosticism, comes from the Greek word *dokesis,* meaning *appearance.* In the first and second centuries A.D., Docetists asserted that Jesus Christ only appeared to be human. They considered the material world, including the human body, so evil and corrupt that God, who is all good, couldn't have assumed a real human body and human nature. He must have pretended.

The Gnostic antagonism between the spiritual and the material worlds led Docetists to deny that Jesus was true man. They had no problem with His divinity, only with believing in His real humanity. So if that part was an illusion, then the horrible and immense suffering and death of Jesus on the cross meant nothing. If His human nature was a parlor trick, then His Passion also was an illusion.

The core of Christianity, and of Catholic Christianity, is that Jesus died for the sins of all humankind. Only a real human nature can feel pain and actually die. Docetism and Gnosticism were considered hostile to *authentic Christianity,* or, more accurately, *orthodox Christianity.* (The word *orthodox* with a small letter *o* means correct or right believer. However, if you see the capital letter *O,* then *Orthodox* refers to the eastern Orthodox Churches, such as the Greek, Russian, and Serbian Orthodox Churches.)

Even today, remnants of neo-Gnosticism are in some modern ideologies and theories of religion. New Age spirituality and Dianetics, which is the Church of Scientology, propose to reveal secrets and unlock secret powers of human nature. Docetism seems to have pretty much died out, however.

Arianism

Arianism was the most dangerous and prolific of the heresies in the early Church. (By the way, the Arianism that we're referring to isn't about modern-day skinheads with swastikas and anti-Semitic prejudices.) *Arianism* comes from a cleric named Arius in the fourth century (A.D. 250–336), who denied the divinity of Jesus. Whereas Docetism denied his humanity, Arianism denied that Jesus had a truly divine nature equal to God the Father.

Arius proposed that Jesus was created and wasn't of the same substance as God — He was considered higher than any man or angel because He possessed a similar substance, or essence, but He was never equal to God. His Son-ship was one of adoption. In Arianism, Jesus *became* the Son, whereas in orthodox Christianity, He was, is, and will always be the Son, with no beginning and no end. Arianism caught on like wildfire because it appealed to people's knowledge that only one God existed. The argument was that if Jesus was also God, two gods existed instead of only one.

Emperor Constantine, living in the Eastern Empire, was afraid that the religious discord would endanger the security of the realm. He saw how animate and aggressive the argument became and ordered that a council of all the bishops, the patriarchs, and the pope's representatives convene to settle the issue once and for all. The imperial city of Nicea was chosen to guarantee safety. In Nicea, the world's bishops decided to compose a creed that every believer was to learn and profess as being the substance of Christian faith. That same creed is now recited every Sunday and Holy Day at Catholic Masses all over the world. It's known as the Nicene Creed, because it came from the Ecumenical Council of Nicea in A.D. 325.

The punch line that ended the Arianism controversy was the phrase "one in being with the Father" in the Nicene Creed (the phrase that has recently been replaced by "consubstantial with the Father"). The more accurate English translation of the Greek and Latin, however, is *consubstantial* or *of the same substance as the Father.* This line boldly defied the Arian proposition that Jesus was only similar but not equal in substance to the Father in terms of His divinity.

Nestorianism

Another heresy was Nestorianism, named after its founder, Nestorius (c. 386–451). This doctrine maintained that Christ had two *hypostases* (persons) — one divine and one human. Nestorius condemned the use of the word *Theotokos,* which was Greek for *bearer* or *mother of God.* If Jesus had two persons, the most that could be said of Mary was that she gave birth to the human person of Jesus and not to the divine. Nestorius preferred the use of the word *Christotokos* or Christ-bearer to *Theotokos.*

Another Ecumenical Council was convened, this time in the town of Ephesus in A.D. 431, where the participants ironed out the doctrine that Jesus had one person, not two, but that two natures were present — one human and one divine. Because Christ was only one person, Mary could rightly be called the Mother of God because she gave birth to only one person.

In other words, Jesus didn't come in parts on Christmas Day for Mary and Joseph to put together. He was born whole and intact, one person, two natures. The Church says that because Mary gave birth to Jesus, the Church could use the title Mother of God *(Theotokos),* realizing that she didn't give Jesus His divinity. (This concept is similar to the belief that your mother gave you a human body, but only God created your immortal soul. Still, you call her *mother.*)

Monophysitism

The last significant heresy about Jesus was known as *Monophysitism.* This idea centered on a notion that the human nature of Jesus was absorbed into the divine nature. Say, for example, that a drop of oil represents the humanity of Jesus and the ocean represents the divinity of Jesus. If you put the drop of oil into the vast waters of the ocean, the drop of oil, representing His humanity, would literally be overwhelmed and absorbed by the enormous waters of the ocean — His divinity.

The Ecumenical Council of Chalcedon in A.D. 451 condemned Monophyistism. A simple teaching was formulated that one divine person with two distinct, full, and true natures, one human and one divine, existed in Jesus. These two natures were *hypostatically* (from the Greek *hypostasis,* for *person*) united into one divine person. Thus the *Hypostatic Union,* the name of the doctrine, explained these things about Jesus:

✔ **In His human nature,** Jesus had a human mind just like you. It had to learn like yours. Therefore, the baby Jesus in the stable at Bethlehem didn't speak to the shepherds on Christmas Eve. He had to be taught how to speak, walk, and so on. Likewise, His human will, like yours, was free, so He had to freely choose to embrace the will of God.

In other words, in His humanity, Jesus knew what He learned. And He had to freely choose to conform His human will to the divine will. (*Sin is when your will is opposed to the will of God.*) Any human knowledge not gained by regular learning was infused into His human intellect by His divine intellect. Jesus knew that fire is hot just as you've learned this fact. He also knew what only God could know, because He was a divine person with a human and a divine nature. The human mind of Christ is limited, but the divine is infinite. His divinity revealed some divine truths to His human intellect, so He would know who He is, who His Father is, and why He came to earth.

✔ **The divine nature** of Jesus had the same (not similar) divine intellect and will as that of God the Father and God the Holy Spirit. As God, He knew and willed the same things that the other two persons of the Trinity knew and willed. Thus, in His divinity, Jesus knew everything, and what He willed, happened.

✔ **As both God and man,** Jesus could bridge the gap between humanity and divinity. He could actually save humankind by becoming one of us, and yet, because He never lost His divinity, His death had eternal and infinite merit and value. If He were only a man, His death would have no supernatural effect. His death, because it was united to His divine personhood, actually atoned for sin and caused redemption to take place.

It's a mouthful to be sure, but the bottom line in Catholic theology is that the faithful fully and solemnly believe that Jesus was one divine person with a fully human nature and a fully divine nature. Each nature had its own intellect and will. So the divine nature of Jesus had a divine intellect and will, and the human nature of Jesus had a human intellect and will.

Some modern scholars have proposed that Jesus didn't know that He was divine, as if His human nature were ignorant of His divinity. But the Catholic Church points to Luke 2:42–50, which says that when Jesus's parents found the 12-year-old Jesus preaching in the Temple, the young Jesus responded that He was in His Father's house and that He was about to do the work of the Father. So even the young Jesus knew that He was divine. To the Church, "I and the Father are one" (John 10:30) and "before Abraham was, I am" (John 8:58) dispel any identity crisis in Jesus.

Chapter 5

Defining "The Church" and What Membership Means

In This Chapter

▶ Building the Church on the rock of Peter

▶ Working together as an organic whole

▶ Embracing the four marks of the Church

▶ Recognizing the Church's missions

▶ The spiritual perks of membership

he Gospels were originally written in Greek; the Greek word *ekklesia* translates into the English word "church." But *ekklesia* isn't limited to a building where believers worship. The Gospels' notion of church is much more organic and people-related — it's not just a physical structure with a steeple and bell tower.

In the fuller sense of the word, the Church is an assembly of people who share a common faith or belief; it is a building made not of stones but of flesh and blood (called "living stones" in the Bible). In other words, *people* make the Church what it is. In this chapter, we explain how the Church was established, its mission, the benefits of membership, and much more.

Establishing a Foundation: Built on Rock

Jesus said in Matthew 16:18 that Simon, son of John, is to be called Peter (*Petros* in Greek) and that upon this rock (*petra* in Greek), Jesus will build His church (*ekklesia*). Here is the passage from Matthew 16:18–19:

> And I tell you, you are Peter, and on this rock I will build my church, and the powers of death (some versions of the Bible read "gates of hell") shall not prevail against it. I will give you the keys of the kingdom of heaven, and whatever you bind on earth shall be bound in heaven, and whatever you loose on earth shall be loosed in heaven.

This passage makes clear that Christ founded the Church; the Church belongs to Christ. However, Christ gave Peter the authority to care for it. For Catholics, this passage is extremely important because the pope is the successor of St. Peter and the *Vicar* (representative) of Christ on earth. The pope does not replace Christ; he represents Him much like an ambassador represents the president or prime minister who sends him to a foreign nation.

Notice in the Scripture that Jesus gives Peter the keys to the kingdom of heaven. These keys are symbolized in the papal flag, which shows silver and gold keys crossing each other. In the time of Christ, keys were given to prime ministers by the king. The gold key provided access to the treasury where the prime minister kept the king's gold (levied by taxes). The silver key offered access to the royal prison where the enemies of the king were kept.

While Jesus did not give Peter actual, physical keys, He gave him the same authority any king would give his prime minister. That authority is full, supreme, immediate, and universal, as expressed in the phrase "whatever you bind on earth shall be bound in heaven, and whatever you loose on earth shall be loosed in heaven."

Immediately following the death of Peter, the Holy Spirit guided the Church in the election of the next pope, Linus, followed by Cletus, Clement, and so on. Since that time, 266 popes have sat in the Chair of St. Peter — an unbroken line of apostolic succession. Read more about the pope in Chapter 6.

Seeing the Church as the Body of Christ and Communion of Saints

The Church is sometimes called the Mystical Body of Christ, and that analogy comes from the writings of St. Paul. He writes in 1 Corinthians 12:12–13, "Just as the body is one and has many members, and all the members of the body, though many, are one body, so it is with Christ. For by one Spirit we were all baptized into one body." It is in baptism that unity of the Body of Christ is most expressed under the head, Jesus Christ. The Church is one Body, the Church has Christ as her head, and the Church is the Bride of Christ.

Paul refers to Christ as the head of the Church and to the baptized members as the body of the Church. Think of your own body: While you have eyes, ears, hands, and feet, there is only one of you; you're the sum of your parts. Likewise, the Church is the union of all her members, who have unique roles but work together to make a complete whole.

If you're a baptized member of the Church, you have a part to play in the Body of Christ. Here are some examples:

- ✔ **The laity** preach the good news of salvation by the way they witness to Christ in the workplace, marketplace, school, and society. Also, through Holy Matrimony (see Chapter 9) they become supporters of their spouses to become saints and bring forth children to populate heaven.

- ✔ **The consecrated religious** give witness to the Kingdom of God by living their religious vows of poverty, chastity, and obedience. These vows are a visible sign for people on earth of the Lord they hope to meet at the end of their lives.

- ✔ **The clergy,** by virtue of Holy Orders (see Chapter 9), share in the task of Christ in dispensing the mysteries of God, the sacraments, to fortify the pilgrim. Through teaching and preaching they instruct the wayfarer toward the correct path to heaven.

The Mystical Body of Christ is also called the *communion of saints* (read more in Chapter 2). Like Paul's body analogy, the communion of saints model of the Church indicates an organic unity of parts working together — the Church Militant, the Church Suffering, and the Church Triumphant:

- ✔ **Militant** refers to the Church's living members on earth who are in a daily battle against the world, flesh, and devil; the war is against evil, not other religions.

- ✔ **Suffering** refers to the holy souls in purgatory, who died in the state of grace with no mortal sin on their souls but still had some attachments to their venial sins and to previously forgiven mortal sins. The soul realizes that it is in need of further purification before it can enter into the glories of heaven.

- ✔ **Triumphant** refers to the angels and saints in heaven around the banquet table of God. They were victorious in the good fight against sin and evil and are now experiencing the joys of paradise.

Understanding the Four Marks of the Church

In Chapter 2, we walk you through the Nicene Creed, which is professed every Sunday and holy day. It speaks of four essential marks, or identifiers, of the Church: "I believe in *one, holy, Catholic* and *apostolic* church." These four elements are the foundation of Catholic Christianity. They are signs to the world that the Church is the work of God and that the Church is of divine origin. Here's what each mark means:

- ✔ **One (unity):** As we explain in the preceding section, the Church is one body with many members, each of whom plays a vital role, and all of whom are united. The Church is an organic unity and not artificial, synthetic, or man-made. The pope is the visible head of the global Church, which has more than 1 billion members worldwide. He appoints the local bishops, who in turn assign the local pastors and parish priests and deacons. The Church has one governing authority (hierarchy) and one teaching authority (Magisterium). The Church has one body of truths she teaches (found in the Catechism) and one body of divine worship (the seven sacraments).

- ✔ **Holy (sanctity):** The Church is holy because her founder is Jesus Christ, the Son of God and second person of the Holy Trinity. She is also the Bride of Christ and is considered the Mystical Body of Christ as well. That association and union with divinity itself makes the Church holy. But she also has been given by God Himself all the necessary divine revealed truths and all the necessary divine grace to save souls (help people get to heaven). This does not mean that members have it made and need to do nothing else except belong. It does mean that holiness is possible and promoted by the Church at the will and command of her founder, Jesus Christ. One becomes a saint through, with, and in the Church.

- ✔ **Catholic (universality):** The word *Catholic* derives from the Greek *katholikos,* which means universal. The church's mission is universal. It is to spread the good news about Jesus (also called the *gospel*) to all men and women all over the world. The Church is not confined to any one nation or country. That's why it's not called the Church of Italy, the Church of England, the Church of America, or the Church of Europe. It is the Catholic Church, which belongs to Christ and is found everywhere around the world. Embracing all languages, continents, cultures, and races, the Church is universal and promotes universality. Human beings belong to the same human race even though they live in different parts of the world and speak different tongues.

- ✔ **Apostolic (continuity):** The last mark refers to the fact that the Catholic Church can trace its foundations to Christ Himself and to the 12 apostles. Also, every deacon, priest, and bishop can trace his ordination lineage back to one of the original apostles; this is called *apostolic succession.* A verifiable and direct connection exists between the apostles whom Jesus handpicked and their direct successors, the bishops. Also, there is direct succession of all the popes, from Saint Peter to his 265th successor, Pope Benedict XVI.

Fulfilling Its Mission

The mission of the Church is the continuation of Christ's mission: to proclaim the Gospel to the entire world for all generations. Christ gave the mission to His church when He said, "Go therefore and make disciples of all nations, baptizing them in the name of the Father and of the Son and of the Holy Spirit, teaching them to observe all that I have commanded you" (Matthew 28:19–20). Evangelization is the mission, and all baptized Christians are involved. So if you're a member of the Church, your life's work is intertwined with the salvific duty of the Savior: to reconcile fellow people with God.

Christ won salvation for humanity on the cross, on Good Friday, by shedding His precious blood. He is the great mediator between the Father and mankind. The Church, as the bride of Christ, continues this work through proclaiming the Word of God, teaching revealed truths, dispensing grace through the sacraments, and gathering the multitude into unity.

As we explain in Chapter 19, all members of the Church are commissioned to perform the Corporal Works of Mercy which are to feed the hungry, give drink to the thirsty, clothe the naked, give shelter to the homeless, visit the sick, ransom the captive, and bury the dead. The baptized also continue the mission of Christ by exercising the Spiritual Works of Mercy, which are to instruct the ignorant, counsel the doubtful, admonish the sinner, bear wrongs patiently, forgive offenses willingly, comfort the afflicted, and pray for the living and the dead.

The mission of the Church is the mission of Christ. Christ Himself was a priest, a prophet, and a king. The *priestly office* of Christ's mission was to sanctify the world. The *prophetic office* of His mission was to teach the truth to the world. His *kingly office* was to be the Good Shepherd and provide governance and leadership. He used all three aspects to achieve the one mission: proclaiming the Good News. The Church, which is an extension of Christ on earth, fulfills that same work via the same three aspects, which we detail next.

Jesus chose 12 apostles and 70 disciples to help continue His mission after He died, rose, and ascended to heaven. Before being able to evangelize, His men needed to be taught the message, sanctified so they could receive the message worthily, and organized to effectively achieve success in the mission. Christ the priest, prophet, and king therefore sanctified, taught, and shepherded His disciples and apostles. The Church continues that process today.

The priestly office: Sanctifying through the sacraments

Jesus Christ the priest instituted the seven sacraments (see Chapters 8 and 9) in order for the faithful to become holy, to receive His divine life, and to become stronger on earth in their journey to heaven. *Sanctifying grace* makes the soul holy and pleasing to God; given at Baptism, this grace is the indwelling of the Triune God (Father, Son, and Holy Spirit) in the soul of the individual person. The priestly (sanctifying) office of Christ and His Church makes the human soul disposed to the gift of divine grace, which makes one holy in the eyes of God.

The sacraments are the visible signs instituted by Christ to confer grace. For the faithful, the sacraments are the necessary vehicles of grace for the sole purpose of salvation. In an analogous way, the Church is what theologians call the *primordial* sacrament, that is, the sacred institution where the seven sacraments are bestowed. The Church and the sacraments both continue the sacred work of Christ's redemption. The effects of the sacraments on the faithful create a bond of unity that is most visible in the Mystical Body of Christ, the Church.

The prophetic office: Teaching through the Magisterium

The official term for the teaching (prophetic) office of the Church is the *Magisterium* (from the Latin *magister*, meaning teacher). The Magisterium is made up of the pope and all the bishops around the world in communion with Him. When the Church teaches on matters of faith and morals, she is *infallible* (free from error). But on matters of science, economics, astronomy, athletics, and so on, she has no *charism* (gift) of infallibility.

The Church's teachings are infallible, but that doesn't mean the Church never updates or refines the explanations of dogmas and doctrines so Catholics can understand them better. Scripture never changes (though the translations do), but teachings can be put in a better context or shown in a different perspective.

As we detail in Chapter 6, there are two levels of infallibility — ordinary and extraordinary — and the same levels apply to the Magisterium. Therefore, we have an Ordinary Magisterium and an Extraordinary Magisterium. Both are infallible in content, but here's how they differ:

✔ **Ordinary Magisterium:** These teachings deal with the consistent and perennial common teaching of all the popes and bishops (in union with the pope) throughout history. Examples from this office include papal teachings on birth control or the ordination of women; these are just retellings of guidelines that have always been taught by popes and bishops throughout Catholic history.

✔ **Extraordinary Magisterium:** The name says it all; these teachings are rare. This level proclaims the Church's stance on doctrines formulated by ecumenical councils, after meetings of all Church bishops, or after the pope has made an *ex cathedra* decree. There have been only 21 ecumenical councils and two *ex cathedra* decrees.

Church history buffs: Turn to Chapter 6 for the lowdown on what kind of teachings you can expect to come from the pope. Suffice it to say that the Church has a responsibility to its members to make sense out of the faith, and the Ordinary and Extraordinary Magisteria help Catholics get the word straight from the Vatican's mouth.

The kingly office: Shepherding and governing through the hierarchy

Christ the King provided governance and leadership to his followers. The kingly office of the Church is to make sure that the Church stays organized with the right people in charge, just like Jesus set it up. The Catholic Church is an institution, and as with any organization, it has rules, procedures, and a hierarchy of authority.

The basic structure of the Church was given by the Lord when He formed His Church by calling the 12 apostles, who became the first bishops. Out of the 12, he chose a leader, Peter, the first pope (flip to the section "Establishing a Foundation: Built on Rock" for more details). That's still the example the Church follows.

Bishops and *presbyters* or priests (successors to the 70 disciples) are ordained to celebrate the sacraments (especially the Mass), to preach, to teach, and to minister in a local church (known as a *parish*). A collection of parishes in a geographical location is known as a *diocese*. The Catholic Church is made up of many different dioceses and archdioceses throughout the world. In addition to priests, there are ordained *deacons* who assist priests and bishops in their local parishes and dioceses.

The pope is the head of the church and the bishop of Rome; as such, his seat of authority *(cathedra)* is the Basilica of St. John Lateran. He is also the head of the Universal Church, and his seat of authority is the Basilica of St. Peter, Vatican City. Cardinals are appointed by the pope and make up the College of Cardinals. As a body, this college advises the pope and, on his death, elects a new pope.

Because the structure of the Catholic Church is such a complex subject, we devote an entire chapter of this book to the subject: Chapter 6. For the whole scoop on the many people and departments that carry on the work of Christ's kingly office, be sure to check out that chapter.

Membership Has Its Benefits

An old axiom states that the whole is greater than the sum of the parts. Belonging to the Church — being a member of the Mystical Body of Christ — has benefits beyond the imagination. Scripture says that eye has not seen and ear has not heard what God has in store for us (1 Corinthians 2:9). While we may not be able to comprehend fully what total union with God fully means, because we are united together, as brothers and sisters, our joy will be more full and intense than if we were all by ourselves.

Although the Church is sometimes called the *societas perfecta* (perfect society), members of the Catholic Church are not in any way perfect or sinless. They are not better than people who do not belong to the Church. Instead, the phrase means that the Church is the source of all necessary divine truth and of all necessary divine grace. It's one-stop spiritual shopping, you could say.

The Church provides for all the spiritual needs of a believer. For spiritual food, there is Holy Communion (also called the Holy Eucharist). For knowledge, there is divine revelation as found in Sacred Scripture and Sacred Tradition, entrusted to the Magisterium (teaching authority of the Church). For spiritual healing, there is the sacrament of Penance and Reconciliation, as well as the sacrament of Anointing the Sick. The Church hierarchy provides necessary leadership, and canon law is the source of justice and discipline. The needs of the individual and the needs of the community are perfectly fulfilled, meaning that members do not need to go anywhere else to fulfill their spiritual requirements.

If all this sounds pretty good to you, and you're not yet a baptized Catholic, we encourage you to check out your local parish's RCIA (Rite of Christian Initiation of Adults) process. It'll give you ample opportunity to learn more about the faith, help find a sponsor for the sacraments of Baptism and Confirmation, and perform all the necessary rites so you can officially join the Church. The process usually takes about nine months, from early fall to spring (Easter), but in some cases can be done privately as well. Baptized Protestants aren't re-baptized, but after instruction are brought into full communion by professing the faith, going to confession, being confirmed, and then receiving their First Communion. Only unbaptized persons can be baptized.

Chapter 6

Who's Who in the Catholic Church

In This Chapter

▶ Looking at the Church's hierarchy

▶ Finding out about papal elections in the Vatican

▶ Discovering the long line of papal succession

▶ Understanding the duties of the clergy

Chain of command: Every structured environment has one — from governments to corporations to schools to sports programs. The Catholic Church is no exception. This chapter explains who's who in the Catholic Church and gives you a glimpse into the authority and duties of its various members. Check out Table 6-1 for a quick look at who's in charge, from highest to lowest (top to bottom) in terms of rank.

Table 6-1	The Catholic Church Chain of Command
Clergy Members' Titles	**What They Do**
The pope	He's the bishop of Rome and the head of the whole Church.
Cardinals	They elect the pope and work in different departments as his right-hand men.
Bishops and archbishops	They take charge of the churches in their respective geographical areas, called dioceses.
Vicar generals	They are priests who help the bishop govern the local churches.
Parish priests, or pastors	They take care of all the big day-to-day duties in their churches, from leading Mass to hearing confessions.
Monks and nuns	They choose to live together, work together, and spend many hours devoted in prayer.

Getting to Know the Pope

Best known throughout the world and among more than 1 billion Catholics as *the pope,* the bishop of Rome is the supreme and visible head of the Catholic Church. The word *pope* is actually an English translation of the Italian *il Papa,* meaning *father,* which leads you to another title for the pope — *Holy Father.* Just as a Catholic priest is called "Father" in a spiritual sense, the pope is called "Holy Father" by Catholics all over the world.

He has a slew of other titles, too: Successor of St. Peter, Vicar of Christ, Primate of Italy, Supreme Pontiff, Roman Pontiff, Sovereign of the Vatican City State, and Head of the College of Bishops. The most common and best-known titles, however, are pope, Holy Father, and Roman Pontiff.

Think you're under pressure at work? The pope has *two* big jobs: He's the bishop of Rome (see the section "Bishops and archbishops" for more about bishops) *and* the head of the entire Catholic Church.

How the pope gets his job

The *College of Cardinals* elects the pope. Nope, that's not a university where priests and bishops learn how to become cardinals. Unlike Notre Dame and The Catholic University of America, the *College of Cardinals* merely refers to all the cardinals around the world, just as the *College of Bishops* is a way of describing all the world's Catholic bishops.

The pope handpicks bishops to become *cardinals,* and their primary function in life is to elect a new pope when the old pope dies or resigns. Because most modern popes live at least ten years in office (except Pope John Paul I, who lived only one month), cardinals do have other work to do instead of just waiting around for the boss to pass on. (For details about cardinals and their jobs, see the section "Cardinals," later in this chapter.) Cardinals under the age of 80 are eligible to vote for the next pope.

The limit of electors is set at 120, but at one point Pope John Paul II (who was pope from 1978 to 2005) had appointed so many that the number of eligible voters reached 137. With retirements and deaths, only 117 eligible voting cardinals remained when Pope John Paul II died in 2005. His successor, Pope Benedict XVI, has so far created 50 new cardinals in three consistories (2006, 2007, 2010), yet with retirements and deaths, in 2011 there were again only 117 electors. (We explain consistories in the upcoming "Cardinals" section.)

Uh, Cardinal, sir? What's that mallet for?

When the pope dies, an ancient but simple ceremony is performed before the cardinals are called to Rome to elect a new pope. The most senior-ranking cardinal enters the room of the dead pontiff and gently strikes his forehead with a silver mallet, calling the pope by his baptismal name. If he doesn't answer by the third time, he's pronounced dead.

Today, however, the pope's personal physician is called in first, and he makes the medical determination that the man is dead before the senior-ranking cardinal is summoned to perform the ceremonial ritual with the mallet. Then the pope's ring (the Fisherman's Ring) and his papal insignia are smashed so that no one can affix the seal on any documents until a new pope has been elected.

The electors can vote for any other cardinal or any Catholic bishop, priest, deacon, or layman, anywhere in the world and of any liturgical rite, such as Latin, Byzantine, and so on. Normally, the cardinals select another cardinal, both because they know each other better and because the number of cardinals to choose from is small compared to the 5,000 bishops around the world and more than 410,000 priests. Although extremely rare, if a layman is elected pope (as in the case of Benedict IX), he first has to be ordained a deacon, then a priest, and then a bishop before he can function as pope, because the authority resides in his office as bishop of Rome. If a priest is chosen, he needs to be ordained a bishop prior to being installed as pope.

Are there pope primaries?

The government of the Catholic Church, called the *hierarchy,* is more like a monarchy than a democracy. Catholicism is hierarchical in that one person, the pope, is supreme head over the universal Church. Yet bishops govern the local churches in a geographical district called the *diocese,* and pastors (or priests) represent the bishop in each local parish. Individual Catholics don't vote for the next pope or for their bishop or pastor. The Catholic hierarchy operates like a military chain of command as opposed to an elected, representative government. So nope — no local primaries, no election campaigns, no debates, no political ads, and no popular vote.

Other religions and Christian churches allow for lay participation in positions of authority from a little to a lot, but Catholicism has been predominantly monarchical since the appointment of St. Peter. (See Chapter 21 for more on St. Peter, the first pope.) Laypersons are encouraged to participate in other ways. While they aren't allowed to have jurisdictional power, laity serve as consulters and advisors to pastors and bishops. Parish councils and finance committees are composed of lay parishioners who advise the pastor before he makes important decisions. Laity also even serve in the Vatican to advise, counsel, and represent the Holy See to organizations like the United Nations.

You may have heard the saying: He who enters the conclave a pope leaves a cardinal. The meaning? When a pope becomes sick or elderly or dies, rumors run rampant as to who will take the Chair of St. Peter. Often, the press names certain cardinals as the most likely candidates; they're called *papabile* (meaning *pope-able*) in Italian. But the *papabile* are usually the ones that the other cardinals *never* elect. So if a man enters the *conclave* — the private meeting of all the cardinals for the specific purpose of electing the pope — as a favorite (or worse yet, if he comes off as wanting the job), chances are he will leave a cardinal because his fellow cardinals will choose someone more humble.

Dimpled, pimpled, or hanging chads?

No sooner than 15 days and no later than 20 days after the death or resignation of the pope, all the cardinals are summoned to Rome for the secret conclave. *Conclave* comes from the Latin *cum clave,* meaning *with key,* because the cardinals are literally locked into the Sistine Chapel, the pope's private chapel at the Vatican, until they elect a new pope.

After the cardinals from around the world assemble inside the conclave, they begin discussions and deliberations. Almost like a sequestered jury, the cardinals are permitted no contact with the outside world during the conclave. Under pain of excommunication (see Chapter 11), no cardinal is ever allowed to discuss what transpires at these elections — to keep the element of politics and outside influence to a bare minimum.

Historically, the election of a new pope could take place in one of three different forms:

- ✓ **Acclamation:** A name is presented, and everyone unanimously consents without the need of a secret ballot.

- ✓ **Compromise:** Each cardinal casts a secret ballot. If no one achieves a two-thirds majority after several rounds of voting, then the entire College of Cardinals may choose one or several electors to select a candidate, and the entire body is bound to accept that choice. A unanimous vote to employ compromise is necessary for it to be valid.

- ✓ **Scrutiny:** Each cardinal proposes a candidate and gives reasons for his qualifications before the individual cardinals cast their secret ballot. A two-thirds majority decision is needed to elect a new pope.

This is the only valid method currently permitted in papal conclaves.

Want a peek at what's going on behind those closed doors? When voting for a new pope, each cardinal writes a name on a piece of paper, which is placed on a gold *paten* (plate). The paten is then turned upside down, so the ballot can fall into a *chalice* (cup) underneath. This symbolism is deep, because the paten and chalice are primarily used at the Catholic Mass to hold the wafer of bread and cup of wine that, when consecrated, become the body and blood of Christ during the Eucharistic Prayer. (See Chapter 10 for the scoop on the Mass and Eucharistic Prayer.)

If no one receives two-thirds of the votes or if the nominee declines the nomination, then wet straw is mixed with the paper ballots and burned in the chimney. The wet straw makes black smoke, which alerts the crowds gathered outside that a two-thirds majority decision hasn't yet been made. One vote occurs in the morning and one in the evening. The election continues twice a day, every day. In 1996, Pope John Paul II introduced a variation in which if no one was elected by a two-thirds majority after 21 votes, then on the 22nd ballot, the man who received a simple majority (50 percent plus one) was elected pope. Pope Benedict XVI subsequently rescinded that change in 2007 and returned the requirement of two-thirds no matter how long the conclave takes. If someone receives two-thirds of the votes and he accepts, the ballots are burned without the straw, which blows white smoke to alert the crowds.

After a cardinal has received a two-thirds majority vote, he's asked whether he accepts the nomination. If he accepts, he's then asked, "By what name are you to be addressed?"

Pope John II (A.D. 533) was the first to change his name when he was elected pope because he was born with the name Mercury after the pagan god. So he chose the Christian name John instead. But it was not until Sergius IV (1009) that all subsequent popes continued the tradition of changing their name at the time of election. So, for example, Pope Pius XII (1939) was originally Eugenio Pacelli, John XXIII (1958) was Angelo Roncalli, Paul VI (1963) was Giovanni Montini, John Paul I (1978) was Albino Luciani, John Paul II (1978) was Karol Wojtyla, and Benedict XVI (2005) was Josef Ratzinger.

Is he really infallible?

Catholicism maintains that the pope is *infallible*, incapable of error, when he teaches a doctrine on faith or morals to the universal Church in his unique office as supreme head. When the pope asserts his official authority in matters of faith and morals to the whole church, the Holy Spirit guards him from error. Papal infallibility doesn't mean that the pope can't make *any* mistakes. He's not infallible in scientific, historical, political, philosophical, geographic, or any other matters — just faith and morals.

It boils down to trust. Catholics trust that the Holy Spirit protects *them* from being taught or forced to believe erroneous doctrines by preventing a pope from issuing them. Whether the Holy Spirit's intervention is as subtle as getting the pope to change his mind or as drastic as striking him dead, in any event, Catholics firmly believe that God loves them and loves the truth so much that he would intervene and prevent a pope from imposing a false teaching upon the whole Church. This belief doesn't mean that personally and individually the pope is free from all error. He could privately be wrong as long as he doesn't attempt to impose or teach that error to the universal Church, because at that point the Holy Spirit would somehow stop him from doing so.

So what does infallibility mean?

Infallibility is widely misunderstood. It's *not* the same as the Catholic beliefs of *inspiration* or *impeccability:*

- ✔ **Inspiration** is a special gift of the Holy Spirit, which He gave to the *sacred authors,* those who wrote the Sacred Scripture (the Bible), so that only the things God wanted written down *were* written down — no more, no less. So the pope isn't inspired, but Matthew, Mark, Luke, and John were when they wrote their Gospels.

- ✔ **Impeccability** is the absence and inability to commit sin. Only Jesus Christ, being the Son of God, and His Blessed Mother had impeccability — via a special grace from God. Popes aren't impeccable, so they're capable of sin — which, by the way, was visible in the case of the first pope, St. Peter, when he denied Christ three times just before the Crucifixion (Matthew 26:69–75).

Everything the sacred authors wrote in the Bible is inspired, but not everything every pope says or writes is infallible. *Infallibility* means that if the pope attempts to teach a false doctrine on faith or morals, the Holy Spirit prevents him (even by death) from imposing such an error on the faithful. So, for example, no pope can declare, "As of today, the number of commandments is nine instead of ten." Nor can he declare, "Jesus was not a man" or "Jesus was not the Son of God."

Infallibility also doesn't mean perfection. Infallible statements aren't perfect statements, so they can be improved so that subsequent popes can use better or more accurate language. Yet infallible statements can never be contradicted, rejected, or refuted.

So according to Catholicism, an immoral pope (you'll find several in Church history) can sin like any man and will answer to God for his evil deeds. However, as supreme head of the Church, the pope retains his infallibility on matters of faith and morals as long as he remains pope.

No pope in 2,000 years has formally and officially taught an error of faith or morals to the universal Church. Individually, some may have been poor or inadequate theologians or philosophers, and some may have had erroneous ideas about science. That has nothing to do with papal infallibility, however, because the main objective is to preserve the integrity of Catholic faith for all the members at all times and in all places.

The pope can exercise his papal infallibility in two ways. One is called the *Extraordinary Magisterium,* and the other is called *Ordinary Magisterium.* The word *magisterium* is from the Latin word *magister* meaning *teacher,* so the *Magisterium* is the teaching authority of the Church, which is manifested by the pope alone and or the pope along with the bishops all over the world.

The Extraordinary Magisterium

Extraordinary means just that, out of the ordinary. When an Ecumenical (General) Council is convened, presided over, and approved by the pope, and he issues definitive decrees, they're considered infallible because they come from the Extraordinary Magisterium. The Church has held an all-time total of only 21 councils. These are gatherings of the world's bishops and cardinals. Sometimes priests, deacons, and laity are invited to observe, but only bishops and the pope can discuss and vote. The culmination of these councils is a written letter that explains the faith, interprets Scripture, or settles disputed topics of faith and morals. They never contradict the Bible but apply biblical truths to contemporary concerns and problems, as well as giving more understanding to essential core beliefs. The names and years of the councils throughout Church history are as follows:

1. Nicea (325)
2. First Constantinople (381)
3. Ephesus (431)
4. Chalcedon (451)
5. Second Constantinople (553)
6. Third Constantinople (680–81)
7. Second Nicea (787)
8. Fourth Constantinople (869–70)
9. First Lateran (1123)
10. Second Lateran (1139)
11. Third Lateran (1179)
12. Fourth Lateran (1215)
13. First Lyons (1245)
14. Second Lyons (1274)
15. Vienne (1311–12)
16. Constance (1414–18)
17. Basel-Ferrara-Florence (1431–45)
18. Fifth Lateran (1512–17)
19. Trent (1545–63)
20. First Vatican (1869–70)
21. Second Vatican (1962–65)

The Ecumenical Councils have defined doctrines such as the divinity of Christ (Nicea); the title of Mary as the Mother of God (Ephesus); the two natures of Christ, human and divine, being united in the one divine person (Chalcedon); *transubstantiation* (see Chapter 10) to describe how the bread and wine are changed at Mass into the Body and Blood of Christ (Lateran IV); the seven sacraments, Sacred Scripture and Sacred Tradition (see Chapter 2), and other responses to the Reformation (Trent); and papal infallibility (Vatican I). These conciliar decrees and *ex cathedra* papal pronouncements form the Extraordinary Magisterium.

Ex cathedra (Latin for *from the chair*) pronouncements from the pope are considered infallible teachings. The only two *ex cathedra* pronouncements in 2,000 years have been the dogmas of the Immaculate Conception (1854) and the Assumption (1950). When the pope teaches *ex cathedra,* he's exercising his universal authority as Supreme Teacher of a doctrine on faith or morals, and he's incapable of error. Catholics consider the Assumption of Mary and the Immaculate Conception infallible teachings because they involve the solemn, full, and universal papal authority. (See Chapter 17 for more information on Mary, the Immaculate Conception, and the Assumption.)

The word *cathedral* comes from the Latin *cathedra* because it's the church where the bishop's chair *(cathedra)* resides. The chair is symbolic of authority going back to Roman days when Caesar or his governors sat on a chair and made public decisions, pronouncements, or judgments. When the pope teaches *ex cathedra,* he's not physically sitting on a particular chair but exercising his universal authority as Supreme Teacher.

Unlike governments that separate their executive, legislative, and judicial branches, in the Catholic Church, the pope is all three rolled into one. He's the chief judge, the chief lawmaker, and the commander in chief all at the same time. That's why the triple crown (also known as a *tiara* or *triregnum*) was used in papal coronations — to symbolize his three-fold authority and that he's higher in dignity and authority than a king (one crown) or even an emperor (double crown). (Pope Paul VI was the last pope to wear the tiara. It's a matter of personal choice and preference now.)

The Ordinary Magisterium

The second way that an infallible teaching is taught to Catholics is through the *Ordinary Magisterium,* which is the more common and typical manner, hence the reason why it's called *ordinary.* This teaching of the popes is consistent, constant, and universal through their various documents, letters, papal encyclicals, decrees, and so on. It's never a new doctrine but rather one that has been taught *ubique, semper et ab omnibus* (Latin for *everywhere, always and by all).* In other words, when the pope reinforces, reiterates, or restates the consistent teaching of his predecessors and of the bishops united with him around the world, that's considered the Ordinary Magisterium and should be treated as infallible doctrine.

When popes write papal documents (anything authored by a pope), the title they use to refer to themselves the most is *Servant of the Servants of God* (*Servus Servorum Dei* in Latin). St. Gregory the Great (590–604) was the first pope to use this title. Check out the different types of papal documents from the most solemn on down:

- ✔ Papal Bulls
- ✔ Papal Encyclicals
- ✔ Papal Briefs
- ✔ Apostolic Exhortations
- ✔ Apostolic Constitutions
- ✔ Apostolic Letters
- ✔ Motu Proprios

Prior to the Second Vatican Council (1962–65), more commonly known as Vatican II, the type of papal document the pope chose determined how much authority he intended to exercise. (See Chapter 10 for more on Vatican II.) The preceding list indicates the order of authority that various papal documents traditionally had. For example, the lowest level was the *Motu Proprio,* which is a Latin phrase meaning *of his own initiative.* Somewhat like an international memo, it's a short papal letter granting a dispensation or making a modification applying to the whole world but on a disciplinary matter only, such as an issue that has nothing to do with doctrine. An example of Motu Proprio was when John Paul II granted permission to celebrate the Tridentine Mass (the order and structure of the Mass as it was celebrated between the Council of Trent and Vatican II). On the other hand, *Papal Bulls* were considered the highest authority.

Since Vatican II, however, the *content* and *context* of the document determine the degree of authority and not just the type of papal document. If the pope intends to definitively teach the universal Church on a matter of faith or morals, then he is expressing his supreme authority as head of the Church. When John Paul II issued his Apostolic Letter *Ordinatio Sacerdotalis* in 1994, he officially declared that the Catholic Church has no power to ordain women. (See Chapter 14 for more on the role of women in the Church.) *Ordinatio Sacerdotalis* was *not* an ex cathedra papal statement, but it's part of the Ordinary Magisterium, and thus, according to the Prefect for the Sacred Congregation for the Doctrine of the Faith, the teaching is infallible. The Cardinal Prefect is the pope's watchdog to investigate all suspected cases of *heresy* (false teaching) and to explain official church dogma.

Papal encyclicals are letters addressed to the world on contemporary issues and concerns. *Encyclical* comes from the Latin word for *circular,* because these documents are meant to circulate around the world. The name of each letter consists of the first two words of the letter in Latin, because every official document coming from the Vatican is still written in Latin. Encyclicals aren't *ex cathedra* pronouncements. Some examples of popes who put encyclicals to good use include:

✔ **Leo XIII** wrote *Rerum Novarum* in 1891, which discusses capital and labor. It defends private property and business, as well as the right of workers to form trade unions and guilds.

✔ **Paul VI** presented the Church's teaching on abortion and artificial contraception in *Humanae Vitae* in 1968. It's not an *ex cathedra* statement, but *Humanae Vitae* is a part of the constant, consistent, and universal teachings of the popes and bishops over the ages. (For more about the church's stand on artificial contraception, as well as other sticky issues, turn to Chapter 14.)

> ✔ **John Paul II** wrote *Laborem Exercens* in 1981 on human work; *Veritatis Splendor* in 1993 on the natural moral law; *Evangelium Vitae* in 1995 on the dignity, sanctity, and inviolability of human life and the things that threaten it, such as abortion, euthanasia, and the death penalty; and *Fides et Ratio* in 1998 on the compatibility of faith and reason.
>
> ✔ **Benedict XVI**'s first encyclical was *Deus Caritas Est* (2005) on the biblical passage that "God is Love." It explains that divine love and human love are based on the same premise: All love must be both "give and take," sacrificial and possessive.

Encyclicals are the routine, day-to-day, consistent teaching of the Ordinary Magisterium, which is equally infallible when it concerns faith and morals and reiterates the constant, consistent, and universal teaching of the popes and bishops. Their content requires religious submission of mind and will of faithful Catholics around the world. So-called dissent from papal teaching in encyclicals isn't part of Catholic belief. The Catholic faithful willfully conform to papal teaching and don't dispute it.

Now that's job security

Popes are elected for life unless they voluntarily — without pressure or coercion — resign from office. (Pope Pontian was the first one to abdicate from the office in A.D. 235. Pope St. Peter Celestine V was the most famous one to resign, going back to monastic life in 1294. Pope Gregory XII was the last one to quit in 1415.) No one can depose a pope even if he becomes insane, sick, or corrupt. No ecumenical council has the authority to remove him from office. So when a bad pope gets in (and from time to time, a bad pope has been elected), the only course of action is to pray to St. Joseph for a happy death of the pope in question. (St. Joseph is the patron of a happy death, because he probably died of natural causes in the arms of Mary and Jesus.)

Although even one bad pope is one too many, Jesus himself picked 12 imperfect sinners to be his apostles. The first pope, St. Peter, weakened and denied Christ three times, and Judas, one of the first bishops, betrayed him for 30 pieces of silver. One repented; the other hanged himself instead of seeking mercy.

This is our two cents' worth: Of the 265 popes in history, only a dozen were real scoundrels and caused great scandal. Seventy-eight popes are recognized as holy saints (see Chapter 18), leaving 175 pretty good, all right guys. Better stats than for presidents, prime ministers, or monarchs around the world.

The good, the bad, and the ugly

Catholicism regards St. Peter as the first pope, handpicked by Jesus Christ himself, according to the Gospel of St. Matthew (16:18), when Jesus said, "You are Peter and on this rock I will build my church." If you count St. Peter as the first pope, then Benedict XVI is the 266th pope or the 265th successor of St. Peter, depending on where you begin. And you thought that memorizing the names of all the world leaders was hard when you were 10 years old?

Probably the worst pope ever, Alexander VI (1492–1503) was a Borgia. The name is infamous; the Borgias were a notorious yet influential Italian family during the Renaissance when no unified Kingdom of Italy existed — only small principalities, dukedoms, and city-states. Pope Alexander VI had several illegitimate children before and during his reign as pope, two of whom are noteworthy: Cesare Borgia and his sister Lucrezia Borgia. Cesare grew up to be a ruthless autocrat, and Lucrezia is reputed to have been the most famous poisoner. Alexander VI is the epitome of nepotism, bribery, deceit, debauchery, and anything else you can imagine. The Borgias were the Sopranos of

their time. The list of Borgias included 11 cardinals, 2 popes, a queen of England, and a saint.

And Benedict IX (1032–1045) was a close second to the worst pope. Assuming the throne of St. Peter in his late teens or early twenties, this playboy pope incited a riot in Rome because the people were so disgusted with his antics.

Lady pope? Hardly. The so-called Pope Joan never existed except in myth from the 13th to 17th centuries. French Protestant David Blondel (1590–1655) disproved the myth once and for all in a scholarly refutation, but the story is so bizarre that some still believe it despite the lack of any credible evidence. The legend goes that a woman named Joan impersonated a man so that she could enter the clerical life and rise through the ecclesiastical ranks of the hierarchy, which she allegedly did with ease. Supposedly, her short hair and manly dress fooled everyone until one day, while riding a horse, she gave birth to a child and was exposed as a fake — only to be stoned to death by the angry mob. And if you believe that, we'll tell you another one. . . .

Where the pope hangs his hat

The pope's home is *Vatican City,* an independent nation since the Lateran Agreement of 1929, when Italy recognized its sovereignty. Vatican City covers only 0.2 square miles (108.7 acres), has fewer than a thousand inhabitants, and rests in the middle of Rome.

After 300 years of Roman persecution, the Emperor Constantine legalized Christianity in A.D. 313 with the Edict of Milan and thus formally ended the state-sponsored persecutions of the Christians. In A.D. 321, he donated the imperial property of the Lateran Palace to the bishop of Rome, which began a trend of donating property in recompense for all the land and possessions that the Romans took from the early Christians during the pagan era.

The donation of large estates stopped around A.D. 600, but 154 years later, King Pepin (the Short) of the Franks (who was also the father of Charlemagne) issued the Donation of A.D. 754: The pope would govern the territory of central Italy (16,000 square miles). From 754 to 1870, Vatican City was part of the Papal States, also known as *Patrimonium Sancti Petri* (the Patrimony of St. Peter). During the unification of Italy, Giuseppe Garibaldi and Count Camillo Benso di Cavour, the two men most responsible for creating the Kingdom and modern nation of Italy in 1870, seized the Papal States and, for all practical purposes, ended the secular rule of the popes. Today, Vatican City is the smallest independent nation in the world. Ironically, it also has the largest number of embassies and ambassadors around the globe. Guglielmo Marconi, the inventor of radio, built a radio for Pope Pius XI; thus Vatican Radio began in 1931. Now, in addition to a radio and short-wave antennae, the Vatican also has television and Internet programming.

The only real citizens of Vatican City, aside from the pope, are the cardinals who live in Rome, directors of other Vatican offices, and full-time diplomats who work for the *Holy See* (the pope and the various offices of Church government in the Vatican). These diplomats, clergy and laity alike, come from countries all over the world. They still retain their own nationality and citizenship but are given a Vatican passport while employed to represent the Vatican. Originally sent to Rome in 1506, about 107 Swiss guards protect the pope, decorating the *Piazza* (outdoor square where people gather) with their colorful costumes. In addition, plain-clothes Swiss guards, with electronic surveillance and sophisticated weapons, also keep a close eye on the Holy Father, especially since the attempted assassination of John Paul II in 1981.

Who's Next in the Ecclesiastical Scheme of Things

Because the Catholic Church has a billion-plus members, the pope depends on many helpers to govern the vast institution. The ranking system goes like this: The pope's at the helm, followed by cardinals, archbishops/bishops, vicars general, monsignors, and priests. The rest of the Church is made up of deacons, monks, nuns, brothers, sisters, and laypersons. (The latter — lay men and lay women — make up 99.9 percent of the Church.)

Cardinals

Although the primary responsibility of the College of Cardinals is to elect a pope (see the section "How the pope gets his job", earlier in this chapter), cardinals have many other responsibilities as well. The *Roman Curia* is the whole group of administrators (Cardinal Prefects) who head up their departments (congregations, tribunals, and so on), working together as the right hand of the pope. The pope governs through the Roman Curia, something like cabinet members who assist the president or department ministers who assist the prime minister. For example, a Cardinal Secretary of State represents the Holy See to foreign governments, because Vatican City is the world's smallest independent country. And you can find a different cardinal heading up each congregation, such as the Congregation for

- ✔ Doctrine of the Faith
- ✔ Bishops
- ✔ Catholic Education
- ✔ Causes of the Saints
- ✔ Clergy
- ✔ Divine Worship and Discipline of the Sacraments
- ✔ Evangelization of Peoples
- ✔ Institutes of Consecrated Life and Societies of Apostolic Life
- ✔ Oriental Churches

A different cardinal also heads up each of several commissions and councils, as well as three high courts of the Catholic Church: the Apostolic Penitentiary, the Apostolic Signatura, and the Roman Rota, all of which deal with canon law (see Chapter 11) and its application and interpretation.

Cardinals who don't work in the Curia run an archdiocese, mostly functioning as an archbishop would — ordaining, confirming, and doing the day-to-day business of being chief shepherd of the archdiocese. These cardinals are also often the *metropolitans,* which means that they supervise the province of two to several dioceses, usually all in the same state or region. (We define archdiocese and diocese in the next section.) A metropolitan doesn't have immediate authority over neighboring bishops or their dioceses even though they're within the cardinal archbishop's province as metropolitan.

A metropolitan does report to Rome, however, if one of the bishops in his province is derelict in his duties, commits scandal or crime, and so on. Often, the *apostolic nuncio,* the papal ambassador to that country, consults with the cardinal when vacancies appear in his province, as in the case of a bishop dying or retiring. For example, the Cardinal Archbishop of Philadelphia is the Metropolitan for Pennsylvania, which incorporates the eight dioceses of Philadelphia, Pittsburgh, Erie, Harrisburg, Scranton, Allentown, Greensburg, and Altoona-Johnstown.

The pope personally selects the men who become cardinals. The ceremony where new cardinals are created is called a *consistory,* and it usually occurs every few years to replace those who have retired (or will soon retire), as well as those who have died since the last consistory. This way, the goal of 120 cardinal electors is more likely achieved should the pope die, in which case a conclave is called to elect a new pope. Since the pontificate of John Paul II, a concerted effort has been made to have a diverse spectrum of cardinals from all continents and from both Latin and Eastern Catholic Rites.

Bishops and archbishops

Besides being the head of the Catholic Church, the pope is also the bishop of Rome. The pope isn't more a bishop than any other bishop, but his authority covers more territory. The pope has supreme, full, immediate, and universal jurisdiction all over the world, whereas a local bishop, who may also be an archbishop or a cardinal, possesses jurisdiction only in his *diocese,* which is the typical geographical designation in Catholic governance — an administrative territory.

Dioceses and archdioceses: The areas that bishops govern

Each individual bishop retains his own authority, which comes from episcopal ordination and consecration. *Episcopal* refers to anything that has to do with a bishop or bishops, and episcopal ordination and consecration is the sacrament by which a priest becomes a bishop. It's the third and fullest level of the Sacrament of Holy Orders. (The first level is the ordination of a deacon, and the second is the ordination of a priest. Deacons, priests, and bishops are all considered *clergy.*)

The local bishop runs the diocese. He's not an ambassador of the pope but governs the local diocese as an authentic successor of the apostles, just as the pope governs the universal Church as the successor of St. Peter.

The pope appoints the bishops, and they must make a visit to the Holy Father every five years and give a report on their particular diocese. The rest of the time, the bishop goes around the diocese confirming adults and teenagers, ordaining men to the *diaconate* (the office of deacon), and ordaining men to the priesthood once a year. Only bishops have the authority to administer the Sacrament of Holy Orders whereby men are ordained deacons, priests, or bishops. Bishops make pastoral visits to the parishes and chair numerous meetings with their staff. (See Chapter 8 for more on the Sacrament of Confirmation, and see Chapter 9 for more on the Sacrament of Holy Orders.) A bishop is like a pastor of an extra-large parish. (See the section "The parish priest" for details about pastors.)

The local diocese is a collection of local parishes, just like a state is a collection of counties and cities. Many dioceses are comprised of several state counties, and in a few places, the entire state makes up one diocese.

In general, you can think of a local parish as being like a town or city, and the local pastor as being like the mayor. The diocese is like a state or province, and the bishop is like the governor. (The pope is like the prime minister, governing the entire nation, except that he governs the universal Church all over the world.)

An archbishop runs a really large diocese, known as an *archdiocese*. For example, an archbishop is given authority in each of the following archdioceses: Newark, San Francisco, Denver, Hartford, Miami, St. Louis, and Omaha. Sometimes, though, the archbishop is also a cardinal, which is often the case in Philadelphia, New York City, Boston, Chicago, Baltimore, Los Angeles, Detroit, and Washington, D.C.

The bishops within an entire country or nation get together at least once a year in a gathering known as an *episcopal conference*. The American bishops belong to the United States Conference of Catholic Bishops (USCCB); the Canadian Bishops belong to the Canadian Conference of Catholic Bishops (CCCB); in Australia, it's the Australian Catholic Bishops Conference (ACBC); and in Great Britain, it's the Catholic Bishops' Conference of England and Wales (CBCEW).

Cathedrals: The place where bishops hang out

The cathedral is to the local diocese what the Vatican is to the universal Church. The cathedral is the official church of the diocese where the bishop's chair resides, and his chair (*cathedra* in Latin) is a symbol of his authority as a successor to the apostles.

Ironically, St. Peter's Basilica in the Vatican, where the pope celebrates most of his Masses, isn't technically the pope's cathedral church. The cathedral for the diocese of Rome is actually St. John Lateran, where the popes originally lived before moving to the Vatican in the 14th century.

Bishops celebrate most Masses at the cathedral church. In addition, it's often the place where the Chrism Mass (also known as the *Mass of the Oils*) takes place — unless the bishop decides to have it elsewhere in the diocese. (Curious? See the sidebar "Nope, the Mass of the Oils has nothing to do with your car's engine" for details about this special Mass.)

Cathedrals also have daily and weekly Mass like other parishes, as well as weddings, funerals, baptisms, and such. But the pride of the cathedral is in the ordinations to the episcopacy, priesthood, or diaconate, as well as the Chrism Mass. (For more on ordination and Holy Orders, see Chapter 9.)

Note: Only the bishop may sit in his *cathedra*, so any other priest celebrating Mass must use another chair.

Nope, the Mass of the Oils has nothing to do with your car's engine

The Chrism Mass takes place on Holy Thursday or some other day of Holy Week (the week before Easter), and all the priests of the diocese are asked to be present if possible. At this Mass, the bishop formally blesses olive oil in enormous multi-gallon containers to be distributed to all the parishes and priests throughout the diocese. Three oils are blessed at this annual Mass:

✔ **The Oil of Catechumens** *(Oleum Catechumenorum)* is used to bless people prior to their Baptism and during enrollment as *catechumen,* students of the faith preparing for Baptism.

✔ **The Oil of the Sick** *(Oleum Infirmorum)* is appropriate when administering the Sacrament of the Anointing of the Sick, formerly known as Extreme Unction.

✔ **Chrism Oil** *(Sacrum Chrisma),* also called Sacred Chrism, is for newly baptized persons, and the bishop also uses Chrism Oil when administering the Sacraments of Confirmation or Holy Orders and to consecrate altars, churches, chalices, and so on. Balsam is added to olive oil to make it more fragrant.

The vicar general

Vicars general aren't military leaders like Generals Montgomery, De Gaulle, and MacArthur. They're priests who are second in command in the diocese and appointed by the bishop to help him govern the local Church. Sometimes, episcopal vicars are also appointed to assist the bishop in certain areas, such as vocations, the marriage tribunal, clergy personnel, Hispanic or minority ministries, and so on. In large dioceses, such as New York or London, vicars general are often *auxiliary bishops,* ordained bishops who assist the bishop of the diocese in the same way any other vicar general does except that they can help the bishop ordain deacons and priests and celebrate the Sacrament of Confirmation.

Often, these priests are given the honorary title of *monsignor* at the request of the local bishop. This title has no extra authority, dignity, or salary. You can recognize a monsignor by the color of his *cassock* — a long, close-fitting garment worn by clerics. This honorary title may be bestowed in three different forms:

✔ **Papal Chamberlain:** Also known as *Chaplain of His Holiness,* this is the lowest ranking of the title of monsignor. These monsignors wear black cassocks with purple buttons and trim.

- ✔ **Domestic Prelate:** These monsignors are also known as *Prelates of Honor,* and they wear purple or black cassocks with red buttons and trim.
- ✔ **Protonotary Apostolic:** This is the highest ranking of the title. It's designated by a purple *ferraiolone,* a silk cape worn over the cassock.

The parish priest

The *parish priest* (also known as a *pastor*) is the next clergy in the hierarchy after the vicar general. Pastors are appointed by the bishop and represent the bishop to the local *parish,* which is a collection of neighborhoods in one small region of the county within a given state.

Some pastors are helped by a priest called a *parochial vicar* (formerly known as a *curate* or an *assistant pastor*) and/or sometimes by a permanent deacon, religious sister, or a lay parishioner as a *pastoral associate.* The parish council and finance committees, which are made up of lay parishioners for the most part, advise and counsel the pastor but don't have administrative or executive authority.

Tough training

The typical Catholic priest isn't what you see in movies or on TV. Priests are expected to obtain a graduate, post-graduate, or doctoral degree, and they often spend anywhere from 4 to 12 years in the *seminary,* which is the equivalent of Protestant divinity school. Most have at least a master's degree in divinity or theology, if not a higher academic degree on par with medical doctors and attorneys.

Besides scholastic training, seminarians also receive practical experience from *apostolates,* which are weekly or summertime assignments in parishes, hospitals, nursing homes, prisons, classrooms, and such, to unite pastoral education with theological and philosophical education.

A busy job

A parish priest celebrates daily Mass, hears confessions every week, gives marriage counseling, provides prenuptial counseling, gives spiritual direction, anoints and visits shut-ins and the sick in hospitals and nursing homes, teaches *Catechism* (a book that contains the doctrines of Catholicism) to children and adults, baptizes, witnesses marriages, performs funerals and burials, attends numerous parish and diocesan meetings, prays privately every day, does spiritual and theological reading, and finds time to relax now and then with family and friends. And once a year, he's expected to make a five-day retreat in addition to doing his regular spiritual direction and daily prayer. Yeah, it's a busy job.

With 1.18 billion Catholics worldwide and only about 410,593 priests to minister to their spiritual needs, that leaves an average of about one priest per 2,874 Catholics. Some areas have as many as 6,000 or more people per priest.

The hub in the wheel: The parish church

The parish church is where the priest does his job and where most Catholics hang out on Saturday evening or Sunday morning to attend Mass.

The local Catholic parish is often named after a title of the Lord Jesus Christ, such as *Blessed Sacrament* or *Sacred Heart;* after a title of the Blessed Virgin Mary, such as *Our Lady of Good Counsel* or *Our Lady of Seven Sorrows;* or after one of the saints, such as *St. Ann, St. Bernadette,* or *St. Joseph.* The parish is the heart of the diocese because it's where most Catholics get baptized, go to confession, attend Mass, receive Holy Communion, are confirmed, get married, and are buried from.

Some American parishes have a parochial school connected to them, but few of them have a convent of nuns who staff the school, although you can still find them here and there. Catholic grade schools were once the bread and butter of vocations and often fed into Catholic high schools and colleges. In other words, these parish schools encouraged boys and girls to consider becoming priests and nuns, and most students continued their Catholic education all the way through college even if they didn't have a religious vocation. But economics, demographics, and declining numbers of religious sisters and brothers have resulted in the consolidation and closing of many parish schools. Public schools in many places are well staffed, well funded, and more accessible.

An even rarer occurrence is the parish cemetery. Nowadays, the diocese has centralized schools and cemeteries, but a few old country parishes still have a graveyard in the back of the property.

Father, are you a diocesan or religious priest?

Catholic priests are *diocesan* (secular) or *religious* (regular). Diocesan priests belong to the diocese that they're located in, but religious order priests, such as Franciscan or Dominican, belong to that order.

Diocesan (secular) priests

The typical parish priest is usually a diocesan priest, meaning he belongs to the geographical area of the diocese, which often comprises several counties in one state. He makes a promise of obedience to the local bishop and a promise of celibacy. Diocesan priests are also called *secular* priests to distinguish them from the priests who belong to communities and orders.

A diocesan priest gets a modest monthly salary from the parish. In addition, the parish or diocese normally provides room and board (meals and lodging) and health insurance, but only a few dioceses also provide car insurance. Diocesan priests live in parishes alone or with another priest, but basically have their own living quarters inside the *rectory* — the house where the parish priests live. They do their own work and relax on their own, usually just sharing one meal together.

Diocesan priests are responsible for buying and maintaining their own automobiles as well as personal property — clothing, books, computers, televisions, and so on. The individual diocesan priest pays his federal, state, and local taxes, including Social Security taxes. After making monthly car payments, paying for insurance, and possibly paying off banks loans from college, not much is left of the monthly salary, but the parish or diocese provides his necessities. Honoraria and gifts from baptisms, weddings, and funerals differ from parish to parish and from diocese to diocese, but it's *very important* to note that a priest never charges any fees for his services. Free will offerings are often made to him or to the parish, but it's sinful, sacrilegious, and rude for any cleric to ask for money while performing his sacred ministry.

Canon law (see Chapter 11) guarantees every priest one day off per seven-day week and one month (30 days) of vacation per year, not including the one-week annual retreat. If you think 30 days of vacation every year seems like a lot, keep in mind that most people get two days off per week. Priests work an extra 52 days each year to earn their 30 days of vacation!

Religious (regular) priests

Religious priests are referred to as *regular* because they follow the *regula,* which is Latin for *rule,* the structured life of a religious community. The Rule refers to how a religious order trains, lives, governs itself, and practices. Religious priests are more commonly known as *order priests* after the religious *order* that they belong to, such as the Franciscans, Dominicans, Jesuits, Benedictines, and Augustinians. They wear particular *habits* (religious garb) and take solemn vows of poverty, chastity, and obedience. They don't own their own cars or personal possessions. Many use community automobiles that everyone in the order shares. They have the clothes on their back and little else. They don't get salaries like diocesan priests but are given an extremely modest monthly allowance to buy toiletries and snacks, as well as to go out for dinner or a movie once in a while. If they need to buy something expensive or want to take time off for vacation, they must ask permission of the superior who authorizes the money to be given them or for the bill to be paid.

They normally live together with three or more (sometimes more than 20) members of the community in the same house, sharing everything: one television, one computer, and so on. This arrangement encourages them to recreate together, because they must also live together, pray together, and work together. Unlike diocesan (secular) clergy who get small salaries and pay taxes, religious clergy own nothing. If they inherit anything whatsoever, it goes to the community or to the order, whereas a diocesan priest could inherit the family home but would also have to pay all the taxes and upkeep.

Deacons

Deacons are the clergy next in the hierarchy, right after priests. *Permanent deacons* are men ordained to an office in the Church who normally have no intention or desire of becoming priests. They can be single or married.

If the latter, they must be married *before* being ordained a deacon. If their wife dies before them, they may be ordained a priest if the bishop permits and approves. Married deacons cannot remarry if their wife dies unless they petition the Pope for a dispensation (for example, when there are small children to be raised).

Transitional deacons are *seminarians,* students in training for the priesthood, at the last phase of their formation. After being a deacon for a year, they're ordained a priest by the bishop.

Deacons can baptize, witness marriages, perform funeral and burial services outside of Mass, distribute Holy Communion, preach the *homily* (the sermon given after the Gospel at Mass), and are obligated to pray the Divine Office (150 psalms and Scriptural readings for clergy) each day.

Permanent deacons, especially those who are married, have secular jobs to support their families. They help the local pastor by visiting the sick, teaching the faith, counseling couples and individuals, working on parish committees and councils, and giving advice to the pastor.

Monks and nuns, brothers and sisters

Technically speaking, monks and nuns live in *monasteries* (from the Greek *monazein,* meaning *to live alone*), buildings that have restricted access to the outside world, allowing them to spend as much time as possible in work and in prayer. Monasteries are places where only women as nuns reside or where only men as monks live. Few monasteries have guest accommodations, and the monks or nuns live a monastic type of spirituality, such that they all gather in the chapel to pray together, they all eat together, and they all work somewhere in the monastery — cooking, cleaning, and so on.

The celibacy issue

Celibacy has been normative for the Latin (Western) church since the 4th century and mandatory since the 11th. Married clergy, however, always existed in the Byzantine (Eastern) churches. The Latin Church has allowed some married clergy from other Christian denominations to get ordained to the Catholic priesthood if they convert to Catholicism, but typically, Catholic priests of the Latin (Western) Church are celibate.

A man may be ordained when he's single or married if he's Eastern Catholic, but after ordination, a single cleric can't marry, and a married cleric can't remarry if his wife dies, unless they have small children and he receives a dispensation from Rome. Marriage must precede ordination according to Eastern tradition, or it can never be received. This is the ancient tradition of both the Catholic and the Orthodox churches. So even if celibacy were made optional in the Latin Church, it wouldn't affect those who were unmarried at the time of their ordination.

Some Anglican, Episcopalian, and certain Lutheran ministers who are married and wish to convert to become Catholic priests have been allowed to enter the sacred ministry because their marriage occurred *prior* to their ordination as Catholic clergy. But celibacy has been so much a part of the Western Catholic Church that even scandal won't erode its role and importance.

Religious sisters, on the other hand, live in *convents,* a word that comes from the Latin *conventus* meaning *assembly.* Convents offer more open access inside and out to the secular world. Residents typically live and pray in the convent but work outside in schools, hospitals, and so on. *Friaries* (from the Latin word *frater* meaning *brother*) are the male version of convents, a place where religious men called *brothers* live and pray together. Their work is done outside the friary.

St. Dominic and St. Francis of Assisi both founded the first group of friars in the Church. Friars bridged the gap between the urban parish and the monastery, and they aren't as cloistered or semi-cloistered as their monk and nun counterparts. How cloistered the group is depends on the religious order or community and the founder who started it.

You can find hundreds of different religious orders, communities, and congregations in the world today. Each community and order bases its spirituality on the founder of its congregation; for example, St. Francis founded the Franciscans, St. Clare founded the Poor Clares, St. Lucy Filippini founded the Religious Sisters Filippini, and Mother Teresa founded the Missionaries of Charity. Some communities specialize in teaching and others in hospital work. Some engage in several active apostolates, and a few devote themselves to a cloistered life of contemplative prayer.

For example, the Sisters of St. Joseph, the Sisters of Mercy, Religious Sisters Filippini, Dominican Sisters, Daughters of Charity, and Sisters of Saints Cyril and Methodius often work in schools, hospitals, and nursing homes. But Carmelite, Dominican, Poor Clare, and other nuns stay in the monastery and pray, fast, and work for the sanctification of souls. You may have seen Mother Angelica and the other Poor Clare nuns on television from time to time and noticed that even while they're in the chapel, they're separated *(cloistered)* from the general public. Cloistered nuns live and stay in the monastery whereas religious sisters work outside the convent.

In contrast, the sisters in parochial schools aren't nuns but religious sisters; they don't live in a cloistered monastery but in a convent, and they teach in the parish school.

You can tell the order of the monk, nun, sister, or friar by their *habit* (religious garb). Franciscans typically wear brown, the Dominicans wear white, the Benedictines wear black, and the Missionaries of Charity wear white with blue stripes. Some communities of women no longer wear a veil on their head but wear a pin that identifies them with their order instead. The style, size, and color of the women's veils also designate their community.

Religious brothers and sisters aren't members of the clergy, but they aren't members of the lay faithful, either. They're called *consecrated religious,* which means that they've taken sacred vows of poverty, chastity, and obedience. They share all meals together and try to work together, pray together, and recreate together. Because they take a vow of poverty, they don't own their own cars (no insurance, loan payments, or gasoline to buy either), and they have no personal savings or checking accounts. The religious order provides all these things, and they must ask their superiors when they need or want something. This is where that vow of obedience kicks in.

Part II
Celebrating the Mysteries of Faith

The 5th Wave   By Rich Tennant

"I'm not sure, but I think he just tweeted the homily."

In this part . . .

Catholic ritual is mysterious, but in this part, you take a peek behind the curtain and see what's going on. This part begins by explaining why and how the whole person — body and soul — gets into the act during Catholic worship. The Seven Sacraments speak to both body and soul, and we give each of them — Baptism, Communion, Confirmation, Marriage, Holy Orders, Penance, and Anointing of the Sick — in-depth attention in this part.

In this part, you discover the connection between what's believed and how that belief is expressed in worship, especially during the most central and sacred act of worship in Catholicism: the Mass.

Chapter 7

Body and Soul: Worshipping Catholic Style

In This Chapter

▶ Worshipping God with both body and soul

▶ Understanding Catholic gestures, objects, and symbols

▶ Using the five senses to worship God

▶ Getting a glimpse of the seven sacraments

*O*ne of the most familiar and yet mysterious aspects of Catholicism is its way of worship, which is chock-full of ancient rites and rituals. Catholic worship is based on the principle that humankind stands between the worlds of matter and spirit. In other words, human beings belong to both the material world, which the body interacts with through the five senses, and the spiritual world, which the soul interacts with by divine grace.

So Catholic worship — from kneeling to burning incense to using symbols — centers on the dynamic relationship between the material and spiritual worlds. This chapter shows you what worshipping Catholic style is all about.

Getting Your Body and Soul into the Act

Christians believe that a human being is made up of a body and a soul, both of which are created by God and are, therefore, good. In addition, because Jesus, the Son of God, had a human body and a human soul united in His divine nature, connecting the body and soul in worship is essential to the Catholic faith.

To capitalize on the dynamic relationship between body and soul — between the material world and the spiritual world — Catholic worship engages the entire human person in its rites and rituals.

✔ **Rites:** *Rites* are the necessary words and actions of a particular religious ceremony. For example, the Rite of Baptism requires that water be poured over the head (or that the person be immersed in water) while a priest says, "I baptize you in the name of the Father and of the Son and of the Holy Spirit." Each of the seven sacraments has its own proper rite.

On a broader scale, *rite* also refers to the four main Liturgical traditions (Roman, Antiochian, Alexandrian, and Byzantine or Constantinopolitan, which originated in the four patriachates) in which the Holy Eucharist is celebrated (see Chapter 8).

✔ **Rituals:** *Rituals* are the official books that contain the essential words and actions of particular religious ceremonies. For example, the Roman Ritual is the book that priests and deacons use when they celebrate rites. It tells them what materials to use, what sequence of events to follow, and what words and actions to say when celebrating rites. The Roman Ritual used to be one volume, but it's now printed in individual volumes for each sacrament — one volume for performing weddings, one for funerals, one for Baptisms, and so on.

During a Catholic Mass, the priest and the congregation engage their bodies by speaking aloud and by sitting, standing, or kneeling. They also perceive tangible symbols that exist outside the body — the water used for baptizing, for example, or the oil used for anointing — through one or more of the five senses. These outward symbols and ritual actions remind the faithful of the internal action of invisible divine grace entering the human soul.

Understanding Some Symbols and Gestures

Kneeling and making the sign of the cross, hanging crosses depicting a crucified Jesus, and sprinkling holy water on this and that are telltale Catholic practices. In this section, we explain the meanings behind these symbols and gestures as they relate to the body and soul.

The sign of the cross

The most common Catholic gesture is the sign of the cross. Latin (Western) Catholics make the sign of the cross by using their right hand to touch the forehead, then the middle of the breast, then the left shoulder, and finally the right shoulder. As they make this gesture, they say, "In the name of the Father and of the Son and of the Holy Spirit, Amen." This one complete gesture makes a cross. Eastern Catholics say the same thing as they make a similar sign of the cross; the only difference is that they go to the right shoulder first and then to the left.

No matter which shoulder Catholics touch first, the sign of the cross has the same meaning. It symbolically reaffirms two essential Christian doctrines: The Holy Trinity — Father, Son, and Holy Spirit — and humankind's salvation through the cross of Christ.

The genuflection

Another telltale sign of Catholic worship is *genuflection,* which is the act of touching the right knee to the floor while bending the left knee, and making the sign of the cross at the same time.

Catholics genuflect only in front of the Holy Eucharist. Why? Because the Holy Eucharist *is* the real body and blood of Jesus and Catholics want to show the ultimate form of respect by genuflecting or kneeling before Him. Catholic churches keep the Holy Eucharist in a large metal container or vault called a *tabernacle,* or sometimes they display the Eucharist behind glass in a gold container called a *monstrance.* (See Chapters 8 and 10 for more on the Eucharist and Chapter 19 for more on the tabernacle and monstrance.)

The crucifix

The *crucifix,* a cross bearing an image of Jesus being crucified, is a typical Catholic symbol. Protestant Christians usually have crosses with no *corpus* (that's Latin for *body*) of Jesus attached. The graphic symbol of the crucifix became predominant in the Western Church to remind Catholics that Jesus was true man as well as true God and that His suffering and death were very real and painful. The crucifix calls attention to the high price paid for human-kind's sins and inspires believers to repent of their sins and be grateful for the salvation that Jesus offered through His death on the cross. The *rubrics* (liturgical laws for celebrating Mass) require a crucifix to be visible to the people during divine worship. The faithful are encouraged to have a crucifix in their homes, and many wear a small one around their neck to remind them of the supreme love Christ showed in dying for our sins.

Holy water

Holy water, which is water blessed by a priest, bishop, or deacon, is a *sacramental,* or a religious object or action that the Catholic Church — not Jesus — created. (To find out more about sacramentals, see Chapter 19.) Helpful and beneficial but totally optional, sacramentals are subordinate to the seven sacraments, which are necessary for believers to live a life made holy by the gift of grace from God. In other words, sacraments give grace no matter what the spiritual state of the recipient. For example, a groom who is in the state of mortal sin when he gets married (the Sacrament of Matrimony) is still validly married. On the other hand, a groom who has a mortal sin on his soul gets no grace from the blessing (a sacramental) the priest gives to the newly married couple after they pronounce their vows.

Think of the sacraments as food for the soul and sacramentals as supplemental vitamins.

Holy water is the most widely used sacramental. Non-Catholics may think of holy water as the stuff that burned the face of the possessed 12-year-old in the movie *The Exorcist.* Although the Church does use holy water to drive out demons on rare occasions (see Chapter 19), it more regularly uses holy water to *sanctify* (bless) objects, to protect people from supernatural evil, and to serve as a symbolic reminder of Baptism.

When entering or leaving a church, Catholics dip their right hand, usually with two fingers, into a *font,* a cup of holy water that's on a wall near the doors of the church. Then they make the sign of the cross, wetting their forehead, breast, and shoulders. In doing so, they visibly remind themselves that they're entering the House of God. Plus, blessing with holy water is good preparation for worship.

Catholics also take small quantities of holy water home with them to fill fonts on their walls. They then bless themselves whenever leaving home, because the home is the *domestic Church* for Catholics. Home is where the family lives, and it's from the family that the Church grows and lives. After all, priests, deacons, and bishops must come from families, and churches can't grow without the families who attend church and support them.

At some Masses, the priest sprinkles holy water on the congregation in place of the Penitential Rite. (See Chapter 10 for what's what at the Mass.) And anytime a priest or deacon blesses a religious article, such as rosary beads, a statue, or a medal of one of the saints, he sprinkles holy water on the object after saying the prayers of blessing. The holy water reminds the owner that the object is now reserved for sacred use — to enhance prayer life, for example — and shouldn't be used for profane (nonreligious) use. This is why the blessed cup, called a *chalice,* that the priest uses at Mass to hold the wine that he consecrates can't be used for any other purpose, like to drink wine or juice at the dinner table.

In case you're wondering, a priest, bishop, or deacon blesses holy water when they celebrate in the church, particularly at the Easter Vigil (or Holy Saturday night), which takes place the evening before Easter Sunday. They can also bless holy water anytime during the year when the quantity runs out or evaporates.

Sensing God

Catholic worship incorporates all five senses — sight, touch, smell, hearing, and taste. Catholics believe that they can't see, feel, smell, hear, or taste the internal action of divine grace entering the human soul. But because the senses can perceive external symbols, Catholics can use many external symbols for the human body to perceive while the soul receives the divine grace.

Through sight

If you've been blessed with a good set of eyes, you gather more information by the sense of sight than any other. From the words you read to the pictures and images you look at, the ability to see impacts your perception of the world significantly.

Depicting God

Catholicism teaches that God the Father has no human body. He's pure spirit and totally invisible. But because of the importance of sight, people have felt the need to represent God visually somehow — to create a visible symbol of the invisible God. One problem with representing visible symbols of God is that the First Commandment forbids *graven images,* which are objects of worship, or idols.

The pagans, such as the ancient Babylonians, Egyptians, Persians, Greeks, and Romans, had many gods and goddesses, which they represented in stone or metal and worshipped. The Hebrew people, on the other hand, were one of the few ancient cultures to have a *monotheistic* religion (*mono* meaning *one* and *theos* meaning *god*). Although their pagan counterparts had plenty of idols to worship, the Hebrews were forbidden from making an image or idol of God.

From Abraham until Moses, no one even knew the name *God.* He was the *nameless* or *ineffable One.* This invisible, imageless deity was different from pagan gods because he had no name. According to the ancient way of thinking, after a person knew the name of the god — or of the evil spirit or demon, for that matter — he could control it somehow. So invoking the name and having an image of the god gave the believer some influence over that being. But the one true God had no name and couldn't be depicted by any image.

After paganism died out in Western culture and the Roman Empire embraced Christianity, the danger of distorting the nature of the one true God evaporated. After God the Son took on a human nature in the person of Jesus, who had a real and true human body, fear about symbolically representing God the Father or God the Holy Spirit in Christian art disappeared.

Today, you can see God the Father, Jesus, and the Holy Spirit portrayed in paintings on walls and canvases, as well as in stained glass. God is most often represented in visible form as follows:

- ✔ *God the Father* is usually depicted as an old man with a long flowing beard, an image that came from the early Europeans. In modern and contemporary Christian art, however, artists also represent God the Father with Asian or African features, for example. The modern reasoning is that if God is a spirit, why portray Him just as a Caucasian man?

- ✔ *Jesus (God the Son)* had a face and a body, but with no pictures of Him to draw from, artists have used their own creativity to depict the Savior — often as a young man with a full beard. Many works of art have been modeled on the image of the Shroud of Turin, which is considered by many to be the actual burial cloth of Jesus and has a miraculous image of His face and body on it.

- ✔ *God the Holy Spirit* is almost always portrayed as a dove because the Bible speaks of a dove descending on Jesus at His baptism by John the Baptist.

Conveying meaning through colors and symbols

The Catholic Church uses symbols to show us the connection of the material and spiritual worlds because human beings are both body and soul. One of the most well-known symbols used in the Catholic Church is the stained-glass window. Some of the most popular churches, like St. Patrick's Cathedral in New York City and the Cathedral of Notre Dame in Paris (not the football shrine), contain hundreds of magnificent stained-glass windows full of color, light, and symbolism.

Originally, churches used stained-glass windows to teach the Catholic faith to illiterate peasants. Unable to read, these peasants could look at the pictures and symbols depicted in the stained glass and learn all about salvation history from biblical stories to Church history to the seven sacraments.

You see another important symbol in the priest's garb. Depending on the occasion, priests and deacons wear different-colored liturgical *vestments* (garments for worship services) for Mass — green, white, red, purple, black, rose, or gold. Vestments often have symbols on them, such as a cross; the first and last letters of the Greek alphabet (the *alpha* and *omega*), which represent Jesus, who is the beginning and the end; and the letter *M* for Mary, the Mother of Jesus.

Marble altars and floors often include engraved symbols, such as

- ✔ **Two keys:** This image symbols St. Peter and comes from the Gospel of Matthew, which describes Jesus entrusting the keys of the kingdom to Peter.

- ✔ **An eagle:** This symbol represents St. John the Evangelist (see Chapter 4 for more details).

- ✔ **A pelican pecking her own heart to feed her young with her blood:** This image symbolizes Christ, who feeds Catholics with His blood in Holy Communion.

In addition, Catholic architecture and art use visual symbols to enhance the faith. For example, the gothic cathedrals spiral up toward heaven to remind the faithful to remember their destiny in the next world — and not to get too comfortable in this earthly one. To literally see the beauty of Catholic worship, you can visit the Shrine of the Most Blessed Sacrament in Hanceville, Alabama (see Chapter 22). The marble, the gold, the stained glass, the light, the altar, the tabernacle, and especially the 7-foot-tall monstrance surrounded by gold and jewels all attract the human eye and inspire the human soul to aspire to heaven. These symbols, which are attractive to the five senses, also help the soul transcend the material world into the spiritual realm.

Through touch

Just as no one has seen God because He's invisible, no one has touched Him either. Yet everyone knows how vital the sense of touch is to human beings from the moment they're born. Being held by a parent and feeling tender, loving hands offers a sense of security.

Like the sense of sight, the sense of touch is also an important part of Catholic worship. For instance, each of the following sacraments incorporates the sense of touch in some way:

- ✔ **Baptism:** You literally feel the water that the priest pours over your head.

- ✔ **Anointing of the Sick:** You feel the oil that the priest applies to your forehead and the palms of your hands.

- ✔ **Matrimony:** The bride and groom join right hands before pronouncing their vows.

- ✔ **Confirmation:** You feel the chrism oil being put on your forehead.

- ✔ **Holy Orders:** Men being ordained feel the two hands of the bishop touching the top of their heads.

A priest's vestments of many colors

A priest's colorful vestments (Latin Rite) help Catholics know which celebrations are at hand:

✔ **Green:** The color of vestments used during ordinary time.

✔ **Purple or violet:** Used during Advent and Lent.

✔ **White or gold:** Most appropriate for Christmas and Easter.

✔ **Red:** Worn on feasts of the Passion of Jesus and for the Holy Spirit, representing red tongues of fire, in addition to being worn for the feasts of martyred saints, who shed their red blood for Christ.

✔ **Rose:** May be worn as a sign of anticipated joy on the third Sunday of Advent and the fourth Sunday of Lent. If you take the somber color of purple or violet and brighten it with some white, it changes into rose; hence the notion of using this color as a visible sign that Christmas or Easter is soon to come.

✔ **Black:** May be worn for funeral Masses (as can purple or white) and on All Souls' Day.

We go into the nitty-gritty details about each of the sacraments in Chapters 8 and 9. Another way that Catholics embrace the sense of touch in prayer is by saying the Rosary (see Chapter 16). They can feel the beads as they pray the Hail Marys and meditate on the mysteries of Jesus and Mary. Catholics also encounter the sense of touch on Ash Wednesday when they feel the ashes of burnt palms (from last year's Palm Sunday) being spread on their foreheads in the sign of the cross. On the Feast of St. Blaise, which is February 3 (see Chapter 19), Catholics feel two crossed candles on their throats when the priest blesses them. Plus, holy water fonts are at every entrance and exit of Catholic churches, so believers can touch the holy water with their right hands and bless themselves.

Through smell

The sense of smell is as much a part of human beings as the other four senses, so Catholic worship also appeals to this function of the body.

Burning incense

The most obvious appeal to the nose in Catholic worship involves burning *incense,* which is the powder or crystalline form you get when you dry the aromatic resins of certain trees. When you place incense on burning charcoal, it produces a visible smoke and a recognizable aroma that fills the church. The smoke represents prayers going up to heaven, and the sweet aroma reminds people of the sweetness of God's divine mercy.

Incense has been a part of worship since biblical times. In the Old Testament, Psalm 141 speaks of prayers rising up to heaven "as incense." God commanded Moses to burn incense on the altar before the Ark of the Covenant, which held the Ten Commandments.

On a more practical level, churches burned incense in the Middle Ages when they didn't have decent air circulation and parishioners didn't wear deodorant. On a hot summer Sunday, the smell in the church became quite potent unless the clergy burnt plenty of incense and thoroughly swung it around the entire congregation. Yep, in pre-air-freshener days, incense was the best thing going. Keep in mind, though, that this practical application of incense didn't take away from its symbolic significance.

Incense remains an integral part of Catholic worship today. Eastern Orthodox Catholics use incense every day and every week during liturgical worship. Latin (Western) Catholics may use it on special holy days (like Easter and Christmas), maybe once a week at Sunday Mass, and almost always at Catholic funerals.

Note: At funerals, Catholics burn incense at the coffin as well as the altar because the body was a temple of the Holy Spirit when the soul lived inside. Jesus will reunite the body with its soul at the resurrection of the dead.

Anointing with oil

Another familiar smell to Catholics is *chrism oil,* sometimes called *oil of chrism.* Chrism is olive oil that the local diocesan bishop has blessed. Catholic worship uses this oil to consecrate bishops, anoint the hands of priests, confirm Catholics, baptize Catholics, bless bells, and consecrate altars and churches. The strong but pleasant odor comes from *balsam,* an aromatic perfume that's added to the oil.

The local bishop blesses three oils during Holy Week (the week before Easter) at a special Mass called the *Chrism Mass,* or *Mass of the Oils.* At this special Mass, the bishop blesses Chrism Oil, the Oil of the Sick, and the Oil of Catechumens. The bishop blesses all three olive oils in multigallon containers. Then he distributes the oil to the priests and deacons of the diocese. Chrism oil is the only one that has balsam added to it.

Through sound

Catholics use their sense of hearing in worship by listening to the Word of God read aloud. Catholics hear the words of the Bible read aloud at every Catholic Mass, whether it's Sunday or daily Mass. Readings come only from the Bible because Catholics believe that no other poetry or prose can replace the inspired Word of God. The readings come from both the Old and New Testaments. After the Old Testament reading and before the New Testament Epistle reading, the congregation normally sings or recites a Psalm. Then, after the Epistle reading, the priest or deacon reads a passage from one of the four Gospels. In addition, many of the hymns Catholics sing throughout the Mass are based on scriptural citations.

Although the words of Scripture are the primary way that Catholic worship incorporates the sense of hearing, the prayers of the priest and congregation are also important, so the congregation pays attention to these prayers and responds at the appropriate times. The *homily,* or sermon, that the priest, deacon, or bishop gives immediately after the Gospel is another important sense-of-sound part of the Catholic Mass because it offers the congregation an application of the Gospel.

The Catholic Church also uses plenty of music, especially organ music, choirs, and *Gregorian chant* (Latin chant named after Pope St. Gregory the Great, who was pope from A.D. 590–604). The beautiful sounds of the pipe organ and the delicate tones of the human voice are also reminders of God that the congregation can physically hear.

Through taste

Catholicism even employs the sense of taste in its worship at Communion time. The Holy Eucharist is the most important, sacred, and pivotal aspect of Catholic worship because it is when the bread and wine become the real, true, and substantial body and blood, soul and divinity of Christ. The appearance of the bread and wine appeals to and is perceived by the sense of taste.

When it's time for Communion, believers receive the Holy Eucharist, which still tastes like unleavened bread and grape wine. (The Latin Church uses unleavened bread, but the Eastern Church uses leavened bread.) The believers' sense of taste doesn't perceive the change of substance, hence the term *transubstantiation* (see Chapter 10), from bread and wine into the body and blood of Christ — which is definitely a good thing because if the Holy Eucharist tasted like flesh and blood, no one would take it.

The appearances of the bread and wine during Communion are sometimes called the *accidents,* but they have nothing to do with mishaps or car crashes. Catholic theology uses the philosophical term *accident* to distinguish outward appearances from the invisible but underlying essence.

Chapter 8

Entering the Church: Baptism, Communion, and Confirmation

In This Chapter

▶ Defining the three Sacraments of Initiation

▶ Baptizing in the name of the Father, Son, and Holy Spirit

▶ Understanding the threefold meaning of the Holy Eucharist

▶ Confirming the promises made at Baptism

hree of the seven sacraments — Baptism, Holy Eucharist, and Confirmation — are classified as *Sacraments of Initiation.* Through Baptism, people enter (are *initiated* into) the Catholic Church. Through Holy Eucharist, which is also called *Holy Communion,* they express their unity with the Church — all her doctrines, laws, and practices. Through Confirmation, they're considered personally responsible for their faith.

The Eastern Catholic Church administers all three Sacraments of Initiation at the same time — at infancy. The Latin (Western) Catholic Church separates the three sacraments into completely different celebrations at different ages. Normally, *infants* are baptized, *children* receive Holy Eucharist at the age of reason (around 7 years of age), and *adolescents* or *young adults* are confirmed at ages ranging from 7 to 18 years old, but many Catholics are confirmed at around 14 years old. This chapter explains the Sacraments of Initiation and offers insight into the ceremonies of Baptism, First Communion, and Confirmation. (Chapter 9 explains the rest of the seven sacraments.)

Come On In — The Water's Fine

Baptism is the first of the seven sacraments. It's the one sacrament that all Christian denominations share in common, even though each faith community baptizes at different ages and some only in one way, such as immersion. A few Christian denominations only baptize by completely immersing or dunking the person head to toe in the water, but most allow immersion or infusion such as the pouring of water over the head of the new Christian.

Like the Sacrament of Confirmation and the Sacrament of Holy Orders (see Chapter 9), you're baptized only once. These three sacraments confer an indelible mark on the soul, which can never be repeated and is never removed. So, no one can ever be unbaptized or re-baptized.

In the eyes of the Catholic Church, any Baptism that uses water and the invocation of the Holy Trinity, as well as the intention to *do* what the Church *does* — that is, "I baptize you in the name of the Father and of the Son and of the Holy Spirit" — is a valid sacrament. So Catholicism regards Episcopalian, Anglican, Lutheran, Methodist, Presbyterian, Baptist, United Church of Christ, Assembly of God, Church of the Nazarene, Church of the Brethren, Amish, Church of God, Disciples of Christ, Adventist, and Evangelical Baptisms to be valid. And if a follower of one of these Christian churches wants to become Catholic, he doesn't have to be re-baptized.

That said, Catholicism doubts the Baptisms in the following faith communities to be a valid sacrament: Christian Scientists, Quakers, Salvation Army, Jehovah's Witnesses, Unitarians/Universalists, Christadelphians, and Mormons (Church of Jesus Christ of Latter Day Saints). The reason has nothing to do with the religions themselves or their members, because all espouse a true love of God and neighbor. The reason merely has to do with what Catholicism considers to be a valid sacrament.

Becoming Christ's kith and kin

Your first birth from your mother's womb made you a member of the family established by your parents and their respective families. You have an immediate family of parents and siblings and an extended family of grandparents, aunts, uncles, cousins, in-laws, and such.

Just as natural birth ushers people into blood and marriage relationships, Baptism — as a supernatural birth — establishes ties to spiritual families. By being baptized, *born again* of water and the Spirit, new Christians become children of God by adoption. In other words, they're adopted into the family of God; they can't be born into that family because they're human and God is divine. Jesus Christ, God and man, divine and yet human, becomes their brother. Mary, the Mother of Jesus, becomes their spiritual mother because siblings share a relationship with the parents. If Jesus is their brother by adoption, then His mother, Mary, becomes their mother by adoption.

Baptism also connects the new Catholic to the Church. The title *Father* is given to the priest because he typically does the baptizing. The Holy *Mother* Church, the Catholic Church, gives birth to the new Christian from the spiritual womb of the baptismal font. The water of the baptismal font has been likened to the waters that surround the baby in the womb — thus the reason it's called the *spiritual womb*. A person is reborn through the waters of Baptism with the assistance of the priest doing the baptizing. It's only an analogy, but it has endured for 2,000 years.

At the moment of Baptism, a new Catholic joins the local parish and diocese as well. The *parish* is the faith community of a neighborhood, composed of Catholic families in that area; the *diocese* is the faith family of many parish communities in one geographic region of the state. So, if you were baptized at Notre-Dame de Paris in France, for example, you'd be a member of the Roman Catholic Church at large, a member of the Archdiocese of Paris, and a member of the Notre-Dame Cathedral Parish, all at the same time.

Washing away original sin

More than making connections and relationships, Baptism also washes away *original sin,* the sin of the original parents of the whole human race: Adam and Eve. The Book of Genesis (1:26–27) says that God created man in his own image and likeness, male and female. The first man was called Adam, and the first woman, the wife of Adam, was called Eve. They were the prototype man and woman, and their sin affected all men and women after them. And the Bible says that their sin was disobedience.

Biology has shown that you inherit many physical characteristics from your natural parents — eye and hair color, facial features, body shape, and so on. Good and bad traits and some diseases are handed down from generation to generation. In the same way, original sin is transmitted from generation to generation by birth.

Original sin doesn't mean that a baby in the womb somehow commits a sin before being born. If Junior kicks too much inside, he's not being a bad boy, for example. Mom just may have had too much spicy Italian sausage. To the Catholic Church, original sin isn't a personal sin of the unborn but a sin transmitted from generation to generation by birth. All men and women are born with original sin, and only Baptism can wash it away.

Catholicism sees original sin differently from *actual sin,* which is what a rational person does when she consciously, deliberately, and willingly disobeys God. Original sin is the natural inclination to sin.

Think of it this way: Nobody is born with polio, measles, or chicken pox, but folks aren't born with any immunity to these diseases, either. A baby needs to be vaccinated so the human body can produce its own antibodies and fight these diseases when it's exposed to them. Likewise, on the spiritual level, human beings are born with a weakened resistance to temptation and sin, and this condition is part of original sin.

Baptism is to original sin what the polio vaccination is to the polio virus. Baptism restores what should have been — a spiritual resistance to sin and temptation. The first sin of the first parents, Adam and Eve, wounded human nature, and everyone inherited that wounded nature from them. Baptism washes it away.

In addition to getting rid of original sin, Baptism also imparts or infuses *sanctifying grace,* a special free gift from God. Sanctifying grace makes the new Christian a child of God and applies the merits of Jesus Christ, His suffering and death for sins, to the new Christian personally because the person being baptized is mentioned by name. Catholicism believes that sanctifying grace allows human beings to enter heaven. It justifies them in the eyes of God by uniting them with the Savior and Redeemer, Jesus Christ. Without sanctifying grace, one can't stand before the utter holiness of God who is sanctity personified. Normally, you receive this special grace only through the sacraments, but God does provide some means to make sure all men and women have the potential and possibility of salvation (that is, baptism by blood or baptism of desire).

Baptizing with water

The most common form of Baptism is by water (we explain what blood and desire have to do with Baptism later in this section). The Gospels say that one must be born again of water and the Holy Spirit (John 3:5). The early Christians and their successors have been baptizing with water for almost two millennia but with some slight differences:

- ✔ **Immersion:** Some Christian denominations fully immerse a person in water up to three times while saying the invocation of the Holy Trinity, also known as the *Trinitarian formula,* "I baptize you in the name of the Father and of the Son and of the Holy Spirit."

- ✔ **Aspersion:** Other Christians sprinkle water on the forehead of the one being baptized and then invoke the Trinitarian formula.

- ✔ **Infusion:** Catholics (mostly Latin) baptize by pouring water over the head of the one being baptized while the Trinitarian formula is pronounced.

All three methods use water and the invocation of the Holy Trinity. Water (good old H_2O) is the only liquid that can be used for this form of Baptism. (The priest or bishop can't use oil, milk, or any other liquid.) Immersion or infusion is preferred to aspersion.

Many people ask why Catholics baptize infants whereas other Christians wait until the individual is old enough to decide for himself whether he wants to be baptized. Fair question. Think of it this way:

- ✔ At your birth, you were given a name by your parents. You had no choice in the matter. Once you're 18 and a legal adult, you can change your name, but from the day you are born, you need an identity. Imagine if your mom and dad waited until you were old enough to choose your own name. Not practical, is it? Similarly, Baptism defines you as a child of God. Your identity as a Christian is established at baptism.

✔ Where you're born and/or the nationality of your parents determines your citizenship; it isn't deferred until you can decide for yourself. Citizens have rights and obligations. Likewise, Baptism makes you a member of the family of faith called the Church. As a member, you benefit from your rights from day one (see Chapter 11).

In the past, infant mortality was so high that many babies didn't survive birth or early childhood, so Baptism as an infant insured that their souls wouldn't be denied heaven. In ancient times, there was no firm teaching on baptism of desire. Medieval theologians developed a theory of Limbo being a place where unbaptized infants went. Later came a fuller and expanded understanding of the baptism of desire and the universal salvific will of God (that all men and women be given the possibility of salvation). Today, with modern medicine and progress, it's not the fear of death but rather the hope for great potential and wonderful possibilities that encourages Catholic parents to baptize their children. It gives them an identity and a spiritual beginning. Anyway, the New Testament affirms that _entire households_ were baptized, which meant the parents and children as well. So infant Baptisms have occurred from the very beginning.

Recognizing the role of sponsors or godparents

Every child or adult about to be baptized must have a sponsor unless he or she is in danger of death. The sponsors in Baptism have traditionally been called _godparents._ The minimum requirement is one sponsor, but usually when infants are baptized, they get two, one of each gender.

Canon law permits only one godparent of each gender — a godmother and godfather. For an adult or a child being baptized, these sponsors

✔ Can't be the parents of the one being baptized

✔ Must be at least 16 years old

✔ Must be practicing Catholics who go to Mass every week, are not invalidly married, and live a good Christian life

✔ Must be already confirmed

If someone can't find two practicing Catholics to be the godfather and godmother, then one sponsor can be Catholic and the other a Christian witness if that person is a baptized Protestant Christian in good standing.

Being a godparent carries with it no legal right or ecclesiastical authority to the custody of the children. Prior to the medical advances of the 20th century, when people died at an earlier age because of illness, godparents were the practical choice to raise a child if both parents died before the son or daughter grew up. Babies had two godparents in case one would not be able to fulfill the job of raising the child. Nowadays, however, custody is a strictly legal matter that parents must decide with their attorney. Being a godparent means more than giving Christmas and birthday gifts every year. It means actively being a good Christian witness and example, a role model, and a supporter by regularly and faithfully practicing the religion.

What goes on at a Baptism?

Baptisms in the Catholic Church usually take place on Sundays, during the parish Mass or in the early afternoon after all the Masses are over. It all depends on the parish, the pastor, and the parents. Adults who were never baptized are an exception to this rule; they're highly encouraged to be baptized with other adults on Holy Saturday evening, during a service known as the Easter Vigil, because it's held on the night before Easter Sunday. Children, however, are baptized once a month or every Sunday, depending on the diocese and parish.

The person being baptized is asked to dress in white. Some parishes put a small white garment on the child, especially if she isn't already dressed in white. When adults are baptized, they typically put on a full-length white gown known as an *alb,* from the Latin word for *white.*

The white garment symbolizes the white garments that Jesus wore when he was placed in the tomb after his death on Good Friday. When the women and disciples returned on Easter day, they found the tomb empty except for the white robes. So it represents the promise of the Resurrection, made at Baptism. The promise is that the baptized body will one day die, like Christ's did, but it'll be raised from the dead someday by Christ. White also symbolizes purity of faith and cleansing.

The priest or deacon is usually the minister of Baptism, but anyone can baptize in an emergency, such as in a hospital or whenever someone's life is in danger. Here are the steps that occur during both infant and adult Baptism:

1. **During the Baptism of an infant, the priest or deacon asks the parents, "What name do you give your child?"**

   He doesn't ask this question because he's too senile to remember or too blind to read the child's name on the card in front of him, but because that person becomes a child of God by name and Jesus becomes her brother by name as soon as the person is baptized. The parents respond aloud, ideally with a Christian name, such as one of the saints or heroes of the Bible.

   In adult baptism, skip this step.

2. **The priest or deacon asks, "What do you ask of God's church for your child?"**

   The parents respond, "Baptism." If an adult is being baptized, she answers the same.

3. **In infant baptism, the priest or deacon asks the parents and the god-parents whether they're willing and able to fulfill their duties to bring up this child in the Christian faith.**

4. **As a symbolic gesture, the priest or deacon makes the sign of the cross with his thumb gently on the forehead of the child or adult.**

   This sign is made to show that the cross of Christ has saved her.

   The parents and godparents do the same.

5. **A particular passage from the Bible is read, usually from the New Testament, where Baptism is mentioned or alluded to.**

6. **After some other prayers, the first anointing takes place.**

   The infant's white garb is pulled slightly beneath the neck so the priest or deacon can smear a little *Oil of Catechumens* (blessed olive oil) on the infant's neck with his thumb. The same anointing takes place for an adult.

   The oil symbolizes that the person, born into the world, is now being set apart from the world by the anointing. She is soon to be baptized and therefore belongs not to the world but to God and heaven.

7. **The priest or deacon blesses the water of Baptism.**

   The prayer recalls how water has played an important role in salvation history as recorded throughout the Bible: It represents a sign of new life, the washing of sin, deliverance from slavery, and a new beginning.

8. **The first part of the baptismal promises are made: renunciation of evil.**

   Because an infant can't speak for herself, mom, dad, and the godparents answer for her. The priest or deacon asks, "Do you renounce Satan? And all his works? And all his empty promises?" If things go well, everyone says "I do." If not, you have to check for devil worshippers among the crowd. Later, probably when she's 14 years old, the child answers those same questions on her own before the bishop. Adults who are being baptized answer for themselves.

9. **The second part of baptismal promises follows, with the *Apostles' Creed* put in question form: "Do you believe in God, the Father Almighty, Creator of heaven and earth?"**

   Again, the hoped-for response is "I do." Then the other two persons of the Trinity are mentioned: "Do you believe in Jesus Christ. . . ?" and "Do you believe in the Holy Spirit. . . ?" And, once again, parents and godparents answer for infants; adults answer for themselves.

10. The actual Baptism takes place.

In infant Baptism, the immediate family gathers around the baptismal font (see Figure 8-1), and the child is held over the basin while the priest or deacon pours water three times over the child's head and says his first and middle name, and then, "I baptize you in the name of the Father and of the Son and of the Holy Spirit. Amen." Usually, the baby cries, because the water tends to be a little cool. (In the Eastern Catholic Church, the formula is: "The servant of God, [name], is baptized in the name of the Father, and of the Son, and of the Holy Spirit." Confirmation (Chrismation) and Holy Communion are also given at the ceremony when one is baptized in the Eastern Church.)

In adult baptism, the catechumen holds her head over the basin, and the priest pours water over her head; or, if baptized by immersion, she enters the pool, and the priest dips her head into the water three times.

11. The priest or deacon anoints the top of the new Christian's head with chrism oil.

Flip to Chapter 7 to find out where chrism oil comes from.

The anointing symbolizes that the newly baptized Christian is now exactly that — a *Christ*ian. The word *Christ* means *anointed,* and a *Christian* is someone who's anointed in Jesus Christ. This anointing also means the person is now to share in the three-fold mission of Christ — to sanctify, proclaim, and give Christian leadership and example to the world. Now, a white garment is usually presented to the newly baptized.

12. A Baptismal candle is lit from the burning Easter Candle, which is present throughout the ceremony.

It symbolizes that the new Christian is a light to the world.

13. The Our Father is said and a blessing is given for mom, dad, and the family, and everyone celebrates.

If you're invited to a Baptism

✔ You don't need to be Catholic or even a Christian to attend. Your presence is a sign of love, support, and friendship for the parents and for the baptized.

✔ If you're a Christian, you may want to join in the renewal of baptismal promises when they're asked.

Figure 8-1:
A baptismal
font.

Receiving the sacrament of Baptism in other ways

Every person must be baptized to receive salvation. Baptism by water is probably what you think of when you imagine Baptism, but people can still receive the sacrament of Baptism sans the water, white garment, and priest. Baptism by blood and by desire are two valid forms of Baptism under certain circumstances.

Shedding blood for Christ

From A.D. 60 to the end of the third century, the Romans violently persecuted the early Christian Church. Christianity wasn't even legal until after Emperor Constantine's Edict of Milan in A.D. 313. During those first 300 years of Roman persecution, many who believed in Christ as the Son of God weren't yet baptized with water. These unbaptized believers were called *catechumens,* which meant that they were preparing for Baptism by study and prayer but were not yet baptized. After all, people coming from a decadent pagan lifestyle needed time to clean up their act before being baptized, and some took several weeks, months, or even a year or two to prepare for their Baptism. After Baptism, they renounced their pagan ways and did no more dabbling in the idolatry and immorality of their secular contemporaries.

These catechumens and students of Christianity, otherwise known as the pre-baptized, were treated just as if they were full-fledged baptized Christians. The Roman gladiators and animals in the arena didn't distinguish between baptized Christians and those preparing for Baptism. Both were violently persecuted.

The notion of being baptized by shedding your own blood for Christ and/or His Church grew up during the Roman persecutions. And the Catholic Church has always revered these unbaptized *martyrs* — people who are killed because of their faith — maintaining that the divine mercy of God wouldn't penalize them or ignore their sacrifice merely because they died before their Baptism by water.

In addition, Herod killed many infants (Matthew 2:16) in a failed effort to kill the newborn Christ. Those infants, known as the *Holy Innocents,* are martyrs, too, because they shed their blood so Christ could live. So Baptism by blood is as valid as Baptism by water. The following quote from the *Catechism of the Catholic Church* shows what the Church has to say about Baptism by blood:

> The Church has always held the firm conviction that those who suffer death for the sake of the faith without having received Baptism are baptized by their death for and with Christ. This *Baptism of blood,* like the *desire for Baptism,* brings about the fruits of Baptism without being a sacrament. (1258)

Having the will but not the way

Part of Catholic theology is the *Universal Salvific Will of God,* which is just a fancy way of saying that God basically would like for everyone, all men and women, to join Him in heaven. Men and women have free will, though, so He *offers* the gift of grace, but men and women must freely accept and then cooperate with it.

St. Augustine (A.D. 354–430) taught that God offers everyone *sufficient* grace to be saved, but it only becomes *efficacious* (successful) for those who freely accept and cooperate with that grace. In other words, God gives every human being the chance and possibility of going to heaven. Whether they get beyond the pearly gates, however, depends on the individual person. (For more on St. Augustine, see Chapter 18.)

The official church doctrine of God's desire that everyone have the possibility of going to heaven is clearly stated in a document from a declaration by the Congregation for the Doctrine of the Faith (the Vatican office in charge of defending and explaining the faith) in 2000, which says:

> "The universal salvific will of God is closely connected to the sole mediation of Christ: 'God desires all men to be saved and to come to the knowledge of the truth.' (1 Tim 2:4)" (Dominus Iesus, #13).

The whole truth and nothing but the truth

The late Archbishop Fulton J. Sheen said that few people reject Christ or even hate the Catholic Church, but many reject and hate false notions and erroneous ideas about Christ, Christianity, and Catholicism. (See Chapter 20 for more on Archbishop Sheen.)

The Catholic Church doesn't see itself as being right and all other religions as being wrong, but Catholicism does firmly believe that Jesus Christ Himself founded the Catholic Church, and therefore, the Church possesses all the truths and graces necessary for salvation, whereas other faiths possess only some (partial) truth and grace. You can think of it like this: Catholicism sees itself more like someone who knows everything about mathematics versus someone who knows only algebra, geometry, or trigonometry. The Church believes that all religions know some truth, but it knows more. She doesn't claim perfect or total knowledge of science, philosophy, or other disciplines, but in the area of faith and theology, the Church believes that she has been given the fullness of truth and the mission to teach it to all nations.

So, on the one hand, you have the doctrine of the necessity of baptism, and on the other hand, you have the doctrine of the universal salvific will of God. How can God impose a requirement if, at the same time, he wants everyone to have the same chance?

As long as a person doesn't explicitly reject Christ and his Church and deliberately refuse Baptism, he can be saved. Nonbelievers can have an implicit desire to know and accept Christ. People who lack any knowledge of Christ and His teachings are sometimes called *anonymous Christians*.

Therefore, the Church believes in Baptism by desire, which allows salvation for non-Christians who, through no fault of their own, do not know or have never heard about Jesus Christ. God, being all-knowing, also knows with certitude if any person would have accepted or rejected Christ had they been given the chance and opportunity.

The Catechism of the Catholic Church has this to say about Baptism by desire:

> Since Christ died for all . . . we must hold that the Holy Spirit offers to all the possibility. . . . Every man who is ignorant of the Gospel of Christ and of his Church, but seeks the truth and does the will of God . . . can be saved. It may be supposed that such persons would have *desired Baptism explicitly* if they had known its necessity. (1260)

So while the Church consistently teaches the absolute necessity of Baptism for salvation, she also understands that it can be accomplished by water, blood, or desire.

The Holy Eucharist

The Holy Eucharist refers to the consecrated bread and wine consumed by Catholics during Communion. Like Baptism, the Holy Eucharist is also considered a Sacrament of Initiation because new members are encouraged to participate regularly and often in Holy Communion.

Of all seven sacraments, the Holy Eucharist is the most central and important to Catholicism because of the staunch belief that the consecrated bread and wine are actually, really, truly, and substantially the body and blood, soul and divinity of Christ. For Catholics, the presence of Christ in the Holy Eucharist is not just symbolic, allegorical, metaphorical, or merely spiritual. It's real. That's why it's also called the *Real Presence* — because Christ *really is present.* (For more on consecrated bread and wine, the Real Presence, and the Mass, see Chapter 10.)

Understanding the consecrated host

Catholicism maintains that Christ's body and blood are present in the *consecrated host* (the wafer of bread upon which the priest says the words of Jesus from the Last Supper: "This is my body") and in the consecrated wine (over which the priest says the words of Jesus: "This is the chalice of my blood"). *Holy Eucharist* refers to the three aspects of Christ's body and blood — as *sacrifice* during the Consecration of the Mass, as Holy *Communion,* and as *Blessed Sacrament.* These three aspects form the core of Catholic belief on the Holy Eucharist.

In Chapter 10, we discuss the parts of the Mass in detail and the Holy Eucharist as a sacrifice, but this section focuses solely on the sacred meal of Communion and the Blessed Sacrament.

The word *Eucharist* comes from the Greek *eucharistein,* meaning "thanksgiving." Catholics are grateful and give thanks to God for providing the Holy Eucharist to feed and nourish the soul.

Only wheat bread and grape wine can be used. The moment the priest or bishop says the words of consecration — the words of Christ at the Last Supper, "This is My body" and "This is My blood," (Matthew 26:26–29) — Catholics believe that the bread and wine become the body and blood, soul and divinity of Christ.

On the natural level, whatever we eat becomes part of us (that is, until there's too much of us, and then we must go on a diet). On the supernatural plane, when Catholics eat the body and blood of Christ, they're supposed to become more like Christ in his obedience to the Father, humility, and love for neighbors.

To Catholics, the physical act of eating the consecrated host or drinking the consecrated wine from the *chalice,* a blessed cup (see Figure 8-2), is secondary to the underlying invisible reality that the human soul is being fed by the very body and blood, soul and divinity of Christ. The body merely consumes the *appearances* of bread and wine while the soul receives Christ personally and totally.

Figure 8-2:
A chalice
from which
Catholics
drink
consecrated
wine.

The Holy Eucharist is food for the soul, so it's given and eaten during Holy Communion at the Mass. However, the form and manner of distribution bear slight differences, depending on whether you attend a Latin (Western) Rite Mass or an Eastern Rite Mass:

- **Latin (Western) Rite:** Holy Communion is in the form of consecrated unleavened hosts made from wheat flour and water, just like the unleavened bread used by Jesus at the Last Supper. The host is flat and the size of a quarter or half-dollar. Latin Catholics may receive the host on their tongue or in their hand if the local bishop and the national conference of bishops permit.

- **Eastern Rite:** Catholics receive consecrated leavened bread (the yeast or leaven symbolizes the Resurrection), which is placed inside the chalice (cup) of consecrated wine. The priest takes a spoon and gingerly places a cut cube of consecrated bread soaked in the consecrated wine inside the mouths of the communicants without ever touching their lips or tongue.

Discovering who can receive Holy Communion

The word *Communion* comes from Latin: *Co* means "with" and *unio* means "union." *Communio* means "union with." Catholics believe that Communion allows the believer to be united with Christ by sharing His body and blood. The priest and deacon, sometimes with the assistance of *extraordinary ministers* (nonclerics who have been given the authority to assist the priest), distribute Holy Communion to the faithful (see Chapter 10 for more on what happens during Mass). Because this is really and truly the body and blood, soul and divinity of Christ, receiving Holy Communion, God's intimate visit with His faithful souls, is most sacred.

When believers receive Holy Communion, they're intimately united with their Lord and Savior, Jesus Christ. However, Communion isn't limited to the *communicant* (the one receiving Holy Communion) and Jesus Christ. By taking Holy Communion, the Catholic is also expressing her union with all Catholics around the world and at all times who believe the same doctrines, obey the same laws, and follow the same leaders. This is why Catholics (and Eastern Orthodox Christians) have a strict law that only people who are *in communion* with the Church can receive Holy Communion. In other words, only those who are united in the same beliefs — the seven sacraments, the authority of the pope, and the teachings in the Catechism of the Catholic Church — are allowed to receive Holy Communion.

In the Protestant tradition, Communion is often seen as a means of building unity among various denominations, and many have open Communion, meaning that any baptized Christian can take Communion in their services. Catholics and Eastern Orthodox Christians, on the other hand, see Communion not as the means but as the final fruit of unity. So only those in communion can receive Holy Communion. It has nothing to do with who's worthy.

Think of it this way: If a Canadian citizen moves to the United States, lives in Erie, Pennsylvania, works in Erie, and has a family in Erie, he can do so indefinitely. However, he can't run for public office or vote in an American election unless and until he becomes a U.S. citizen. Does being or not being a citizen make you a good or bad person? Of course not. But if citizens from other countries want to vote, they must give up their own citizenship and become U.S. citizens.

Being a non-Catholic in the Church is like being a non-citizen in a foreign country. Non-Catholics can come to as many Catholic Masses as they want; they can marry Catholics and raise their children in the Catholic faith, but they can't receive Holy Communion in the Catholic Church until they become Catholic. Becoming Catholic is how a person gets united with and experiences union with the whole Catholic Church. Those in union can then receive Holy Communion.

Similarly, Catholics who don't follow the Church's laws on divorce and remarriage, or who obstinately reject Church teaching, such as the inherent evil of abortion, shouldn't come forward to receive Communion because they're no longer in communion. This prohibition isn't a judgment on their moral or spiritual state because only God can know that. But receiving Holy Communion is a public act, and therefore, it's an ecclesiastical action requiring those who do it to be united with all that the Church teaches and commands and with all the ways that the Church prays.

Partaking of First Holy Communion

When boys and girls (usually in second grade) make their First Holy Communion, it's a big occasion for Catholic families. Like their Baptism, the day of First Communion is one filled with family, friends, and feasting after the sacred event has taken place in church.

Girls typically wear white gowns and veils and often look like little brides, and boys wear their Sunday best or new suits and ties bought just for the occasion. Some parishes have the entire class make their First Communion together at a Sunday or Saturday Mass, but other parishes allow each child to go on a different weekend.

The children are generally too young to appreciate all the theological refinements of *transubstantiation,* the act of changing the substances of bread and wine into the substances of the body and blood of Christ, but as long as they know and believe that it's not bread or wine they're receiving but the real body and blood of Jesus Christ, they are old enough to take Holy Communion. (For more on transubstantiation, see Chapter 10.)

Like Penance and the Anointing of the Sick, Holy Eucharist can be received more than once. (However, Baptism, Confirmation, and Holy Orders can't be repeated.)

First Penance (see Chapter 9), which is going to confession for the first time, *must come before* First Communion.

Adult converts normally make their First Communion at the Easter Vigil, the same night they are baptized and confirmed.

Coming of Age: Confirmation

The final Sacrament of Initiation is Confirmation. Soon after babies are born and get fed, they start to grow. Growth is as vital to human life as nourishment. The body and mind must grow to stay alive. Catholics believe that the soul also needs to grow in the life of grace. Just as the human body must grow through childhood, adolescence, and then adulthood, the human soul needs to grow into maturity.

Catholics believe that Confirmation is the supernatural equivalent of the growth process on the natural level. It builds on what was begun in Baptism and what was nourished in Holy Eucharist. It completes the process of initiation into the Christian community, and it matures the soul for the work ahead. The Eastern Catholic Church confirms *(chrismates)* at Baptism and gives Holy Eucharist as well, thus initiating the new Christian all at the same time.

Too often, Confirmation is the bribe to get Catholic kids who go to public school to attend CCD (Confraternity of Christian Doctrine), also known as religious education classes. As long as they attend eight years of CCD, they're eligible for Confirmation.

But Confirmation is more than a carrot on a stick to keep kids in CCD classes. This Sacrament of Initiation means that they become young adults in the Catholic faith. During an infant's Baptism, parents and godparents make promises to renounce Satan and believe in God and the Church on behalf of the child. At Confirmation, before the bishop, the young adult renews those same promises, this time in her own words.

So what occurs during Confirmation? The Holy Spirit is first introduced to a Catholic the day that she's baptized, because the entire Holy Trinity — Father, Son, and Holy Spirit — are invoked at the ceremony. During Confirmation, God the Holy Spirit comes upon the person, accompanied by God the Father and God the Son, just as he did at *Pentecost.* The Feast of Pentecost commemorates the descent of the Holy Spirit from heaven to earth upon the 12 apostles and the Virgin Mary, occurring 50 days after Easter and 10 days after Jesus's Ascension (Acts 2:1–4).

This sacrament is called *Confirmation* because the faith given in Baptism is now confirmed and made strong. Sometimes, those who benefit from Confirmation are referred to as *soldiers of Christ.* This isn't a military designation but a spiritual duty to fight the war between good and evil, light and darkness — a war between the human race and all the powers of hell.

Traditionally, the 12 fruits of the Holy Spirit are charity, joy, peace, patience, kindness, goodness, generosity, gentleness, faithfulness, modesty, self-control, and chastity. These are human qualities that can be activated by the Holy Spirit. The seven gifts of the Holy Spirit are wisdom, understanding, counsel, fortitude, knowledge, piety, and fear of the Lord. These gifts are supernatural graces given to the soul. With these fruits and gifts, confirmed Catholics are now equipped to live out their baptismal call to holiness as adult members of the faith.

A bishop is the ordinary minister of the Sacrament of Confirmation. However, priests can be delegated by the bishop to confirm young people of the parish or adult converts being brought into full communion.

The following occurs during the Sacrament of Confirmation:

✔ The ceremony may take place at Mass or outside of Mass, and the bishop usually wears red vestments to symbolize the red tongues of fire seen hovering over the heads of the apostles at Pentecost.

✔ Each individual to be confirmed comes forward with his sponsor. The same canonical requirements for being a godparent in Baptism apply for sponsors at Confirmation. At Baptism, Junior's mom and dad picked his godfather and godmother; for Confirmation, he picks his own sponsor. The sponsor can be the godmother or godfather if they're still practicing Catholics, or he may choose someone else (other than his parents) who's over the age of 16, already confirmed, and in good standing with the Church. One sponsor is chosen for Confirmation.

✔ Each Catholic selects his own Confirmation name. At Baptism, the name was chosen without the child's consent because the child was too little to make the selection alone. Now, in Confirmation, another name — in addition to the first and middle names — can be added, or the original baptismal name may be used. It must be a Christian name, though, such as one of the canonized saints of the Church or a hero from the Bible. You wouldn't want to pick a name like Cain, Judas, or Herod, for example, and no secular names would be appropriate.

✔ The Catholic being confirmed stands or kneels before the bishop, and the sponsor lays one hand on the shoulder of the one being confirmed. The Confirmation name is spoken, and the bishop puts chrism oil on the person's forehead, says his name aloud, and then says, "Be sealed with the gift of the Holy Spirit." The person responds, "Amen." The bishop then says, "Peace be with you." And the person responds, "And with your spirit" or "And also with you."

Latin (Western) Rite Catholics are usually baptized as infants, receive First Communion as children, and are confirmed as adolescents. Adult converts who've never been baptized are baptized when they become Catholic; they're confirmed and receive their First Communion at the same time. Or, if adult converts were baptized in a Protestant Church, they make a Profession of Faith, are confirmed, and receive Holy Eucharist — typically at the Easter Vigil Mass on Holy Saturday. Eastern Rite Catholics are confirmed at the same time they are baptized.

Confirmation means accepting responsibility for your faith and destiny. Childhood is a time when you're told what to do, and you react positively to reward and negatively to punishment. Adulthood, even young adulthood, means that you must do what's right on your own, not for the recognition or reward but merely because it's the right thing to do. Doing what's right can be satisfying, too. The focus is on the Holy Spirit, who confirmed the apostles on Pentecost (Acts 2:1–4) and gave them courage to practice their faith. Catholics believe that the same Holy Spirit confirms Catholics during the Sacrament of Confirmation and gives them the same gifts and fruits.

Chapter 9

The Sacraments of Service and Healing

In This Chapter

▶ Making marriage vows stick

▶ Caring for the Church community through Holy Orders

▶ Spilling your guts in the confessional

▶ Strengthening the spirit through the Anointing of the Sick

*T*he seven sacraments are the most sacred and ancient Catholic rites of worship. They mark seven sequential stages of spiritual development, so if you missed the first three — Baptism, Confirmation, and Holy Eucharist — head over to Chapter 8 before hearing all about Catholicism's final four (sacraments, that is).

In this chapter, we discuss the two Sacraments of Community and Service: Matrimony and Holy Orders. They're all about uniting and ministering. Then we make sure you're clear on the last two sacraments — Penance and the Anointing of the Sick — which are Sacraments of Mercy and Healing.

The Sacraments of Service and Community

Following the three sacraments for the sake of initiation (see Chapter 8) are the two sacraments for the sake of social development. The Sacrament of Matrimony takes care of the family, and the Sacrament of Holy Orders takes care of the society of the Church. Both are of service to others.

Marriage — Catholic style

The Catholic Church distinguishes between a legal, state-recognized marriage and the Sacrament of Matrimony. Marriage is regulated by the civil government, which has certain rules that must be followed to make a marriage legal. But being legally married doesn't necessarily mean that two people have participated in the Sacrament of Matrimony. The Sacrament of Matrimony means becoming husband and wife through a sacred covenant with God and each other. In this section, we explain what must occur for the marriage to be a valid sacrament in the eyes of the Church.

Responding to the vocation

A Christian (Protestant, Catholic, Orthodox) marriage is between one baptized man and one baptized woman. A Catholic marriage is a Christian union where one or both parties are of the Catholic faith. The sacrament of Matrimony is a vocation, a calling from God, from the Latin *vocare,* to call. Just as priests, deacons, religious sisters and brothers, nuns and monks have a calling from God, so do married people, as well as single persons.

Being a good husband or wife — then a good father or mother — is as much a sacred calling from God as the call to become a monk or nun. Married people are to be sanctified as much as clergy and religious brothers and sisters.

Because marriage is a vocation *and* a sacrament, marriage imparts a special grace that gives the recipients the strength and ability to assume and fulfill all the duties and responsibilities of Christian marriage. Three elements are required for a marital union to be a valid sacrament: The participants must enter the Sacrament of Matrimony with the intention that their union will be

- **Permanent:** Unto death
- **Faithful:** Without adultery
- **Fruitful:** Open to the possibility of children if God wills it

The term *fruitful* means only that both bride and groom have to be open to the *possibility* of children. They do not have to give birth to as many children as biologically possible, but they cannot purposefully avoid having any kids whatsoever.

The Sacrament of Matrimony gives the bride and groom the necessary graces to bring those vows to fruition. However, getting married in the Catholic Church isn't as complicated as some may think. At least one person must be Catholic, but the other person can be any other religion. If the non-Catholic was baptized in a non-Catholic church, the non-Catholic needs documentation verifying Baptism. If the non-Catholic is unbaptized, unchurched, or of a non-Christian religion, a special dispensation from the local bishop is needed. The priest or deacon doing the ceremony can obtain it.

If two baptized but non-Catholic Christians get married in a civil ceremony or in any religious denomination, the Catholic Church does recognize that as being valid as long as it's the first marriage for both of them.

Committing to a lifetime and avoiding annulments

Like the Sacraments of Baptism, Confirmation, and Holy Orders, the Sacrament of Matrimony can take place only once in someone's life, unless his or her spouse dies. Due to the lifelong commitment that's required for the Sacrament of Matrimony, Catholics can only marry someone who's widowed or wasn't married before. If a person was previously married and the spouse is alive, it must be demonstrated that the marriage was invalid so the previous union can be declared null and void through an annulment.

In most dioceses, Catholics who want to marry are asked to meet with a priest or deacon at least 9 to 12 months before the wedding. This period is called *Pre-Cana* after the name of the town, Cana, where Jesus and his mother, Mary, went to a wedding feast, and Jesus changed water into wine. During the Pre-Cana period, the priest or deacon offers practical financial and emotional advice to the couple, as well as instructions on the spiritual nature of marriage and Natural Family Planning (NFP), which, by the way, is not the old, forsaken Rhythm Method. (Because the Catholic Church forbids artificial contraception, regulating birth must be based on morally allowable means. Chapter 14 has the scoop on NFP.)

Why so much time spent in preparation? Why can't weddings be spontaneous? Because the Sacrament of Matrimony is a vocation for life. The Catholic Church wants to prevent impulsive, shotgun weddings, or anything done in haste, rashness, or imprudence.

An *annulment* is not a Catholic version of divorce. Divorce is a civil decree from the state that a legal marriage is no longer in force. An annulment, on the other hand, is an ecclesiastical decree that a marriage, even if entered in good faith, was determined to be an invalid sacrament from the first moment (when vows were exchanged at the wedding ceremony).

How could this sacrament be invalid? When a baptized man and a baptized woman marry for the first time, the Church presumes the marriage to be valid unless proven otherwise in a Church court. That same assumption applies for all baptized persons: Catholic, Protestant, or Eastern Orthodox. If, however, one or both of the participants did not intend on their wedding day to enter a *permanent, faithful,* and *fruitful* union, then no sacrament took place, and the Church can declare the marriage null and void. If that happens, both parties are free to marry someone else — the Church hopes *validly* this time.

Food, flowers, and faith

Some brides call the caterer first and the priest last when they're wedding-planning, but we think it should be the other way around. Granted, caterers, florists, photographers, and other folks in the wedding biz may book up 12 to 18 months ahead of time. But the food, photos, and flowers aren't the required elements of the Sacrament of Matrimony, so it makes sense to contact the Catholic Church and the priest or deacon *first* — before making any other wedding plans. Besides, most dioceses ask Catholics to meet with a priest or deacon beginning up to a year before the wedding. So if you're getting ready to walk down the aisle, make sure that you give your faith at least as much consideration as the decision to serve chicken or beef.

Likewise, if one or both parties had a lack of due competence or a grave lack of due discretion, the marriage is invalid. The latter concerns the requisite knowledge and comprehension of the essential rights and obligations of marriage, whereas the former concerns the emotional and psychological ability to fulfill them.

Keep in mind that because Church annulments are *not* a form of divorce, they have no effect whatsoever on the legitimacy of children because that's a purely legal matter. Annulments *don't* make the children born of that union illegitimate.

Making it valid

A valid Sacrament of Matrimony requires the presence of a priest or deacon, a bride and groom (no same-sex marriages), and two witnesses of any religion. All the other stuff is icing on the wedding cake — the ushers, bridesmaids, groomsmen, parents, grandparents, photographer, videographer, caterer, ring bearer, flower girl, organist, and soloist. (See the sidebar "Food, flowers, and faith" for our opinion on prioritizing wedding preparations.)

The bride and groom are the real ministers of the sacrament because their "I do" makes them husband and wife. The priest or deacon is just an official witness for the Church — necessary, yes, but just a witness.

Only Scripture readings from the Bible can be read and only approved vows recited during the ceremony. Secular or other writings from other faiths can be read at the wedding reception before grace is prayed and the toast given, but they don't belong in church.

Three types of Catholic wedding ceremonies are available. The first is a wedding at Mass; the second is a wedding without a Mass; and the third is a *convalidation* ceremony, in which a couple who was previously married invalidly in the eyes of the Church (perhaps by a Justice of the Peace or Protestant minister) now seeks to have that marriage recognized by the Church or, as the canon lawyers call it, *convalidated.*

Getting the full treatment with a Nuptial Mass

A *Nuptial Mass,* the Sacrament of Matrimony with a Mass, normally occurs on Saturdays (and sometimes Friday evenings and Sundays, with special permission from the bishop). The Nuptial Mass is highly recommended and encouraged when *both* the bride and groom are Catholic because two sacraments are received at this ceremony: the Sacrament of Matrimony and the Sacrament of the Holy Eucharist. Participating in two sacraments is a great way to start the marriage.

Just like a Sunday parish Mass, the wedding Mass has four Scripture readings: one from the Old Testament read by a friend or relative, a Psalm that's sung, one from the New Testament Epistles read by a friend or relative, and one from the Gospels read by the priest or deacon. Then the priest or deacon gives the sermon and proceeds to witness the vows.

Just before the formal vows, the priest or deacon asks the couple three important questions:

1. **Have you come here freely and without reservation to give yourselves to each other in marriage?**

2. **Will you love and honor each other as husband and wife for the rest of your lives?**

3. **Will you accept children lovingly from God and bring them up according to the law of Christ and his Church?**

Assuming that both say "Yes!" to all three questions, the priest or deacon can proceed to the marriage vows.

The vows may be stated by the priest or deacon and repeated by the bride and groom, or the vows may be addressed as a question, to which the bride and groom merely respond, "I do." Following are examples of the two accepted versions:

> I, Concetta, take you, Salvatore, to be my husband. I promise to be true to you in good times and in bad, in sickness and in health. I will love you and honor you all the days of my life.

Or:

> Do you, Salvatore, take Concetta for your lawful wife, to have and to hold, from this day forward, for better, for worse, for richer, for poorer, in sickness and in health, until death do you part?

After the vows, the rings are blessed. Then the groom places one ring on the bride's finger and says, "Take this ring as a sign of my love and my fidelity, in the name of the Father and of the Son and of the Holy Spirit. Amen." The bride takes the other ring and places it on the groom's finger and says the same words.

The couple become husband and wife at the moment they exchange consent, not rings. Rings are merely a symbol.

After the exchange of rings, the prayers of the faithful are said (just like at Sunday Mass), followed by an offertory hymn and the preparation of the gifts on the altar. A relative or friend may bring up the bread and wine, and Mass proceeds as normal. (See Chapter 10 for a detailed look at the Mass.) After the Our Father, the priest gives a special nuptial blessing to the couple. Then they stand, give a sign of peace (hug or kiss) to their respective parents, and return to the sanctuary. Communion proceeds as usual.

Often, after Communion and the final prayer, the bride and groom walk to a statue of Mary. They place some flowers before the statue, while a soloist sings *Ave Maria,* the *Hail Mary* sung in Latin, or another song in honor of Mary (See Chapter 16 for details on the *Hail Mary.*) This custom arose from a pious practice of newlyweds asking for Mary's prayers because Mary's intercession at the wedding feast of Cana prompted her son, Jesus, to change water into wine. The new husband and wife ask Mary, the Mother of Jesus, to pray to Jesus for them as well.

Finally comes the big announcement: The priest or deacon introduces "Mr. and Mrs. Nicastro." Then they smooch and exit down the main aisle.

Opting for a wedding without a Mass

The Catholic wedding ceremony without a Mass is often celebrated when the bride or groom isn't of the Catholic faith. Without a Mass, Communion doesn't take place. If Communion took place, the non-Catholic wouldn't be able to receive it, because you must be Catholic to receive Communion. (See Chapter 8 for more on Communion.) So to spare any embarrassment, misunderstandings, or hurt feelings, the Church usually suggests a wedding ceremony without Mass for a Catholic and non-Catholic.

The ceremony (formally called *Rite of Marriage Outside of Mass*) is the same as the Nuptial Mass in that selections from the Old Testament and New Testament are read, along with a Psalm and a Gospel. The priest or deacon preaches a sermon after proclaiming the Gospel, and then the wedding vows are pronounced, followed by the exchange of rings. Some prayers are offered on behalf of the new husband and wife, followed by the Our Father, after which the priest or deacon gives the nuptial blessing to the couple. Then comes the sign of peace (a hug and/or kiss), a final prayer, and the big announcement. The difference between the two ceremonies is that in the Nuptial Mass, right after the vows are pronounced and rings exchanged, the Mass continues.

Do's and don'ts at Catholic weddings

Want some tips about what to do — and not to do — at a Catholic wedding? Don't feel awkward or embarrassed if this is your first time in a Catholic Church! Don't feel like you have to keep up with all the Catholic gymnastics; if you don't feel comfortable kneeling, stay seated.

Do arrive early, and dress as you would for any religious ceremony or special event. Show good taste and modesty. Limit all food, beverages, party activity, and gum-chewing to the reception. Don't smoke or consume any alcohol on church property, either. Be aware that traditionally, the bride's side of the church is on your left as you face the altar and sanctuary, and the groom's side is on the right. Weddings and funerals are the few occasions when no collection baskets are passed at Mass, but *do* give the newlyweds a gift.

Don't come late, especially after her dad has already walked the bride down the aisle. It's rude to the bride and groom, and it's disrespectful to the Church and God because the wedding is taking place in His house. And keep the couple in your prayers.

Making it Catholic: Convalidation

A *convalidation ceremony* is needed when a Catholic couple gets married in a civil or non-Catholic ceremony, which makes it an invalid marriage in the eyes of the Church. Even if only one of them is Catholic, it's an invalid sacrament because Catholics must always follow Church law, which says they must be married in a Catholic church.

After the mandatory waiting period of six months or more, if the couple decides to have their civil marriage recognized (sometimes erroneously called having it *blessed*) by the Catholic Church, then a *convalidation* is in order. This is a simple and private ceremony involving the couple, two witnesses, and the priest or deacon. The vows are pronounced, and the rings may be exchanged. If the rings can't be taken off, then they're simply blessed. It's not a renewal of vows but a making of the vows for the first time in the eyes of the Church. The convalidation makes a merely civil marriage a Sacrament of Matrimony.

Convalidations are a way to remedy a hasty decision to marry too soon. If a couple marries in haste but later realizes that, yes, they will remain together, the couple can have the union recognized by God and the Church through convalidation. It's not considered an option but a remedy to an unfortunate situation, because the Church prefers couples to marry validly the first time.

Sadly, some couples run off and get married in a modest non-Catholic ceremony just to avoid an expensive Catholic wedding. The Church *never* demands or even suggests big weddings with huge bridal parties, stretch limousines, and country club receptions. Brides and grooms are allowed that, but if a couple wants a simple, dignified, and reverent ceremony with a few family and friends and without all the high-priced, big-ticket items, they can still opt for that in the Catholic Church. The Nuptial Mass or the Rite of Marriage Outside of Mass is appropriate in either situation: expensive or economical. The choice is that of the bride and groom.

If a Catholic gets married by a Justice of the Peace, a captain on a ship, a mayor, or a Protestant minister, and hasn't obtained a dispensation from the local Catholic bishop, then that marriage is invalid, and the Catholic isn't allowed to receive Holy Communion until that union is sanctioned by the Church in a convalidation. This situation often happens when a nonpracticing Catholic doesn't realize that a non-Catholic minister can still marry the couple in a non-Catholic ceremony with the Catholic Church's blessing as long as the couple meets with a priest or deacon and still fulfills all the same Pre-Cana preparations as everyone else. A dispensation from the local bishop is possible and can allow a Catholic bride or groom to be validly married in the eyes of the Church, by a non-Catholic minister, and in a non-Catholic church of the non-Catholic spouse, but the Catholic priest or deacon must fill out the necessary forms, and the couple still has to make the same preparations as other Catholic couples.

Occasionally, a Catholic goes against the advice and laws of the Church and marries a divorced person who hasn't obtained an annulment. This marriage takes place in a civil ceremony or by a non-Catholic minister, but it's not considered valid in the eyes of the Catholic Church. If an annulment is granted later on, and the couple wants to have their union recognized and sanctioned as a valid sacrament, then a convalidation is the appropriate and only remedy.

Because annulments aren't guaranteed, Catholics shouldn't *presume* that they'll get a convalidation after marrying in an invalid civil ceremony.

The Sacrament of Matrimony entails a lot more than just getting hitched. Society often places more emphasis on the wedding and less importance on the entire marriage. What the Church cares about is the sacrament's spiritual dimension, and the fact that marriage is a lifelong vocation.

Holy Orders

Along with Matrimony, the other sacrament of community and service is *Holy Orders.* In the Catholic Church, *sacred ministers,* those who serve the spiritual needs of others, are ordained by a bishop by means of Holy Orders, which creates the hierarchy of deacon, priest, and bishop. Chapter 6 provides detailed information about the rank and file of the Catholic Church and the specific duties of deacons, priests, and bishops.

This sacrament can be received only once, just like Baptism and Confirmation, but a man may also be ordained to a higher order up to the third degree. A man must first be ordained a deacon before being ordained a priest, and he must be ordained a deacon and then a priest before being ordained a bishop. So every priest and every bishop has experienced the Sacrament of Holy Orders more than once, yet he can never be re-ordained a deacon, priest, or bishop, because it's for life.

Only baptized men can receive the Sacrament of Holy Orders. (For an explanation of why the priesthood is exclusively male, see Chapter 14.)

Celebrating the sacrament

Jesus Christ instituted the Sacrament of Holy Orders at the Last Supper simultaneously with His institution of the Sacrament of Holy Eucharist. To change bread and wine into the body and blood, soul, and divinity of Christ, you need priests who've been given this power by virtue of their ordination. (See Chapter 5 for a discussion of the Holy Eucharist.)

Bishops receive the highest level of Holy Orders, and it's often said in the Church that bishops have the "fullness of the priesthood" because they alone have the authority to offer all seven sacraments: Baptism, Penance, Holy Eucharist, Matrimony, Anointing of the Sick, Holy Orders, and Confirmation. Priests have the power and authority (also known as *faculties*) to celebrate only five: Baptism, Penance, Holy Eucharist (Mass), Matrimony, and Anointing of the Sick. Deacons can celebrate only two: Baptism and Matrimony (provided that the wedding is without a Nuptial Mass).

Preparing for the responsibility

Deacons, priests, and bishops receive plenty of pastoral and theological training. Catholic clergy candidates attend *seminary,* the Catholic equivalent to Protestant divinity school. A college degree, however, is a prerequisite for seminary, and then most *seminarians,* students who attend a seminary, start work on a master's degree — Master of Divinity (MDiv) or Master of Arts (MA) — in Theology. Post-college studies can range from four to eight years, depending on the candidate and the diocese he's studying for. Now and then, a few students go farther and earn a Doctorate in philosophy (PhD), theology (STD or ThD), or canon law (JCD).

Having a similar academic background as physicians, lawyers, and Protestant ministers gives the Catholic clergy a good foundation, but the academic background must also be complemented with solid prayer life. Seminarians must also receive *pastoral formation,* which is learning how to listen to people, counsel them, work with others (especially the sick and the needy), and so on, so they can function as good pastors, as well as adequate theologians.

The Sacrament of Holy Orders doesn't make a man a Church aristocrat, but it does confer the dignity of the sacrament, which entails the obligation to obey the pope and be of service to the people of God. In previous ages, though, some opportunistic and ambitious men rose through the clerical ranks and used their office of deacon, priest, or bishop to abuse ecclesiastical authority and satisfy personal needs. Nevertheless, the original purpose of Holy Orders was not to create an upper class but to provide spiritual leadership. Pastors are to see their role as shepherds who love and know their sheep instead of seeing their people as servants and peasants.

Removing the clergy from service, but not the sacrament from the clergy

Holy Orders impart an indelible mark on the soul (much like Baptism and Confirmation), which means this sacrament cannot be removed or undone. Hence, deacons, priests, and bishops cannot have their ordination removed or dissolved. What can happen, though, is that their sacred ministry can be constrained in such a way that they're not allowed to dress or function like clergy.

What is commonly called being "defrocked" is technically known as an *involuntary laicization* or formal dismissal from the clerical state. This step is taken as a punishment for crime and to remove from public ministry a cleric who either promotes heretical teaching and/or engages in immoral and abhorrent behavior. While still having the power to validly celebrate the sacraments, a laicized cleric is not legally permitted to do so. The only exception is if the defrocked priest is the only one available to anoint a dying person or hear a confession before death. Otherwise, laicized clergy are forbidden to function as clergy.

In addition, an ordained man may, of his own accord, request being dispensed from his vows of celibacy in order to marry validly in the Church — a step called *voluntary laicization.* This request is not automatically granted. The priest in question must demonstrate that being ordained either was a mistake in the very beginning or that he is now involved in a serious relationship with serious obligations (in other words, he has a pregnant girlfriend or she recently gave birth to his child). It is not enough for him to say that he's bored with being a priest or tired of living as a single man and now wants to try married family life.

Laicized priests can't wear the Roman collar, be called "Father," or publicly celebrate the sacraments. All requests for laicization must go to Rome, and only the Vatican can approve them. A voluntarily or involuntarily laicized cleric isn't given a salary, housing, or insurance. He can validly and licitly get married in church, but he can never celebrate any of the sacraments publicly.

The Sacraments of Mercy and Healing

The two Sacraments of Healing are Penance and the Anointing of the Sick. The following sections provide the details of these sacraments.

Penance

Catholics believe that the Holy Mother Church gives birth in the Sacrament of Baptism, nourishes in Holy Eucharist, helps Catholics grow in Confirmation, and heals in the *Sacrament of Penance.*

Healing the spirit

Medicine and therapy can heal a wounded body, but Catholics believe that only God's grace can heal a wounded soul. That's why Jesus left the Sacrament of Penance to heal our spiritual wounds, which we call *sin.* Often, people think of sin only as breaking God's laws. Sure, stealing, lying, and murdering break some of the Ten Commandments and are considered sinful. But Catholics believe that God said, "You shall not" because he knew these sinful actions would wound spiritually.

Sin is like a bacteria or virus to the soul. When a person lies, cheats, steals, or murders, it's like being infected with millions of deadly germs. The longer the infection is left untreated, the more it spreads and worsens. It wounds and can even kill the life of grace that enables entry into heaven.

Just as tumors are benign or malignant, Catholics believe that sins are venial or mortal. In other words, some sins aren't considered as serious as others and merely inflict a slight wound to the soul, but others are so intrinsically evil that they're considered deadly. The latter are called *mortal sins* because they can kill grace. (For more on mortal sin, see Chapters 11 and 13.)

The Sacrament of Penance (also known as the *Sacrament of Reconciliation* or *Confession*) is for spiritual healing. According to the Gospels, after the Resurrection, Jesus appeared to the apostles, breathed on them, and said, "Receive the Holy Spirit. If you forgive the sins of any, they are forgiven; if you retain the sins of any, they are retained" (John 20:22–23).

Because Jesus gave the apostles the power to forgive sins, he must have wanted them to use it. So the Sacrament of Penance has been the very will of Christ from day one.

Understanding penance in the past

The actual confession of sins (verbally admitting the wrongs you have done) is — and always has been — done privately to a priest or bishop. Private or secret confession of sins ensures the absolute confidentiality (also called the *Seal of Confession*) of the *penitent:* the sinner. However, the *penance* (acts of sorrow) performed as part of the Sacrament used to be done in public for *public sins* (those done openly and known by the community). For example, in the early Church, penance for *apostasy* — denying the faith — was done publicly before the entire Church community. (People who denied their Christian faith [called *lapsi* in Latin] in court to be spared from death in the arena during the Roman persecution period might perform public acts of penance.) A public penance may have involved making a pilgrimage to the Holy Land and visiting the places where Jesus lived, visiting a local shrine, or wearing sackcloth and ashes. The idea was that to repair the scandal caused by public sin, public penance was done to encourage others to repent and be reconciled with God and the Church.

On the other hand, for *private sins* (sins nobody else knew about), the penance was performed privately. Private penance would entail saying some prayers quietly in church, doing a good deed anonymously, reading passages from the Bible, giving alms to the poor, and so on.

In reality, because Christians were clustered into small groups at first, everyone knew what everyone else did anyway. But as Christianity's status changed from persecuted religion to the state religion, more and more members filled the ranks, and admitting faults before a large crowd became more embarrassing and delicate.

Also, more sins became private and less public, so the need for private and discreet penances arose. In the ancient church, believers lived in close-knit communities, and everyone knew what you said and did, whether it was cheating on your spouse or getting drunk. Later, as Christianity was no longer illegal in the Roman Empire, behavior became more private. Discreet penances meant that no one could figure out your sins by merely observing your performed penance.

Absolving sins

Whether a sin was public or private, only a priest (or bishop) had the power and authority to absolve sin in the name of Jesus Christ. Additionally, the penance had to be completed before the absolution took place. So a sinner would first confess his sins to the priest, who would impose a penance. Then the penitent would go and do the prescribed acts of sorrow. Once finished, he would then return to the same priest and receive sacramental absolution.

The Irish monks of the sixth and seventh centuries refined the practice of private confessions, which became the norm for the rest of the Church. The monks gave absolution immediately after confession but before the penance was performed. This practice took place because the monks were *itinerant,* meaning they traveled from place to place and would not be in the same area later on.

You gotta confess

Just like the Sacrament of the Holy Eucharist, the Sacrament of Penance may be received many times throughout a person's life. However, the first time that a young Catholic confesses his sins is before his First Communion, which in the Western Church is around the age of reason: 7 years old.

Catholics must confess all known mortal sins to a priest.

To receive the Holy Eucharist without having gone to confession and without receiving absolution for mortal sins makes matters worse. Receiving the Eucharist with mortal sin on your soul is a *sacrilege,* the use of something sacred for an unworthy purpose. A sacrilege expresses disrespect for the sacrament and is another mortal sin.

If you're in danger of death and no priest is available, you can make a *perfect act of contrition.* A perfect act of contrition (which can be as easy as saying "Jesus, have mercy on me, a sinner" to the more elaborate act of contrition said by penitents in the confessional) means that the sinner is sorry for his sins out of love for God and remorse for offending Him rather than just a fear of punishment in the afterlife. Hence, the reason for the sorrow determines whether it's a perfect act of contrition. The sinner must have the absolute intention of going to confession to a priest or bishop as soon as possible if she survives. In situations where no threat to a person's life exists, however, the Church believes that mortal sins can only be forgiven in the Sacrament of Penance. Otherwise, the soul damns itself to hell without absolution from a priest.

Assuming that your death is not imminent and you *can* make it to confession, the perfect act of contrition doesn't apply. Instead, you go to see a priest, confess your sins, and express your remorse and desire to avoid sinfulness in the future. One way to do so is to say aloud the Act of Contrition prayer that we include in Appendix B.

Trusting in absolute secrecy

Telling sins to a priest isn't as scary as people think. Most people tell sensitive, delicate, and confidential information to their physicians and attorneys, so why not to their pastor? The priest is bound by the most absolute secrecy and confidentiality known to humankind. Not even the pope can get a priest to tell who went to him for confession or what was confessed. The priest must be willing to endure prison, torture, and death before violating the *Seal of Confession,* the secrecy of the sacrament. (See the "Offering his life in defense of the Seal" sidebar in this chapter.)

Offering his life in defense of the Seal

The patron of confessors, St. John Nepomucene (1340–1393), known as the Martyr of the Confessional, was put to death for his unwillingness to reveal a woman's sins. Around 1393, King Wenceslaus IV, apparently one of those jealous types, demanded that St. John tell him what the queen had revealed in the confessional. But St. John, honoring the Seal of Confession, wouldn't say a word about it. The king had him tortured, but still, St. John wouldn't reveal the queen's sins. Then the king commanded that St. John be drowned in the river.

Over 2,000 years, many bad, immoral, unethical, and unscrupulous priests have existed, and many of them left or were thrown out of the priesthood. But none have ever revealed the secrets they knew from hearing confessions. The fact that even the bad or mediocre ones throughout all history haven't done so — even after they've left the active ministry or the Catholic religion — is, to Catholics, a great sign of the power of the Holy Spirit protecting the dignity and sanctity of the Sacrament of Penance. C'mon, priests *never* blab about what they hear in confession? Nope. Never.

The confidentiality of the sacrament is so strict and sacred that even enemies of the Church are often in awe of its endurance. The absolute secrecy ensures that anything can be confessed without fear of any retaliation, reaction, or response. Knowing that the priest can never tell anyone anything he hears gives penitents the strength and courage to confess everything.

 If a priest does violate the seal of secrecy of the Sacrament of Penance, he's automatically excommunicated, and only the pope can give him absolution for such a crime. (For more on excommunication, see Chapter 11.)

Confessing in three ways

Confession may take place in one of three different ways:

- ✔ **Private confession** is the most common form of confession. The *penitent* (person telling his sins) goes into a Catholic church and enters a *confessional,* also known as a *reconciliation room* or *penance room.*

  Although some older confessionals don't allow the penitent the option of seeing the priest and confessing face-to-face, the newer penance rooms give the penitent the choice of kneeling behind a screen (just like in the older confessionals) and maintaining anonymity, or confessing face-to-face, thus revealing the penitent's identity (if only by face) to the priest.

  The penitent confesses all known and remembered mortal sins since the last confession. See the section "Are you really, truly sorry?" for more on what to confess.

This form of confession happens almost every Saturday afternoon or evening in every parish around the world. A priest sits in a confessional every week, waiting for parishioners to confess. St. John Vianney (1786–1859), the patron saint of parish priests, heard confessions for nearly 20 straight hours, but most priests hear confessions for about 30 to 90 minutes straight every weekend.

But Catholics don't have to wait for Saturday to go to confession. They can ask the priest to hear their confession anytime it's convenient. It's just easier and more practical for people to take advantage of the "man in the box" whenever possible.

✔ **Parish Penance services** are the second form of confession. Usually during Advent (before Christmas) and Lent (before Easter), parishes get several priests to visit as *confessors* — priests hearing the confessions. The whole congregation sings a hymn, listens to a Scripture reading, hears a brief sermon, and then everyone prays the *Act of Contrition* together as a group. Next, people individually go to a priest of their choosing, verbally confess *at least* all mortal sins in confidence, get a penance, and receive absolution.

This form of confession is helpful, because often before Christmas and Easter — times of year when faith is foremost on people's minds — the lines for confessions on Saturdays are longer than the check-out lines in the stores.

✔ **General confession and absolution** is the third and rarest form. In a time of war, natural disaster, or when lives are in danger, if a large number of sinners can't logistically get to confession because only one priest is available to hear the confessions of hundreds of penitents and time is of the essence, the priest can ask the bishop for permission to give general absolution without individual confession.

Simply having a large crowd and one priest isn't a serious enough reason to give general absolution. It's not like a spiritual car wash. General absolution without individual confession is valid only if the local bishop gives permission *and* for a grave and serious reason, such as when the Three Mile Island nuclear power plant incident occurred in 1979. And the proviso is stated that all persons taking advantage of general absolution make a private confession as soon as possible — first chance they get if they survive — and confess at least all their mortal sins, including those that they had on their souls when they participated in the general confession.

Soldiers and sailors going off to battle are often given general absolution by the Catholic chaplain. If they survive, they must make a private confession as soon as possible.

Spiritual ER

When you go to the doctor's office for a visit, you must tell the physician what's wrong before she can diagnose the problem and prescribe the remedy. Confession is like a spiritual checkup. The penitent, the person telling her sins, must tell the confessor, the priest hearing Confession, what her sins (symptoms) are, so the confessor can offer the proper advice and prescription. A confessor isn't a spiritual attorney or lawyer, but a spiritual physician. He does judge an appropriate penance, but only God judges whether the person is truly sorry for her sins. People can fake it and lie to the confessor and merely claim to be sorry (have contrition) for their sins, but they only fool the priest and not God. Without real sorrow, the sacrament doesn't work.

Are you really, truly sorry?

Confessing all known and unconfessed *mortal* sins (any acts or thoughts that turn away from God and turn toward a created thing instead) is absolutely necessary. Any and all *venial* sins (lesser violations than mortal sins) committed since the last confession may be and are encouraged to be confessed as well. If a person has no mortal sins or simply wants to include her venial sins with the mortal sins she needs to confess, then telling the priest all her sins is a helpful thing (like telling the doctor about your minor aches and pains as well as the serious injuries). The best part is that any forgotten sins are also forgiven. Only the ones intentionally withheld make the sacrament invalid.

Being truly sorry for your sins should go without saying, but we want to say it anyway: The *contrition* (sorrow) for sins must be genuine. The priest gives everyone the benefit of the doubt, but no one can fool God. If a man confesses the sin of adultery but isn't sorry — just sorry that his wife caught him — then none of his sins are absolved (forgiven), venial or mortal, because he made a bad confession. Verbal confession must coincide with interior contrition for the sin.

Perfect contrition is being sorry for your sins merely because God is good and sin offends him. *Imperfect contrition* is being sorry because you fear the pains of hell. The church believes that either will do, but perfect is obviously better. Still, when you're in a weak moment, those images of fire and brimstone can help keep you on the straight and narrow.

After you list your sins, the priest asks you to say an Act of Contrition (see a sample in Appendix B) but you have to really mean what you're saying. Just as the responsibility for receiving the Holy Eucharist without being in the state of mortal sin rests with the conscience of the individual, the validity of the penitent's confession rests with the penitent and his own conscience. The priest doesn't know whether you're in the state of mortal sin, whether you're telling all your sins, whether you're really sorry, or whether you really don't intend to avoid committing sin again, but *you* know. Only you and God know the exact state of your soul.

Doing penance

After you confess your sins, the priest gives you a penance to perform. A penance may be to do something nice for your enemy every day for a week or every week for a month. It may be to visit a nursing home or hospital one day a week for a month. It may be to donate time to a soup kitchen or clothing bank. It may involve any one of the corporal or spiritual works of mercy (see Chapter 13). On the other hand, quite often, the penance is a set of prayers, such as saying the Our Father or the Hail Mary (see Chapter 16) five to ten times.

Whatever the penance, it's merely a token, because Catholics believe that the sacrifice of Christ on the cross is what made atonement for our sins. Your penance is for your benefit — to remind yourself that God comes first and you come last.

Absolving the sinner

After you're told what the penance is and you agree to do it (if you really can't perform the penance the priest assigns, tell him and he'll give you a different one), the priest gives his sacramental absolution:

> God the Father of mercies through the death and resurrection of His Son has reconciled the world to Himself and sent the Holy Spirit among us for the forgiveness of sins. Through the ministry of the Church may God give you pardon and peace, and I absolve you from your sins, in the name of the Father, and of the Son, and of the Holy Spirit. Amen.

If the person shows no sorrow or no firm purpose of amendment, then the priest can't give absolution. For example, if a man confesses to being in an adulterous relationship but refuses to end it and go back to his wife, the priest can't give absolution because the man not only fails to feel sorrow but also intends to continue committing this sin — he has no firm purpose of amending his life. Also, if the person fakes out the priest by only pretending to be sorry, the absolution is invalid because you can't fool God.

Only a priest or bishop (which includes cardinals and popes) can give absolution. Deacons don't have the power to celebrate this sacrament.

Anointing of the Sick

Paired with penance, the second sacrament of mercy and healing is *Anointing of the Sick.*

Receiving strength, not a death sentence

In the past, Anointing of the Sick was called *Extreme Unction,* or last anointing, because it was the last anointing a person received in this life (Baptism and Confirmation are the first two times a person is anointed). This sacrament was also commonly called *Last Rites* because before antibiotics and penicillin, more people died than recovered from disease and injury.

Modern medicine has given folks tremendous hope for recovery and remission from diseases, and many surgeries are now quite successful, unlike in the days before blood transfusions, sterile instruments, and anesthesia. Back when sickness and injury usually resulted in death, Catholics called for the priest to anoint based on St. James's Epistle: "Is any among you sick? Let him call for the elders of the church, and let the them pray over him, anointing him with oil" (James 5:14).

When the sick and injured weren't expected to survive, Extreme Unction was the sign that no more could be done, so the sick and injured were spiritually preparing for death. That's why even today, many of the elderly get a bit nervous when the Catholic hospital chaplain brings his purple stole and oils. They may presume the worse and only see the sacrament as the beginning of the end.

In reality, the Anointing of the Sick is to offer prayers for possible recovery, but the more important intention is to give strength to the soul of the sick person. Often, when people are sick, they get discouraged, depressed, angry, annoyed, and afraid. The Church believes that the sacrament offers a special grace to calm the spirit. If physical recovery is God's will, so be it. If not, then the person needs the grace, strength, and encouragement to bear the illness with dignity. The Sacrament of Anointing of the Sick also remits (absolves) all sins the person is sorry for but did not previously confess in the Sacrament of Penance. On occasion, there isn't time for the person to make a confession, or the person is unconscious or not lucid enough to make a confession, so the anointing compensates by forgiving sins, which the person would have confessed were he able to do so. Because of this aspect of absolving sins, deacons can't anoint, but priests and bishops can.

The Catholic notion of redemptive suffering — that is, uniting your own suffering with the crucified Jesus — gives a person's unavoidable suffering meaning and purpose. This notion is explicitly and implicitly expressed in the Sacrament of the Anointing of the Sick. Most of the time, the innocent are the ones who suffer, and guilty sinners seem to escape pain and misery. So instead of seeing suffering as a punishment, Catholics are asked to see suffering as (in the words of Mother Teresa of Calcutta) being personally kissed and embraced by the Crucified Lord. He holds us so close and so tight; we can feel the nails and thorns in our own body (analogously, of course).

Administering the sacrament

The Anointing of the Sick involves using Oil of the Sick *(oleum infirmorum)* — olive oil blessed by the bishop during Holy Week. Anointing with oil is not a magical or good-luck gesture but a sincere sign of supernatural assistance to coincide with the physical medicine and treatment already being given. Those suffering are reminded of St. Paul's words: "Now I rejoice in my sufferings for your sake, and in my flesh I complete what is lacking in Christ's afflictions for the sake of his body, that is the church," (Colossians 1:24), and "For we share abundantly in Christ's sufferings, so through Christ we share abundantly in comfort too" (2 Corinthians 1:5). Catholic Christians firmly believe in *redemptive suffering,* whereby a person willingly offers up his personal aches and pains, trials and tribulations with Christ on the Cross.

Because many sick and injured people recover nowadays, or at least go into remission, Catholics are able to receive the Sacrament of Anointing of the Sick more than once — as many times as needed. The elderly, people with many ailments, and those with a deadly or serious disease, chronic pain and suffering, or recurring illness can and should be anointed often.

Some Catholics see Anointing of the Sick as a spiritual oil change and feel that every three months (or 3,000 miles) is a good time to anoint the bedridden, people in nursing homes, and others with chronic and pathological conditions. Coauthor Father Trigilio relates, "When my brother Michael was alive and suffering from muscular dystrophy, and when my dad was alive and endured his leukemia, I often anointed them whenever I came home to visit, which was often every three months or so."

Some parishes have a Mass of Anointing once or twice a year for the sick of the parish. (That's not people who are sick of the parish. It's parishioners who are sick.) The only caveat is that often, people with minor illnesses, aches, and pains and those suffering from nonphysical conditions that aren't life threatening want to be anointed, but the sacrament is for those in danger of death or in critical condition medically speaking. In minor cases, a prayer for healing is appropriate. The sacrament shouldn't be overused or trivialized for every upset stomach and toe ache.

Many older Catholics have a "sick call set" crucifix hanging on the wall. This special crucifix opens up in preparation for the priest to make a *sick call,* a visit to the sick to anoint them, and inside are two white beeswax candles, a bottle of holy water, and a white cloth. The cloth is placed on a table near the sick person before the priest arrives to anoint him. The crucifix is laid on top of the cloth, and the two candles are put in their holders and lit, unless the patient is on oxygen, in which case, *no candles.* A family member greets the priest and escorts him to the sick person's room, which is *quiet.* In other words, the television isn't blaring *Wheel of Fortune.* The priest anoints the sick person, and if the person is dying, the priest also administers *viaticum*. Viaticum is Latin for *something for the journey*. Viaticum offers a dying person that last opportunity on earth to have intimate union with Christ by receiving his body and blood in Holy Communion. This conveys the teaching that death is but a journey from this life to the next, where the union with Jesus is forever. If a person is unconscious or is unable to eat and swallow the sacred host, then the priest doesn't administer viaticum. Whether or not Holy Communion has been administered, the Anointing of the Sick closes with the priest sprinkling holy water on the person and room.

The Catholic Church suggests that a dying person have a crucifix nearby to meditate on, a rosary, a Bible, holy water, and candles, if safe to use. These items make the setting sacred because the suffering person is going through his own form of Calvary and literally walking with the Lord as he approaches the place where Jesus was crucified.

The priest sticks his finger in the oil stock, which often has cotton squished inside to absorb the oil and keep it from spilling and going bad. He dabs some on his thumb and then anoints the head, saying, "Through this holy anointing may the Lord in his love and mercy help you with the grace of the Holy Spirit." Then, if possible, he anoints the palms of the person, saying, "May the Lord who frees you from sin save you and raise you up." If it's an emergency, such as a patient in the trauma center, the priest can anoint any part of the body that's available if the doctors and nurses are working on the head and hands of the injured person.

Priests and bishops aren't anointed on the palms when given the Sacrament of the Anointing of the Sick because their hands were already anointed at their ordination. Priests and bishops are anointed on the back of the hands instead.

Chapter 10

Celebrating the Catholic Mass

. . . .

In This Chapter

▶ Re-presenting Christ's sacrifice in the most important form of Catholic worship

▶ Discovering the various parts of the Mass

▶ Knowing when to stand, sit, or kneel

▶ Following the Church calendar

. . . .

*T*he *Mass,* or more precisely, the *Holy Sacrifice of the Mass,* is the most important, central, and sacred act of worship in Catholicism. The Mass is of the utmost significance because Catholics take the Holy Eucharist only by means of the Mass, and the Holy Eucharist is "the source and summit of Christian Life" (Vatican II: *Lumen Gentium;* 1964). Catholics believe that during the Mass, the priest changes the bread and wine into the body and blood of Christ; the *Holy Eucharist* describes the liturgical act of worship itself and the end result or fruit of it.

The Mass is the primary worship ceremony celebrated by Catholics all over the world, in exactly the same way, every day of the week. The Mass sums up all the doctrines of the Church, expresses how Catholics should live, and gives them the means to do it. To understand the Mass is to understand Catholicism. In this chapter, we help you do just that.

Additionally, you may have heard about the *Roman Missal, Third Edition,* which includes changes to the prayers said in Mass; we explain what all that means in this chapter. You can also get more information in our book *Catholic Mass For Dummies* (Wiley).

What Exactly Is the Mass?

The *Mass* is the sacred rite — the formal, official worship service of Catholicism. It incorporates the Bible (Sacred Scripture), prayer, sacrifice, hymns, symbols, gestures, sacred food for the soul, and directions on how to live a Catholic life — all in one ceremony.

Because the Mass is such a big deal, it's no wonder that the Mass is sometimes referred to as the *Eucharistic Liturgy.* The word *Eucharist* comes from the Greek *eucharistein,* meaning "thanksgiving," and the word *liturgy* comes from the Greek word *leitourgia* meaning "public worship." In addition to Eucharistic Liturgy, several other terms describe this essential and vital part of Catholic worship and belief:

- ✔ Breaking of the Bread
- ✔ Divine Liturgy
- ✔ Gathering or Synaxis
- ✔ Holy Eucharist
- ✔ Holy Mass
- ✔ Holy Sacrifice of the Mass
- ✔ Lord's Supper

Don't be misled by the phrase *Sacrifice of the Mass;* Catholics aren't trying to add to the one sacrifice of Christ on the cross on the original Good Friday. Rather, the mass is a reenactment (in an unbloody manner) of the one and same sacrifice — a sacrifice so perfect and powerful that it can never be ended or repeated. It's eternal, because sins are still being forgiven even two millennia after Jesus's death.

The Church maintains that without all the blood and gore of the physical Crucifixion, the Sacrifice of the Mass re-presents (*not* represents) the same

- ✔ **Offering:** Jesus is the *Victim* at the Mass
- ✔ **Person making the offering:** Jesus is the *Priest* at the Mass
- ✔ **Effect:** The remission of sins

Jesus actually offers himself through the priest, making the offering on behalf of the people to God the Father. As victim, he's also the one being sacrificed. By virtue of the Sacrament of Holy Orders, the priest acts *in Persona Christi* (in the Person of Christ) as an *alter Christus* (another Christ).

In the English language, the word *mass* describes a large group of people or a scientific characteristic of matter. But the word means something completely different in the context of the Holy Sacrifice of the Mass. The English word "Mass" comes from the Latin phrase spoken at the end of the Sacred Liturgy. The priest or deacon says *"ite missa est,"* which has been translated in English as "go, the Mass is ended," but literally means "go [the congregation] is sent." In other words, it's not an ending as much as a commencement. The worship of God continues throughout the week by each believer in his or her own way until the community gathers again for Sacred Liturgy. In this section, we bring you up to speed on the importance of Mass.

Honoring the Sabbath publicly

Mass, being the supreme act of worship, is the only way that a Catholic can fulfill the Third Commandment to keep holy the Sabbath day. (See Chapter 12 for more on the Ten Commandments.) Even though the Jewish Day of the Lord (Sabbath) is Saturday, the main focus of Christianity is that Christ rose from the dead on Easter Sunday. Therefore, for Christians, Sunday is the day that Catholic Christians go to church to participate in the Mass. In many languages, the word *Sunday* is translated as "Day of the Lord" (*Domenica* in Italian; *Domingo* in Spanish and Portugese; *Kyriaken* in Greek).

You can pray anywhere and anytime and read the Bible alone or with others whenever and wherever you want, but you must go to church to attend Mass. Catholics can't just get together and hold Mass at home or someplace that's mutually convenient. The Mass can only occur through the exercised authority of an ordained priest, bishop, or pope. Missing Mass on Sunday or on a holy day of obligation is a mortal sin, unless bad weather, illness, or a real emergency prevents it. (For more on mortal sin, see Chapter 9.)

The Church professes that at the Mass, the three levels of the Church (all those in heaven, on earth, and in purgatory) converge and are united with one another in what's called the *communion of the saints.* This social dimension is central to Catholicism. It's definitely not a religion of individualism but one of community. (See Chapter 18 for more information about the communion of saints.)

Participating fully

Catholicism asks for more than the mere physical attendance of the congregation at Mass. The full, conscious, and active physical participation of the faithful is required by singing, praying, speaking, sitting, kneeling, and so on (don't worry if you don't know when to do what just yet; we cover all the bases in the upcoming section "The Two Parts of the Mass"). Both the priest and the congregation participate through their own respective gestures and responses. Full, active, and conscious participation is required; Catholics can't just sit in a pew and read the newspaper or bulletin during Mass.

In addition to participation through verbal responses and physical gestures, interior participation, which counts more than anything else, also occurs. Every person should be communicating with God at Mass. Being disposed to, cooperative with, and willing to accept the supernatural divine graces being bestowed at the Mass should be the goal of all present. The music may be a little flat, the singing slightly off key, and the preaching sometimes boring, but the bottom line is that which can't be seen or heard — the spiritual benefit to the soul.

Uniting past, present, and future

The Catholic Church professes that the Mass isn't just a reenactment of the Last Supper, when Jesus took bread and wine and said the words, "This is my body," and "This is my blood" (Matthew 26:26–29). More than a ceremonial reenactment of an ancient ritual, the Mass combines past, present, and future at the same time:

- ✔ **Past:** The exact words and elements that Jesus used at the Last Supper on Holy Thursday are used faithfully and precisely.

- ✔ **Present:** The Mass brings grace, nourishment, and instruction for the people who are present.

- ✔ **Future:** The Mass foreshadows the sacred banquet in heaven. Jesus often spoke of a heavenly banquet or wedding feast where guests would be well-fed, lasting for eternity, and surviving well after the world ends.

The Mass transports the participants back in time to Christ's Last Supper with His apostles, Christ's Passion and death on the cross, and His Resurrection and the empty tomb on the first Easter Sunday. The same *risen* Christ comes to enter the soul of each person at Holy Communion when the congregation eats and drinks His *living* (risen, not dead) flesh and blood.

St. Thomas Aquinas (see Chapter 21), a 13th-century Dominican theologian, said that the Holy Eucharist, particularly at Mass, reminds the faithful of what Jesus did for humankind in the *past,* makes Him *present* in the *Real Presence* (the consecrated bread and wine), and promises the faithful the *future* glory of heaven by giving food for eternal life. (See the section "Saying the Eucharistic Prayer," later in this chapter, for more details.)

The Two Parts of the Mass

By now, you've gathered that Mass is central to the Catholic faith, and you know it's a ritual with a set schedule. But what really happens during this sacred rite at a Catholic parish? The first part of the Mass in the Western (Latin) Church is the *Liturgy of the Word,* and its main focus is on Bible readings as an integral part of daily and weekly worship. The second part is the *Liturgy of the Eucharist,* and its main focus is the holiest and most sacred part of the Mass — Holy Eucharist. We cover those two main parts in depth in this section.

Eastern Catholics call their Mass the *Divine Liturgy,* but it's essentially the same.

Eastern Catholics also use the two-fold division of *Liturgy of the Catechumens* and *Liturgy of the Faithful,* which coincide with the *Liturgy of the Word* and the *Liturgy of the Eucharist.* The differences arise from the fact that in the West, the Mass follows the tradition of the Roman liturgy, but in the East, it's the liturgical tradition of Constantinople.

The Roman Missal is the official book the priest uses at Mass. It contains all the prayers that he must say, as well as instructions of what to do and how to do it. The Catholic Church implements the *Roman Missal, Third Edition* in English on November 27, 2011, and the prayers and creeds in this section follow the newest English translation. For more on what this Missal is all about, see the section "Checking Out the *Roman Missal, Third Edition.*" In this chapter, we look more closely at the Western liturgy because it's the most common, keeping in mind that both are full and equal rites in the Catholic Church.

Beginning the Mass

Before the first main portion of the Mass, the Liturgy of the Word, a few introductory rites serve to begin the Mass and help Catholics prepare for it mentally and spiritually. These introductory parts aren't a separate part of the Mass, but help prepare Catholics for the two main parts. To signal the beginning, a bell may be rung; the congregation, often led by an organist and choir, stand and sing an entrance hymn; and the priest, deacon, reader, servers, and (if needed, and in some parts of the country) *extraordinary ministers of Holy Communion* (laypersons who help the priest distribute Holy Communion) march down the aisle from the back of the church to the altar area in front. An opening song sets the proper mood and perspective for sacred worship. If the tabernacle (see Chapter 19) is in the center of the sanctuary, the priest and anyone passing in front of it genuflects as a sign of respect and recognition that Christ is truly present in the Holy Eucharist. Then the priest kisses the altar, and the priest and deacon bow before it because it represents Christ. The belief is that the Holy Eucharist *is* Christ, and the altar only *represents* Christ. Then the priest, deacon, and servers go to their respective seats in the sanctuary but stay standing while the sign of the cross officially begins the Mass.

Catholics begin and end every prayer and sacrament with the sign of the cross. It's one of the trademarks of Catholicism.

Greeting (Introductory Rite)

The priest celebrant says "In the name of the Father, and of the Son and of the Holy Spirit" while tracing a cross over his torso: He places his right hand first on his forehead and then moves it down to his breast; then he moves his hand across to his far left and then to his far right. The people make the same gesture and respond, "Amen."

Next, the priest may say one of the following: "The Lord be with you," "The grace of our Lord Jesus Christ, and the love of God, and the communion of the Holy Spirit be with you all," or "Grace to you and peace from God our Father and the Lord Jesus Christ." When a bishop presides at a Mass, his greeting is "Peace be with you."

For 40 years, the response given by the congregation to the celebrant's greeting was "and also with you." But now, the people say "and with your spirit" in response to any of the greetings. Why the change? The Latin text reads *et cum spiritu tuo,* which literally means "and with your spirit." This biblical phrase is rooted in Galatians 6:18 and 2 Timothy 4:22.

Acknowledging sin (Penitential Act)

The priest or deacon then initiates the *Penitential Act.* This isn't a general confession or general absolution. It doesn't replace the Sacrament of Penance, and it doesn't count as going to confession. (See Chapter 9 for details about the Sacrament of Penance.) The Penitential Act is merely a public acknowledgement that everyone is a sinner and has sinned to some degree during the week, be it big or small. Often, the rite starts with everyone saying the *Confiteor,* which is Latin for *I confess:*

> I confess to almighty God
> and to you, my brothers and sisters,
> that I have greatly sinned,
> in my thoughts and in my words,
> in what I have done and in what I have failed to do,
> through my fault, through my fault,
> through my most grievous fault;
> therefore I ask blessed Mary ever-virgin,
> all the angels and saints,
> and you, my brothers and sisters,
> to pray for me to the Lord our God.

Regardless of whether the Confiteor is said, the *Kyrie* is always said (in Greek or English) as part of the Penitential Act. *Kyrie* is Greek for *Lord* (as in *Kyrie eleison* or "Lord have mercy"). The rite expresses public guilt and shame for any sins against God because committing sin is also an offense and a wound to the faith community.

The Church renews an ancient petition: "Lord, have mercy; Christ, have mercy; Lord, have mercy." This part of the Mass in the Latin Church is one where the Greek text often remains intact (though the English may be used as well):

> *Kyrie, eleison; Christe, eleison; Kyrie, eleison.*

Gloria

On Sundays (except during Advent and Lent), holy days, and at all solemnities and feasts, the Gloria is recited or sung by the celebrant and congregation. It begins with the angelic salutation given to the shepherds at the first Christmas when Jesus was born in Bethlehem, "Glory to God in the highest" (*Gloria in excelsis Deo* in Latin), as found in Luke 2:14.

Glory to God in the highest,

and on earth peace to people of good will.

We praise you,

we bless you,

we adore you,

we glorify you,

we give you thanks for your great glory,

Lord God, heavenly King,

O God, Almighty Father.

Lord Jesus Christ, Only Begotten Son,

Lord God, Lamb of God, Son of the Father,

you take away the sins of the world,

    have mercy on us;

you take away the sins of the world,

    receive our prayer;

you are seated at the right hand of the Father,

    have mercy on us.

For you alone are the Holy One,

you alone are the Lord,

you alone are the Most High,

Jesus Christ,

with the Holy Spirit,

in the glory of God the Father.

Amen.

Opening Prayer (Collect)

The Opening Prayer (also called the *Collect,* pronounced COLL-ect instead of coll-ECT) sets the tone for the liturgical act of divine worship. It reminds the assembly that adoration of God is directed to the Father through the Son and in the Holy Spirit. In other words, it is always Trinitarian because the one God is in Three Persons.

As we explain in Chapter 15, Catholicism traditionally has four kinds of prayer:

- **Adoration:** Praising God
- **Contrition:** Asking for God's forgiveness
- **Petition:** Asking God for a favor
- **Thanksgiving:** Showing God gratitude

The Church believes that the Mass is the highest and supreme form of prayer, so it has all four elements in it. The Gloria is the adoration part of prayer, whereas the Confiteor and Penitential Rite are the contrition part. Later in the Mass, after the homily (sermon) and the Nicene Creed, comes the Prayer of the Faithful, also known as the General Intercessions, which is a prayer of petition. The thanksgiving part comes after Holy Communion, when gratitude is shown for all the graces given at Mass.

In a sense, the opening prayer provides a theme for the Mass. Every Sunday, holy day, and feast day (honoring a saint) has its own unique prayers and readings depending on the time of year or priority of the feast. (See the section, "Spiritual Seasons of the Year," later in this chapter.)

The priest, deacon, and congregation stand throughout each element of the beginning of the Mass that we've described so far.

The Liturgy of the Word

Now that the introductory part is over and the people are ready to really celebrate Mass, the Liturgy of the Word begins. We explain what this part of the Mass entails in this section.

Reading Scripture

Any qualified *lector,* a layperson trained for the task of reading at Mass, can read the Old and New Testament. Lectors prepare each day or week to read Sacred Scripture at Mass. Everyone sits during the readings, while the lector stands in front near the altar and reads aloud. On Sundays, a selection from the Old Testament is read, as well as a Psalm, which is usually set to music and sung, and then a selection from one of the New Testament Epistles or from the Acts of the Apostles is read.

Then, a musical arrangement of the word *Alleluia* is usually sung just before the reading of a passage from the New Testament Gospels of Matthew, Mark, Luke, or John. *Alleluia* is the Latin version of the Greek word *allelouia,* an expression of praise and joy that, in turn, comes from the Hebrew *hallelujah* for "praise the Lord." This is the high point of the Bible readings, and it's the cue to stand. (Or the cue is when the priest or deacon stands up.) This change from sitting to standing shows the preeminence of the Gospels in their relationship to the other books of the Bible. The entire Bible is inspired, but the Gospels are special because they contain the very words and deeds of Christ. So Catholics stand when the Gospels are read but remain seated while the other parts of the Bible are read at Mass.

Only a deacon, priest, or bishop can read the Gospel at Mass. Sometimes, the Gospel book is also *incensed,* meaning that incense is burned in a container (called a *thurible* or *censor*) over the pages of the Gospel about to be read. Incense is a symbol of prayer rising up to heaven and recognition of the presence of divinity. The Gospels are incensed because Christ is present whenever his words are read from the Bible.

The Bible plays an important role in daily Catholic prayer. The words of the Mass aren't just made-up mumbo jumbo; they're carefully selected from the Bible. The Gloria, Psalm, Old and New Testament readings, and so on, are all straight out of Scripture, which is also read during each of the seven sacraments.

The Church chooses the sacred texts to be read during a specific Mass; the choice isn't up to the priest or deacon. Each Sunday, the readings follow a three-year cycle (A, B, and C); the Gospels of Matthew, Mark, and Luke take precedence, with the Gospel of John sprinkled in here and there. After three years, if you go to Mass every Sunday, you'll have heard and been exposed to all four Gospels as well as most of the New Testament writings and Epistles. But the readings at the weekday Mass (Monday through Saturday morning) work a little differently. The weekday Mass uses a two-year cycle (I and II) because only two readings are done during the week versus the three on the weekend. All even-numbered years (2012, 2014, and so on) are Year II for daily biblical readings.

Because, on any given day, the readings are the same in every Catholic Church all over the world — and also to prevent having Bible pages flipped all over the place — the Catholic Church uses a book called the *Lectionary.* This book, usually bound with a red cover, contains only readings from Sacred Scripture — nothing else. If it's not a book in the Bible, it's not in the Lectionary. The difference between the Lectionary and the Bible is merely the order and sequence of the writings. Lectionary readings are usually excerpts (*pericopes* or *cuttings*), not necessarily complete whole chapters.

The option exists to use a Book of the Gospels, which is exactly that: a book just containing the Gospels (Matthew, Mark, Luke, and John). The Lectionary is still used in this case for the Old Testament, Psalm, and New Testament Epistle, but the priest or deacon reads from the Gospel Book rather than the Lectionary. Doing so gives more solemnity to the most special part of the Bible for Christians, the Gospel.

As we discuss in Chapter 2, Catholicism is a religion based on the complete written and unwritten Word of God. Therefore, more emphasis is placed on the Word as it is *proclaimed* (read aloud) than as *read* by people in their pews. Yet, to help those who can't hear too well and for those who want to read along, many Catholic parishes have a people's version of the altar *missal* (books containing all the prayers and Scripture readings used at Mass) or abridged seasonal versions in the pews to help the congregation follow the prayers (including those of the priest) and Scripture readings.

Whether you attend Mass or not, you can go online to see what the readings are for any day of the month at the United States Conference of Catholic Bishops website (www.usccb.org). You may notice that even though the selected readings for a particular day are from different parts of the Bible, they share a common theme. Several places on the Internet allow you to see and hear the Mass online as well. While not satisfying your Sunday obligation, televised Mass does provide a help to the bedridden, the sick, and those who are physically incapable of travel.

Hearing the homily

After standing for the Gospel, the congregation sits and listens to the homily, which is different than a sermon:

- **Sermon:** Any explanation and reflection on the Word of God, on any topic chosen by the minister.
- **Homily:** A sermon that's preached at Mass after the Gospel is read. Only clergy — deacons, priests, or bishops — can preach a homily. According to canon law, the local bishop may allow laity and religious brothers and sisters to preach a sermon under certain conditions, but they're never allowed to preach the homily itself.

The priest or deacon connects the Scripture readings to the daily lives of the people, the teachings of the Church, or the particular celebration at hand, such as a wedding or funeral.

Reciting the Creed

On Sundays and holy days, the homily is followed by the *Creed* (Profession of Faith), which is ordinarily the ancient Nicene Creed of A.D. 325. The Apostles'

Creed, an ancient symbol of Baptism, *may* be used anytime, but especially during Lent and Easter time and occasionally at Masses for children. (You can read the Apostles' Creed in Chapter 2.) The entire congregation stands to sing or recite the Creed.

Here is the Nicene Creed:

> I believe in one God,
>
> the Father almighty,
>
> maker of heaven and earth,
>
> of all things visible and invisible.
>
> I believe in one Lord Jesus Christ,
>
> the Only Begotten Son of God,
>
> born of the Father before all ages.
>
> God from God, Light from Light,
>
> true God from true God,
>
> begotten, not made, consubstantial with the Father;
>
> through him all things were made.
>
> For us men and for our salvation
>
> he came down from heaven,
>
> and by the Holy Spirit * was incarnate of the Virgin Mary,
>
> and became man.
>
> For our sake he was crucified under Pontius Pilate,
>
> he suffered death and was buried,
>
> and rose again on the third day
>
> in accordance with the Scriptures.
>
> He ascended into heaven
>
> and is seated at the right hand of the Father.
>
> He will come again in glory

to judge the living and the dead

and his kingdom will have no end.

I believe in the Holy Spirit, the Lord, the giver of life,

who proceeds from the Father and the Son,

who with the Father and the Son is adored and glorified,

who has spoken through the prophets.

I believe in one, holy, catholic and apostolic Church.

I confess one baptism for the forgiveness of sins

and I look forward to the resurrection of the dead

and the life of the world to come. Amen.

At the words *by the Holy Spirit* * . . . *became man,* all make a profound bow to show respect for the *Incarnation,* from the Latin word *caro* for flesh. The *Incarnation* refers to Jesus's taking on human flesh — being conceived in the womb of His mother. On Solemnities of the Annunciation (March 25) and Christmas (December 25), everyone kneels instead of just bowing.

Some changes have been made to the previous English translation of the Nicene Creed. Most importantly is the use of the word *consubstantial* to replace *one in being.* This word more accurately expresses what is meant by the original Greek word *homoousios* and the Latin *consubstantialem.* The Ecumenical Council of Nicea defined that Jesus Christ (as God the Son) had the same substance as God the Father and not just a similar one, as the heretic Arius had proposed.

The other change is more modest. *Born of the Virgin Mary* was replaced with *incarnate* of the Virgin Mary. Again, this word more precisely conveys what the official Latin text says, namely that Jesus's mother not only gave birth to Him but also gave Him His human nature. Theologically speaking, this mystery of God becoming Man is called the *Incarnation.*

The Creed succinctly sums up all that the *Magisterium* (the teaching authority of the Church; see Chapter 6) has taught for the past 2,000 years.

Like the Boy Scout oath or the Hippocratic oaths that medical professionals recite, the Creed is a Christian oath, stating what Catholics believe as revealed to them by God through Sacred Scripture and Sacred Tradition.

Praying the General Intercessions

After the Creed, the *General Intercessions* (Prayer of the Faithful) takes place. The lector or deacon reads several petitions aloud, and the people respond to each one with "Lord, hear our prayer" or "Hear us, O Lord." The petitions are for the pope, the Church, the civil authorities, current concerns, and so on. For example, you may hear the lector say, "For Pope Benedict and all religious leaders, that they may preach the Word of God and teach the truths of our faith with fidelity and courage, let us pray to the Lord."

The Liturgy of the Eucharist

The second half of the Mass focuses on offering: the collection offering, the offering of the bread and wine to be consecrated, the sacrifice itself, the Consecration by the priest, and the Holy Communion of the faithful.

Gathering the offerings

As the Liturgy of the Eucharist begins, everyone sits down for the collection of offerings. Sometimes, a basket is passed from one end of the pew to the next, person by person. Traditionally, however, ushers pass the basket: Starting in front of the church and moving pew by pew to the back, the ushers extend a collection basket with a very long handle in front of each person. Either way is acceptable.

If there is an Offertory Procession (usually just on weekends or holy days of obligation in most parishes) while the collection is being taken, a few parishioners often go to the back of the church where a cruet of plain drinking water, a cruet of grape wine, and a container of unconsecrated *hosts* (unleavened bread made from wheat flour and water) have been placed. Usually, two to four people bring the bread and wine (called *gifts*), along with the collection, in an offertory procession up to the altar area. The organist and choir lead the congregation in an offertory hymn.

Preparing the gifts on the altar

The priest, deacon, and servers meet the procession at the foot of the altar and receive the gifts. The deacon (or, if none is present, the priest) prepares the gifts on the altar in an action called, suitably enough, *the preparation of the gifts.* The deacon or priest pours wine into the *chalice* (the gold or silver cup that holds the wine that will become Christ's body and blood) and adds a few drops of water to symbolize the union of the divinity and humanity of Christ.

The priest lifts the hosts of bread above the altar and says, "Blessed are you, Lord, God of all creation, for through your goodness we have received the bread we offer you: fruit of the earth and work of human hands, it will become for us the Bread of Life." The people respond, "Blessed be God forever." Then the priest lifts the wine-filled chalice above the altar and says, "Blessed are you, Lord God of all creation, for through your goodness we have received the wine we offer you: fruit of the vine and work of human hands, it will become our spiritual drink." The people again respond, "Blessed be God forever."

Washing hands

The priest may incense the gifts and then washes his hands with water at the side of the altar. The washing is a ceremonial relic of the Jewish tradition present at the time of Jesus. At that time, the high priest washed his hands before making the sacrifice of killing an unblemished, spotless lamb in the Temple of Jerusalem on the day of Passover. So, too, celebrating Mass today, the priest prepares to offer up the Lamb of God (Jesus Christ) to God the Father, so he ceremonially washes his hands to offer a spotless sacrifice.

Some observers associate the priest's hand washing with the hand-washing act by Pontius Pilate (the Roman Governor of Judea who condemned Christ to death on the Cross) before the Crucifixion and death of Jesus on Good Friday. But the Church views that scene as a symbolic gesture in which Pilate claims that he's washing his hands of the death of an innocent man (Jesus). The hand washing of the priest isn't a connection with Pilate but a ritual purification, such as a connection with the high priest who made a symbolic sacrifice in the Temple of Jerusalem.

Praying on behalf of the people

Next, the people stand, and the priest says more prayers, addressing God on behalf of the people. Prayers are said over the gifts, and then the people and the choir normally sing the words of the *Sanctus* (Latin for "holy"): "Holy, holy, holy Lord God of hosts. Heaven and earth are full of your glory. Hosanna in the highest. Blessed is he who comes in the name of the Lord. Hosanna in the highest." These words are taken from Isaiah 6:3 and Revelation 4:8 as well as from Mark 11:9–10.

Preparing for the Holy Eucharist

After the Sanctus, the congregation kneels for the first time. Now comes the holiest part of the Mass.

Saying the Eucharistic Prayer

The *Eucharistic Prayer,* which only the priest can say, recalls what happened at the Last Supper. The priest narrates the sequence of events until the part where Jesus takes the bread. Then the priest changes from third person narration to first person and acts in the person of Christ *(in persona Christi)* as an *other Christ (alter-Christus).* The priest doesn't say, "This is Christ's body" or "This is Jesus's blood." He uses the pronoun *my* because at the moment of consecration, the priest speaks in the person of Jesus.

The priest uses the same words that Jesus used at the Last Supper at the Consecration: **"Take this, all of you, and eat of it, for this is my body, which will be given up for you."** He elevates the Host above the altar for everyone to see. The priest genuflects, takes the chalice of wine, and continues in first person, speaking as Christ: **"Take this, all of you, and drink from it, for this is the chalice of my blood, the blood of the new and eternal covenant, which will be poured out for you and for many for the forgiveness of sins. Do this in memory of me."** He elevates the chalice, and he genuflects.

The ringing of bells at the Consecration signifies the holiest moment of the Mass, an appropriate symbol of reverent rejoicing. In the Middle Ages, before stereo audio-microphones, people way in the back of a Gothic cathedral could barely hear anything that the priest was saying, so they needed a signal that the Consecration was happening. That signal was the ringing of bells. Often, bells are still rung today when the priest elevates the Host, and again when the priest elevates the chalice.

Transubstantiation

Catholicism professes that during the Consecration, a miracle occurs — the priest *consecrates* the bread and wine: Just as Jesus did at the Last Supper, the priest takes the bread in the form of a Host and says, "This is my body." Then he takes the chalice of wine and says, "This is my blood." Now it's the body and blood of Christ; it still has the appearances (also called *accidents*) of bread and wine, but it's not. It's the real body and blood of Christ, and this change is called *transubstantiation*.

The Bible says that God created merely by speaking: "God said, 'Let there be light'; and there was light" (Genesis 1:3). Likewise, by merely speaking the words of Christ over the bread and wine during Holy Communion, the priest changes them into the body and blood, soul and divinity of Christ through the authority given to him by the Sacrament of Holy Orders. Only an ordained priest has the authority to say Mass and consecrate the bread and wine.

Kneeling before the Eucharist

Catholics kneel before the consecrated bread and wine — called the *Eucharist* — because it's not a piece of bread and wine anymore; it truly is Christ. If the Holy Eucharist were just a symbol — such as bread and wine — then kneeling down and adoring it would be considered idolatry, but the Catholic Church has staunchly asserted for 2,000 years that the Holy Eucharist isn't a symbol. The Holy Eucharist is His body and blood, whether on the altar or in the *tabernacle,* a locked metal receptacle usually on an altar or table. (To see what a tabernacle looks like, go to Chapter 19.)

Tracing the biblical roots of transubstantiation

The miraculous changing of what was bread and wine into the body and blood of Christ that occurs during the Consecration at each and every Mass is called *transubstantiation.* It refers to the changing of substances: in this case, the substances of bread and wine into the substances of the body and blood of Jesus. Catholicism bases this belief in the transubstantiation on two points:

✔ In the Gospels of Matthew, Mark, and Luke, each writer uses the same phrase to describe the Last Supper on Holy Thursday, the day before Jesus was crucified. Jesus took the bread, blessed it, broke it, and gave it to his disciples and said, "This is My Body" (*touto estin to soma mou* in Greek; *hoc est corpus meum* in Latin). The verb *to be* is used such that an equality exists between *This* (which refers to the bread) and *My Body.* So the bread becomes the body of Christ. Because all three Gospels (Matthew 26:26, Mark 14:22, and Luke 22:19)

meticulously repeat the exact same phrase, as does St. Paul (1 Corinthians 11:24), these sacred words must be taken literally.

✔ The words of the Last Supper spoken by Christ over the bread and wine are consistent with the New Testament: Jesus explicitly and graphically commanded, "Eat My flesh and drink My blood," (see John 6:54) more than a few times. He also said, "My flesh is food indeed and my blood is drink indeed." Some in the crowd said, "How can this man give us his flesh to eat?" (John 6:52), and he responded, "Unless you eat the flesh of the Son of man and drink his blood, you have no life in you," (John: 6:53). "After this, many of his disciples drew back and no longer went about with him," (John: 6:66). The Church reasons that if Jesus had meant this to be symbolic, He wouldn't have allowed so many of His followers to leave with a serious misunderstanding.

Eastern Catholics, such as the Byzantine, don't kneel because standing is their normal posture for reverence, but in the Latin (Western) Church, kneeling is the most profound sign of reverence. In the United States, Catholics kneel throughout the Eucharistic Prayer, but in Europe and elsewhere, they're only obligated to kneel during the Consecration.

The Eucharist has other names, too:

✔ Holy Eucharist

✔ Communion and Holy Communion

✔ Sacrament and Blessed Sacrament

✔ Sacrifice and Holy Sacrifice

✔ True Presence and Real Presence

Catholics believe that the Eucharist is always simultaneously an object of adoration and worship, being the Real Presence; it's the same Holy Sacrifice of God the Son to God the Father for the remission of sins; and it's sacred food to nourish the soul. In a sense, the Holy Eucharist is the Last Supper, His death on the cross on Good Friday, and His Resurrection on Easter Sunday all rolled into one:

- ✔ **Holy Thursday:** Jesus gave the sacrament of Holy Eucharist at the Last Supper.

- ✔ **Good Friday:** He sacrificed His life to save humankind from our sins.

- ✔ **Easter Sunday:** Christ reunited His body and blood, rose from the dead, and established the promise of eternal life.

The Mystery of Faith

Note that just as Christ did at the Last Supper, the priest consecrates the bread and wine separately. He doesn't combine the two into one action by taking the bread and wine together and saying, "This is My body *and* My blood." He separates bread and wine, body and blood. The reason? When a person's body is separated from his blood, what happens? Death. A person bleeds to death. The separate consecration of the bread and wine re-presents the separation of body from blood that happened on the cross on the first Good Friday.

But Catholics don't receive dead flesh and blood in Holy Communion because Christ rose from the dead. Catholics receive His living and risen flesh and blood in Holy Communion because after Good Friday came Easter Sunday. After death came Resurrection.

Therefore, immediately after commemorating His death through the separate consecrations, the Mystery of Faith is said or sung. According to the Third Roman Missal, Catholics may say one of three texts for the Mystery of Faith:

- ✔ We proclaim your death, O Lord, and profess your Resurrection until you come again.

- ✔ When we eat this Bread and drink this Cup, we proclaim your death, O Lord, until you come again.

- ✔ Save us, Savior of the world, for by your Cross and Resurrection you have set us free.

So at Mass, body and blood are reunited as they were at the Resurrection.

The Lord's Prayer and sign of peace

The rest of the Eucharistic Prayer follows, and the priest concludes with: "Through Him, and with Him and in Him, O God, Almighty Father, in the unity of the Holy Spirit, all glory and honor is yours, for ever and ever." The people sing or say, "Amen," then stand and say the Our Father (Lord's Prayer), which you can read in Chapter 15.

Then the priest or deacon may say, "Let us offer each other the sign of peace," and each parishioner gives those standing next to and near to him a simple handshake to show solidarity as one family of faith before the real and most intimate sign of unity — Holy Communion.

The Church has never officially recognized the practice of holding hands as a sign of unity during the Our Father. This practice originates from non-Catholic tradition. Catholics think that holding hands to symbolize unity is unnecessary because at Holy Communion the unity is real. The word *communion* comes from the Latin *cum + unio* meaning "united with." The sign of unity is the act of taking Communion because it signifies that the person is in union with all that the Catholic Church teaches, does, and prays.

Agnus Dei

The *Agnus Dei* (Lamb of God) is then said or sung: "Lamb of God, you take away the sins of the world: have mercy on us. Lamb of God, you take away the sins of the world: have mercy on us. Lamb of God, you take away the sins of the world: grant us peace," and then the people kneel. This title of Jesus, Lamb of God, comes from the words of St. John the Baptist (John 1:29).

The priest holds the consecrated Host over the chalice of consecrated wine and says: "Behold the Lamb of God, behold Him who takes away the sins of the world. Blessed are those called to the supper of the Lamb." Responding to this, the people say: "Lord, I am not worthy that you should enter under my roof, but only say the word and my soul shall be healed."

Here is another change from the previous English translation of the Latin. The new text goes back to the biblical reference of the Centurion, who said he was not worthy to have Christ under his roof (Luke 7:6–7). Previously, it was said: "Lord, I am not worthy to receive you, only say the word and I shall be healed." The other change is the substitution of the word *soul* for *I*. The Latin text uses *anima mea* (my soul) and it does so to convey that this is spiritual food for spiritual healing.

Holy Communion

The priest first consumes the consecrated Host and then drinks the consecrated wine from the chalice. If a deacon is present, the priest gives him a consecrated Host and then the chalice to drink from.

Sometimes, Catholics refer to the chalice as only containing *the wine*. This terminology is wrong, disrespectful, and sacrilegious because it's no longer wine but the precious blood of Christ.

Offering a sign of reverence

While going in line to receive Holy Communion, Catholics in the congregation who are properly disposed (a phrase we explain in the upcoming section "Being properly disposed and in communion") approach the priest, deacon, or extraordinary minister and are first given a consecrated Host. Sometimes, they may be offered the option of also taking a sip of the Precious Blood (the consecrated wine) from the cup. Before they actually receive either one, however, some sign of reverence for the Real Presence is required, be it a bow of the head, the sign of the cross, a genuflection, or kneeling.

The local bishop and the national conference of bishops for each nation give guidelines on which posture they prefer or suggest. In the United States, for example, standing is the norm, but with a bow of the head; however, it is forbidden to refuse Communion to someone who is kneeling. If the church or chapel has a *Communion* or *altar rail* (a short gate-like structure surrounding the sanctuary where people can kneel during Holy Communion), and people kneel at it, no other sign of reverence is required because kneeling is a sign of reverence.

Receiving the Host

As a Catholic, when you're first presented the consecrated Host, the priest, deacon, or extraordinary minister says "the Body of Christ" to which you reply "Amen," signifying, "Yes, I do believe it is Jesus." Then, you either open your mouth and extend your tongue, or open your hand and allow the Host to be placed on it, depending on the practice of that parish. Then if the Precious Blood is offered, you may choose to go to the person holding it who says, "the Blood of Christ," and you reply again, "Amen." Then you take the cup (called a *chalice*) from the person holding it, drink a few sips of the consecrated wine, and hand the cup back.

Catholics aren't allowed to *self-communicate,* which means going up to the altar and picking up the chalice for themselves. An authorized minister (priest, deacon or extraordinary minister) must give them Holy Communion. Then, after receiving Holy Communion, the faithful go back to their respective pew and pray silently for a few minutes before sitting down.

The whole and entire Christ is in one consecrated Host, one part of the Host, or one drop of the consecrated wine. The faithful are encouraged but not obligated to consume both elements of Communion. If only consecrated Hosts are given, the people aren't being ripped off or cheated. Sometimes, Catholics are given the opportunity to receive both the Host *and* chalice, but those who receive both elements shouldn't think that they *must* have both elements in order to fully receive Communion.

Being properly disposed and in communion

Catholics can participate in Holy Communion if they're *properly disposed,*
which is a fancy way of saying they

- ✔ Are unaware of any mortal sins that aren't yet confessed and absolved.
  (See Chapter 9 for a discussion of the Sacrament of Penance.)
- ✔ Don't publicly dissent from Church teaching, such as the Church's views
  on abortion.
- ✔ Fasted (didn't eat or drink anything but water) for one full hour before
  receiving Holy Communion. The fast is one hour before Communion, not
  before the beginning of Mass.

The Church asks that the following people *not* take Communion:

- ✔ Non-Catholics
- ✔ Catholics in an invalid marriage (see Chapter 9)
- ✔ Catholics who've broken the one-hour fast (unless they're on medica-
  tion, sick, elderly, or in the hospital)
- ✔ Catholics who haven't made their first confession (see Chapter 9) and
  First Communion (see Chapter 8)

You must be in communion to receive Communion. Being *in communion*
means being united with *all* that the Church teaches, prays, and does. Non-
Catholics, for example, obviously aren't in full or complete union; otherwise,
they'd be Catholics.

Unlike customs at the airport, no one checks your ID at Communion time to
make sure you're Catholic. Sometimes, at weddings and funerals, the priest
makes an announcement before Communion that only Catholics who are in
full communion with the Church and who are in the state of grace (no mortal
sins on their soul) should come forward. Even if this isn't said, it's implied
and written in the back or front cover of many Catholic hymnals and missals.

Unless someone displays obvious confusion regarding the procedure of
receiving Holy Communion, normally no questions are asked. If somebody
appears clueless ("What do I do with the Host?"), the priest, deacon, or minister may ask, "Are you Catholic?" The question is not meant to be intrusive
or insulting.

If a Catholic is divorced and remarried outside the Church or is not in
the state of grace because he didn't go to confession to have a mortal sin
absolved, he shouldn't take Holy Communion. Should you receive the
Eucharist while you're in the state of mortal sin, you're doubling the negative
effect of the mortal sin on your soul by committing *sacrilege* — using
something sacred for an unworthy purpose.

Putting the Word of God into practice

Western Catholicism uses Latin and the vernacular as the official languages of worship. At the end of the sacred liturgy, the priest or deacon tells the congregation in Latin: *ite missa est*. This phrase is literally translated as: "Go, [the congregation] is sent." What it means is that after being nourished by the Word of God (Scripture) and Holy Communion (Eucharist), the People of God are commissioned to make Jesus present to others by their thoughts, words, and deeds.

When the Mass was translated into English in 1970, however, someone alternately interpreted the text *(ite missa est)* as "Go, the Mass is ended." While technically acceptable, this translation gave people the notion that the worship was over when it was time to go home, but it's really more of a commencement than an ending. Hence, the *Roman Missal, Third Edition* allows these four alternate options:

- ✔ "Go in peace."
- ✔ "Go forth, the Mass is ended."
- ✔ "Go and announce the Gospel of the Lord."
- ✔ "Go in peace, glorifying the Lord by your life."

Vatican II and the Celebration of Mass

Commonly known as *Vatican II,* the Second Vatican Council (1962–65) was opened by Pope John XXIII and closed by Pope Paul VI. The Sixteen Documents of Vatican II were responses of the Catholic Church to reiterate the traditional teachings of the Church and to address contemporary concerns. The Sacred Liturgy, Revelation, Ecumenism, the Church, the World, the Laity, the Priesthood, the Diaconate, Social Communication, and so on were all discussed.

Presenting and explaining a 2,000-year-old religion to a modern world in contemporary terms was the primary goal of the council. Included was the renewal of the sacraments, especially the Holy Mass. No new dogmas or doctrines were proclaimed or defined, but the old ones were restated and reemphasized with modern vocabulary and context. In other words, the *content* of Faith was not changed, but the *context* in which it was explained and the manner in which it was communicated was adapted for the modern era. Previous councils sought to define theological doctrine and resolve conflicts, but the Second Vatican Council was primarily a pastoral one in that it sought to promote greater spirituality while still defending the traditional teachings and practices of Catholicism.

In this section, we explain the influence of Vatican II on the modern Mass.

Allowing worship in vernacular languages

Vatican II allowed the introduction of the *vernacular* (native tongue) into the public worship of the Church, even while preserving the rich Latin language and tradition. Today, Mass is said in the native language of the local place (though with the *Roman Missal, Third Edition*, the prayers are translated into a more accurate and reverent wording; see the section "Checking out the *Roman Missal, Third Edition*" for more).

Before Vatican II, Mass in the Latin Catholic Church was always in Latin. Since the Council of Trent 400 years beforehand (1545–63), the universal norm for the Western Church was Latin. Having the Mass in one language anywhere and everywhere all over the world made it easy for Catholics to travel and feel truly *catholic* (from the Latin word *catholicus* and the Greek *katholikos* meaning *universal*). But Latin wasn't universally taught in the schools like it used to be, so many people didn't know any Latin at all. That's why the Church allowed for the native language — to promote a full, conscious, and active participation of the faithful in all the prayers, hymns, and responses of the Mass all over the world.

Latin is still the official language of the Catholic Church, so anything coming from the Vatican and applying to the universal Church is written in Latin. For example, papal encyclicals and ecumenical council decrees (see Chapter 6), the Code of Canon Law (Chapter 11), and so on are first written in Latin and then translated. This same process applies to all official documents concerning doctrine, worship, and law.

The Church never intended to drop Latin completely. The Church still asks that Latin be used to preserve the Catholic heritage, much like Hebrew, Greek, Old Slavonic, and Arabic are used by other religions even today.

Pope Benedict XVI has renamed the new Mass of Paul VI (formerly known as the *Novus Ordo* or *Vatican II Mass*) as the *Ordinary Form of the Roman Rite*. It can be celebrated entirely in Latin, entirely in the vernacular, or mostly in the vernacular with common parts in Latin. He also designated the old Mass (formerly known as the *Traditional Latin Mass* [TLM] or *Tridentine Mass*) as the *Extraordinary Form of the Roman Rite*. This Mass can be celebrated by any priest, anywhere, but he must use the 1962 Missal of John XXIII.

Other changes resulting from Vatican II

In addition to allowing the priest to say the Mass in the native language of the congregation, Vatican II also made some other changes to the Mass:

✔ The first half of the Mass is now called the *Liturgy of the Word* to emphasize the Scripture readings that take place during this part.

✔ Catholics attending Mass in the Latin (Western) Rite have been allowed the occasional option to receive both forms of Holy Communion: the consecrated bread and the consecrated wine. However, it's not necessary or mandatory that the faithful receive both because the consecrated Host and the consecrated wine are both the body and blood, the soul and divinity of Christ.

Checking out the Roman Missal, Third Edition

As of November 27, 2011, the first Sunday of Advent, the *Roman Missal, Third Edition*, is used throughout the Roman Catholic Church in the United States and in most English speaking countries. The new Roman Missal is a revised English translation of some of the prayers used in the *Order of Mass* (texts and rites used in the celebration of the Eucharist), as well as of prayers for seasons of the church year, memorials of saints, celebrations of the other sacraments, funerals, and various needs and circumstances.

The new Missal replaces the previously used *Sacramentary* (or Mass book), which contains the collection of prayers that the priest uses in the celebration of the Mass and the responses of the people. The Roman Missal contains essentially the same prayers as the Sacramentary, but with new English translations and a few additional prayers.

The main reason for the changes in the *Roman Missal, Third Edition*, is to make the English translations more accurately reflect the original Latin prayers, reflecting the depth and richness of the prayers and their biblical origins.

Understanding the Latin roots

In 1970, Pope Paul VI released the Roman Missal of the Second Vatican Council, with a second edition being released in 1975. Each edition of the Roman Missal, including the new Third Edition, is first published entirely in Latin, the preferred language of the church and biblical scholars for centuries; this Latin version is called the *Missale Romanum*.

While Latin remained the preferred language, the reforms of Vatican II allowed for translations of the Latin into the vernacular, or common language, of Catholics around the world. In the United States, this resulted in the first English-language edition of the Sacramentary published in 1973. A revised edition of the Sacramentary went into use in 1985 in the U.S. and was a translation of the second edition of the *Missale Romanum*. Nearly thirty years later, in the Jubilee Year 2000, Pope John Paul II issued the third edition of the *Missale Romanum,* which first became available in Latin in 2002 (it takes a while after the time the pope issues or *promulgates* an edition for it to actually take shape). The *Roman Missal, Third Edition* is the English translation from this Latin edition that the Catholic Church in the United States will be using beginning on November 27, 2011, almost ten years after it became available in Latin. Why all that time in the interim? The new revised Missal went through a lengthy process of translation that involved several groups including the International Commission on English in the Liturgy (ICEL) and the United States Conference of Catholic Bishops (USCCB), receiving final approval by the Vatican.

Seeing why change was necessary

At the end of Vatican II, the Latin edition of the Roman Missal was quickly translated into the languages of the local people. This was done using the principle of *dynamic equivalence*, or translation attempting to convey the spirit or overall meaning of the text rather than a literal translation. After nearly forty years of celebrating the Mass in the vernacular languages and with new understanding of the principles of translation, the Vatican felt that improvements to the text could be made using the principle of *formal equivalence,* a more accurate and word-for-word translation.

In many cases, the new translations make the biblical origins of the prayers more apparent, deepening the appreciation for the connections between the Eucharist and Scripture. Plus, the updated translation also encourages a more formal and reverential way of praying the liturgy, enhancing the appreciation of the mystery of the Eucharistic celebration. The principle of *formal equivalence* also helps the prayers of the Roman Missal in English be more consistent with other languages, like Spanish and French.

Knowing what it means for you in the pew

Here's what's new in the *Roman Missal, Third Edition*:

- ✔ Updated and revised instructions for the celebration of the Mass
- ✔ Updated translations of prayers, responses, and acclamations including the Greeting, Gloria, the Nicene Creed, and the Mystery of Faith
- ✔ Prayers for the observances of recently canonized saints
- ✔ Additional prefaces for the Eucharistic Prayers
- ✔ Additional Masses for various needs and special occasions

The Mass itself isn't changing with the *Roman Missal, Third Edition* — just the English translation of some of the prayers used during the Mass. Many prayers, like the Lord's Prayer, aren't changing at all, and the translations of the Scripture readings aren't changing.

Adjusting the Mass for the Occasion

The Mass has some variety. The main focus of each Mass is the same, but slight differences exist depending on the occasion. This section gives you some background so you know what to expect from a particular Mass.

Weekday and Sunday

The basic difference between Masses lies in whether a given Mass is on a weekday (also known as *daily Mass*) or a Sunday. Weekday Mass obviously takes place Monday through Friday but also includes Mass on Saturday morning. Sunday Mass can be held Saturday evening and at any time on Sunday.

Saturday evening counts as Sunday using the ancient Hebrew practice of considering the new day to begin at sundown rather than sunrise. So as soon as the sun sets on Saturday evening, liturgically speaking, it's Sunday.

Sunday (or Saturday evening) Mass is obligatory for all Catholics, but weekday Mass is optional. Sunday Mass is the *parish Mass,* meaning the whole parish is expected to participate. Sunday Masses include a reading from the Old Testament, a reading from the New Testament, a Psalm, and a Gospel reading as well as the Gloria and Creed. At the weekday Mass, however, only one selection is read (either from the Old Testament or the New Testament), along with a Psalm and a Gospel reading.

Often, Sunday Mass often includes an organ and a choir but weekday Mass usually doesn't. Sunday Mass normally takes an hour. Weekday Mass typically takes about a half-hour.

Holy days of obligation

Holy days of obligation are days of the year when Catholics must attend Mass in addition to the normal Sunday Mass. The United States has six holy days of obligation:

- **January 1:** The Feast of Mary, the Mother of God
- **40 days after Easter Sunday:** Ascension Thursday

- ✔ **August 15:** Assumption of Mary into heaven
- ✔ **November 1:** All Saints' Day
- ✔ **December 8:** The Feast of the Immaculate Conception
- ✔ **December 25:** Christmas, the Nativity of Our Lord

The schedule gets confusing sometimes. If certain holy days fall on a Saturday or Monday, they *aren't* considered holy days of obligation because they're back-to-back with Sunday. The concern is that it would be burdensome to many Catholics to have to go to Church two days in a row.

In the United States, however, Christmas Day (December 25) and the Immaculate Conception (December 8) are always days of obligation even when they fall on Saturday or Monday. The reason is that Christmas and Easter are the highest-ranking holy days, and the Immaculate Conception is the patronal feast for the United States. But if All Saints' Day, the Assumption, or the Feast of Mary, the Mother of God falls on a Saturday or a Monday, the obligation to attend Mass is lifted. If either of those days falls on a Tuesday, Wednesday, Thursday, or Friday, though, attending Mass is obligatory. Believe us, Catholics get confused with this formula — including the priests. And to make it even more perplexing, some parts of the United States have moved holy days, such as the Ascension, from Thursday to the closest Sunday. If in doubt, it's best to call the local Catholic parish or just go to Mass anyway. Attending Mass is never a waste of time, even if it ends up not being a holy day of obligation. Holy days differ around the world, so if you're traveling abroad, check in with those local parishes to make sure you're not missing something important.

Note that some countries, including Vatican City, have more holy days of obligation which are often civil holidays as well. That could mean a national day off and closed government offices. These other days include: January 6 (Epiphany), March 19 (St. Joseph), Corpus Christi (Thursday after Trinity Sunday, which is the Sunday after Pentecost, which is 50 days after Easter), and the Solemnity of St. Peter and St. Paul (June 29).

Holy days are like Sundays in that Catholics must attend Mass and, if possible, refrain from unnecessary servile work. Some Catholic countries, such as Italy, Spain, and Ireland, give legal holiday status to some of these holy days so that people can attend Mass and be with family instead of at work.

Simple and solemn celebrations

Catholics believe that Mass can be celebrated in both simple and solemn ways. Simple celebrations, such as weekday Mass, usually have little or no music and singing. They're fairly low-key occasions that attract smaller numbers of parishioners than solemn celebrations.

Solemn celebrations, such as Sunday and holy day Mass, use singing and music. Solemn celebrations may also include the use of incense at different parts of the Mass, the use of gold vestments, the presence of the bishop, or a procession with the Gospel book. This solemnity is given to a holy day not declared a holy day of obligation. For example, the feast day of the saint in whose name the parish is taken (such as St. Ann or St. Bernadette) isn't a day when Catholics must attend Mass, even if they're from that parish; however, the Mass of that feast day can be celebrated with solemnity. In addition, weddings, funerals, ordinations, first Masses of priests, and anniversary Masses honoring the years of marriage (silver and gold) or the years of priesthood are reasons for more solemnity. During these types of celebrations, the Gospel and the Our Father may be chanted to add to the solemnity.

Some feasts of Jesus and Mary — such as the Feast of the Sacred Heart of Jesus (the third Friday after Pentecost) and the Feast of the Annunciation (March 25) — aren't holy days of obligation but are solemnities, which means that the Gloria and the Creed are said at Mass even if it's on a weekday.

Spiritual Seasons of the Year

The *liturgical year* (Church calendar) is as different from the calendar year as the fiscal year is for most people. The Church calendar begins on a different day than the civil year, but it still contains the same 12 months and 365 days. The liturgical year begins on the first Sunday of Advent, which is four Sundays before Christmas. The last Sunday of the year, the Feast of Christ the King, is the Sunday before the first Sunday of Advent.

The Catholic liturgical year revolves around two feasts: Christmas and Easter. They're high holy days because they commemorate the birth and Resurrection of the Church's founder, Jesus Christ. The first half of the liturgical year focuses on the theme *Christ Our Light* and is epitomized by Christmas. The second half focuses on the theme *Christ Our Life,* epitomized by Easter.

Christ Our Light: The first half of the liturgical year

According to the Catholic Church calendar, Advent, Christmas, Epiphany, and the Baptism of the Lord all form the Christ Our Light theme. *Advent,* the season before Christmas, and Christmas itself occur in the winter when, in the Northern Hemisphere, the days are short, and light is often longed for. Candles decorate the Advent wreath — a wreath of evergreen with four candles, three purple or violet and one rose or pink. Each week of Advent, a candle is lit until the fourth week when all four are ablaze. The colors correspond to the vestments the priest and deacon wear on the Sundays of Advent. Advent wreaths are used in Churches and private homes just to remind people to spiritually prepare for Christmas and to give light during these days of less daylight, and to remind the faithful that Jesus is the Light of the World.

Advent is a time for the faithful to prepare for Christmas spiritually in the midst of all the shopping, decorating, baking, and parties. Advent tones down the festivity for Catholics so the real celebration can take place on the birthday of Jesus, Christmas Day. During Advent:

- Catholics typically go to confession to prepare for Christmas.
- Some attend weekday Mass.
- Most try to pray more and practice patience and tolerance (while the rest of the world often goes crazy having Christmas sales in October and bringing out Santa before Halloween).

Usually, by December 25, people have been saturated with Christmas parties and carols. In Catholic parishes, though, no Christmas hymns or music are sung or played until December 25. Then they're sung all the way to New Year's, Epiphany (January 6 — when the Wise Men or Magi came to worship the Christ-child), and ending on the Baptism of the Lord (the Sunday after Epiphany — when John the Baptist baptized Jesus at the River Jordan).

Christ Our Life: The second half of the liturgical year

According to the Church calendar, Lent, Easter, Ascension (40 days after Easter when Jesus ascended into heaven, body and soul), and Pentecost (50 days after Easter when the Holy Spirit came upon the 12 Apostles and the Blessed Virgin Mary in the Upper Room) form the Christ Our Life theme in the liturgical year. *Lent,* the season before Easter, occurs in the spring when new life appears after the death of winter. Easter takes place the first Sunday after the first full moon after the equinox, which means Easter floats every calendar year (as the Jewish Passover does).

Lent is a more penitential time than Advent, but both seasons prepare the faithful for a big feast. Lent begins with Ash Wednesday and lasts for 40 days. Catholics are asked to do modest mortifications and acts of penance during Lent for the purification of the body and soul. Lent is a time of confession, fasting, abstinence, more prayer, more Bible and spiritual reading, and more spiritual and corporal works of mercy. It culminates at Easter when Christ rose triumphant from the dead.

Part III
Living a Saintly Life

The 5th Wave   By Rich Tennant

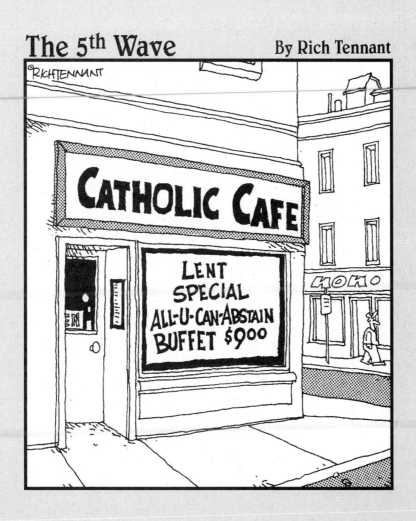

CATHOLIC CAFE

LENT SPECIAL
ALL-U-CAN-ABSTAIN
BUFFET $9.00

MOMO

In this part . . .

Catholics are law-abiding people. We begin this part by explaining God's laws and the Church's rules, both of which its members must follow. We then focus on the most famous divine laws — the Ten Commandments — and discuss why adhering to them is so crucial.

But being good requires more than just avoiding evil; just obeying the Ten Commandments isn't enough. We also have a moral duty to do good and be virtuous. In Chapter 13, we examine good habits every Catholic should cultivate and seven deadly sins to actively fight against. Finally, in Chapter 14 we look at some controversial contemporary issues (real hot-button topics such as abortion, war, and capital punishment) and discuss the Church's commitment to her convictions.

Chapter 11

Obeying the Rules: Catholic Law

● ●

In This Chapter

▶ Defining the different types of laws

▶ Thumbing through canon law

▶ Laying down the law with a few house rules

● ●

*L*aws aren't just arbitrary rules made by those in authority. Governments, clubs, organizations, families, and religions have laws for the common good of their members. Whether for professional baseball or a friendly game of basketball in someone's driveway, an Elks meeting or a session of Congress, all groups have rules of behavior to protect their members from possible abuse or neglect, as well as to preserve the unity and integrity of the whole group.

The Church is considered the family of God, and rules exist to protect that family as a whole, as well as the individual members. Specifically, Catholics are obligated to follow all the divine laws of God, the natural moral law, Church law (also known as *canon law*), and all the legitimate and ethical civil laws of their city, state, and nation as long as they don't contradict the laws of God or the Church. In short, a Catholic is expected to be a law-abiding citizen. This viewpoint is reinforced by what Christ said: "Render to Caesar the things that are Caesar's and to God the things that are God's" (Mark 12:17).

Every morally binding law must make sense, be known, and be of benefit to people. This chapter covers such laws, as they're understood by the Church.

Following the Eternal Law of God

In the 13th century, philosopher and theologian St. Thomas Aquinas (see Chapters 2 and 21) defined *law* as "a command of reason promulgated by a competent authority for the common good." He divided it into the three categories that follow under the main title *the Eternal Law of God:*

✔ Divine positive law

✔ Natural moral law

✔ Human positive law

- Civil (also known as *secular*) law

- Ecclesiastical (also known as *canon*) law

Note that human positive law also comprises civil and ecclesiastical law. But first, we want to explain what *eternal law* means. From all eternity, God has willed that all things act according to their nature. Created things must obey the laws of nature (physics, mathematics, chemistry, gravity, and so on), animals must obey their instincts, and humans must act according to their nature, which is rational. Being rational creatures, humans must also obey authentic laws that conform to reason, are made known, and exist for the common good. So the eternal law is nothing more than the combination of all laws that conform to reason and exist for the common good of everyone.

Only rational beings can know philosophical, theological, and moral laws — so only rational beings are obligated to obey them. Catholics regard these laws as chemists regard formulas, cooks regard recipes, and pharmacists regard prescriptions: If you follow the rules, the results are guaranteed. If you fudge the figures or disregard the directions, the end product is in danger. The soul needs God's laws to find eternal happiness, and obeying them is as crucial for Catholics as following the correct formula is for scientists.

The divine positive law

According to Exodus in the Old Testament, God issued his own set of laws, known as the *Ten Commandments,* which were given to Moses on Mount Sinai. God didn't give Moses ten suggestions or ten proposals but Ten Commandments. These laws aren't negotiable, and they apply to every human being who's at least 7 years old (the age of reason).

The first three commandments deal with your personal relationship with God: Love but one God, honor His name, and honor His day. The last seven deal with interpersonal relationships: Honor your parents and honor other people's lives, property, spouses, and their right to know the truth. Chapter 12 spells out all the details concerning the Ten Commandments.

Because God himself revealed the Ten Commandments, they're considered *divine* law. And because they were spelled out specifically with no room for ambiguity, they're also *positive* law. Hence the term *divine positive law*. For many people, the Ten Commandments — whether or not they're classified under the term *divine positive law* — are still treated as rules and regulations.

But the divine positive law isn't abstract or arbitrary. It's simple and explicit: Thou shall not kill; Thou shall not commit adultery; Thou shall not steal; and so on. The Ten Commandments are all simple and clear. Although the last seven of the ten can be known by reason alone via the natural moral law (see "The natural moral law" section, coming up next), God chose to reinforce and equalize the playing field by divinely revealing them, too, instead of just leaving them for people to figure out on their own.

Think of it like the sticker on a hair dryer that says, "Do not immerse in water while plugged in to outlet." Even though most people know via common sense not to do so, some people don't know that it's dangerous and lethal to let a plugged-in hair dryer fall into water. That's the reason for the stickers. Common sense should also tell folks to honor their parents, not to take an innocent life, not to cheat on their spouses, not to lie, not to steal, and so on. But for some people, common sense doesn't do it. So in His divine mercy, God revealed His divine positive law to remove all doubt and ambiguity.

The natural moral law

The Bible tells the story of Cain murdering his brother Abel centuries before Moses ever received the Ten Commandments, which included the injunction "Thou shall not kill." So if he'd had a good lawyer, such as *Rumpole of the Bailey* or the Dream Team — F. Lee Bailey, Johnny Cochran, and Barry Scheck — could Cain have had his day in court and been acquitted, because the law hadn't been promulgated until *after* the alleged crime took place?

> But your Divinity, my client is innocent of murder because he didn't have access to a Bible, and there's no way he could've known about the Fifth Commandment because it wasn't written down by You and given to Moses until centuries after my client allegedly committed the deed.

Case closed? Not.

The Bible explains that because Cain *knew* he did something wrong, immoral, and sinful, he hid from the Lord. And Moses broke the same commandment (Exodus 2:12) before he got the Ten Commandments. After killing an Egyptian, Moses fled into the desert because he *knew* he did wrong — even though he didn't get the Fifth Commandment for another 18 chapters.

So how did both Cain and Moses know it was wrong to murder an innocent person? And why did other civilizations, such as the Egyptians, Persians, Assyrians, Babylonians, Greeks, and Romans, all have laws forbidding murder, stealing, adultery, perjury, and so on, if they didn't have the revealed Word of God like the Hebrews did? How could Nazi soldiers and officers be condemned at the Nuremburg War Trials for crimes of genocide if they and their government had no religion and no belief in God, let alone any respect for His chosen people? Can all men and women be aware of an unwritten law merely by the use of reason? Does this naturally knowable law apply to all human beings at every time and in every place?

A century before Christ, the Roman stoic philosopher Cicero wrote:

> There is truly a law, which is right reason, fitted to our nature, proclaimed to all men, constant, everlasting. It calls to duty by commanding and deters from wrong by forbidding, neither commanding nor forbidding the good man in vain when it fails to move the wicked. It can neither be evaded nor amended nor wholly abolished. No decree of Senate or people can free us from it. No explainer or interpreter of it need be sought but itself. There will not be found one law at Rome and another at Athens, one now and another later, but one law, everlasting and unchangeable, extending to all nations and all times. (*De Republica*, III, xxii, 33)

And St. Paul the Apostle said:

> When Gentiles who have not the law do by nature what the law requires, they are a law to themselves, even though they do not have the law. They show that what the law requires is written on their hearts (Romans 2:14–15a).

Natural moral law is unwritten but is known by all men and women who have the use of reason. It uses basic common sense, prudence, and justice. Because it's known by reason, not written in stone or on paper, like the Commandments or the Bible, the moral law is *natural*. It's *moral* because it applies only to moral acts — actions of human beings that involve a free act of the will. (It doesn't apply to animals because they don't have the use of reason.)

Because of the natural moral law, Cain and Moses knew it was wrong to commit murder before the Fifth Commandment ever came along. And because of the natural moral law, trials for war crimes can be conducted against anyone who commits genocide or mass murder regardless of the person's religion or lack thereof. A Nazi couldn't have used the defense that he didn't recognize the authority of the Bible because even the most evil of Nazis still had the use of reason, and reason is what discovers the natural moral law for each and every man and woman.

Just obeying orders or following the civil law won't cut it either. An immoral act violates the natural moral law even if it conforms to the local civil law. Slavery was immoral and contrary to natural moral law even though the U.S. Supreme Court (1857) upheld it until it was overturned by the 14th

Amendment (1868) after the Civil War. The Nuremburg Laws of Nazi Germany (1935) also violated the natural moral law because they deprived Jews of their citizenship; paved the way for confiscation of personal property, deportation, and incarceration; and doomed many to the concentration camps. Apartheid is another example: The legalized racial segregation in South Africa from 1948 to 1991 defied the natural moral law. In all these cases, the civil law endorsed, tolerated, or promoted horrible injustices precisely because the natural moral law was being violated. A government, a constitution, a law, or an amendment doesn't grant personhood. It comes from human nature made in the image and likeness of God. Jew and Christian, born and unborn: The natural moral law exists despite what political parties and civil authorities legislate to the contrary.

The human positive law

People — not God or nature — create *human laws*. The Church maintains that natural and divine laws are immutable and eternal because they come from God. However, human laws — whether they come from the Church or the government — are conditioned by contemporary circumstances, such as time, place, and culture. They're *positive* in that they're clearly written and promulgated.

Speed limits of 15 miles per hour in a school zone, income tax laws, and the Patriot Act are all human laws. They're not perfect and can always be improved, changed, interpreted, dissolved, or re-created.

Human laws apply to humans, obviously, so when an animal does damage to property or people, the owners are often responsible. Also, human laws aren't meant to restrict activity and behavior but to protect and defend the inalienable rights of life and liberty of all people. So even though one of the Commandments is "Thou shall not steal," and the natural moral law tells people with reason that taking something that doesn't belong to them is unethical and wrong, civil laws also make theft a crime — a punishable one.

Human positive law comprises both civil law and canon (Church) law.

Civil law

Civil laws are all the laws written and enforced by cities, states, nations, and international communities, such as the United Nations (UN) and the North Atlantic Treaty Organization (NATO). Calgary, Alberta, has laws that apply only to residents of the municipality, but Alberta has laws that apply to all the cities and towns in the province. The Canadian Parliament makes laws that are binding in all its provinces because the Canadian government oversees the whole country.

Some civil laws apply only to residents of the area, and other laws apply to anyone who works at or visits that place, too. For example, speed-limit laws are for everyone, regardless of where you live, vote, or have citizenship, but laws for where and when you vote depend on exactly where you live. Because civil laws (being human laws) aren't perfect, they can and must be interpreted and applied by a recognized authority.

Canon (Church) law

Canon law is the supreme law of the Church, and it specifies the universal norms and regulations for the entire Church. The Catholic Church is a religion and an institution. With more than 1 billion members worldwide and thousands of cardinals, bishops, priests, and deacons to govern the Church, having laws that pertain to activities and people in the Church is both a necessity and a matter of justice.

Getting a taste of canon law

The word *canon* comes from the Greek *kanon,* which means *rule* and refers to decrees that are binding on all persons. *Canon law* refers to the laws that apply to all members of the Catholic faith. The Roman Church has 1,752 canons, and 1,546 canons are in the Eastern Catholic Church. That's quite a few more than the Ten Commandments, eh? It could be worse — the number of Roman Catholic canons actually decreased in 1983; 2,414 canons filled the Code from 1917 to 1982! The *Code of Canon Law* is the book containing the laws of the Catholic Church. The edition for the Western (Latin) Church is separate from the Eastern (Byzantine) Church edition.

The Code of Canon Law is patterned according to the Vatican II document *Lumen Gentium* (Dogmatic Constitution on the Church), which describes the Catholic Church as the living and continuing presence of Christ on earth — his mystical body and spotless bride. The Church that Christ himself founded continues his three-fold mission as priest, prophet, and king — to sanctify, teach, and govern. Laws allow the Church to govern.

Some laws protect rights and privileges; others define obligations and duties. Following are some examples:

- Canon 226 reminds parents that they're the primary teachers of their children and, therefore, they are responsible to God for their sons' and daughters' religious education and practice.

- Canon 208 emphasizes the genuine equality of dignity and action among all of Christ's faithful. This means that clergy aren't better than laity, and both have equal importance, although they have different functions.

- Canon 212 guarantees that everyone has a right to make known their spiritual needs to their pastors.

✔ Canon 221 states that all the faithful (laity and clergy) have a right to due process in church tribunals and ecclesiastical courts.

✔ Canon 281 guarantees clergy fair wages, and Canon 283 assures them reasonable time off — one weekly day off and 30 days of annual vacation (533).

✔ Canon 276 highly encourages priests, deacons, and bishops to participate in daily Mass and obliges them to daily pray the Liturgy of the Hours, make an annual retreat, go to confession often, and honor and venerate the Virgin Mary.

Facing punishment for violations

Law exists to protect the common good, and sometimes that requires disciplining those who violate the rules and thereby endanger the community as well as themselves. Sanctions are medicinal punishments meant to encourage a person to stop doing something harmful. Normally, the penalty is removed soon after the offender repents and ceases to break the law.

Some of the punishments handed down by the ecclesiastical court system include interdict, suspension, and excommunication.

✔ **Interdict:** This is a temporary penalty that can be applied to one or more persons, either of the clergy or laity. Under this punishment, the persons named can't receive the sacraments, but they aren't excommunicated, so they still can receive income, hold office, and so on. The sanction is lifted when the person repents and seeks reconciliation.

✔ **Suspension:** Applying to clergy only, the Church forbids priest, deacon, or bishop to exercise his ordained ministry and to wear clerical garb. However, suspension doesn't deprive the cleric of receiving the sacraments.

✔ **Excommunication:** The most severe form of penalty, *excommunication,* which means being outside of the Church, is used only as a last resort, with the hope that the excommunicated person, whether cleric or layperson, will repent and seek reconciliation. Excommunicated people are deprived of the sacraments, such as receiving the Holy Eucharist at Mass. The excommunicated are also forbidden from employment or holding any position of authority in a diocese or parish and are deprived of a Catholic burial. However, penalties are suspended in danger of death. If the excommunicated person shows a sign of repentance before he dies, then he's allowed Catholic funeral rites.

Some excommunications are automatic and occur as soon as the offense is committed, without formal declaration by the Church. Others are imposed by the local bishop by formal decree.

Taking it to the top

Because the pope possesses full, supreme, immediate, and universal ordinary power (authority) to govern the Catholic Church (Canon 331), no member of the Church or its clergy can appeal a papal decision (Canon 333), and even an attempt to appeal to an ecumenical council is forbidden (Canon 1372). Even though no higher authority exists on earth than the *Holy* *See* (the term used to describe the pope and his staff), every single baptized Catholic has the right to appeal directly to Rome and to the pope (Canon 1417). This appeal is sometimes called *the appeal to Caesar* based on the ancient right of every Roman citizen to plead his case before the emperor.

Of the three, excommunication is the most serious and most severe. Often people ask, "Why, then, are not murder, rape, or sexual abuse of children listed as crimes worthy of excommunication?" The main reason is that these horrible sins are also violations of civil law and already incur serious penalties that only the state can impose, such as imprisonment.

Sins that violate divine, natural, and/or Church law are not always in violation of civil law. Abortion is legal in many places but is still considered a grave evil because it's the direct and actual killing of an innocent human life. The sin of abortion incurs an automatic excommunication (Canon 1398) for all direct participants and necessary accomplices as long as each one knows there is a serious penalty for that crime.

Canon 1323, however, stipulates that no one can be excommunicated who

- ✔ Has not turned 17
- ✔ Was, without fault, ignorant of violating the law
- ✔ Acted under physical force or under a chance occurrence that could not be foreseen or avoided
- ✔ Acted under compulsion of grave fear
- ✔ Lacked the use of reason

Some penalties (for example, those for heresy, pretended celebration of the Holy Eucharist, or procuring an abortion) can be lifted by any priest when the offender goes to confession in the Sacrament of Penance. Other penalties are so serious that only the local bishop or, in some grave offenses, only the pope can remove them. For example, only the pope can remove the offenses of desecration of sacred species (Holy Communion) or physical attack on the pope himself. To find out more about punishment for different offenses, check out the Code of Canon Law.

Playing by the Church's Rules

While the 1983 Code of Canon Law has 1,752 laws, the Church has only five *precepts,* which are the Catholic Church's house rules — the basic recipe for spiritual health for each and every Catholic. Just as schoolchildren must at least attend school daily in order to remain in school and employees must show up for work each day to keep their paychecks coming, so, too, Catholics must do the minimum by following these five precepts. These simple precepts are, of course, in addition to the Ten Commandments, which apply to every Christian (Protestant, Catholic, and Orthodox) and Jew alike. But the precepts of the Church are binding only on Catholics. To be a good, practicing Catholic means believing what the Church teaches and obeying these rules:

- ✔ Attend Mass on all Sundays and holy days of obligation.
- ✔ Receive the Holy Eucharist during Easter season.
- ✔ Confess your sins at least once a year.
- ✔ Fast and abstain on appointed days.
- ✔ Contribute to the support of the Church.

In the United States, the American bishops added two more precepts:

- ✔ Observe the marriage laws of the Church.
- ✔ Support missionary work of the Church.

Except for the Ten Commandments and the natural moral law, most Catholics aren't well versed in the 1983 *Code of Canon Law* because so many laws exist. But Catholics are aware of the precepts of the Church, which are personal applications of the numerous canons from the Code.

Nowadays, the minimum requirements for the precepts are manageable — they're not nearly as burdensome as they were in the old, old days (back when monks were monks and nuns were nuns). Of course, personal piety may motivate some people to go beyond the minimum by, for example, praying the Rosary daily, going to confession once a week, or attending Mass once or twice during the week in addition to Sunday.

Attending Mass on all Sundays and holy days of obligation

Catholics must regularly and faithfully attend and participate in a Catholic Mass each and every Sunday and holy day of obligation. Missing Mass on one of these days is a mortal sin. (See Chapters 9 and 13 for more on mortal sin.)

Only inclement weather and bad health that would prevent you from leaving home at all excuse you from the obligation of going to Mass that day.

Even on vacation, Catholics are obliged to attend Mass. Non-Catholic religious services are fine as long as Catholics don't attempt to substitute a non-Catholic worship service for the Mass. So, for example, if you attend a Lutheran Sunday service, you still have to go to Sunday Mass in addition if you're a Catholic. See Chapter 10 for more on the holy days of obligation.

Receiving the Holy Eucharist during Easter season

Catholics must receive the Holy Eucharist at least once during the Easter season, which for U.S. Catholics is from Ash Wednesday to Trinity Sunday. We explain the meaning and importance of the Holy Eucharist in Chapters 8 and 10.

In the Middle Ages, many Catholics, feeling personally unworthy, received the Eucharist only rarely even though the Church never endorsed that they go only occasionally. Pope St. Pius X (he was pope from 1903–1914), however, felt that Catholics should receive Christ every time that they went to Mass as long as they were without the blemish of mortal sin. So Catholics were encouraged and prepared for more frequent reception, which is why this precept was created. The Church requires that Catholics fast for an hour before receiving the Eucharist. This means that Catholics can't eat or drink anything besides water or necessary medication for at least an hour before receiving the Holy Eucharist.

Receiving Holy Eucharist once a year during the Easter season is the minimum requirement for Catholics, and receiving it twice a day — if you attend two Masses — is the maximum allowed.

Confessing your sins at least once a year

Confessing your sins once a year applies only if you're guilty and conscious of a mortal sin. Full consent of the will, full knowledge, and grave matter are all required elements for mortal sin. (See Chapters 9 and 13 for more on mortal sin.) Missing Sunday Mass without a valid excuse (such as really bad weather or serious illness), a sin of the flesh, and blasphemy by using God's name in vain are all mortal sins. These sins and all other mortal sins must be confessed before a Catholic can worthily receive the Holy Eucharist. The bare-minimum requirement is that those in a state of mortal sin must go to confession before receiving the Holy Eucharist. Otherwise, they've committed another mortal sin — the *sacrilege* of receiving Communion when in the state of mortal sin, a sort of spiritual double jeopardy. Before Vatican II (see Appendix A), most Catholics went to confession every week before going to Communion.

Fasting and abstaining on appointed days

Today, *abstaining* applies to all Catholics age 14 and older and means that they must not eat meat on Ash Wednesday, Good Friday, and all Fridays in Lent. (Meat is any beef, pork, chicken, or fowl.) *Fasting* applies to all Catholics ages 18 to 59 and means they must eat only one full meal on Ash Wednesday and Good Friday, which means no snacks between meals. However, two smaller meals, such as breakfast and lunch, can be eaten in addition to the one full meal (supper) as long as they don't equal the one full meal if combined.

Some Eastern Catholics and many Orthodox Christians observe the *Great Fast,* meaning they don't eat any meat, egg, or dairy products during all 40 days of Lent, and they often fast every Friday — if not every day — of Lent (from midnight to noon) except on Sundays (to honor the Resurrection).

Before Vatican II, *every* Friday of the year — Lent or not — was a day of abstinence from meat. Today, in most countries, only Fridays in Lent are obligatory, but the Church highly recommends abstinence on Fridays during the rest of the year to show respect for the day Christ died and sacrificed his flesh on the cross. The Church also recommends that if Catholics don't abstain on Fridays outside of Lent, they should do some small form of penance or work of mercy, nevertheless.

Contributing to the support of the Church

Although *tithing,* giving 10 percent of your income to the parish, is mentioned in the Bible (Leviticus 27:30–34), it isn't mandatory in the Catholic Church. Most Catholics are encouraged to donate at least 5 percent of their income to the parish and 5 percent to their favorite charities. Statistically, though, Catholics are notoriously the lowest givers of all Christians, dedicating 1 percent of their incomes to the Church. Mainline Protestants give 2 percent, and Evangelical and Fundamentalist Christians give 5 to 10 percent.

But those who can't give much financial support can and often do donate an abundance of volunteer time to the parish by holding fundraisers and supporting other parish events and projects. Volunteers sometimes teach religious education programs for children, sometimes known as the Confraternity of Christian Doctrine (CCD) classes and the Rite of Christian Initiation of Adults (RCIA) classes (convert classes for adults). Catholic children who can't attend a Catholic school learn about the Catholic faith through CCD classes, and non-Catholics who are interested in the Catholic faith attend RCIA classes, usually at a local parish. Those volunteers who are too old or infirm for other types of service support the parish with their prayers. Giving of one's time and talent, as well as giving of your treasure (financial contributions), are ways that Catholic Christians support their church, from the parish to the diocese.

In the eyes of the Church, nobody goes to heaven merely by earning their way through obedience, because salvation is a free gift from God. But following the laws of God (divine and natural laws) and the laws of His Church help a person be a better person, a better Christian, and a better Catholic. These rules and regulations help promote holiness just as following your doctor's advice and prescriptions helps promote good health.

Observing Church marriage laws

Like we said before, this precept isn't given in the Catechism as one of the five, but Catholics in America are asked to abide by it. Catholics must be married with two witnesses before a priest, bishop, or deacon in a Catholic Church at a Catholic wedding ceremony, unless a special *dispensation* (a special allowance in light of circumstances that warrant it) has been granted from the local bishop for the couple to be married by a non-Catholic minister in a non-Catholic ceremony at a non-Catholic church.

In addition, Catholics ought to take 9 to 12 months to prepare for their marriage. During this prep time, called the *Pre-Cana period,* the couple receives practical advice and instructions from the priest or deacon. Catholics can only marry someone who has never been married before, or the intended spouse must have an official annulment from a previous marriage. And both the bride and groom must intend to enter a permanent, faithful, and (God willing) fruitful union for it to be a valid sacrament. (See Chapter 9 for much more information about the Sacrament of Matrimony.)

Supporting Missionary Work of the Church

American bishops ask that the faithful pray regularly for the success of the Church's missions abroad, provide financial support when possible, and encourage priests, brothers, and sisters to enter *vocations,* or callings, to be missionaries around the world. Spiritual and material support for those who are helping others is a challenge to all the faithful, since Catholics belong to a universal and not just a local church community.

Chapter 12

Loving and Honoring:
The Ten Commandments

In This Chapter

▶ Honoring God, His name, and His day

▶ Loving the folks next door and all down the block

▶ Going neck and neck on the Ten Commandments

The Catholic Church sees the Ten Commandments as one of the four *pillars of faith,* along with the Creed (the Apostles' Creed and the Nicene Creed), the seven sacraments, and the Our Father. They're called the *pillars of faith* because they're the foundations upon which the Catholic Church is built, just as an altar would have four solid pillars to support itself. Each pillar represents a major component of Catholicism, and all four together establish the core of Catholic belief and practice. The Church treats the Ten Commandments as divine laws from God that the Church and pope can never change, add to, or subtract from.

The Church doesn't see the Ten Commandments as arbitrary rules and regulations from the man upstairs but as commandments for protection. Obey them, and eternal happiness is yours. Disobey them and suffer the consequences.

The Ten Commandments have also been called the *Decalogue* (Greek) and the *Debarim* (Hebrew), both of which mean *the Ten Words.*

Many a preacher has said, "These are the Ten Commandments, not the Ten Suggestions." True enough. Just as a prescription tells you how many pills to take and how often, the Commandments tell us what to do and what not to do in the moral life. Disregard the formula in the laboratory, and the chemicals you mix may explode. Ignore grandma's favorite recipe and carelessly fail to measure the ingredients, and the end result won't taste good. Likewise, disobey the Commandments now, and expect eternal misery in the afterlife.

Demonstrating Love for God

The first three commandments focus on the individual's relationship with God. The main objectives are to honor God, His name, and His day.

1: Honor God

The First Commandment is "I am the Lord your God, you shall not have strange gods before Me." This commandment forbids *idolatry,* the worship of false gods and goddesses, and it forbids *polytheism,* the belief in many gods, insisting instead on *monotheism,* the belief in one God. So the obvious and blatant ways to break this commandment are to

- ✔ Worship a false god, be it Hercules, Zena, or Satan
- ✔ Consciously and willingly deny the existence of God, as in the case of atheism or having no religion whatsoever

The Catholic Church looks at the commandment — the letter of the law and the spirit of the law — and tries to apply it to daily life. Granted, in the 21st century, the Church doesn't see many people worshipping idols like they used to do in pagan Greece and Rome. But refraining from building golden calves or statues of Caesar in your house aren't the only ways you can obey the First Commandment.

Rejecting false belief systems

You can break the First Commandment by willingly and consciously being ignorant of what God has revealed in Sacred Scripture (the Bible) and Sacred Tradition (see Chapter 2), as well as by believing in and/or seriously using *astrology* (horoscopes), numerology, and *dianetics,* which refers to the Church of Scientology.

Another way to break this commandment is to become involved with *New Age spirituality,* which is an informal religion of no creed, no liturgy, no doctrine, and no church structure, leadership, or institution. This type of religion blends ancient paganism with the occult, superstition, Gnosticism, and so on. It's extremely different from the three monotheistic religions of Judaism, Christianity, and Islam.

Dabbling in witchcraft, sorcery, devil worship, white or black magic, voodoo, *spiritism* (communicating with the dead), *fortune telling* (which is also known as psychic reading), tarot cards, Ouija boards, lucky charms, and such are all violations of this commandment, too.

Sacrilege, the desecration of holy objects, and *simony,* trying to buy or sell spiritual favors or graces, are also ways in which you can break the First Commandment. The Church believes that all these things are forbidden by the first commandment because they don't put the one, true God before all else — and many of them put credence in superstition.

Tuning out the distractions and putting God first

Today, we think the most common way that the First Commandment is broken is when you put someone or something before God. In other words, God isn't your highest priority. According to Catholicism, when career, fame, fortune, comfort, pleasure, family, or a friend, for example, is your most important object, value, or priority, you're violating the First Commandment.

Even though you're not denying the existence of God or showing contempt for God or things symbolizing the divine, the Church believes that you're showing disrespect by not making God your highest priority and most cherished relationship. When you're too busy to go to church every week or going to church becomes too inconvenient, yet you have time to attend every soccer game for Susie, music recital for Johnny, and football game at your favorite college, then God's no longer *numero uno* in your life.

The Bible, Jesus Christ, and the Catholic Church say that you're to love God "with all your heart, and with all your soul, and with all your strength, and with all your mind" (Luke 10:27). So no one and no thing can be number one in your heart except God.

Spending QT with God

To the Church, the First Commandment implies that if God is the most important person in your life, you'll want to honor Him, spend quality time with Him, and communicate with Him daily through prayer. Prayer enables you to speak to God with your heart and mind — vocally or mentally — and neglecting to pray, or intentionally not praying, violates the First Commandment.

Honoring, not idolizing, Mary and the saints

According to the First Commandment, only God the Father, God the Son, and God the Holy Spirit are entitled to and deserve worship and adoration. Worshipping or adoring anyone or anything else is idolatry and forbidden. Yet Catholics are sometimes accused of idolatry for the prayer and honor they give to the saints — especially the highest honor and respect they give to Mary, the Mother of Jesus. While worship of anyone or anything other than God is idolatry, adoration is only one form of prayer. Intercessory prayer addressed to the Virgin Mary and the Saints isn't worship, but spiritual communication.

In Catholicism, the devotion to and veneration of Mary and the saints aren't considered idolatry because devotion, honor, and veneration aren't considered the same as worship and adoration. The Fourth Commandment, "Honor your father and mother," shows the faithful that honoring a human being, like mom or dad, is permissible — even commanded — because honor isn't adoration or worship. And in the Gospel, even Jesus showed honor to dead people, such as Abraham and Moses, speaking of them with great respect.

Catholics believe that if humans can and must honor their parents, then it's only logical to honor the faithful servants of God who lived holy lives on earth and are now in heaven before the throne of God.

11: Honor God's name

The Second Commandment, "You shall not take the name of the Lord your God in vain," tells the faithful to honor the name of God, which goes hand in hand with the First Commandment saying to honor the person of God by not worshipping anyone else. It makes sense that if you're to love God with all your heart, soul, mind, and strength, then you're naturally to respect the name of God with equal passion and vigor.

Avoiding blasphemy

Imagine a man using his fiancée's name whenever he wants to curse. How can he say that he loves his girlfriend if he shows contempt for her very name? A person's name is part of who that person is, and respect for the name is respect for the person. Disrespect and contempt for the name equal disrespect for the person.

So Catholics believe that using God's name — especially the name *Jesus Christ* — to swear and curse when, say, a car cuts you off in traffic, a bird leaves a little surprise on your new suit, or a stranger waves with his middle finger is disrespectful to God. It's using the sacred name of the Lord and Savior to show anger and hostility. It's ironic that many who claim to be followers of Christ show their anger and animosity by using His name. Think about it. When was the last time you heard someone say *Jesus Christ?* Was it in prayer or shouted from an open window?

Using God's name in a disrespectful manner is *blasphemy,* and it's the essence of the Second Commandment.

Respecting holy things and holy oaths

Any act of disrespect to anything holy — be it a holy image, place, or person — is considered a *sacrilege,* and it's forbidden by the Second

Commandment. The Church believes that you're being irreligious when you show contempt for God, such as by desecrating a holy object or place. When a house of worship — a church, temple, synagogue, or mosque — is vandalized, the Church maintains that the sin of sacrilege has been committed; a house of God was desecrated, and contempt was shown not solely for those who attend the house's services but also and preeminently for the person the place was built for.

You're also violating the Second Commandment if you make jokes, watch movies, or read books that are disrespectful to God or anything considered holy. So for a Catholic, if you ridicule or laugh at a Jewish man for wearing a *yarmulke* (skull cap), a Muslim woman for wearing a *khimar* (head covering), a nun for wearing her religious habit, or a priest for wearing a *cassock* (a long, close-fitting garment, usually black), you're being sacrilegious. Human beings wear certain things out of religious tradition, or they perform certain rituals as an external way of showing their love for God. When others make fun of religious garb or religious practices, it's an insult to the one being honored by them, in other words, God Himself.

The Second Commandment also forbids false oaths and perjury. So to place your hand on the Holy Bible and swear to tell the whole truth and nothing but the truth, "so help me God," and then tell a lie is considered perjury and a serious violation of this commandment. Also, when a couple plans to get married, they meet with a priest or deacon and fill out papers that ask questions, such as "Were you ever married before?" and "Do you intend to enter a permanent, faithful, and, God willing, fruitful union?" They're asked to sign this document, and by doing so, they're placing themselves under oath and saying that they've answered all the questions truthfully. Lying about any of the questions is considered a false oath — a mortal sin. (See Chapter 9 for more about mortal sin.)

III: Honor God's day

The Third Commandment is "Remember to keep holy the Lord's day." The Jewish celebration of Sabbath *(Shabbat)* begins at sundown on Friday evening and lasts until sundown on Saturday. So, basically, Saturday is the Sabbath Day. It's the last day of the week, the seventh day, the day (according to the Book of Genesis) on which God rested after six days of creation. Even modern calendars have Saturday as the last day of the week and Sunday as the first day of the new week.

So why, then, do Catholic, Protestant, and Orthodox Christians go to church on Sunday, treating it as the Lord's Day instead of Saturday? In general, Catholicism and Christianity moved the celebration of the Lord's Day from

Saturday to Sunday because Jesus Christ rose from the dead on Easter Sunday. In other words, Sunday has become the Christian Sabbath, the day of rest, to honor the day Christ rose from the dead. Jesus said in the Gospel that the Sabbath was made for man, not man for the Sabbath. So, Christians who wanted to honor their Risen Lord on the day of the week that He rose from the dead made Sunday their day of worship instead of the former day of Saturday, which the Hebrews had honored from the time of Moses.

Catholics are also bound to attend a Catholic Mass on each and every Sunday or the Vigil Mass on Saturday of every weekend in the calendar year. To miss Mass on Sunday is considered a mortal sin unless the person has a legitimate excuse, such as serious illness.

Ever wonder why some Catholics go to Mass on Saturday evening instead of Sunday morning? Using the Hebrew method of time reckoning, after sundown on Saturday evening is actually the beginning of Sunday, so the Church allows parishes to offer a Saturday evening *Vigil Mass* to satisfy the Sunday obligation.

But just going to a Christian Sunday worship service isn't good enough. In order for Catholics to satisfy and fulfill the Third Commandment, they must attend a valid Catholic Mass. Going to another denomination for a Sunday worship service is nice, but Catholics must also attend Mass the evening before or sometime during the day on Sunday. The reason is that the Church maintains that only the Mass has the real, true, and substantial presence of Christ in the Holy Eucharist. Even if a Catholic doesn't receive Holy Communion, she still satisfies the Sunday obligation by attending and participating at Mass.

The Third Commandment also forbids doing any servile work — unnecessary hard labor — on the Lord's Day, because it's a day of rest. And Pope John Paul II wrote a document about Sunday, *Dies Domini* (Latin for *Day of the Lord*), in which he reminded Catholics of the serious obligation to attend Mass each and every weekend and to refrain from doing unnecessary manual work.

To meet this obligation, all Catholics would optimally have Sunday off, so they'd have the opportunity to go to church and spend time with family. But in reality, some people must work frequently on Sundays — doctors, nurses, pharmacists, police officers, firefighters, and so on. Pastors can transfer the obligation to another day, but only on an individual basis and only for serious reasons.

Loving Your Neighbor

The last seven of the Ten Commandments focus on the individual's relationship with others. The main objectives are to honor your parents, human life, human sexuality, the property of others, and the truth.

IV: Honor your parents

The Fourth Commandment, "Honor your father and mother," obliges the faithful to show respect for their parents — as children *and* adults. Children must obey their parents, and adults must respect and see to the care of their parents when they become old and infirm.

Therefore, the Catholic Church believes that adult children who abandon, abuse, or neglect their elderly parents are violating the Fourth Commandment as much as teenage children who refuse to show respect or obedience to their parents. Likewise, being ashamed or embarrassed of your parents is considered as much a sin as disobeying them when you're a child or harboring feelings of hatred or revenge for them even if they weren't the parents they should have been.

This commandment is meant to protect the dignity and integrity of the family, which consists of a father, a mother, and their children. Obviously, some families are headed by a single parent because of the death or illness of the absent parent or because the absent parent was abusive or delinquent; in such sad circumstances, some people manage to do a terrific job at parenting solo. However, many single-parent households exist simply because the parents never married in the first place. Catholicism teaches that this commandment frowns on the option of freely and willingly choosing to establish a single-parent family. Voluntary single parenthood is considered an abuse because, all things being equal, a child deserves both a loving mother and a loving father.

Whether it's adopting a child or having your own, parenthood should be sought and tried within the context of the family, which means a husband and a wife to be the mother and the father, rather than just being a parent by yourself. Just as the Church discourages parenthood outside of marriage, she also condemns artificial insemination — especially from donors not married to the potential mother.

According to the Church, children deserve (if possible) to have both parents. The Church also believes that even if the children are adopted, parenthood means both genders. So two men or two women can't replace the divine plan that everyone deserves — a father and a mother. Check out Chapter 14 for more details on these touchy, but important, family matters.

The Catholic Church believes this commandment means more than just keeping order in the home and preventing the kids from establishing anarchy. It also entails and implies a respect and honor for everyone in legitimate positions of authority — be they civilian, military, or *ecclesiastical* (church-related). Teachers, employers, police officers, and so on have some degree of authority over others, and the Fourth Commandment requires that respect be shown to those given the responsibility of taking care of others. Whether you like or dislike the person who was elected president or prime minister, for example, the office demands some respect and dignity if, say, the prime minister enters the room. To show contempt or disrespect is considered sinful.

In the same line of thinking, this commandment also involves respect and love for your country. Patriotism isn't the same as nationalism. The former is a healthy love and respect for your country, but the latter is blind, total, and unrestricted support for any and all legislation, policies, or activities of a nation. Nationalism is the extreme, whereas patriotism is the goal, because good patriots know when to challenge their political leaders, laws, and policies when they become unjust or immoral.

For Catholics, this commandment recognizes the natural right of the family and of the state to form society. The family is the primary and fundamental building block from which comes the civil union of many families into a local and national government. And the family is the basis for the faith community of the Church, which is the family of God and the union of all the natural families around the world.

V: Honor human life

In English, the Fifth Commandment is read as "You shall not kill," but the Hebrew word *ratsach* (murder) was used rather than *nakah* (kill), so the better translation would be "Thou shalt not murder." And St. Jerome used the Latin word *occidere* (to murder) instead of *interficere* (to kill) when he translated the Hebrew into the *Latin Vulgate,* which was the first complete Christian Bible combining the Old and New Testaments in one volume and translated.

It's a subtle distinction but an important one to the Church. Killing an innocent person is considered murder. Killing an unjust aggressor to preserve your own life is still killing, but it isn't considered murder or immoral by any means. The use of deadly force is morally permitted *only* if it's the last resort and if the person isn't innocent — he or she must be guilty of a most serious offense or threatening to commit such horrible evil.

Forbidding unjust killings

The Catholic Church believes that murder is the sin prohibited in the Fifth Commandment. Killing in self-defense has always been considered justifiable and morally permissible. This distinction is the reason that when God ordered the Israelites to kill sometimes in the Old Testament, it wasn't a violation of the Fifth Commandment. Only unjust killing (taking innocent life) or murder is forbidden. Likewise, police officers and soldiers may have to use deadly force in certain well-defined and restricted circumstances. Again, this is morally permitted. Yet the legitimate taking of life isn't casual, unlicensed, unrestricted, or uncontrolled. The Church sees it as only a last resort — rare rather than common.

In broader terms, the Church believes that the intentional taking of innocent life includes murder (homicide or manslaughter), abortion, euthanasia, suicide, in most cases the death penalty, and even the old custom of dueling. The Church also condemns terrorism, violence, and any unjust war or physical abuse.

Taking issue with capital punishment

Capital punishment, whereby the death penalty is inflicted on someone guilty of a grisly murder, is obviously not the same as the murder of an innocent person. The pope and the Catechism acknowledge the theoretical right of the state (civil government) to resort to this extreme measure, but its actual implementation must be morally done across the board.

Because capital punishment is not currently performed universally, uniformly, and equitably, the Church claims that very few if any circumstances or situations today fulfill the moral criteria to allow the death penalty to be carried out. Because some countries outlaw it and others do not; some states and provinces allow it and others do not; location has plenty to do with capital punishment. How just is it to put criminals to death based on where the crime took place? Is life more or less sacred in one location than another? Also, several means of capital punishment are more humane than others. Does making it *painless* make it more acceptable?

Finally, it's often the poor who get executed because the rich and famous can hire expensive lawyers to appeal their cases. The poor people are given public defenders and don't have the money to make appeals. Based on the inequities of place, diversity of means, and unfairness of economics as to who has access to aggressive attorneys and long appeal processes, the reality of the death penalty overrules the theory that some criminals can be morally executed as a last resort. Although not totally condemning capital punishment, the Catechism does strongly discourage it. Whenever an innocent life is unjustly taken, it is always condemned as murder.

Recognizing other violations

More subtle violations of this commandment, according to the Church, include growing angry in your heart with your neighbor, harboring feelings of hatred or revenge, being criminally negligent (such as refusing to save someone's life when you're able to do so), and committing personal abuse (which is intentionally neglecting to take care of your own health and safety).

Abusing drugs and alcohol is considered breaking the Fifth Commandment because it recklessly endangers the user's life and potentially endangers others if someone under the influence becomes violent and irrational. Drunk driving is considered a violation because drunk drivers are jeopardizing their own lives and the lives of others by using an auto under the influence.

Mutilation and torture of human or animal life is also considered breaking the Fifth Commandment. Using animals for medical and scientific research is permitted as long as no suffering or unnecessary death is involved. To boot, psychological or emotional abuse is considered forbidden because such abuse attacks the victim with unjust consequences.

Because the natural moral law (see Chapter 11) tells anyone with the use of reason that the intentional, direct taking of innocent life is immoral and wrong, the Fifth Commandment is no secret nor is it a change from general human experience. In the Bible, Cain knew it was wrong to murder his brother Abel, even though it was centuries before Moses ever received all Ten Commandments. And the Nazis who were convicted of war crimes, such as genocide, were found guilty not by reason of the Fifth Commandment but because of the natural moral law, which also outlaws such atrocities.

VI and IX: Honor human sexuality

The Sixth Commandment is "You shall not commit adultery," and the ninth is "You shall not covet your neighbor's wife." Both deal with honoring human sexuality.

The Sixth Commandment forbids the actual, physical act of having immoral sexual activity, specifically adultery, which is sex with someone else's spouse or a spouse cheating on his or her partner. But this commandment also includes *fornication,* which is sex between unmarried people, prostitution, pornography, homosexual activity, masturbation, group sex, rape, incest, pedophilia, bestiality, and necrophilia.

The Ninth Commandment forbids the intentional desire and longing for immoral sexuality. To sin in the heart, Jesus says, is to lust after a woman or a man with the desire and will to have immoral sex with that person. Committing the act of sex outside of marriage is sinful, and wanting to do it is immoral as well, just as hating your neighbor is like killing him in your heart (Matthew 5:21-22). Just as human life is a gift from God and needs to be respected, defended, and protected, so, too, is human sexuality. Catholicism regards human sexuality as a divine gift, so it's considered sacred in the proper context — marriage.

Taking the cake: Marriage

The Church believes that sexual intercourse was ordained by God and designed exclusively for a husband and wife. Marriage is the best, most sacred, and most efficient union of man and woman because God created marriage. It's a sign of the permanent, faithful, and hopefully fruitful covenant that's made on the day that the man and woman make their vows and exchange consent. Human sexual activity is designed to promote love (unity) and life (procreation). And whenever that formula is altered or divided, the Church believes that sin enters the equation.

Only sex between a husband and wife is considered moral, and even then, the couple must be mutually respectful of each other. If the sole objective is personal pleasure and nothing more, then even a husband or wife sins by reducing his or her partner to a sex object or just a means to self-gratification. For example, using pornography or any kind of sex toy is strictly forbidden in the eyes of the Church.

So married sex is considered holy and sacred when it focuses on the unity of the couple as husband and wife — two human people who deserve dignity, respect, communication, honesty, fidelity, and compassion. To the Church, human sexuality isn't an end but a means to an end — the greater unity between husband and wife and the possibility of new life.

Planning a family the natural way

Catholicism doesn't teach that married couples *must* have as many children as biologically possible. It allows for Natural Family Planning (NFP), which is *not* the old, archaic, and unreliable rhythm method. So responsible parents can morally decide how large or small a family they can reasonably afford, raise, and maintain, as long as moral means are employed to do so.

Contraceptive sex, the Church says, divides the bond of love and life, unity and procreation — isolating the dimension of human sexuality that unites two people from the possible procreative level. Likewise, any form of human reproduction that results from anything other than sexual intercourse, such as surrogate mothers, sperm banks, in vitro fertilization, human cloning, and all methods of artificial conception are equally sinful because they isolate and separate the God-intended bond of the unitive and procreative. Sex outside of marriage and conception outside of sex are considered violations of the unity within human sexuality. For more info about the Church's stand on these and other sticky issues, turn to Chapter 14.

Cheating and philandering don't cut it

The Church teaches that sex outside of and/or before marriage is considered sinful and immoral, but strictly speaking, *adultery* is having sex with someone else's spouse or cheating on your own spouse by having sex with someone else. Catholicism says that adultery is primarily a sin against justice because all married couples make a solemn oath, a sacred covenant, to be faithful to each other until death. So marital infidelity is an injustice as well as a selfish and irresponsible sin of the flesh. Don Juans and desperate housewives needn't apply.

Playing footsie with fire

Even though the average Joe may think nothing of experimenting with sex before marriage, the Church says that true love means wanting what's best for the other person — body and soul. Having sex before or outside of marriage, whether it's a one-night stand or a long-term shack-up, isn't sanctioned or blessed by God and lacks respect for the people involved. True love and respect mean you'd never want to lure the one you love into a sinful situation any more than you'd intentionally lead that person into a scenario that would endanger his or her life or health. So having sex supposedly just to show your love is considered a lie.

It's all about a covenant — the glue that bonds

Catholic teachings on sexuality are based on the biblical notion of covenant: A man and woman enter a permanent, faithful, and hopefully fruitful covenant of marriage. So, too, marriage is often a metaphor that describes the covenant relationship between God and the Hebrew people and between Jesus Christ and His Church. The sign of that marriage covenant between two people is licit sexual activity that honors and respects each as a human person and doesn't treat either one as a mere sex object or tool for personal use. Animals have sex out of instinct to perpetuate the species, but human beings have the use of reason and free will, which makes humankind "in the image and likeness of God" (Genesis 1:27). Unlike animals, humans can choose when, with whom, and why to have sex.

Engaging in sexual intercourse without a lifelong commitment blessed by God is also dishonest. Having sex before or outside of marriage is considered dishonest because the people involved deserve only the best, and the best is the total gift of self — lifelong commitment, fidelity, and openness to the possibility that God may use this couple to bring a new human life into the world.

VII and X: *Honor the property of others*

The Seventh Commandment, "You shall not steal," and the tenth commandment, "You shall not covet your neighbor's goods," focus on respecting and honoring the possessions of others.

The Seventh Commandment forbids the act of taking someone else's property, and the Tenth Commandment forbids wanting to do so.

Explicitly, these two commandments condemn theft and the feelings of envy, greed, and jealousy in reaction to what other people have. The Catholic Church believes that, implicitly, these commandments also denounce cheating people of their money or property, depriving workers of their just wage, or not giving employers a full day's work for a full day's pay. Embezzlement, fraud, tax evasion, and vandalism are all considered extensions of violations of the Seventh Commandment. Showing disrespect for the private ownership of someone else's property — be it money or possessions — occurs when these sinful acts take place.

In addition, the Church believes that governments have no right to usurp private property and nationalize businesses, and they do have an obligation to protect private property and to help individuals and other nations in great need.

The Church maintains that personal property is a fundamental right, but it's not considered an absolute right. If a person owns more food than he needs, and someone comes along who is starving, the person with more food than he needs is obligated to share with the one who's starving. In the same way, governments and corporations have no right to deny the individual his inalienable right to private property. But although private property is a right, it's subservient to higher values, such as human life and national security.

VIII: *Honor the truth*

The Eighth Commandment, "You shall not bear false witness against your neighbor," condemns lying. Because God is regarded as the author of all truth, the Church believes that humans are obligated in the Eighth Commandment to honor the truth. The most obvious way to fulfill this commandment is not to *lie,* to intentionally deceive another by speaking a falsehood.

Low blows and cheap shots

Lies come in many different forms, and sometimes even the truth can be sinful, depending on your intentions. For example:

✔ **Calumny** is telling a lie about someone with the purpose of ruining his reputation.

✔ **Detraction** is telling the truth about someone, usually something embarrassing and confidential, with the intent and purpose of ruining her reputation.

✔ **Slander** is verbally telling lies about someone.

✔ **Libel** is publishing a lie in print, such as in a book, magazine, or newspaper. People in the public eye are often victims of libel.

Figures of speech, metaphors, hyperboles, fairy tales, and such aren't considered lies because the listener isn't expecting accurate facts or exclusive truth, and the speaker isn't intending to deceive but to make a point.

Keep reading, because you haven't heard it all yet. *Mental reservation* is considered a means by which you can withhold some aspects of the truth without telling a lie, usually by not telling all the details. The Church believes it can be used in very limited circumstances:

✔ When someone isn't entitled to know all the facts and seeks to know them for evil purposes

✔ To protect the safety of self or others

✔ To protect confidentiality of penitent and confessor, doctor and patient, or attorney and client

This line of thinking is why the Church considers it moral to keep certain secrets confidential. For example:

✔ Catholicism regards the secrecy of the confessional as absolute, and no priest can ever reveal who went to confession or what was confessed. This is what's known as the *Seal of the Confessional.* Yet a priest can't lie to protect the penitent because the ends can never justify the means. He can and must simply remain silent rather than tell a falsehood.

✔ Doctor-patient and lawyer-client confidentiality is considered close to, but not synonymous with, the Seal of Confession and priest-penitent secrecy.

✔ The government can have secrets to protect the national security of the country and all its citizens, but just like the individual, the government isn't allowed to tell a lie even to save lives. Governments can use mental reservation to keep strategic information from enemies.

Concealing the truth (or some details of it) is different from distorting it, which would be a lie. Telling bedtime stories, writing fiction, using figures of speech, and using mental reservation are all permissible acts when done in the proper context. But intentionally lying is always considered sinful, even if the reasons may be noble. According to the Church, God created the human intellect to know the truth, just as He made the human will to seek the good.

Coming Out Even Steven

Certain differences exist between the Catholic and Lutheran version and the Protestant version of the Ten Commandments. The content is just the same, but the numbers differ. See Table 12-1 for a side-by-side comparison.

The Bible doesn't number the Ten Commandments; it merely states them in Exodus 20:1–17 and Deuteronomy 5:6–21. Both Roman Catholics and Lutherans use a numbering sequence devised by St. Augustine in the fifth century, because Martin Luther (1483–1546), a German theologian, had been an Augustinian priest before he left the priesthood in favor of his new Lutheran religion. The Augustinians were followers of St. Augustine. (For more on St. Augustine, see Chapter 18.) Protestant denominations other than the Lutheran Church, however, use the sequence of commandments devised by English and Swiss reformers in the 16th century.

Table 12-1	Comparing the Catholic/Lutheran and Protestant Ten Commandments
Catholic/Lutheran	*Protestant*
1. I am the Lord your God, you shall not have strange gods before Me.	1. I am the Lord your God who brought you out of the land of Egypt. You shall have no other gods before Me.
2. You shall not take the name of the Lord your God in vain.	2. You shall not make unto you any graven images.
3. Remember to keep holy the Lord's day.	3. You shall not take the name of the Lord your God in vain.
4. Honor your father and mother.	4. You shall remember the Sabbath and keep it holy.
5. You shall not kill.	5. Honor your father and mother.
6. You shall not commit adultery.	6. You shall not murder.
7. You shall not steal.	7. You shall not commit adultery.

(continued)

Table 12-1 *(continued)*

Catholic/Lutheran	Protestant
8. You shall not bear false witness against thy neighbor.	8. You shall not steal.
9. You shall not covet your neighbor's wife.	9. You shall not bear false witness against your neighbor.
10. You shall not covet your neighbor's goods.	10. You shall not covet your neighbor's house, nor his wife, nor anything that belongs to him.

The Catholic/Lutheran version has the First Commandment prohibiting idolatry (no strange gods = no graven images). The Protestant version separates false worship and graven images into the First and Second Commandments. Additionally, in the Catholic/Lutheran version, one commandment forbids you to covet your neighbor's wife and another commandment forbids you to covet your neighbor's goods. Contrarily, the Protestant version combines all forms of coveting into one commandment.

Chapter 13

Being Good When Sinning Is So Easy

In This Chapter

▶ Practicing virtue in thought, word, and deed

▶ Striking a balance between deprivation and excess

▶ Avoiding the seven nasty no-no's

▶ Knowing what antidotes to apply

Catholic morality is more than just avoiding what's sinful. Just as peace is more than the mere absence of war and good health is more than the mere absence of disease, holiness is more than the mere absence of sin and evil. Being able to say, "I've committed no sin today" isn't enough. A cat could say the same.

If a doctor gives you a prescription to cure a disease or infection, you must choose to follow the directions — such as "Take twice daily with plenty of water" — to make it work. If you don't, you can't blame the doctor if you don't get better. Similarly, God gave humans the Ten Commandments — a prescription for protection from spiritual disease (sin). But consciously choosing to follow the directions is up to the individual.

A good doctor does more than just give a prescription to cure the infection. She also gives overall directions for good and sustained physical health, such as "Drink plenty of fluids and get plenty of sleep and exercise," and "Stay away from high-fat and high-cholesterol foods." Likewise, Catholics believe that God did more than give the Ten Commandments for protection from sin. He also gave overall directions for good and sustained spiritual health — specifically, how to cultivate good habits, eliminate bad habits, and recognize the difference between the two. In this chapter, we tell you all about the four cardinal virtues Catholics cling to and the seven biggest sins they steer away from to keep their souls pure and disease-free.

Cultivating Good Habits

A *virtue* is a habit that perfects the powers of the soul and disposes you to do good. Catholics believe that divine grace is offered to the soul because, without God's help, humans can't do good on their own due to *original sin:* the sin of Adam and Eve, the first human beings and the parents of the human race. Their disobedience wounded human nature, and we all inherit that sinful nature from them. Grace, which is God's intervention, bolsters a person's soul, providing the necessary oomph to do the right thing — that is, *if* the recipient recognizes grace's value. Catholics believe that virtues prepare and dispose people so that when grace is offered, people readily recognize, accept, and cooperate with it. In other words, God's grace is necessary, and virtues make it easier to work with.

Traditionally, the Catholic Church recognizes four cardinal virtues, but you don't have to be a cardinal in the Catholic Church to possess them. The root meaning of *cardinal* is *cardo,* which is Latin for *hinge.* These four virtues are the hinges on which the rest of the moral life swings:

- ✔ Prudence
- ✔ Justice
- ✔ Temperance
- ✔ Fortitude

The four cardinal virtues are also called *moral virtues* to distinguish them from the *theological virtues* of faith, hope, and love (charity), which are given to the soul at Baptism.

Taking virtuous actions doesn't make you a virtuous person. A virtuous person is able to do what's virtuous because he's committed to doing the right thing for the right reason. Doing good merely because it's the right thing to do — instead of for profit, fame, or esteem — is the motivation for a virtuous person to do virtuous acts.

Prudence: Knowing what, when, and how

Too many people today carelessly blurt out statements that, although true, aren't spoken in charity and compassion but with cold, deliberate, and calculated harshness. That's where prudence can help.

Prudence is basically practical common sense. It's saying or doing the proper thing at the proper time and in the appropriate manner. It's also the ability to know and judge whether to say something or nothing at all.

You don't need a high IQ to be prudent. Prudence, like wisdom, isn't measured by intelligence but by the willingness of a person to think, discern, and then act. For example, asking a friend for the $500 he owes you while you're both at a funeral parlor for the viewing of his deceased brother isn't prudent. Knowing what to say, how to say it, and when to say it is prudence.

As another example, prudence can help you find the right time to appropriately confront a family member or friend who has an eating disorder. With prudence, you're not negligent, saying nothing at all, but neither are you abrupt or rude, saying something like "Hey, you look anorexic!" or "You really need to eat a cheeseburger!"

An alcoholic practices prudence when declining an invitation to lunch at a bar, even though the person doing the inviting assures the alcoholic that they won't sit at the bar but merely eat at a table. Prudence tells the alcoholic that entering a room where the aroma of booze permeates the air, where old drinking buddies hang out, and where she has memories of getting plastered is too dangerous for her. Prudence tells the alcoholic to decline or offer an alternative — a restaurant with no bar or, better yet, one where no alcohol is served.

Prudence takes time and practice. In the olden days, when good manners were more important, noblemen and peasants alike strove to show respect for their fellow man through the practice of prudent speech. Today, manners often come in two extremes: Some people are politically correct, live in fear of offending anyone, and, as a result, say nothing controversial — even when someone is in danger; other people adopt the shock-jock approach, which is to bludgeon you over the head with the raw, unadulterated truth, hoping to hurt your feelings and get a violent reaction from you rather than help you. Prudence lies in the middle of these two extremes. Prudent people speak the truth when it's needed and appropriate, in an inoffensive way, but they never lose their force and conviction.

Acting prudently requires mature deliberation, wise choice, and the right execution:

- **Mature deliberation:** When you exercise mature deliberation, you think carefully before acting or not acting. Mature deliberation involves contemplating past experience, examining the current situation and circumstances, and considering the possible results or outcome of your decision. Mature deliberation means that you're not content with just personal knowledge, either. You seek the good advice of others — the opinions of well-respected, good, and morally upright people whom you respect and admire. You consult with peers and colleagues, and research authoritative sources and documents. For Catholic Christians, these sources include both the Bible and the Catechism of the Catholic Church. In any event, mature deliberation means not just depending on your own personal experience and opinion but also testing your knowledge and beliefs and getting good advice.

✔ **Wise choice:** Making a wise choice involves determining which of the available options is most feasible and appropriate. Getting input is the first step, and deciding which course to take after examining all the possibilities is the second. This route may not be the quickest or easiest one, but prudence enables you to judge the most beneficial path to take.

✔ **The right execution:** The right execution is one in which you don't delay after you make a wise choice, but swiftly and thoroughly follow through on what you've decided to do. Procrastination and haste are the two foes to look out for. The right execution means that you've planned and prepared and now know what to do. You don't hesitate; you follow through.

Justice: Treating others fairly

Justice is the virtue that seeks to promote fair play. It's the desire and resolve to give each person his due. It demands that you reward goodness and punish evil. Justice can be one of three different types: commutative, distributive, and social.

Quid pro quo: Commutative justice

Commutative justice concerns the relationship between individuals — between two people, such as a customer and a merchant. Commutative justice demands, for example, that the customer be asked to pay a fair price for a product and that the merchant be honest about the condition and history of the item, so the buyer can know whether the price is indeed fair. So if a merchant tries to sell a coin that allegedly belonged to Abraham Lincoln, the consumer needs some proof to verify the claim. It's unfair to charge an enormous amount of money for something that can't be authenticated or, worse yet, isn't really as old as or in as good condition as advertised.

Forgive thine enemies, but do what justice demands

Christians are taught that they can and must forgive their enemies. And doing so was demonstrated when Pope John Paul II personally forgave Mehmet Ali Agca, the man who attempted to assassinate him in 1981.

Showing mercy and forgiveness, the pontiff also realized that justice demanded that the criminal be punished for his crime by spending time in jail — which he did. But later, the pope asked the Italian President to pardon the man, so he could return to Turkey during the Jubilee Year of 2000. The would-be assassin was pardoned and released, but when returned to Turkey, he was taken to a Turkish jail to resume a previous sentence for the murder of a newspaper editor.

Commutative justice is based on the principle *quid pro quo,* which is Latin for *this for that.* I'm willing to pay you the price that you ask for this item, and you're willing to sell it to me at that price. But the item must actually be what it's advertised to be. If the advertised price isn't correct or facts about the item are wrong, then commutative justice is violated.

Cheating the consumer *and* cheating the merchant are both ways of violating commutative justice.

Another situation in which commutative justice comes into play is when you're robbed. Commutative justice demands that the thief make restitution by giving back the stolen money or property or, if that's impossible, recompensing you in another way, such as giving you something equal in value or providing services. So when you were a kid and smashed your next-door-neighbor's window, your mom or dad rightfully enforced commutative justice. And after apologizing to Mr. Wilson, you had to save your allowance until you could pay for the replacement window.

All for one and one for all: Distributive justice

Distributive justice involves the relationship between one and many — between an individual and a group. This kind of justice is most obvious in the relationship between a citizen and her government. The city, state, and federal governments are required by distributive justice to levy fair taxes to pay for services provided. Charging excess taxes is a violation of distributive justice, as is not charging enough taxes to pay for services, resulting in cuts to essential services. A flip-side violation is when a citizen refuses to pay her fair share of taxes and yet often benefits from the government's services.

Distributive justice means that taxpayers have a right to know where their money goes, who spends it, and on what. The government has a right to ask citizens to financially support police, ambulance, firefighter, national defense, and other social services.

Here's another example of how distributive justice comes into play. Suppose that Fred and Barney belong to the Loyal Order of Water Buffaloes, a private club. They pay their annual dues, and in return they get a monthly newsletter, an annual membership card made of bedrock, and an invitation to the annual convention. Distributive justice demands that members pay their dues and that the board of directors be responsible for the monies collected, giving an accounting each year so that everyone knows where the loot went. If Mr. Slate skims some money off the top for personal use or if favoritism or nepotism creep in, this type of justice has been violated. All members should be treated fairly and equally.

Fair play from Dan to Beersheba: Social justice

Social justice concerns the relationship of both individuals and groups between one another and everyone. The bottom line is the common good — the public welfare of all. Social justice is concerned with the environment, the economy, private property, civil rights, and church-state relations.

Although businesses have the right to make a profit by manufacturing and selling goods and services, increasing profit share at the harmful expense of others is unacceptable. For example, polluting the local water system just to make a greater profit is a violation of social justice. At the same time, environmental extremists violate social justice when they take the law into their own hands and perpetrate property damage or seek to close a business, which results in many lost jobs that families depend on for survival. Cooperating and communicating in order to balance the needs of the community and the needs of the business are better for both sides.

Note that neither the right to profit nor the right to property is absolute. So if a community is suffering from a severe drought, for example, a company that has access to drinkable water is obliged to share with those who are dying of thirst.

Social justice demands that everyone be treated fairly and equally under the law. It also recognizes the inalienable right and duty of every human being to work and receive a fair and just wage for that work. This type of justice defends the right of workers to form unions, guilds, and societies. And it defends the right of managers to expect reasonable and fair requests that won't put them out of business or make them lose money rather than make it.

Treating all citizens — regardless of gender, color, ethnicity, or religion — with the same dignity and human rights is a mandate of social justice to all governments. For their part, citizens are expected to support their governments and nations in return for the protection and services they provide.

Temperance: Moderating pleasure

Feast or famine. Many people live at extremes — too much or too little. Some party hearty, and some are party poopers. From Puritans to Hedonists, the practices of self-deprivation and self-indulgence run the gamut, but the choice doesn't have to be an either/or proposition. Having some fun, enjoying your leisure time, taking pleasure, and relaxing aren't sinful, immoral, illicit, or juvenile. Really!

Christians can and ought to have fun without it degenerating into depravity and debauchery. That's where temperance comes in.

Temperance is the virtue by which a person uses balance. It's the good habit that allows a person to relax and have fun without crossing the line and committing sin.

The Catholic Church believes that human beings are permitted to participate in legitimate pleasures but that, often, society and culture lure people into excesses in the direction of either extreme. For example, enjoying a good meal is a good thing, but if you continually eat more than you need and become obese, that's gluttony. On the other hand, if you deprive yourself of food until your health suffers, all for the sake of looking good, well, that's vanity.

Temperance is nothing more than moderation and balance in using lawful pleasures. Temperance is having an alcoholic beverage without abusing it. Drinking to get drunk and drinking and driving are violations of the virtue of temperance. So are eating, sleeping, or recreating to excess.

Temperance is the habit of using prudence and restraint and doesn't require total abstinence unless someone has a problem. For example, an alcoholic can never have one or two social drinks. An alcoholic must forever abstain from booze, but she can still have a good time at parties with soft drinks instead.

Practicing temperance isn't about Carrie Nation and the Women's Christian Temperance Union and a bunch of old ladies banging a drum and decrying the evils of gin and rum. Rather, practicing temperance means knowing when to say when. It's knowing your limits and sticking to them. For example, a kiss and a hug don't have to end in passionate sex, and an argument doesn't have to deteriorate into a fistfight. Temperance is establishing, respecting, and enforcing boundaries. Self-control is the key. Having a good time without it becoming an occasion of sin or a sinful act is what temperance is all about.

Fortitude: Doing what's right come hell or high water

Fortitude isn't about physical strength or mental intelligence, nor is it about being macho or bullying people around. Instead, this cardinal virtue centers on strength of character.

Fortitude is the ability to persevere in times of trial and tribulation — the strength to hang in there when the going gets tough. It's having the courage to do the right thing no matter what the cost.

It's not enough to be fair, use self-control, and be prudent. The virtue of fortitude gives you the strength to fulfill your commitments to God, family, and friends. This virtue enables

✔ You to keep your promise and your word even when the world and everyone else is telling you to forget it

✔ Teenagers to combat peer pressure, avoiding drugs and sex

✔ Adults to remain chaste, abstaining from sexual relations until marriage despite the social pressures to have premarital relations

✔ People of conscience to speak up and out when injustice occurs at work or in society

When practiced faithfully and consistently, fortitude empowers people to remain courageous and overcome even the fear of death in order to help others and/or do the right thing for the right reason.

The Seven Deadly Sins

As you may have guessed, along with cultivating good habits, you need to avoid some bad habits. The Church maintains that seven vices in particular lead to breaking one or more of the Ten Commandments. These particular bad habits are called the seven deadly sins because, according to Catholicism, they're *mortal sins* — sins that kill the life of sanctifying grace. The Church believes that if you commit a mortal sin, you forfeit heaven and opt for hell by your own free will and actions. (See Chapter 9 for more on mortal sin.) Remember, too, that the Catholic Church teaches that God can and will forgive any sin if the person is truly repentant (through the Sacrament of Penance, Baptism, and Anointing of the Sick, or a perfect act of contrition in extreme necessity). Don't commit the vices described in this section. But you can always seek God's grace and mercy (read more in Chapter 9).

A mortal sin is any act or thought of a human being that turns away from God (*aversio a Deo* in Latin) and turns toward a created thing instead (*conversio ad creaturam* in Latin). In other words, mortal sin is completely turning away from God and embracing something else in His place. It's deadly to the life of grace because it insults the honor of God and injures the soul of the sinner himself. Mortal sin is like a malignant tumor or a critical injury that's lethal to the spiritual life. Three conditions are necessary for mortal sin to exist:

✔ **Grave matter:** The act itself is intrinsically evil and immoral. For example, murder, rape, incest, perjury, adultery, and so on are grave matters. These actions are in and of themselves deadly to the life of grace.

✔ **Full knowledge:** The person must *know* that what he's doing or planning to do is evil and immoral. For example, say someone steals a postage stamp, thinking that it's worth only 50 cents. She knows that it's sinful,

> but if she's unaware that the stamp is rare and actually worth $1,000, she's not guilty of mortal sin but of venial sin (more on that is coming up in this section).
>
> ✔ **Deliberate consent:** The person must *freely choose* to commit the act or plan to do it. Someone who's forced against his will doesn't commit a mortal sin. For example, a man who is drugged and brainwashed to assassinate a leader hasn't done so of his own free will; therefore, he's not guilty of mortal sin.

Venial sins are any sins that meet only one or two of the conditions needed for a mortal sin but do not fulfill all three at the same time, or are minor violations of the moral law, such as giving an obscene gesture to another driver while in traffic. Venial sin is less serious than mortal sin. Like a benign tumor or a minor infection, venial sin only weakens the soul with sickness; it doesn't kill the grace within. Venial sins aren't deadly to the life of grace, but like minor infections in the body, if casually ignored and left untended, they may deteriorate into a more serious condition. For example, someone who tells so-called "white lies" commits venial sin, but if he does it long enough, he'll be much more easily tempted to tell a big lie later on that would, in fact, be a mortal sin, such as cheating on a test or on his income tax return.

In the sixth century, Pope Gregory the Great made up the list of the seven deadly sins, which are pride, envy, lust, anger, gluttony, greed, and sloth. Later, in the 14th century, Geoffrey Chaucer popularized these sins in his *Canterbury Tales*.

In this section, we cover the seven deadly sins. As a bonus, we tell you about the remedies. Yep, *remedies*. Some specific virtues, lesser known than the four cardinal virtues, have traditionally been linked with a particular deadly sin. These virtues (listed in Table 13-1) help to defeat their counterparts.

Table 13-1	The Seven Deadly Sins and the Virtues That Defeat Them
Deadly Sin	*Conquering Virtue*
Pride	Humility
Envy	Kindness or meekness
Lust	Chastity
Anger	Patience
Gluttony	Periodic fasting and abstinence
Greed (avarice)	Generosity
Sloth (acedia)	Diligence

Pride goeth before the fall

Parents and teachers say to be proud of yourself, so why is pride considered a deadly sin? In the context they're talking about, it's not a sin. Parents and teachers are talking about healthy pride, such as taking joy from belonging to a family, a church, or a nation. Being proud to be an American, a Canadian, a good student, a hard worker, and so on isn't sinful.

The sin of *pride* is an inordinate love of self — a super-confidence and high esteem in your own abilities. It's also known as vanity. It exaggerates your abilities, gifts, and talents, and ignores your weaknesses, frailties, and imperfections.

In Catholicism, sinful pride is the deviation or distortion of the legitimate need of self-affirmation. Liking yourself isn't sinful; in fact, it's healthy and necessary. But when the self-perception no longer conforms to reality, and you begin to think that you're more important than you actually are, the sin of pride is rearing its ugly head.

The sin of pride gives you a fat head. You think you're better and more important than anyone else. It leads to resenting others whom you consider inferior, and you become impatient with others because you think they're not perfect like you.

Pride is the key to all other sins because after you believe that you're more important than you actually are, you compensate for it when others don't agree with your judgment. You rationalize your behavior and make excuses for lying, cheating, stealing, insulting, ignoring, and such, because no one understands you like *you* do. In your mind, you're underestimated by the world.

That's the extreme expression of pride. A subtler example is when you refuse to accept the authority of someone else over you, be it a parent, teacher, employer, pastor, bishop, or pope. The refusal to obey others is a by-product of pride. Showing disrespect for those in authority is pride as well. The ego can't stomach someone else having more power, intelligence, influence, or authority, so it rebels against the lawful superiors.

Pride also prevents you from seeking, listening to, or applying advice from others. Do you ever wonder why it is that most men refuse to ask for directions when they're lost? Pride prevents them from admitting that they can't read a map or follow directions properly. They can't let their wives, girlfriends, or mothers know the truth, so they drive on and on, hoping that something familiar appears before it gets too dark or too late.

The devil's downfall

Many spiritual writers, such as St. John of the Cross, St. Teresa of Avila, and St. Catherine of Siena, considered pride to be a form of idolatry, making yourself divine. Instead of being made in the image and likeness of God, the prideful make God in their own image and likeness and then they become a god.

Pride was considered to be the sin of Lucifer. According to pious tradition, he was the most intelligent and beautiful of all the angels, but his pride wouldn't allow him to embrace humility, and he rebelled against God. So St. Michael the Archangel fought and defeated Lucifer, and God cast Lucifer and all the fallen angels into hell. From then on, he was known as Satan or the Devil, and his compatriots were called demons.

The Catholic Church teaches that *humility* is the best remedy for pride. It's not a false self-deprecation, where you beat yourself up verbally only so others can say otherwise. It's not denying the truth. If you have a good singing voice, for example, responding to a compliment with "Oh, no, I can't carry a tune" isn't humility. Catholicism regards humility as recognizing that the talent is really a gift from God and responding with, "Thank you — I've been blessed by the good Lord." Pride would say, "You're darn right I have a good voice. It's about time you realized it."

In other words, although acknowledging your talents is good, humility reminds you that your talents come from God. Pride fools you into thinking that you're the source of your own greatness.

Envying what others have or enjoy

Envy, another deadly sin, is the resentment of another person's good fortune or joy. Catholicism distinguishes between two kinds of envy:

- ✔ **Material envy** is when you resent others who have more money, talent, strength, beauty, friends, and so on, than you do.

- ✔ **Spiritual envy** is resenting others who progress in holiness, preferring that they stay at or below your level instead of being joyful and happy that they're doing what they're supposed to be doing. Spiritual envy is far worse and more evil than material envy.

Note that spiritual writers and moralists make a distinction between envy and jealousy. Envy is the resentment of what others have, such as possessions, talent, fame, and so on, whereas jealousy is the fear of losing what you already have. So a jealous husband fears that he may or will lose his wife to another man. If he happens to think Julia Roberts is the most beautiful woman in the world, then that same husband may also be envious of Julia Roberts's husband. Jealousy is considered to be as much a sin as envy because it closely resembles that deadly sin.

Jealousy among professional people is common, because they often fear losing their own status, position, notoriety, or esteem to rival colleagues. Jealous people are insecure, apprehensive, and fearful of peers taking what they have, surpassing them, or leaving them behind with less than they started out with. The same fears exist among students. A student ranked with the best grades in his class is jealous when he fears losing that ranking to another student who's getting better grades day by day and is moving up the list faster and faster. On the other hand, a B student is envious when he resents a straight-A student.

The Church maintains that *meekness* or *kindness* can counter envy. For example, Genesis 37–47 tells the story of Joseph's brothers, who were envious of Joseph because he was the favorite son of their father, Jacob. They sold Joseph into slavery, but Joseph rose through the ranks from slave to personal advisor to pharaoh. Later, when he met his brothers again, instead of seeking revenge, Joseph showed them kindness and brought them and their father into Egypt.

Lusting after fruit that's forbidden

The Catholic Church believes that being attracted to and appreciating the opposite sex is normal and healthy. That's not lust, and it's not considered a sin.

Lust is looking at, imagining, and even treating others as mere sex objects to serve your own physical pleasures, rather than as individuals made in the image and likeness of God. Lust is having someone become something merely to please you, in fantasy or reality.

The Church says that lust depersonalizes the other person and the one having the lustful thoughts. It makes both parties nothing more than instruments of enjoyment instead of enabling them to focus on the unique gift of personhood. And it seeks to separate, divide, and isolate what God intended to be united — love and life, the unitive and procreative dimensions of marriage.

The pleasure that lustful thoughts provide is only a sign of the human condition and its wounded nature from original sin, which is *concupiscence,* the proclivity to sin, especially the tendency toward sins of the flesh. The fact that you're entertained by impure thoughts isn't sinful; rather, sin comes into play when you entertain them — you engage in the conscious and deliberate act of having lustful thoughts. The sin occurs when you initiate, consent to, and/or continue fantasizing about sexual activity with another person, because all sin involves a free act of the will. Spontaneous thoughts — especially during puberty and adolescence — are primarily involuntary and aren't considered sinful. Such thoughts become sinful when the person recognizes them and has the ability to dismiss and reject them as soon as possible, yet doesn't do so.

Chastity, the virtue that moderates sexual desire, is the best remedy for lust. Chastity falls under temperance and can help to keep physical pleasure in moderation.

Without chastity, men and women become like animals that copulate when in heat. Animals have sex driven by instinct, but men and women have the gift of reason and can choose when and with whom to be intimate. Desirous of chastity, men and women can freely abstain from sexual activity until the wedding night. If they allow lust to drive their actions, however, they sin and commit *fornication* (sex between two unmarried people) or they commit *adultery* (having sex with someone else's spouse or cheating on your own spouse). Cultivating and clinging to chastity separate them from the animals.

Anger to the point of seeking revenge

You have no control over what angers you, but you do have control over what you do after you become angry. The deadly sin of *anger* is the sudden outburst of emotion — namely hostility — and sustaining thoughts about the desire for revenge. The key here is that the wrath persists for more than a moment. You want harm to come to someone else. In the worst case, anger can lead to willfully inflicting suffering on others.

If someone sticks you with a needle or pin, for example, or slaps you in the face, your initial reaction is probably one of anger. You resent what was done to you. The sin of anger occurs when you react by swearing, cursing, shouting, ranting, or raving. (Don't confuse these last three reactions with the shouting, ranting, and raving that occur at a typical Italian meal. Everyone screams and yells at those.) In the same vein, if you brood over injuries and insults others have heaped on you and begin to yearn for revenge, the Church asserts that you're committing the sin of anger. Inordinate, violent, and hateful anger is always a mortal sin. Bloodthirsty revenge also comes from anger.

But what if, say, someone robs you? In that case, wouldn't those feelings be merited? No. Being upset that someone robbed you is normal and is properly called *righteous indignation,* but seeking revenge and desiring to see the culprit suffer isn't. Instead, with the virtue of justice, you can desire for the police to catch the thief and for a court to sentence her to a fair punishment.

Patience, the virtue that allows you to adapt and endure evil without harboring any destructive feelings, is the best countermeasure for anger. When you give yourself the time and opportunity to cool off, anger dissipates and more practical concerns come to the front line.

Gluttony: Too much food or firewater

Gluttony is immoderate, excessive eating, and/or drinking too much alcohol. Enjoying a delightful dinner isn't sinful, but intentionally overeating to the point where you literally get sick to your stomach is. So, too, having an alcoholic beverage now and then (provided that you don't suffer from alcoholism) is *not* sinful in the eyes of the Church. Responsible consumption of alcohol is allowed. Making a champagne toast to a bride and groom or having a mixed drink with friends at a dinner party is all fine and well — that is, as long as you aren't a recovering alcoholic. But drinking to the point of drunkenness *is* a sin. Abusing alcohol is sinful, and it doesn't necessarily mean only getting drunk. People who use alcohol to lessen their own (or others') inhibitions are committing sin. Driving under the influence or while intoxicated or impaired is a grave matter and can be a mortal sin (if you meet all three conditions for a mortal sin we talk about in the section "The Seven Deadly Sins"), because you endanger your own life and the lives of others. Underage drinking is also considered a serious sin.

Legitimate eating disorders, such as anorexia and bulimia, aren't gluttony; they're medical conditions that require treatment and care. The sin of gluttony is freely choosing to overconsume.

Like lust, gluttony focuses on *pleasure.* Gluttony finds it in food and drink, whereas lust finds it in sexual activity. Both enslave the soul to the body, even though the soul — being superior to the body — should be in charge. Gluttons don't eat out of necessity or for social reasons, but merely to consume and experience the pleasure of taste.

Gorging yourself on appetizers, several courses, desserts, and so on — with no concern for the possibility of getting sick or the reality that millions of people are starving around the world — is the ugliness and evil of gluttony. In addition, gluttony endangers your life by jeopardizing the health of your body.

Periodic *fasting,* restricting the amount of food you eat, and *abstinence,* avoiding meat or some favorite food, are the best defenses against gluttony. Unlike dieting where the goal is to lose weight, fasting and abstinence purify the soul by controlling the desires of the body. Occasionally giving up favorite foods and beverages promotes self-control and temperance. In addition, deciding ahead of time what and how much to eat and drink is considered prudent and helpful.

Greed: The desire for more and more

Greed is the inordinate love of and desire for earthly possessions. Greed entails cherishing things above people and relationships. Amassing a fortune and foolishly trying to accumulate the most stuff is greed, which is sometimes called *avarice.* "It's never enough. I have to have more." That's the battle cry of greed.

Greed is also a sign of mistrust. "I doubt that God will take care of me, so I try to gather as much as possible now in case no more is left later." The Gospel relates the parable about such a greedy man. He had so much grain that he tore down his bin to hold more — only to die that very night (Luke 12:16–21). But you can't take it with you. That saying was true then, and it's true now. Some time ago, a rich woman stipulated in her will that she be buried in her Rolls Royce. Where's she going to drive that thing?

Greed, the apex of selfishness, has ruined marriages, families, and friendships. *Generosity,* however, is the best weapon against greed. Freely giving some of your possessions away, especially to those less fortunate, is considered the perfect antithesis to greed and avarice. Generosity promotes detachment from material things that come and go. Things can be broken, stolen, destroyed, or lost. They can be replaced, but people can't.

Sloth: Lazy as a lotus-eater

Sloth (sometimes called *acedia*) is laziness — particularly when it concerns prayer and spiritual life. It centers on doing nothing or doing just trivial things. A slothful person always wants to rest and relax, with no desire or intention of making a sacrifice or doing something for others. It's an aversion to work — physical, mental, and spiritual. Sloth inevitably leads to lukewarmness and tepidity and then deteriorates into disinterest, discouragement, and finally despair. Sloth breeds indifference, which prevents joy from ever being experienced.

The Church says that the evil habit of being inattentive at religious worship services — being physically present but not consciously participating — or being careless in fulfilling your religious duties is a sin of sloth. Other examples include never getting to Church on time, before Mass starts; just sitting in church but not singing, praying, kneeling, or standing; never reading the Bible or the Catechism of the Catholic Church; and not praying before eating a meal or going to bed.

Proverbs has something to say about sloth:

- ✔ **Proverbs 10:26:** Like vinegar to the teeth, and smoke to the eyes, so is the slothful to those who send him.

- ✔ **Proverbs 18:9:** He who is slothful in his work is a brother to him who destroys.

- ✔ **Proverbs 19:15:** Slothfulness casts into a deep sleep, and an idle person will suffer hunger.

- ✔ **Proverbs 19:24:** A slothful man hides his hand in the dish, and will not even bring it back to his mouth.

Spiritual laziness can only be overcome by practicing the virtue of *diligence,* which is the habit of keeping focused and paying attention to the work at hand — be it the work of employment or the work of God. Diligent prayer and diligent worship can make you more reverent. Diligence in all things ensures that you don't become idle and then start daydreaming, leaving reality for Fantasy Island.

Catholics, like all other human beings, are asked to practice virtue and avoid vice. Going even farther, religion and faith ask God's children to seek holiness and avoid all sin and evil at the same time. The motivation for believers is simple: the choice of heaven or hell — eternal happiness, joy, and peace, or eternal pain, misery, and damnation.

Chapter 14

Standing Firm: The Church's Stance on Some Sticky Issues

In This Chapter

▶ Realizing why priests must remain single

▶ Finding out why it's no dice for women priests

▶ Grappling with issues of life and death

▶ Going through married life naturally with NFP

Catholicism may appear at times to go against the grain, risk unpopularity, or even chance rejection and persecution of some of its beliefs and practices. Like most religions, Catholicism seeks to conform to the Almighty rather than go along with the hoi polloi. Moods change, tastes differ, and crowds can be fickle, ugly, or just plain apathetic. Whether something is popular doesn't determine whether it's true or good. When most of the people thought the world was flat, their belief didn't make it so. Moral and spiritual leaders have an obligation to conform to a higher authority than their own. Even though they serve and minister to the common folk, they owe their obedience not to the *vox populi* (voice of the people) but to the *vox Dei* (voice of God).

Most religions have some controversial teachings, doctrines, disciplines, and policies that the outside world rejects or misunderstands. A few members may even dislike or oppose some doctrine or another. Yet these positions remain part and parcel of the official religion because at the very core is an obligation to speak the truth "in season and out of season" because there will always be those who'd rather have their ears tickled than hear what's true (2 Timothy 4:2–3). For this reason, the Catholic Church stands by her convictions and teachings on artificial birth control, abortion, euthanasia, capital punishment, and the like. In this chapter, we explain the Church's position on a number of controversial issues that people face today.

Celibacy and the Male Priesthood

Even before the advent of clergy sex scandals, the issue of celibacy intrigued non-Catholics. Some claim it contradicts nature and goes against biblical teachings on marriage and the ministry, such as "Be fruitful and multiply" (Genesis 1:28) and "Do we not have the right to be accompanied by a wife?" (1 Corinthians 9:5). Although the number of Catholics in the world continues to increase (there are more than 1 billion Catholics worldwide), the number of priests to minister to all of them has decreased. Because of this vocations crisis (not enough shepherds to take care of the sheep), many people are questioning celibacy and the restriction of ordination to males only. Married clergy and women priests, some contend, would alleviate the shortage of personnel and bring a fresh perspective to the vocation. Protestant Christians have had both for decades now and wonder when Catholics will catch up. Legitimate questions and valid points to be sure, but Catholicism has some good answers and replies, as we point out in this section.

To address these issues, we must differentiate celibacy from the male priesthood. They're two separate and distinct issues and entities, even though they overlap in practice. Celibacy is a discipline of the Church that isn't absolute; exceptions and modifications have been made through the centuries. But the male priesthood is a part of doctrine and divine law that can never be changed or altered by any pope or council.

Flying solo for life

Celibacy is the formal and solemn oath never to enter the married state. Celibate men and women willingly relinquish their natural right to marry in order to devote themselves completely and totally to God and His Church.

Only in the United States

At the turn of the last century, many Eastern European immigrants came to America and brought their clergy with them. Some influential and shortsighted Irish-American bishops feared (with no foundation) that a married priesthood among Eastern Catholics would cause tension and animosity among the Western (Latin) Roman Catholic clergy and laity. So they asked Rome if they could force the Byzantine clergy to mandate celibacy in North America, even though it would remain optional in the rest of the world.

Before that, every single Ruthenian, Ukrainian, Melkite, Maronite, Coptic, and Romanian Catholic priest had the option of being celibate or married all over the world. Today, only the United States still pushes mandatory celibacy on the Eastern Catholic clergy.

The Catholic Church doesn't teach (and never has taught) that *all* clergy must be celibate. From day one, clergy of the Eastern Catholic Churches, such as the Byzantine, have consistently and perennially had the option of marrying. Only in the United States was celibacy imposed on the Byzantine Catholic clergy. (See the sidebar "Only in the United States" for details.)

Celibacy isn't necessary for valid Orders in the Roman Catholic Church. It's a *discipline* of the church, not a doctrine. The East never made it mandatory. The Western (Latin) Church made it normative in A.D. 306 at the Council of Elvira and mandatory in 1074 by Pope Gregory VII. The Second Lateran Council reaffirmed it in 1139. Although the Eastern Catholic and Orthodox Churches have always had an optional celibacy for clergy, both have a celibate episcopacy, meaning that only celibate priests can become bishops. So although they have a married clergy, the upper hierarchy remains celibate and, to a degree, quasi-monastic. (They live and pray more like monks than like parish priests.)

A rolling stone gathers no moss

Celibacy is legitimate for both the East and the West, even though it's optional for the former and mandatory for the latter. But why the difference between the two? Well, politics and culture. Even before East split from West in 1054 and formed the Orthodox Church, the Eastern part of the Holy Roman Empire operated differently from the Western part. (See Appendix A in this book for more on the history of Catholicism.)

In the East, a close association existed between the secular and religious spheres, which was dramatically different from the situation in the West. After Rome fell in A.D. 476, no single, powerful, and influential secular ruler arose until Charlemagne was crowned Holy Roman Emperor in A.D. 800.

So from the fifth to the eighth centuries, the most powerful and influential person in the West was the bishop of Rome. As pope and head of the world-wide Catholic Church, he became the icon of stability and power as Western Europe survived the fall of the ancient Roman Empire, the barbarian invasions, and the so-called Dark Ages.

Instability in the secular realm meant that the clergy, especially the bishops, took on more than just spiritual leadership, just as the pope wielded more than pastoral power in Rome and around the world. And the West found that celibacy among the clergy was beneficial and helpful because that meant no divided loyalties.

Kings, princes, barons, earls, dukes, counts, and other nobility married first to make political alliances and second to establish families. Mandatory celibacy prevented the clergy from getting involved in the intrigue of who marries whom. Mandatory celibacy ensured that the priests were preoccupied with Church work and had no ties or interests in local politics among the fighting factions, which were trying to establish the infant nation states.

Priests with families would have been vulnerable to the local nobility, because their extended families would have been under secular dominion. A celibate clergy made for a more independent clergy, free from earthly concerns and corruption, enabling them to serve the people and the hierarchy with full attention and loyalty.

Biblical background for celibacy

As noted earlier in this section, some people think that celibacy goes against biblical teachings on marriage and the ministry. But the Catholic Church actually uses the Bible as part of its reasoning for priestly celibacy.

Jesus Christ never married and was celibate, and the New Testament affirms the value of celibacy:

- **1 Corinthians 7:8:** To the unmarried and the widows I say that it is well for them to remain single as I do.

- **1 Corinthians 7:27–34, 38:** Are you bound to a wife? Do not seek to be free. But if you marry, you do not sin, and if a girl marries she does not sin. Yet those who marry will have worldly troubles, and I would spare you that. I mean, brethren, the appointed time has grown very short; from now on, let those who have wives live as though they had none, and those who mourn as though they were not mourning, and those who rejoice as though they were not rejoicing, and those who buy as though they had no goods, and those who deal with the world as though they had no dealings with it. For the form of this world is passing away. I want you to be free from anxieties. The unmarried man is anxious about the affairs of the Lord, how to please the Lord; but the married man is anxious about worldly affairs, how to please his wife, and his interests are divided. . . . So that he who marries his betrothed does well; and he who refrains from marriage will do better.

According to Catholicism, to claim that celibacy is nonbiblical is erroneous. Many significant people in the Bible were unmarried, and the preceding passages show that the New Testament and the Early Church didn't frown on or merely tolerate celibacy. They saw it as a gift — as much a gift as the gift of faith and the gift of a vocation to serve the Church.

Mandatory celibacy for the priesthood is a discipline of the Church, not a doctrine or a dogma. Theoretically, any pope can modify or dissolve mandatory celibacy at any time, but it's highly improbable because it has been part of the Western Church's priesthood since the fourth century. (See the sidebar, "Footloose, free, and on the run," in this chapter.) Additionally, the Church teaches and affirms that celibacy isn't just a sacrifice; it's also a gift.

Is celibacy to blame for the priest shortage?

Because of the declining number of newly ordained Catholic priests, some people think that allowing married clergy would alleviate the shortage of personnel. But statistics show that even Protestant ministers and clergy — who *can* be married and, in many cases, can be women or men — are decreasing in numbers, too. The Church believes that relaxing or eliminating celibacy isn't the panacea that would answer the priest shortage in the West.

Socially and culturally, first-world nations, such as the United States, Canada, and most of Western Europe, are having smaller and smaller families. The birth rate has dropped to an all-time low because many couples in these affluent countries are having only one or two children. Big families aren't the only, or primary, source of priests and nuns, but they do bring possible vocations into the world.

But if a pope were to decide to change, modify, or end mandatory celibacy for the Western church, the Church would still maintain and follow the same tradition observed by the Eastern Catholic Church concerning married clergy. Among the married clergy in the Eastern Church, marriage must come before ordination; if a cleric is ordained unmarried, he must remain unmarried. Therefore, ending mandatory celibacy would affect only those yet to be ordained. In addition:

 ✔ Seminarians would have to decide before ordination whether they wanted to be married. They'd have to find a wife prior to their ordination or remain celibate.

 ✔ Anyone having aspirations to be ordained a bishop would have to remain celibate.

 ✔ Catholic priests who were ordained celibate and then later left the active ministry to get married would *not* be allowed back into the active ministry as a married priest.

The pros and cons

Celibacy can be difficult for those who don't come from a large, extended family. An only son may feel anxiety and tension when his elderly parents become sick and need attention, and no other adult children are available to care for them. And a priest who comes from a small family may feel lonely more often during the holidays. He sees married families in his parish sharing the joy of the season with one another, and yet he doesn't have many aunts and uncles, brothers and sisters, and nieces and nephews to visit.

Another sacrifice is not having a lifelong companion to support, encourage, advise, and, of course, correct you at times. Not having a baby to rock to sleep, a son to watch in his first little league baseball game, and a daughter to walk down the aisle on her wedding day are all sacrifices required by celibacy.

But at the same time, celibacy gives a priest the time and opportunity to love hundreds of people and to give 100 percent of his attention, effort, zeal, and talent, whereas a married man must balance family and work. A celibate priest doesn't have to make the painful decision of whether to respond to an emergency phone call at 3 a.m. or stay home with a seriously ill wife or child.

Celibacy can be distorted into being only a sacrifice ("I gave up a wife and children"), or it can be seen as the Church intended — as both a sacrifice and a gift. ("I freely gave up a wife and children so that I can love and serve my parishioners as if they're my children.")

Catholic priests use the title *Father* because they're spiritually considered the father of many children through the sacraments. Catholic Christians are spiritually born in Baptism, fed in the Holy Eucharist, made mature in Confirmation, and healed during Penance and the Anointing of the Sick. The responsibilities of parents parallel those of the priest: Parents give birth to their children, feed them, heal them, and help them grow and mature. So the Church is considered the spiritual mother. Catholics call the Church the *Holy Mother Church,* and the priest is their spiritual father.

Footloose, free, and on the run

Because of the necessity of a priest for major Catholic religious practices to occur (only a priest or bishop has the authority and ability to say Mass, anoint the sick and hear confession), a celibate, all-male priesthood is far more practical. A single priest can move about unencumbered, without having to think about and see after the welfare of a family.

In the late 1800s, Catholic homesteaders would go for weeks and sometimes months without the benefits of Sunday Mass. Then a priest, traveling from town to city and back again, would arrive in say, Helena, Montana, to hear confessions and say Mass. Catholics would come from miles around, sometimes walking all the way and undergoing great hardship to get to confession and Mass.

Priests are obliged to act as pioneers between this world and the next, leading Christ's flock into heaven. To remain focused on their calling, they can't afford to get hung up in worldly (or political) changes. This is particularly true for missionary priests in a foreign country, as well as those priests in any country that's experiencing a change in government that may be hostile toward the Church. In these situations, which have occurred over and over again throughout history and continue to occur, the priests who aren't arrested, thrown in prison, executed (martyred), or compromised are apt to hide and travel throughout the countryside and the byways of the city, saying Mass, hearing confession, baptizing, and so on, in secret and on the run like outlaws.

During England's Reformation, priests were drawn and quartered, and citizens found guilty of hiding a priest were executed. Such was the fate of St. Margaret Clitherow, martyred on March 25, 1586. And today, *Fides,* the Vatican's missionary news source, tallies the number of priests throughout the world who suffer martyrdom annually.

Pope John Paul II's letter *Pastores Dabo Vobis* (I Will Give You Shepherds) reminded Catholic priests that although they have no wife and children of their own, they're not alone. They do have a spouse — the Church. A priest is to treat the people of his parish (and every member of the Church, for that matter) as his beloved bride. The parishioners aren't to be treated as stockholders, employers, employees, servants, customers, or clients. They're to be treated as a beloved spouse. The priest marries the Church because the Church is considered the Bride of Christ, and the priest is considered "another Christ" by virtue of the Sacrament of Holy Orders. So the priest must love the Church as Christ loves the Church. It's a spousal relationship and covenant of love.

When put in this context, celibacy is merely the means to making the reality more possible and more dynamic. Married clergy can do a superb and phenomenal job, no matter what their denomination or gender. But celibacy for the Catholic priesthood in the Latin tradition makes sense, and although it's not always easy, neither is married life.

The sexual abuse issue

Celibate clergy aren't more likely or prone to sexual misconduct (homosexual or heterosexual) than any other group, despite the rhetoric that ensued soon after the blitz of pedophilia cases came to light in the United States a while back. Catholic priests were the focus of much media attention — mostly because of the unconscionable actions of a very small minority of deviant clergy and a few bishops who merely transferred clergy known to be sex offenders from one assignment to another.

Sadly, 80 percent of physical abuse of children is perpetrated by parents, and other family members account for another 7 percent. Teachers, coaches, neighbors, daycare providers, scoutmasters, youth ministers, and clergy are among the remaining 12 percent who know the children. (Complete strangers account for only 1 percent of this abuse.)

The 2004 John Jay Report, a study based on 10,667 allegations of Catholic clergy engaging in sexual abuse of minors between 1950 and 2002, showed that 4,392 priests had been credibly accused. That number amounted to 4 percent of the 109,694 priests in active ministry during that same time period. Estimates indicate that between 2 and 5 percent of Protestant ministers, Eastern Orthodox priests, Jewish rabbis, and Islamic imams use their position of authority to sexually abuse minors as well.

Even one case is one too many, of course, because abusing children is one of the most heinous evils any adult can commit. But this horrible behavior isn't limited to — or even primarily found in — the celibate male clergy. It's an evil that afflicts a few pastors of all denominations, as well as people from all other walks of life.

We in no way think that the statistics take away from the horror, shame, and diabolical evil of a few celibate priests committing the heinous crime and sin of child sex abuse. But it's important to also look at the whole picture — to see that the overwhelming majority of child abuse cases are committed by married laymen who are related to the kids and that the overwhelming majority of celibate priests aren't pedophiles and have never abused any boy, girl, man, or woman.

The evil of child abuse makes no distinction between Catholic or Protestant, Christian or Jewish, celibate or married, black or white, young or old. All ethnic, religious, and racial groups have a few deviants and perverts in their ranks. Indiscriminately associating the Catholic priesthood and its discipline of celibacy with pedophilia doesn't make sense. Yes, sadly, some priests and bishops did abuse children, and more disturbing is that some bishops merely moved these weirdoes from place to place instead of stopping them once and for all. Nonetheless, no credible or logical argument or data supports the notion that celibacy encouraged or promoted sexual misconduct among the clergy. And from now on, those found ought to be — and will be — removed from active ministry, suspended of their ordained faculties, and reported to the civil authorities.

No-woman's-land

With an apparent priest shortage and so many Protestant denominations embracing women ministers, some people wonder why the Catholic Church doesn't allow female priests. First of all, it's *not* because women aren't qualified or that they're somehow not worthy of this calling.

Having a male clergy is a *constitutive element* of the Sacrament of Holy Orders — no pope, council, or bishop can change it. The same is true about the use of water for Baptism and wheat bread and grape wine for Holy Eucharist. The elements of every Sacrament can't be changed because Christ established them. This belief is shared by the Eastern Orthodox, who don't ordain women for the very same reason. It has nothing to do with who's more worthy or suitable for Holy Orders, in the same way that the ban on non-Catholics receiving Holy Communion has nothing to do with any moral or spiritual judgment on the persons involved. It has to do with Sacred Tradition, which is considered as divinely inspired as Sacred Scripture. (See Chapter 2 for details about Sacred Tradition.)

The reason the Roman Catholic and Eastern Orthodox Churches are unable to ordain women — be it to the diaconate, priesthood, or episcopacy — is actually threefold:

> ✔ The Church can't change what constitutes valid matter for any of the seven sacraments.
>
> ✔ Sacred Tradition, nearly 2,000 years old, has never had an instance of women priests.
>
> ✔ Jesus didn't ordain any women or call any of them to be apostles — not even his own mother!

The Sacrament of Holy Orders

No pope, bishop, or council can change the constitutive elements of any of the seven sacraments, and a valid Sacrament of Holy Orders requires a baptized male to be ordained by a validly ordained bishop (flip to Chapter 9 for more on this sacrament). Maleness is as essential to the Sacrament of Holy Orders as wheat bread and grape wine are to the Sacrament of the Holy Eucharist. So just as the pope can't change the requirements of valid matter for the Holy Eucharist, he can't change the requirements of valid matter for Holy Orders.

Sacred Tradition

Both the Catholic and Orthodox Churches believe that the revealed Word of God is both written (Sacred Scripture) and unwritten (Sacred Tradition). When the Bible is silent or ambiguous, Sacred Tradition authentically fills in the gaps. Sacred Tradition shows that women were never ordained, and Pope John Paul II's apostolic letter *Ordinatio Sacerdotalis* (1994) clearly stated that women can't be ordained. (For more on encyclicals and other papal documents, see Chapter 2.)

Ordaining only males is not considered a matter of injustice because not all men are allowed to be ordained. Just having a personal vocation isn't enough. The local bishop must call the man, giving an official recognition from the Church that a man may indeed have a priestly vocation. No man can demand or expect ordination because it's a gift, not a right. Think of it like this: Just as it's not unjust for men not to be able to give birth, it's not unjust for women not to be ordained.

Jesus and his apostles

The Church points to the fact that Jesus was both God and man. From all eternity, He was divine with a divine nature, intellect, and will. But He was also born of a human mother and took on a human nature as well. In His divinity, Jesus was God and pure spirit, but in His humanity, He was a man. His gender was more than accidental because the Church is His bride. And because the priest acts *in persona Christi* (in the person of Christ) as an *alter-Christus* (another Christ), the priest reflects Christ to the entire Church whenever he celebrates any of the sacraments. The maleness of Christ was part of who He was, and therefore, Jesus only called men to be His apostles (even though His mother would have been a far better choice). If a woman were to be ordained, she couldn't be espoused to the Church because the Church is considered *mother.* A mother needs a father to complement the equation.

Catholicism regards Jesus as the groom and the Church as his bride. The priest is another Christ who acts in the person of Christ. The male priest represents the male Christ, and the priest is in a spousal relationship with the Holy Mother Church. Women priests don't fit into that typology.

The changing roles of women

Women have come a long way since the early and medieval Church. Although they can't be ordained priests, women have equal rights to be sponsors at Baptism and Confirmation. In Matrimony, they're treated and regarded as 100-percent full, equal partners with their husbands. Women can serve on the parish council and finance committees. They can be readers at Mass, *extraordinary ministers* (laypersons who assist the priest at Mass to give out Holy Communion) if needed, and ushers. They can work in the parish office, teach religious education courses, and so on, just like their male counterparts. And many parishes have women *pastoral associates* — usually nuns, religious sisters, or laywomen who help the pastor with many spiritual and pastoral duties. In addition, women can even hold positions of influence and power in the diocesan chancery. The Church has women who are canon lawyers, judges, and chancellors across the country. The Church has allowed local bishops and pastors the option to permit female altar servers at Mass. Now many parishes have both altar girls and altar boys.

Matters of Life and Death

The Catholic Church's stand on various life and death issues — abortion, euthanasia, the death penalty, and war — doesn't always go with the flow. To find out exactly what each stand is and the reasoning behind it, keep reading.

Abortion

The Catholic Church opposes and condemns any and all direct abortions. Even pregnancies that result from rape or incest or that present a danger to the life of the mother aren't reasons for abortion. Although the Catholic position on abortion may seem extreme to some, it coincides consistently and completely with Catholic morality, which is based on the natural moral law, the Bible, and the official teachings of the Magisterium. (For more on natural moral law, see Chapter 11; for more on the Magisterium, see Chapter 6.)

Letting nature take its course

St. Thomas Aquinas defined *life* as spontaneous, immanent activity. Once fertilization occurs, the embryo begins to grow. Cells divide, grow, multiply, and follow a predetermined pattern, but the process is also independent to a degree. Although the embryo needs the womb to survive for nourishment and shelter, the process of cell division, growth, and development occur inside from a life force within the embryo itself. Unlike a red or white blood cell that takes orders from the brain to go to one part of the body, the embryo isn't being told what to do by the mother's brain.

It's working on its own initiative, plan, and schedule. Mom is merely giving the unborn child the time, place, and support he needs to complete the process begun at conception. If that internal, spontaneous, automatic, and independent process stops on its own, then the mother's body will eject the dead embryo by itself, which is commonly known as a miscarriage. On the other hand, if that process is intentionally stopped by any outside force, it's an abortion, which Catholics consider immoral because it's the intentional taking of an innocent life.

The ends can never justify the means. Catholics believe that willingly, knowingly, and deliberately committing evil is never justifiable — no matter how good the intention and no matter how noble the cause. This belief is a moral absolute for Catholics, and it can't be diluted or altered one iota. The Church believes that if, in even one circumstance, someone is allowed to knowingly and willingly commit evil so that good may come from it, then Pandora's box is opened for anyone to claim he was merely doing a so-called necessary evil for the greater good in the long run. So the Church teaches that one innocent life can't be taken even if it would save hundreds, thousands, or millions.

The Catholic Church sees abortion as the termination of an innocent, though unborn, life. Therefore, it's always wrong, sinful, and immoral. The circumstances by which that life was conceived are considered irrelevant to the question, "Is this an innocent person?"

The Church teaches that human life is created and begins at the moment of conception. A whole unborn child is growing and living in the womb — not a half-human or pre-human. At the moment of conception, when the father's sperm fertilizes the mother's egg, God infuses an immortal soul into this brand new member of the human race. The embryo may not survive the nine months of pregnancy, but nature — not man — should decide when life should be terminated. The baby's DNA is human and distinct from the DNA of mom and dad, too. That means that only a human being exists in the womb, nothing less.

Often, people say that the Catholic Church opts for the child over the mother. Not the case at all. The real teaching is that each and every innocent life must be protected, and intentionally ending the life of the mother or the unborn child is immoral.

So if a pregnant woman has a heart attack and needs emergency surgery, it's considered morally permissible to put her under anesthesia and operate, even though it's likely that she'll spontaneously abort the unborn fetus on her own as a consequence. The distinction is that her body is doing the act of eject-ing the fetus as an effect of the primary action of the doctors who are trying to save both lives — the mother and the baby. If the baby dies naturally, the Church believes that no sin has been committed. But if the doctor or nurse directly kills the baby, that's considered murder, the taking of an innocent life.

Likewise, say a pregnant woman has a cancerous uterus, and it must be removed immediately or she and the baby will die. It's considered morally per-missible for the uterus to be removed as long as the unborn child isn't directly killed. If the womb is diseased and threatening the life of the mother, the Church permits removing both the uterus and the child while the child is still alive. In this case, the unborn are often too young to survive outside the womb even with the best of prenatal care, and the baby dies a natural death. The sin of abor-tion occurs if the doctor or nurse intentionally causes the death of the unborn while still in the womb or on the way out. The Church sees a drastic difference between causing death and allowing the process of certain death to continue.

The same applies to ectopic pregnancies. This pathologic condition can war-rant the immediate removal of the fallopian tube even though an embryo is attached or embedded to it. As long as the unborn is never directly killed, the Church doesn't consider the procedure an abortion.

Killing an embryo while in the womb or removing an unviable fetus from the womb with the intent and purpose to end its life is considered an abortion. Treating a life-threatening, pathological condition that indirectly results in the unborn child dying naturally is considered a tragedy but not an abortion. So it's not a question of who lives or who dies. It's not a battle of mother versus child.

Even the horror and tragedy of rape or incest isn't considered cause to kill an innocent unborn life. If possible, the woman — who is also considered an innocent victim — can get treatment as soon as possible to try to *prevent* conception from occurring immediately after the rape or incest. Moral theo-logians and doctors say that it takes several hours to a day for the sperm to reach the egg, so the Church permits a female rape victim to be given a con-traceptive *(anovulent) only* if ovulation or conception haven't yet taken place *and* the drug given isn't an *abortifacient* — a so-called contraceptive that doesn't prevent fertilization and conception but rather removes, destroys, or prevents implantation of the embryo. If she waits too long, usually more than 24 hours, conception may take place, and any procedure or treatment to eject the unviable human embryo is an abortion. The Church's stand is that even though she's an innocent victim of a horrible evil, the unborn child is also an innocent victim. No matter what the circumstances that led to the conception, once conceived, that child has an immortal soul and has as much right to live as the mother. In the United States, 98 percent of abortions have nothing to do with rape or incest, and throughout much of the world, the greater percentage of abortions also have nothing to do with rape.

Unborn children in the Bible

The Gospel of Luke tells the story of an encounter between Mary, the mother of Jesus, and her cousin Elizabeth, the mother of John the Baptist. According to Luke 1:39-56, Mary first meets the Archangel Gabriel, who announces to Mary that she's to conceive and bear a son and name Him Jesus. At the very moment that Mary gives her free consent, "Let it be done unto me according to your word" (Luke 1:38), the Holy Spirit overshadows her, and she conceives right then and there. So Mary becomes pregnant while she's engaged but before she marries Joseph. That's why he plans to quietly divorce her rather than expose her to the law. He erroneously concludes that Mary was unfaithful as his fiancée and got pregnant through another man. An angel in a dream tells Joseph not to be afraid and to take Mary as his wife, because it was by the power of the Holy Spirit that she conceived, not through any sexual contact with a man. Joseph's fears are alleviated, and he realizes that Mary remained a virgin, so he takes her as his wife.

The Archangel also informs Mary that her elderly cousin Elizabeth is pregnant. So Mary travels "with haste" from Nazareth to Judah to help Elizabeth. When Mary enters the home, Elizabeth is, as the Archangel told Mary, in her sixth month of pregnancy, and Mary, coming in haste from Nazareth, is only a few days into her pregnancy.

The Gospel says that when Mary enters the room, Elizabeth's unborn baby (John the Baptist) leaps for joy in his mother's womb because he knows that within Mary is the unborn Jesus. So in the Bible, a 6-month-old unborn child recognizes the presence of a 2- to 3-day-old unborn child. It's not inanimate tissue that stirs within Elizabeth, and it's not a blob of protoplasm that the unborn John the Baptist is getting excited about. So not only are the two pregnant mothers — one six months along and one only a few days along — greeting one another, but their unborn children are also very much alive and participating in the event. The unborn John heralds the arrival of the unborn Jesus.

Euthanasia

The same principles used to condemn abortion are also used to condemn euthanasia. Catholicism regards life as sacred, and taking any innocent life is immoral and sinful, whether it's doctors, nurses, family members, or friends who are taking the life.

The Church believes that no one ought to suffer a long, painful death and that the sick must be treated and the dying must be comforted. The dying and those suffering enormous pain from disease or injury can and should have as much painkilling medication as they can tolerate, as long as the medication isn't the cause of death. Modern medicine has created a plethora of chemicals to diminish or even remove pain, even if it means the patient loses consciousness. So giving someone morphine is permitted and encouraged, for example, but the dosage can't be large enough to be the direct cause of death.

The Church distinguishes between two types of euthanasia. In active euthanasia, you're causing death by doing something to hasten death. In passive euthanasia you intend and cause death by not doing what's necessary to preserve or sustain life, as follows:

- ✔ **Active:** Any procedure or treatment that directly causes the death of a patient. Giving someone a lethal injection or drinking poison are examples. This type is always considered immoral and sinful because it's the direct taking of an innocent life. The reasoning is that because the ends can't justify the means, causing the death of someone — even someone you love and hate to see in pain and suffering — is still immoral. Better to make them comfortable and give them pain medication, water, air, and nutrition.

- ✔ **Passive:** Intentionally withholding life-sustaining treatment. If the treatment is sustaining life and stopping or removing it ends life, then doing so is considered passive euthanasia. Omitting medicine that's needed to preserve life — such as not giving a diabetic insulin — or starving someone to death by not feeding her are examples. Like active euthanasia, passive euthanasia is considered immoral and sinful because its primary purpose is the death of an innocent person. The means are different, however.

The Church also distinguishes between direct and indirect passive euthanasia:

- ✔ **Direct passive:** Intentionally causing death by withholding medicine or a procedure or stopping one that has begun. This type is always immoral.

- ✔ **Indirect passive:** Withholding treatment or medicine knowing that doing so may cause death, but death isn't the intent or direct cause of withholding it. This type isn't considered immoral. For example, someone dying of cancer who's also on dialysis can refuse (or his family can refuse) that particular treatment as long as he has already started the dying process and will die of cancer or complications of it well before he'd die of kidney failure. As long as the medicine or treatment being withheld isn't the direct cause of death, it can be refused. Likewise, say that a 98-year-old person in a nursing home is in bad health and bedridden, has cancer, and has begun the dying process (the organs are starting to shut down one by one). It's considered morally permissible to have a Do Not Resuscitate (DNR) order on the chart in case the patient has a heart attack because doing cardio-pulmonary resuscitation (CPR) would be fruitless or would only prolong death by cancer. The Catechism of the Catholic Church clarifies when medical treatment can be refused or stopped: "Discontinuing medical procedures that are burdensome, dangerous, extraordinary, or disproportionate to the expected outcome can be legitimate; it is the refusal of 'overzealous' treatment. Here one does not will to cause death; one's inability to impede it is merely accepted" (2278).

When Pope John Paul II was in his last months of life suffering from Parkinson's disease, he issued a statement that the terminally ill must always be given at least *hydration* (water), *nutrition* (food), and *normal care* (clean clothes, bathing, shelter, and so on). All ordinary means to sustain life and treat disease or injury are to be done, while extraordinary means can be withheld. The only exception is a person whose digestive system has shut down. Then the use of a feeding tube would be redundant because the stomach is no longer working and is therefore unable to absorb any food or drink. Otherwise, ordinary procedures, like performing an emergency tracheotomy or inserting a feeding tube into the stomach, ought to be done to any and all sick persons, whether terminally ill or not. If these are not done and the person starves to death or dies of asphyxiation, it is considered euthanasia. Those directly involved may be guilty of the sin of murder or negligent homicide, even if the state never presses charges against them.

The death penalty

The Catechism of the Catholic Church says, "The traditional teaching of the Church does not exclude recourse to the death penalty, *if this is the only possible way* of effectively defending human lives against the *unjust aggressor*" (2267). This teaching assumes that the truly guilty party's identity and culpability have been firmly established. But the death penalty is not an absolute right of the state as would be the case in defending the right to life of the innocent. Remember: It's always immoral to intentionally take the life of an innocent person, such as in the case of abortion or euthanasia.

If the innocent can never be intentionally killed, then what about the guilty? The Catechism and the pope, quoting St. Thomas Aquinas, affirm that legitimate defense is not only a *right* but may even be a *duty* for someone responsible for another's life. Sadly, sometimes the only way to render an unjust aggressor incapable of causing harm may involve the use of deadly force, such as a policeman in the line of duty may use or a soldier in time of war would do. But the very significant restriction, according to the Catechism, is "if, however nonlethal means are sufficient to defend and protect people's safety from the aggressor, authority will limit itself to such means" (2267).

What does this all mean? It's consistent Church teaching that the state *possesses* the right to impose the death penalty, but there is no unlimited or unrestricted *use* of that right. According to the Catechism, because the state can effectively prevent crime by stopping the perpetrator without the use of deadly force, "the cases in which the execution of the offender is an absolute necessity 'are very rare, if not practically non-existent'" (2267). This severe restriction on the application of the death penalty is rooted in the fact that punishment isn't meant to be revenge but the restoration of justice, deterrence, and possible rehabilitation. Conversion of the criminal is an aspect not often brought into the public debate on the death penalty. (For more discussion on this subject, see our discussion of the Fifth Commandment — honoring human life — in Chapter 12.)

What about terrorists? There is significant evidence, argumentation, and sound reasoning that says you can invoke the rules of a Just War. (The Just War Doctrine is discussed in the next section.) This would mean that you could try terrorists in a military tribunal as enemy combatants. The thinking is that a terrorist is at war with the civilian (and in most cases) noncombatant population. So those who planned and executed the attacks of September 11, 2001, aren't just criminals; they're war criminals.

The Just War Doctrine

Catholicism has a tradition of discerning a Just War Theory, which says that all things being equal, the state has a right to wage war — just like it has a right to use capital punishment. However, just like capital punishment, the right to wage war isn't an absolute right.

St. Thomas Aquinas (1226–74) developed a theory of St. Augustine (354–430) into the now-known Just War Theory. (For more on St. Thomas Aquinas, see Chapter 21; for more on St. Augustine, see Chapter 18.) Its basis is the natural moral law, and it incorporates a moral evaluation before going to war (the reasons for it) and during war (the means used). Everything leading up to war and every act during it must fulfill the criteria listed due to the seriousness of the actions. Otherwise, the war is judged to be immoral. So the Church's stand is that in theory war is justified at times, and a just war can be waged. And the Church believes that throughout history, some wars were morally right, but many wars could've and should've been avoided.

We believe it's actually more accurate to call the Just War Theory the *Just War Doctrine* because theories are ideas not yet proven. The doctrine uses the natural moral law as a litmus test, so its premises and conclusions are sound and morally binding.

The Just War Doctrine can be broken down into two components: *Ius ad bellum* (Latin for *right to war* or moral reasons that justify a country's going to war) and *Ius in bello* (Latin for *right in war* or moral conduct during war). We discuss each component in turn.

Justifying a country going to war

Before war, these issues must be considered:

- ✔ Just cause
- ✔ Competent authority
- ✔ Comparative justice

✔ Right intention

✔ Last resort

✔ Probability of success

✔ Proportionality

Here, we explain each consideration.

Just cause

For a war to be morally permissible, the reasons for going to war must be morally correct. One example of a just cause is to repel invading enemy forces, which are considered unjust aggressors. Imperial Japan's attack on Pearl Harbor in 1941 was sufficient reason to go to war because the enemy was in the process of making attacks on the United States.

Another moral and just cause for going to war is to rescue or assist an ally who was attacked by an unjust aggressor, as Great Britain did in World War II when Poland was invaded by Nazi Germany. Removing or repelling an invading aggressor is sufficient reason to go to war. Gaining new territory or financial or political superiority, however, aren't good reasons.

If citizens are captured, property is seized, land is occupied, or allies are being attacked or invaded, the Church believes that going to war is justified. Defending or protecting lives and territory is considered a just cause. But aggression, revenge, or economic, political, or territorial gain is considered an immoral, or unjust, cause.

Competent authority

Morally speaking, only legitimate, authentic, and authorized leaders can declare and involve the nation in war. Private citizens, corporations, special interest groups, associations, political parties, and so on have no moral authority to declare war. Only presidents and congresses, prime ministers and parliaments, kings and queens — those who wield executive power — have the capacity to engage the entire nation in a war. The press and media may cover the war, but they don't declare it. And they don't sue for peace or have the authority to sign treaties. Individual soldiers, sailors, admirals, or generals have no authority to declare war either.

Comparative justice

Are the values at stake worth the loss of life, the wounding of others, the risk of innocent victims, and damage to property? There must be greater goods at risk, like freedom and liberty, which are in jeopardy if one does not go to war.

Right intention

Morally acceptable reasons for going to war are a just cause, such as the stopping of an unjust aggressor, or having the goal of restoring peace rather than seeking revenge, retaliation, or total destruction of the enemy (without any possibility of surrender).

Last resort

Morally speaking, all viable alternatives must be exhausted before resorting to war. These alternatives include but aren't limited to diplomatic dialogue and debate, quarantine, blockade, sanctions, economics, negotiation, mediation, arbitration, political and public pressure, and sufficient warning. Going to war shouldn't be the first step but the last one. All peaceful attempts must be tried. However, a country can't allow the unjust aggressor who has invaded time to regroup and strike again.

Probability of success

A just war demands that the hope of winning the war is reasonable. Fighting just to make or prove a point or merely defending honor when enemy forces are vastly superior in number, ammunition, or resources is foolish. Sacrificing troops and endangering citizens unnecessarily are irresponsible. The Mutual Assured Destruction (MAD) policy of the former Union of Soviet Socialist Republics and the United States during the Cold War had no probability of success because the goal and objective were to totally destroy the enemy, knowing that the enemy had the same capability; there could be no winners and no survivors.

Proportionality

The evils and suffering that result from the war must be proportionately less than the evils or suffering that would have ensued had there been no conflict. If more misery will result by going to war than deciding not to go, the moral choice is to wait, defer, or use other means. Part of proportionality includes the aftermath and cost of the war — in lives, injuries, property damage, and economic consequences.

Displaying right conduct during war

During war, these two issues are in play:

- ✓ Proportionality
- ✓ Discrimination of noncombatants

Proportionality

A just war uses moral means during the execution of the war. Biological weapons are considered immoral because they disproportionately harm more people and in more severity than is necessary for victory. Furthermore, germ and biological weapons of mass destruction are intrinsically evil because there is little control over the chance of harming innocent noncombatants.

Tactical nuclear weapons are permissible only if employed as a last resort and there are no other means to deter the aggressor; in addition, there must be significant accuracy and control to target only valid sites. Conventional weapons, troops, and tactics should first be tried.

Discrimination of noncombatants

The last criterion for a just war is that collateral damage must be kept to an absolute bare minimum. Military and strategic targets are the only morally permissible sites for attack. Major population centers and any place where noncombatants reside shouldn't be directly targeted. Terror bombing of civilians, for example, is immoral.

The old distinction between *military* and *civilian* no longer applies because not all combatants wear uniforms. Guerilla warfare that uses both military and civilian forces is common, so now the distinction is made between *combatants* (those who carry and use firearms or weapons) and *noncombatants* (those who don't).

Wars are declared, whereas military operations may not require such formality. Rescuing hostages; protecting innocent noncombatants; and making humanitarian deliveries of food, clothing, and medicine are not considered acts of war but still must be done prudently. Certain actions may instigate or be the catalyst for all-out war; hence, nations and their leaders are urged to resort to diplomacy and economic pressure when possible.

The sticky part comes when enemy action is imminent and probable. No one argues that a person or country should not defend itself when attacked. But what happens when there is only the threat and nothing more? What if the enemy is working on a secret weapon or is in the process of planning, preparing, and implementing an attack? Here is where credible intelligence may not be enough. There may not be enough information to determine precisely what the enemy is about to do and when it intends to do it. Preemptive wars normally do not fall into the category of being permissible. Strategic military operations may be necessary, however, if an attack is considered imminent, probable, and potentially devastating to many innocent victims.

Planning Your Family Naturally

Catholicism does *not* teach that wives are to have as many children as biologically possible. Women aren't baby factories. So why, then, is the Church against artificial contraception? Keep reading to get a glimpse of the Church's reasoning and to find out about what the Church considers a morally permissible alternative — Natural Family Planning (NFP).

The moral argument against artificial contraception

Pope Paul VI issued his encyclical *Humanae Vitae* (1968), which articulates and reiterates the Church's moral opposition to the use of artificial contraception. The Catholic Church has always said that artificial contraception is immoral. In fact, until 1930, every Christian denomination in the world — Protestant, Catholic, and Orthodox — believed that artificial contraception was sinful. The Anglican Lambeth Conference in 1930, however, permitted contraception in limited cases. Soon afterward, most Protestant churches followed suit. Today, Catholicism and a few Evangelical and Fundamentalist churches still maintain that the use of artificial contraception isn't part of God's plan.

For the Church, the worst aspect of birth control pills is that many of them aren't true contraceptives; they don't prevent the sperm and egg from conceiving. Instead, they work as an *abortifacient,* causing the uterus to eject a fertilized egg, which, according to Catholicism, is now an embryo and a human person. Many women think that their birth control pills are really contraceptives, when they're actually abortifacients.

The Church also says that artificial contraception is morally wrong because it synthetically divides and separates what God intended to always be together. Morally, each and every sex act can occur only between husband and wife *and* must be directed toward two ends: love and life, that is, the intimate unity between the man and woman (love) and the possible procreation of another human being (life). Married conjugal love — the intimacy between husband and wife — is the most profound union on earth at the natural level. The physical union of bodies in married sex represents the spiritual reality of two becoming one flesh, but that unity is also present to be open to the possibility of new life. Conception and pregnancy don't have to occur each time, but no manmade barriers should prevent what God may intend to happen. For example, if a middle-age woman, having gone through menopause and lost the natural ability to become pregnant, marries, then her marriage is just as valid in the eyes of the Church as those who are young enough to conceive.

When love and life — unity and procreation — are separated, then sex becomes an end in itself rather than a means to an end. Birth control makes sex recreational, and removing what may be perceived as the "danger" of pregnancy means that couples no longer need to communicate about when and when not to have sex and whether they want or can afford another child. The communication and consideration that's necessitated by the possibility of having a child actually strengthens the marriage. Without the necessity for consideration, communication, and cooperation, their ties to one another may weaken or fail to live up to their full potential.

Love and marriage go together

Catholic husbands and wives must pay attention to each other, showing consideration and real Christian love and charity in all aspects of the life that they share together, including the possibility of children. The Catholic Church maintains that sex isn't an absolute right but a gift and a privilege that must be used properly. Neither the Catholic wife nor the husband can demand sex from the other, but both are entitled to regular intimacy unless prevented by illness, disease, or other significant obstacles.

Artificially contraceptive sex denies the couple another opportunity for exhibiting love and extending their love to the possibility of another human being. And who could be better parents than a husband and wife who've learned how to love?

But the challenge is to suspend confidence in easy medical fixes and trust that God will send only as many children as that couple can support. A couple that can rise to that occasion must have faith, and the faith and trust that they have in God will also transfer to one another and to their children. Without the faith and trust that couples must build to keep a marriage together, it falls apart. Using artificial birth control and not having to worry about the possibility of pregnancy, spouses can cheat with less hassle. On the other hand, the possibility of pregnancy keeps many on their toes and less likely to treat a spouse as a mere sex object. Is it any accident that the increased use of artificial contraceptives has coincided with the increase in the rate of divorce, infidelity, and venereal disease?

The ramifications of using artificial birth control aren't confined to couples and families either; the results extend out to society as a whole. Until 1930, everyone in the United States assumed that the population of young people would outnumber the old and that an abundance of young workers would continue to support the government and its institutions, such as Social Security, enough to take care of the numbers of old people retiring and needing care. But that balance has tipped. The percentage of elderly in the total population has grown due to continual advancements in medical technology; at the same time, due to contraceptive sex and abortion, the percentage of youth in the total population has decreased. Combined, these facts have led to the economic concern that the smaller younger population has fewer resources and the elderly have more needs. According to the United Nations, the birth rate among first-world industrialized nations has decreased so rapidly that one European nation has dropped to an all-time low of 1.2 children per family. That's not enough to replace the current generation.

Whether it's the pill, a condom, an intrauterine device (IUD), or a sponge, any artificial method of contraception is deemed immoral because the Church believes that it divides what God intended and may frustrate a divine plan to bring a new life into the world.

The natural alternative to contraception

The Catholic Church permits and encourages married couples to space births and plan how big or small their families will be. But if artificial contraception is out, what's in? Definitely not the archaic and undependable rhythm method. That's not what the Church means by Natural Family Planning (NFP).

Because no two women are exactly alike, no two menstrual cycles are exactly alike, either. But science does show that women are infertile more times during the month than they're fertile. Each woman has a unique cycle in which she goes from producing eggs to being infertile and vice versa. By using natural science — taking body temperature, checking body fluids, and using some computations — a woman can determine with 95 percent accuracy when to have sex without getting pregnant.

Unlike artificial methods, NFP doesn't require foreign objects to be inserted into the woman's body. This method is completely natural, organic, and 100-percent safe, with no chemical side effects, no recalls, and no toxic complications. And it's a *team* effort. When using the pill or a condom, one person takes responsibility for spacing the births and regulating conception. But *both* the husband *and* the wife practice NFP. This makes sense in the eyes of the Church because *both* get married on the wedding day and *both* are involved if a baby comes along.

When practiced properly, NFP is as effective as any artificial birth control method. And it's not difficult to learn. Mother Theresa taught illiterate women how to effectively use NFP. In addition, no prescription and no expensive devices are involved, so it's easy on the budget. Birth control pills, on the other hand, are commodities bought and sold for profit. Pharmaceutical companies have a vested interest as well.

A woman is fertile during approximately seven to ten days per cycle and is infertile the rest of the time. During periods of fertility, a couple seeking to space out their family can abstain from sex.

The Catholic Church believes that these times challenge the couple to remain romantic without becoming sexual. All too often, our culture and society have exclusively united the two so that people can't imagine how someone can be romantic without ending up in bed. Yet men still court women before marrying them. Courtship means being affectionate, romantic, and loving without any sex, because it's saved for the wedding night. The Church says that the brief period of abstinence that's observed by those practicing NFP enables husbands and wives to see each other as more than objects of desire and still encourages them to be close, romantic, and loving toward one another in other, nonsexual ways. It demonstrates that one can be romantic without being sexual.

For more information on this topic, check out The Couple-to-Couple League at www.ccli.org. This international, interfaith, nonprofit organization teaches Natural Family Planning (NFP).

What if you can't conceive naturally?

What about the other side of the coin? What if a man and woman are using Natural Family Planning (NFP) to have a baby but find that they can't conceive? Infertility is one of the most painful and agonizing crosses some married couples have to carry. Just as contraceptive sex is immoral because it divides love and life (unity and procreation), conception outside of normal sexual intercourse is considered immoral, too. The Church teaches that the ends can't justify the means, so immoral means can never be used, even to promote the birth of another human being to two loving parents who desperately want a child. Children are a gift from God and not an absolute right that people can demand. Moral means must be employed when married couples have sex and when they want to have children.

One alternative to using biological procedures to conceive children is the ancient tradition of adoption. Saint Joseph is often invoked as the patron saint of adoptive parents as he wasn't the natural father of Jesus, but as the husband of Mary, the mother of Jesus, he loved her son as if He were his own flesh and blood. Adoption can save many unborn children from a horrible death by abortion and can also bring love and joy to infertile married couples.

That said, fertility drugs aren't per se forbidden, but the warning is that they often lead to multiple births, which then prompts some physicians to play God and say to the mother, "It's unlikely that all will survive, so let's terminate the least likely to survive to increase the chances of the rest." So a selective abortion is done. Kill one to save two, three, or more. To the Church, the end doesn't justify the means. Evil can never be knowingly, willingly, and intentionally done, no matter how great and good the final effect.

When conception occurs artificially, the Church claims that it isn't in God's plan, which is found naturally (in nature as opposed to manmade). Therefore, the following methods of artificially creating new life are considered immoral:

- ✔ **Artificial insemination (AIH):** The husband's sperm are inserted into the wife with a device. And often, because the man's sperm count is low, some of the husband's sperm are mixed with donor sperm. The mixture is used, but it takes only one sperm to fertilize the egg, so it's possible that someone else is going to be the genetic father of the child.

- ✔ **In vitro fertilization (IVF) and embryo transfer (ET):** With in vitro fertilization, several eggs are fertilized with plenty of sperm in a test tube or petri dish. Every fertilized egg becomes an embryo — a human person with an immortal soul. The clinic picks the best-looking embryo(s), transfers one or more into the womb of the mother, and discards the rest, which Catholicism regards as an abortion. The Church believes that at the moment of conception, a human being is created and that freezing or throwing away a person — no matter how small and developing — is gravely immoral.

✔ **Donor sperm and donor eggs:** These methods are forbidden because, again, artificial means are used to achieve conception. Even more importantly, one of the spouses is completely absent from the act of procreation because another person's egg or sperm is being used; a third party becomes involved in the birth. The donor isn't married to the husband and wife, and yet he or she is going to genetically create a new human person with one of them. For the same reason, sperm banks and surrogate mothers are considered immoral because they literally exclude the husband or the wife in the very act of procreating. Also, clinics often overfertilize and then select good embryos from not-so-good ones. The ones that are tossed out are human beings nevertheless.

✔ **Human cloning:** This method attempts to replicate rather than procreate. Using genetic material from mom and/or dad, a healthy egg is wiped clean of DNA, only to have someone else's put inside. Human cloning is an attempt to play God — as if a mere mortal can create life — and Catholicism teaches that it's dangerous and wrong.

Despite the sadness of infertility, the Catholic Church maintains that modern science doesn't offer moral solutions — only immoral alternatives. Natural sex between husband and wife is the only morally accepted means to conceive and have children.

Defending Traditional Family Life

The Catholic Church firmly believes in the sanctity of human life and in the sanctity of the human family. Both the Bible and the Catechism teach that God intended human beings to be born, be raised, and live within the nurturing protection of the family. More than just a social agreement among individuals to live together, family is a covenant relationship blessed by God.

The family is often called the *domestic church* because it is the place where persons first learn about God and His love for His children from the love shown by mom and dad to their kids. It is the building block of society, both church (religious) and state (secular). As such, family has defined parameters, obligations, duties, privileges, and rights.

Family is intimately connected to marriage, which itself reflects the covenant between the Lord and His people. Marriage is the permanent, faithful, and fruitful union of one man and one woman. This institution was created by divine design and cannot be changed or undone by any person, state, or religion. Likewise, family is built on marriage. Parents are supposed to be married to each other so they can best raise their children.

What the Catechism says

The Catechism is a book that spells out the doctrines of Catholicism. Here are some of the doctrines pertaining to marriage and family:

2201 Marriage and the family are ordered to the good of the spouses and to the procreation and education of children.

2202 A man and a woman united in marriage, together with their children, form a family. This institution is prior to any recognition by public authority, which has an obligation to recognize it.

2203 In creating man and woman, God instituted the human family and endowed it with its fundamental constitution. Its members are persons equal in dignity.

2207 The family is the *original cell of social life*. It is the natural society in which husband and wife are called to give themselves in love and in the gift of life.

Biologically, most adults can have offspring, whether they are married or single. Being a mother or father is more than just procreating; it's a vocation that is simultaneously connected to and built on the foundation of marriage. Unmarried parents can certainly love and care for their children as much as married couples; however, the children are deprived of the blessings of full family life when mom and dad are not husband and wife.

The Church does not condone any denial or violation of human rights. All human beings are made in the image and likeness of God and deserve equal treatment and protection. At the same time, there is no inalienable right to redefine or remake marriage and the family.

Marriage is between one man and one woman by divine, natural, and ecclesiastical law regardless of whether the local civil law says otherwise. Hence, homosexual (same-sex) unions cannot become or be considered true marriages. This issue is not a matter of discrimination because not just one group of people is affected. Whether you're talking about an unmarried heterosexual couple or a civilly united homosexual couple, neither of these unions constitute the divinely instituted estate of marriage. And without marriage, there cannot be full family life. Polygamous and incestuous unions are also not considered true marriages.

There may be commitment and even love between adults, and they may have all the financial resources necessary, but being open to an exclusive, permanent, and fruitful union is the foundation of marriage. A same-sex union is no different than a polygamous union or an unmarried couple in the eyes of the Church. None fully coincide with the mandate of God as does the traditional family. Christ Himself is described as the bridegroom and the Church as His bride by Saint Paul in his epistles.

Pope John Paul II said in his letter *Familiaris Consortio* (1981) that individuals are born into a family so they may more easily see their membership in the family of faith, known as the Church. Baptism makes us a child of God and we belong to God's family, being able to call Him Father and seeing Jesus as our brother. Familial relationships are not artificial but organic, like the unity in a body among all its parts.

That is why the family has a natural right to exist as it was intended to be. Unfortunately, human sin and weakness have entered the equation, and all too often innocent victims, namely the children, suffer when families are divided due to broken marriages. Sometimes even the economy and the culture — if not governments themselves — work against family life by making it easier for parents to live together without the grace and stability of marriage. Tragedies like death, illness, abuse, and abandonment also inflict harm on families and family members. All the more reason, Pope John Paul II said, that people need the spiritual family of the Church to sustain them when even their own natural family falls short.

Part IV
Praying and Using Devotions

The 5th Wave By Rich Tennant

Spiritually, I believe I can manifest many good things in my life. But right now I'd settle for being able to manifest a cab.

In this part . . .

Beyond the Mass, Catholics express their faith and morals in many ways. Chapter 15 examines various means of praying (both privately and publicly) that help Catholics deepen their relationship with God. In Chapter 16, we take a look at Catholic *devotions:* prayers that help a Catholic express her personal love for God. Devotions can include novenas, litanies, prayers on the rosary, and even petitions to St. Anthony when your car keys are lost! In Chapter 17, we focus specifically on the ways in which Catholics show their affection for Mary, the mother of Jesus.

Chapter 18 explains how and why Catholics recognize and honor the deceased heroes of the Church: the saints. Finally, the last chapter in this part explains some great Catholic traditions, including adoring Jesus in the Holy Eucharist, using holy water and blessed candles, and taking part in a religious procession.

Chapter 15

Growing in the Faith

In This Chapter

▶ Talking to God through prayer

▶ Performing solitary and communal prayers

▶ Moving through the three stages of spiritual growth

*I*n this chapter, we explain how people can achieve *interior sanctification,* which is a fancy way of saying "becoming holy and growing in the faith." The first step to interior sanctification is to work on your personal connection with God, which depends entirely on prayer. Think of it this way: If you had never spoken with (or texted or exchanged e-mails with) a person, you couldn't claim to have much of a relationship with him or her, right? The same is true with God. If you never attempt to communicate with God, you simply can't have much of a personal relationship with Him. Luckily, you can pray in all sorts of ways, which we explain in this chapter.

And while praying is crucial, it isn't the only means of growing in your faith. In this chapter, we explain the three stages of spiritual growth and the ways in which you achieve them. Of course, God has a direct hand in that growth as well; you can't get far without His grace. But He needs *you* to be an active partner — no spiritual couch potatoes allowed!

Prayer is an art that anyone can do. The more you pray, the better you get at praying. There is no wrong way to pray, just the mistake of not praying at all. Any effort made is helpful, but the main objective is quality, not quantity. In other words, it's not how much time you spend in prayer that matters as much as how well you pray.

Having a Personal Relationship with God through Prayer

Prayer is a type of communication that's not all that different in method from texting or Skyping or (how old-fashioned!) writing an e-mail. But what makes prayer unique is that it allows people to converse with God, and it allows God to communicate with them.

Reading the Bible is a form of prayer. Catholics believe God communicates to us through divine revelation, which is contained in both Sacred Scripture and Sacred Tradition. Making time to read the inspired Word of God is not always easy, but it is essential to the life of faith.

The problem is that people's lives are so busy — and so noisy — that many consider prayer complicated because finding time to pray seems so difficult. As a result, they may have a prayer experience only when they attend Sunday Mass. But the truth is that the soft voice of God can be heard only in the quietness of prayer. And while the *Divine Liturgy* (another name for Mass) is the source and summit of Christian prayer, we are challenged to be prayerful people every day — not just every week, month, or year. Whether you pray mentally or verbally, it all serves to bring you closer to God.

Practicing the four types of prayer

This section shows you how to pray the four types or acts of prayer: adoration, contrition, petition, and thanksgiving. The Holy Sacrifice of the Mass contains all four elements and, therefore, is the most perfect prayer of the Church, but you can practice these four types of prayer in your own quiet time.

Adoration

Adoration is the worship of God, whether private or public. It's a matter of justice that creatures endowed with reason (like human beings) owe worship to the Creator. As His follower, you praise God not for what you can get from Him, but merely because of who He is. As Supreme Being, Creator and Lord of the Universe, King of Heaven and Earth, Redeemer, and Sanctifier, He deserves recognition and praise. In the Holy Sacrifice of the Mass, the *Gloria*, *Sanctus*, and *Alleluia* are prime examples of praise (see Chapter 10).

When you pray, praise and worship God for who He is. Focus your prayer on Him alone and your relationship to Him. You can prayerfully adore God just by thinking of His many attributes, praising His greatness, and being in wonder and awe of His power. Affirming the Lordship of God, that He rules and His will is our objective, is real adoration. Psalm 145 and Daniel 3:56 are classical sources of worship prayer.

Contrition

Contrition is having sorrow for one's sins. With this element of prayer, you express regret for the wrongs you have done and ask God to forgive you and cleanse you of your sins. You seek God's mercy and forgiveness while expressing a firm purpose to change your life. In other words, contrition is a prayer of repentance. In the Mass, prayers of sorrow are expressed in the *Confiteor, Kyrie,* and *Agnus Dei* (see Chapter 10).

When a sinner recognizes his sinful past and is truly sorry for offending God, who is all good and all loving, the sinner's sorrow is known as *perfect contrition.* The opposite, *imperfect* contrition, occurs when the sinner is motivated purely by a fear of punishment.

If you're truly sorry for your sins and want to pray a prayer of contrition, tell God you regret making a mistake. Ask Him to forgive the sins you committed (such as the Commandments you broke, and so on) and also ask for the grace to resist temptations in the future.

Petition

Petition (also called *supplication*) is a specific prayer request that asks for God's assistance. At Mass, the General Intercessions (Prayer of the Faithful) is an example of this type of prayer. Simply ask God to heal someone who is sick; to help a friend who is unemployed to find a job; to bring tranquility to a rocky marriage or friendship; or whatever else is on your mind.

Sacred Scripture says that you are to ask, for in so doing you shall receive (Matthew 7:7-8). However, when making prayer appeals, you must remember that God answers your prayers according to how He sees fit. And the divine perspective always takes the view of your eternal reward in heaven. So if you pray for a new car or a bonus at work, don't be shocked if you don't receive it! The Church advocates using petition to pray for *each other's* needs as well as your own.

Thanksgiving

Prayers of thanksgiving recognize the debt you owe to God for all the blessings and gifts bestowed on you, personally and communally. As you pray, always offer a sincere thank you for all that He has done for you. Too many times, prayers become a laundry list of what an individual needs: forgive me of my sins; please give me the things that I want; Amen. You don't want to be like the nine lepers in Luke 17:12-19 who didn't come back to the Lord to thank Him for their cure!

The Liturgy of the Eucharist, especially the Roman Canon or another Eucharistic Prayer, is an essential prayer of thanks (the word *Eucharist* is derived from the Greek word meaning "thanksgiving"), but you can also thank God by telling him you're grateful for the blessings in your life.

Getting to know spontaneous and formal prayer

After you're familiar with the kinds of prayer to offer to God (see "Practicing the four types of prayer" for a reminder), recognize that your prayer can be either spontaneous or formal. We explain each type in the following sections. You should also take time to pray both communally and by yourself. (Flip to "Praying in Private and in a Community" for more.)

Whether you create the words yourself, as in a conversation or dialogue, or recite words written by someone else, you're still praying, and it's still bringing you closer to God.

Spontaneous

Usually when you call a friend on your cell phone or send a text message, you're not enacting a rehearsed conversation (we digress: phone interviews and breakups are probably exceptions). Instead, you both speak from the heart. The same is true of prayer. *Spontaneous prayer* simply involves expressing what's in your mind and heart. It's called the *direct* approach.

Prayer has been called *cor ad cor loquitur* (heart speaks to heart). Communicating with God can be like having a chat between pals; this approach is as much prayer as is singing in the church choir. Even though you're speaking to the Almighty, Creator of Heaven and Earth, you're also talking to your best friend in the universe.

When you pray spontaneously, you can use the four types of prayer described earlier in this chapter (see "Practicing the four types of prayer") to say exactly what's in your heart in your own words. Write your words down in a journal, speak them aloud, or simply ponder your spontaneous prayer. You can tell God whatever is on your mind; Catholics believe that He's always listening.

Formal

Sometimes you may find it difficult to come up with your own dialogue with God. You may be distracted by earthly problems, or you may just not know what to say. Formal prayer is the answer in this situation. You can depend on the wisdom and holiness of those who have gone before you. *Formal prayers* are those composed by someone else and usually memorized, and they include devotions, novenas, chaplets, litanies, and aspirations.

Head to Appendix B, your local parish, a Catholic bookstore, or a Catholic website to find prayers in these different categories. Prayer books, which have been used by Catholics for centuries, often contain many of these prayers. On the eve of a child's reception of First Holy Communion (see Chapter 8), he or she customarily receives such a prayer book. A popular adult prayer book is the *Raccolta,* which contains many prayers that have certain indulgences granted by the Church to their usage.

An *indulgence* isn't a "get out of purgatory" or "get out of hell" for free card. Instead, it's a remission of temporal punishment due to sin. The Church bestows indulgences on certain prayers and pious acts and uses them to tap in to the infinite merit of Christ's Passion, death, and resurrection.

Praying in Private and in a Community

Human beings don't exist in a vacuum; no one lives completely alone. Catholicism asks believers to take their faith public from time to time. For example, you're asked to worship publicly with other believers each Sunday. But having a relationship with God in public (such as in church) isn't enough. You also need to cultivate a deep, interior, personal relationship with God. This relationship is what folks call *spirituality*.

Private prayer nourishes your public prayer. It creates the environment in which you become receptive to the Word of God proclaimed, the Body of Christ received, and the abundance of graces bestowed at Mass. In turn, your public worship cultivates your relationship with the Lord in personal prayer. Graces received at Mass make you more in tune with the Lord. Private and public prayers aren't in competition with one another; they support each other.

One excellent way to combine your public and private spirituality is the *Holy Hour:* a tradition of spending an hour adoring the Blessed Sacrament outside of Mass. Flip to Chapter 19 for the rundown on this special hour of prayer.

The goal of private and communal prayer is greater understanding, worship, and adoration of God and His message of salvation. Jesus Christ spent time in private and in public prayer. He often prayed by himself, and He prayed many times in the local synagogue and in the Temple of Jerusalem. Both types of prayer are necessary for the life of a Christian to grow in his relationship to — and understanding of — God. We discuss both private and communal prayer in the following sections.

Taking personal time with God: Private prayer

The Gospels give specific accounts of Jesus's private prayer times. For example, Matthew 14:23 says, "[W]hen He had dismissed the crowds, he went up on the mountain by himself to pray." Mark 1:35 says, "[I]n the morning a great while before day, he rose and went out to a lonely place, and there he prayed."

Daily personal prayer is as essential to the soul as daily food and rest are to the body. Spending time with the Lord cultivates a relationship so the believer truly becomes a friend and not just a servant.

Two specific types of private prayer are meditation and contemplation, which we explain in the following sections.

Meditation

Meditation is a form of prayer that allows a person to reflect on God and His plan for salvation. The word derives from Latin and means "to give consideration." In meditation, the Christian consciously focuses his thoughts on the Lord, the Virgin Mary, the saints and angels, or an article of faith. Its purpose is to deepen and increase the personal relationship with the Lord. Meditation can be a part of a Holy Hour (spent in adoration of the Blessed Sacrament). We discuss the Holy Hour earlier in the chapter and again in Chapter 19.

Meditation in the Catholic tradition is quite different from that in the Eastern religions like Buddhism or Taoism. Eastern non-Christian mysticism involves emptying the mind of all thoughts. Catholic tradition meditation is the opposite; it's an active mental task that tries to reach the depth, width, height, and breadth of God.

The end results of meditation are essential for Christian growth. Meditation aids in knowing God, being receptive to His help and direction, and creating an attitude of commitment and determination. When performed properly, meditation can lead to great results in your spiritual life, most specifically the way you grow in consciousness of God in your life. With meditation, you, as the Christian disciple, become better informed about moral choices and major decisions you have to make. You then make better choices because you're allowing God to direct your soul.

A classic form of Christian meditation is *Lectio Divina,* or the Divine (or Holy) Reading. And it's making a comeback. In a 2005 speech, Pope Benedict XVI recommended that Catholics engage in *lectio divina.* Here's the step-by-step guide on this form of meditation, which uses Sacred Scripture as the source of inspiration:

1. **Reading** *(lectio)*: Choose a text from Sacred Scripture and read it slowly.

2. **Discursive meditation** *(meditatio)*: Read the given passage with some thought and reflection.

3. **Affective prayer** *(oratio)*: Converse with God about the content of the Scripture passage.

4. **Contemplation** *(contemplatio)*: Allow the Lord to direct your mind and heart to achieve a set outcome.

Contemplation

Whereas meditation begins with yourself, *contemplation,* which simply means making yourself available to God, originates with God. You can't conjure or summon the Lord; you can only make yourself available and open to His divine action. When you meditate, you're in the driver's seat. Contemplation, on the other hand, requires you to be the passenger who waits for the bus or train to arrive. When it does arrive, that bus or train takes you to the very heart of God.

Contemplative or mystical prayer is a normal part of the Christian prayer life. Everyone — not just clergy and religious brothers and sisters — can experience contemplation. Of course, several religious orders of men and women are especially dedicated to contemplation, such as the Cloistered Poor Clares, Dominicans, Carmelites, Trappists, and Cistercians. Yet, throughout the Old and New Testaments, you find examples of ordinary people who devote some time to this prayer — from Moses to Martha's sister, Mary.

Contemplative prayer usually ensues after meditation. It consists of a more passive and sublime experience of God. If Christian meditation is the soul's inspired quest to discover God, contemplation is God's lifting the soul into Himself so it effortlessly basks in the divine light. The key distinction is that contemplation, in the strict sense, is purely the work of God. Meditation, though aided by God and predicated on the grace and work of Christ, is the result of your seeking Him.

Joining others for communal prayer

In addition to private prayers, a Christian also prays in common with the Church. Doing so means participating in Mass and the other sacraments and reciting the Liturgy of the Hours.

Mass and the other sacraments

The most obvious and regular way Catholics experience communal prayer is in the Holy Mass, especially on Sundays in the local parish church. While keeping the Sabbath holy is a commandment, the Mass also offers a practical way of connecting with a community of believers. Head to Chapter 10 for all the details on what happens during Mass.

Liturgy of the Hours

The Liturgy of the Hours (LOH), also known as the *Divine Office* or the *Breviary,* is considered part of the communal or public prayer of the Church. Because it's part of the official liturgy of the Church, all clergy and religious sisters and brothers have a duty and obligation to pray the Liturgy of the Hours on behalf of others. *Liturgy* is Greek for "work." One of the chief works of the Christian is to give praise and adoration to his Creator, and clergy do so in part through the Sacred Liturgy.

The LOH is a four-volume set of prayer books made up of psalms, hymns, readings from Scripture, and reflections from the saints. It's divided into segments, which originally were categorized by the hours of the day. In ancient times, the monks and nuns of the monasteries would hear the chapel bell ring to remind them to pray. But the luxury of a bell reminding you to pray isn't available to those who live outside the monastery and work throughout the day. Hence, most priests, deacons, religious sisters and brothers, and laity don't follow the original time slots. But they keep the same divisions and designations in the Liturgy of the Hours.

Daily praying of the LOH normally begins with the *Invitatory Psalm,* which can be said at either the Office of Reading or Morning Prayer. Here are the different prayers recited each day according to the LOH:

- ✔ **Office of Readings (Matins):** Many people pray this first thing in the morning. It contains a hymn; three psalms; an extended reading from Sacred Scripture; and another reading. The hour concludes with a prayer taken from the saint of the day or the liturgical season. An Office of Reading recited on a Sunday or Holy Day concludes with a hymn of praise called *The Te Deum.*

- ✔ **Morning Prayer (Lauds):** This prayer can be prayed anytime during the morning. It consists of a hymn, three sets of psalms, a short reading and response, the Song of Zechariah (*Benedictus*), intercessory prayers, the Our Father (Lord's Prayer), and a concluding prayer.

- ✔ **Midday prayer:** This prayer is divided into three sections, and only cloistered religious brothers and sisters have the obligation to pray all three *minor hours,* divided into mid-morning (*Terce*), midday (*Sext*), and mid-afternoon (*None*). These hours consist of a hymn, three psalms, a small reading from Scripture, and a concluding prayer. Everyone else just prays one of the three minor hours.

- ✔ **Evening Prayer:** Evening Prayer (*Vespers*) can be prayed anytime in the afternoon or evening. It has the same structure as Morning Prayer, but instead of including the Canticle of Zechariah, it includes the Canticle of Mary (the *Magnificat*).

- ✔ **Night Prayer:** Night Prayer (*Compline*) can be prayed anytime after supper and before going to bed. It includes an examination of conscience, *Confiteor* (a public act of sorrow for committing sin), a hymn, one or two psalms, the Canticle of Simeon (*Nunc Dimittis*), a closing prayer, and a hymn to the Blessed Virgin Mary.

Saying the Lord's Prayer

The most famous and beloved formal prayer is the one Jesus himself gave Christians, called the Lord's Prayer or the Our Father (*Pater Noster* in Latin).

Taught by Christ to His own apostles, this prayer is the blueprint for all prayer because it tells you what to ask for and why.

The Lord's Prayer contains the essentials regarding the relationship between mankind and God. It's prayed not only in private through devotions such as the Rosary, Stations of the Cross, and various chaplets and novenas (see Chapter 16), but also in public in the celebration of the sacraments (refer to Chapters 8 and 9), Mass (Chapter 10), and Liturgy of the Hours (described earlier in this chapter). The Lord's Prayer is revered by Christians because it was given by Jesus, contains all the basic element of prayer (adoration, thanksgiving, petition, and contrition), and is universal.

The Lord's Prayer is divided into the following parts and petitions:

- **Our Father who art in Heaven:** This invocation recognizes God's authority and your duty to love Him. In Christ and through the grace of the Sacrament of Baptism (see Chapter 8), man becomes an adopted child of God. God condescends to offer humankind a share in His divine life, which is impossible for you to attain on your own.

- **Hallowed be Thy Name, Thy Kingdom Come, Thy Will be done on earth as it is in heaven:** These are three distinct petitions:

  - The first petition acknowledges that in the First Commandment (see Chapter 12), God mandates that His name be treated always as holy and not be used in a profane way. (Man recognizes the holiness of God by obeying His commandments.)

  - The second petition expresses the coming of the Kingdom of Heaven, which has already begun in the Church and will reach its fullness in Heaven. Christians anticipate an event at the end of time that corresponds to the second coming of Jesus (called the *Parousia*).

  - The third petition demonstrates the necessity of humanity cooperating with God's will by observing His moral principles. God makes holy His Name by ruling and implementing His Will throughout the entire universe, which includes both heaven and earth.

- **Give us this day our daily bread:** In mere human terms, bread is food. For Christians, this staple takes on a spiritual meaning as well. With this petition, Christians are praying not only for their daily needs to be met but also for spiritual food, or the *bread of life:* the Word of God and the Eucharist (see Chapter 8). This spiritual bread helps them attain eternal life. They ask for it *today* because the Kingdom of Heaven begins on earth and culminates in Heaven. To share in the culmination, a Christian knows that he needs to be nourished daily with the bread of life.

St. Thomas Aquinas wrote about such nourishment when he composed *O Sacrum Convivium,* a text honoring the Blessed Sacrament: "O sacred banquet at which Christ is consumed, the memory of his Passion is recalled, our souls are filled with grace, and the pledge of future glory is given to us."

✔ **Forgive us our trespasses as we forgive those who trespass against us:** With this petition, the worshipper seeks forgiveness. Often, *trespasses* is replaced by the word *debt,* which denotes a sense of reparation on your part due to your personal sins. Yet, it's impossible for humans to alone make recompense for sin. You're commended to God, who is all merciful and overlooks all things to a humble and contrite heart. The second part of this petition conveys an obligation to forgive others; the phrasing of this petition indicates that God should forgive the petitioner only to the degree that she's able to forgive. Yet, the reality is that human mercy can never compare to the all-embracing mercy of God.

✔ **And lead us not into temptation, but deliver us from evil.** With the first phrase, you ask for the grace of perseverance in order to avoid those people, places, and things that can lead you into sin. With the second phrase, you pray not only to be delivered from temptation but also from falling into sin. If the petitioner asks fervently, God gives him grace to resist temptation not only now but at the hour of death when enticement is most strong. Finally, the deliverance from evil refers to Satan himself. Christians are taught early on the three sources of sin: the world, the flesh, and the devil. They pray to be delivered from all three so they don't fall into sin and separate themselves from the love of God.

When a person converts to Catholicism, she participates in a special rite during Lent that's called "The Presentation of the Lord's Prayer." The Church entrusts this prayer and its fruits to a *catechumen* (an adult who is preparing to be baptized) who will shortly embrace Catholicism at the Easter Vigil.

Taking It to the Next Level: The Stages of Spiritual Growth

So you're a decent Catholic: You've been baptized, you've been confirmed, and you go to Mass every Sunday. Can your relationship with God just sit in that same rhythm for the next 30 years? We say it shouldn't. In this section, we walk you through what Catholicism considers the three stages of spiritual growth: purgative, illuminative, and unitive. In doing so, we explain the ultimate goal of Christian action (including prayer): union with God.

Purgative: Practicing self-denial and sacrifice

No one but God is perfect. Every man and woman has some imperfections, weaknesses, faults, and failures. The first stage of spiritual growth, called the *purgative* stage (based on the need to purge, cleanse, and purify) requires a cleansing or removal of bad habits and evil desires.

This stage has two elements: penance and mortification. It addresses temptations to sin and the intense attraction to satisfying the senses. In this stage, the devout person tries to achieve a purity of soul so he can act freely and not out of slavery to habit, passions, or vices. The individual earnestly avoids the vices: pride, envy, lust, anger, gluttony, greed, and sloth.

Penance

The first means of purgation is to do *penance*. Penance isn't punishment for past misdeeds. Instead, it's an external manifestation of contrition and sorrow for past sins. In other words, it means you have remorse and regret for offending God, and therefore show your repentance by acts of self-denial.

Because a person may go too far and cross the line into behavior that's painful and self-destructive, any and all penance should first be approved by a person's spiritual director or confessor — a sort of personal trainer in the life of faith.

Here are some forms that penance may take:

- **Abstaining:** Avoiding certain foods, like not eating meat on Fridays, is an act of penance.

- **Fasting:** A believer reduces the amount of food consumed in one day. Fasting isn't starvation, and it isn't a bread-and-water diet. Fasting is eating one full meal for the day, two smaller meals (which if combined would be smaller than the one full meal), and no snacks.

- **Almsgiving:** A person makes a financial donation to help the poor and needy. Giving alms means to give a monetary gift, generously and anonymously. It can be to Catholic charities in the diocese or the Saint Vincent de Paul Society in the parish. Both of these help poor people and their families.

Mortification

Like penance, *mortification* is a means of self-denial. Unlike penance, however, it isn't rooted in sorrow for past sins; instead, it's oriented toward future temptations. Mortification uses the same methods of abstinence, fasting, and almsgiving but for the purpose of strengthening your will. It's like spiritual spring training. Athletes deny themselves a lot during practice and training so they're prepared to compete at their best.

Giving up something freely and willingly trains the soul. Everyone has desires and urges. If you give in to all of them completely and immediately, they will ruin you. For instance, if you aren't moderate in how much or how often you eat, you risk becoming overweight. Likewise, if you satisfy every whim that comes your way, you won't have any discipline — and without discipline, you have no safety or security.

Mortification is a modest and temporary means of self-denial that trains your ego to realize that life and reality itself isn't just about you. Other people and their needs may supersede your wants, and, therefore, you must be willing to make that sacrifice. By denying yourself legitimate goods every now and then, you show yourself that you can say no and that you aren't addicted to feeding your ego. Talk to your parish priest to make sure you're choosing the best forms of mortification.

Illuminative: Distinguishing good from evil

As a person makes spiritual progress by avoiding mortal sin and attachment to worldly things, her mind and soul become more enlightened with virtue. She longs to form a closer union with God. She becomes less selfish and more selfless, which is expressed by practicing corporal and spiritual works of mercy (which we outline in Chapter 19). She also has a greater desire for solitude, which comes from meditations and Holy Hours (which we explain earlier in the chapter). Acts of charity flow from her and nourish the works of mercy.

Purifications (spiritual cleansing) are still required at this *illuminative* stage of spiritual progress, and usually they result in boredom or personal trial. God permits these sufferings in order for the person to be strengthened in faith. Meditation is the type of prayer normally associated with this stage.

While the purgative stage focuses on the bad habits to be removed, the illuminative stage centers on positive things to be done — and done often. As the person moves from the purgative to the illuminative stage, bad habits, or *vices,* are eliminated and replaced by good habits, or *virtues,* which we outline next and discuss in more detail in Chapter 13.

Prudence

Prudence is the ability to make good moral judgments — to know what to say or do, when, and how. Prudence is not only about timing but also about technique. There's a proper place, time, and way to do everything. For example, consider *fraternal correction,* which occurs when you give good advice to a friend and counsel him to stop doing an immoral and sinful activity.

Say, for instance, you have a friend who has a gambling or drinking problem; clearly, you need to recommend that he get help. Prudence is the ability and wisdom to know you don't confront the person at the funeral parlor during his grandmother's wake. Or similarly, somebody may owe you five bucks, but prudence tells you not to ask for it by ringing his doorbell at 4 a.m.

Justice

Justice is giving each person his or her due. If you hire someone for $5 to shovel your driveway after a heavy snowfall, justice demands you actually pay him $5 for doing the job. Justice also demands that the person shoveling truly shovel your driveway and not just shovel a few feet of it.

Doing the right thing for the right reason is what justice is about. Justice requires paying fair wages, doing a full day's work, being honest on your employment records, and so on. Cheating on your taxes, cheating employees or employers, and discriminating against people because of their race or religion are violations of justice.

Temperance

Temperance, or moderation, requires that you establish limits. It means knowing when to say no or when to stop. It doesn't demand total abstinence unless something is bad for you. Giving up all sweets forever isn't temperance (although it may be prudent if you're a diabetic or obese). Temperance means aiming for and achieving a happy balance.

For example, temperance means getting the right amount of rest while doing the right amount of work. Temperance avoids extremes, like becoming a workaholic or a couch potato. If someone isn't an alcoholic and isn't about to perform surgery or drive a car, temperance allows her to consume an alcoholic beverage — but not enough to get drunk or be inebriated enough to make bad and dangerous judgments.

Fortitude

Fortitude is the courage to do what has to be done or say what has to be said. Prudence tells you what, how, and when; fortitude is the force that enables you to fulfill that directive. This strength comes from repetition, from reaffirming the plan, and from the desire to pursue it. However, fortitude shouldn't be reckless or irrational. You must use reason, think through what has to be done, and then act prudently. Fortitude builds character; the more reliable you are in doing the right thing, the more confidence people will have in you.

Unitive: Connecting with God

The third stage of spiritual growth, the *unitive* stage, is the level of perfection, where you desire only to do the will of God. Temptation and sin aren't issues at this stage. Whereas meditation is the type of prayer exemplified in the illuminative stage, contemplation is associated with the unitive stage.

Although a person may still experience personal sufferings at this stage, still he has an atmosphere of peace — a joy even in the midst of trial. The soul is united to God by the virtue of love, and the seven gifts of the Holy Spirit (wisdom, understanding, counsel, fortitude, knowledge, piety, and fear of the Lord) are used splendidly.

Yet, a person at this stage can still continue to endure further purifications through sufferings in order to achieve greater purification and thus greater union due to less attachment to lower things. Some of the great saints on earth have experienced mystical ecstasies, such as Teresa of Avila.

The unitive stage is something that takes a lifetime to perfect, but each day is worth the daily effort. It may be slow and incremental, but like mature wine, it takes time to achieve a great end result.

Chapter 16

Showing Your Love for God

. . . .

In This Chapter

▶ Looking at the most popular Catholic devotions

▶ Praying more than the minimum requirement with novenas and litanies

▶ Taking time out with pilgrimages and retreats

▶ Getting a grip on your rosary beads

. . . .

_I_f you're Catholic, you know you need to participate at Mass weekly, believe in Jesus, obey the Ten Commandments, and confess your sins when you fall short of God's glory. So isn't that enough? Do you really need anything more? The answer to both questions is yes. Those _are_ the actions required of every Catholic, but we encourage you to do more. Devotions are a way of going the extra mile to express your personal love for God.

Whether practicing devotions privately at home, in a small group, or in the form of a pilgrimage or retreat, Catholics believe that devotions act like spiritual vitamins to supplement the primary and main form of divine communication — the Mass. This chapter explains how Catholics show their love for God through devotions.

Devotions are optional — Catholics can take 'em or leave 'em — but attending Sunday Mass or the Saturday Vigil Mass is mandatory. Missing Sunday Mass without a legitimate excuse is a grave sin.

Going Beyond Your Basic Duty

Devotions refer to a wide variety of prayers, both long and short, such as the Rosary and novenas, as well as various religious practices that Catholics engage in, such as making a pilgrimage or a retreat. Devotions are generally less official than the Mass, and many different devotions are available so that individuals can find the one(s) to suit them and their personal spirituality.

Knowing when and where to pray devotions

Unlike Sacraments, which are formal, sacred celebrations of the whole church that need to take place on sacred ground, devotions can be done anywhere — in church, at home, or outside. Sacraments were instituted by Christ whereas devotions are classified as *sacramentals,* meaning they were created by the Church.

Devotions are prayed alone or with others. They're done outside of the Sacred Liturgy — in other words, not during Mass, except for the Litany of Saints on special occasions. They can, however, be said in any public setting, such as a cemetery or a prayer gathering.

Separating devotions from Mass

Just like some people think that the Second Vatican Council (see Chapter 10) threw out Latin (which it didn't), some people think that it got rid of or discouraged devotions. Not true. Vatican II didn't pooh-pooh devotions. What it did say was that the separation between the Sacred Liturgy — the Mass — and all forms of public and private devotion must be clear and distinct. No gray area.

Sure enough, Pope Paul VI asserted in his encyclical *Marialis Cultus* (1974) that Catholics shouldn't say the Rosary during Mass. But praying the Rosary *before* Mass as a preparation or *after* Mass as a thanksgiving is allowed and highly encouraged. (See the "Praying the Rosary" section later in this chapter for the Rosary how-to.)

Likewise, the Stations of the Cross, a traditional Lenten devotion, should never be celebrated during adoration of the Holy Eucharist or in the middle of Mass, but it can be said before or after Mass. (See "The Way of the Cross" section later in this chapter.) And adoration of the Holy Eucharist should be separate from Mass to differentiate the two.

Devotions to the Virgin Mary and the saints are also subordinate and auxiliary to the Mass. Of course, plenty of Masses honor the Virgin Mary and the saints. Even though the names of Mary and the saints are mentioned in the Mass, as in the Eucharistic Prayer (see Chapter 10), they're still secondary. References to God are primary; Mary and the saints are honored, but God alone is worshipped and adored.

Running the Gamut of Devotions

To get up close and personal with God, Catholics practice a wide variety of devotions. In this section, we cover some of the most popular ones. Your local Catholic bookstore should have a wide variety of booklets containing novenas, litanies, and other devotions. We recommend checking out the catalog section of EWTN's website (www.ewtn.com).

Praying novenas to the saints

A novena (from the Latin word *novem,* meaning *nine*) is a traditional prayer that's said for nine consecutive days. The practice is based on the concept that nine days passed from the day of Christ's Ascension into heaven (40 days after Easter) until the coming of the Holy Spirit at Pentecost (50 days after Easter). According to Scripture, the apostles, based on Acts 1:14–2:4, accompanied by Mary, prayed during those nine days in the upper room, where the Last Supper took place. And the Church considers that event the first novena.

Novenas are merely short prayers to a particular saint, requesting that the saint pray to Jesus for the person. The prayers are often said nine days before the feast day of the particular saint so that the novena ends on the actual day that the saint is believed to have gone to heaven, which is called the saint's *feast day.* The hope is that after praying for nine days, some special spiritual blessings will be given by God through the intercession of the particular saint that the novena is addressed to. (For more on the saints, see Chapter 18.)

Novenas can also be prayed anytime for a special need, such as in desperate and seemingly hopeless cases. Whenever you find yourself or someone you care about in a desperate or seemingly hopeless situation, consider doing what some Catholics do — pray a novena to St. Peregrine, Patron of Cancer Patients, or to St. Jude (see Chapter 21), Patron of Hopeless Cases, such as the Prayer to St. Jude that follows:

> Most holy apostle, St. Jude, faithful servant and friend of Jesus, the Church honors and invokes you universally, as the patron of hopeless cases, of things almost despaired of. Pray for me, I am so helpless and alone. Make use, I implore you, of that particular privilege given to you, to bring visible and speedy help where help is almost despaired of. Come to my assistance in this great need that I may receive the consolation and help of heaven in all my necessities, tribulations, and sufferings, particularly *[state your request]* and that I may praise God with you and all the elect forever. I promise, O blessed St. Jude, to be ever mindful of this great favor, to always honor you as my special and powerful patron, and to gratefully encourage devotion to you. Amen.

Is saintly intercession non-Christian?

Often, non-Catholics say that the idea of saintly intercession is non-Christian because only Christ should be our mediator. The Catholic response is that intercession isn't mediation.

Catholics believe that only Christ had a complete divine nature with a divine intellect and will and a complete human nature with a human intellect and will united in His one divine person. So Catholics believe that He's the only mediator between God and humans, between heaven and earth.

Catholics believe that intercession is subordinate and optional. Human beings *need* Christ to be their mediator. The intercession of Mary and the saints isn't necessary, but their help is still part of God's plan; *intercession* — someone asking a favor to God on your behalf — is considered helpful. God doesn't need to use these intercessors, but every individual is a member of the family of God, and He wills that the members of his family assist one another. One way of helping others is to pray for them — to ask for God's favor on behalf of someone else. If those on earth can and ought to help their neighbor with prayer, then those in heaven (Mary and the saints) can, too.

The Bible says that at the wedding feast of Cana, Mary went to her son, Jesus, and interceded with Him to help out the groom because they ran out of wine (John 2:1-11). Jesus then changed the water into wine. The Church maintains that Jesus — as God, in His divine intellect, being able to know all things — already knew that they ran out of wine. Yet He chose to allow His mother to intercede.

Loving litanies

A *litany,* from the Greek *lite* (meaning *prayer*), is a long prayer often prayed *antiphonally,* meaning one person recites the first part and the rest of the group responds. For example, the leader says, "Holy Mary, Mother of God," and the people respond, "Pray for us." The leader then says, "St. Michael," and the people respond, "Pray for us." And so on until the end of the litany.

The Litany of the Saints is the one litany that's actually allowed to be used during Mass on certain occasions. Before the Baptism of catechumens at the Easter Vigil, as well as at the Ordination Mass of a deacon, priest, or bishop, you may hear the chanting of the Litany of Saints. Otherwise, litanies are prayed outside of Mass as a private devotion or publicly after Mass on the feast day of the particular saint.

The Contemporary Litany of the Saints, which follows, incorporates some recent saints relevant to U.S. Catholics. The leader's text is in Roman type, and the responses are italicized; at the asterisk, the people respond, "Pray for us."

> Lord, have mercy, *Lord, have mercy.*
> Christ, have mercy, *Christ, have mercy.*
> Lord, have mercy, *Lord, have mercy.*
> Holy Mary, Mother of God, *pray for us.*

St. Michael, *
Holy angels of God, *
St. John the Baptist, *
St. Joseph, *
St. Peter and St. Paul, *
St. Andrew, *
St. John, *
St. Mary Magdalene, *
St. Stephen, *
St. Ignatius of Antioch, *
St. Lawrence, *
St. Perpetua and St. Felicity, *
St. Agnes, *
St. Gregory, *
St. Augustine, *

St. Athanasius, *
St. Basil, *
St. Martin, *
St. Benedict, *
St. Francis and St. Dominic, *
St. Francis Xavier, *
St. John Vianney, *
St. Catherine of Siena, *
St. Teresa of Jesus, *
St. Frances Xavier Cabrini, *
St. John Neuman, *
St. Elizabeth Ann Seton, *
St. Katharine Drexel, *
All holy men and women, *.

> Lord, be merciful, *Lord, save your people.*
> From all evil, *Lord, save your people.*
> From every sin, *Lord, save your people.*
> From everlasting death, *Lord, save your people.*
> By your coming as man, *Lord, save your people.*
> By your death and rising to new life, *Lord, save your people.*
> By your gift of the Holy Spirit, *Lord, save your people.*
> Be merciful to us sinners, *Lord, save your people.*
> Guide and protect your holy Church, *Lord, save your people.*
> Keep the pope and all the clergy in faithful service to your Church, *Lord, save your people.*
> Jesus, Son of the living God, *Lord, save your people.*
> Christ, hear us, *Christ hear us.*
> Lord Jesus, hear our prayer, *Lord Jesus, hear our prayer.*

> Let us pray: *God of our ancestors who set their hearts on you, of those who fell asleep in peace, and of those who won the martyrs' violent crown: We are surrounded by these witnesses as by clouds of fragrant incense. In this age, we would be counted in this communion of all the saints; keep us always in their good and blessed company. In their midst, we make every prayer through Christ who is our Lord for ever and ever. Amen.*

Looking at statues and icons

Catholics have been accused of being idol worshippers because they use statues and icons — paintings on wood of the Byzantine tradition — in church and at home. But unlike the pagan Romans and Greeks, who actually worshipped false gods, Catholics use statues and icons the same way that others use photographs.

Most people have photos of their loved ones — living and deceased — in their wallets and purses, on their desks, and in their homes. The pictures are nothing more than reminders of those people. Neither the images nor the people are worshipped. Likewise, Catholic statues and icons are merely religious reminders of friends and servants of God whom Catholics admire for their holiness, loyalty, and obedience to God. Catholics don't worship a statue any more than they worship the saint it represents. If you see a Catholic kneeling before a statue, she isn't worshipping it or the person it represents. Kneeling is merely a posture of prayer, and the Catholic is praying *to* God *through* the intercession of that particular saint.

Actions like hanging icons or religious pictures on the wall and placing statues of the saints on shelves or on front lawns are nothing more than honoring the memory of heroes who have gone before us. Like the images of native sons and daughters and famous people the community wishes to honor in most national, state, and municipal capitals, Catholics honor past generations of religious heroes by memorializing them in stone or wood.

More than decoration but never an object of worship or adoration, statues and pictures of the saints are meant to remind and encourage the living on earth to imitate the holiness of the holy people who went before them. No specific prayers are said; Catholics just display the image as they would a beloved relative or friend.

Making pilgrimages

Like all devotions, pilgrimages are optional. Jews, Muslims, and Christians all make *pilgrimages,* religious journeys to visit a holy place. For Muslims, it's Mecca, and many Protestant and Orthodox Christians as well as Jews and Catholic Christians make pilgrimages to the Holy Land, visiting the sites mentioned in the Bible. While on the way and during the pilgrimage, people say prayers and hope to have a spiritual renewal. The journey is like a revival but at a more individual, personal, and low-key level.

The fact that Christian pilgrims were prohibited from access to the sacred shrines in the Middle Ages was one of the motivations for the Crusades. But the Crusades deteriorated into an opportunity for some ruthless and ambitious men to seize wealth, land, and power at the expense of many innocent men, women, and children — Jewish, Muslim, and Christian.

When the Holy Land was too dangerous for pilgrimages (sound familiar?), St. Francis of Assisi (1182–1226) erected the *Christmas crèche* (nativity scene) and the 14 stations of the cross in the church so people could imagine they were at the actual place and still pray. To this day, Catholic churches still have the 14 stations on the walls of their churches and still display the nativity scene at Christmastime. (For more on St. Francis, see Chapter 21.)

Catholics like to visit the Holy Land to see where Jesus was born (Bethlehem), grew up (Nazareth), and was crucified and resurrected (Jerusalem). They also make pilgrimages to Rome to see St. Peter's Basilica, where St. Peter is buried, and the Vatican, where the pope lives. See Chapter 22 for more on holy sites.

Going on a retreat

Because many Catholics don't have the time or money to make a pilgrimage to many of the holy places, they often make an annual retreat instead. It can last a week (five to seven days) or be a weekend event at a retreat center. The retreat is a time away from work, school, family, and friends. No radio or TV, no computers or Internet, no cellphones or tablets. Retreats are opportunities for Catholics to get away from the stress and anxiety of the world and just spend time praying, meditating, reflecting, and renewing. Retreats may also give Catholics a chance to go to confession, because priests are often available on-site for that purpose. Priests, deacons, and bishops are required by canon law to make a five-day retreat every year. Some of the different types of retreats that are offered are as follows:

- **Private retreats** are one on one, between a retreat director and the person.
- **Group retreats** include a number of people at the same time.

   Group retreats can be of two varieties:

   - **Silent retreats** are almost completely speechless. Nothing is said — even at meals — except the prayers and responses at Mass and the talks of the retreat master.
   - **Preached and directed retreats** offer some interaction among fellow participants.
- **Days of recollection** are like mini-retreats. They last a day or less and often take up only the morning and/or afternoon. They occur more frequently than retreats, which are annual. Days of recollection often occur every month or at least quarterly.

Priests and nuns of various orders run retreat houses. In addition, many Catholic organizations sponsor retreats.

Wearing sacred gear

Catholics often wear special religious articles, such as medals and scapulars, as a type of personal devotion. *Medals* are small metal disks ranging from about the size of a dime to the size of a 50-cent piece, worn around the neck by a chain. *Scapulars* — coming from the Latin *scapula,* meaning *shoulder* — are worn around the neck and have two pieces of cloth: One piece rests on the chest and the other on the back. (A scapular can be either the garb worn by priests and members of a religious order or devotional items worn by lay members that look like more like necklaces.) These items aren't considered good luck charms or magical amulets. Catholics don't believe that medals and scapulars prevent sickness or stop you from sinning. And they're not a get-out-of-hell-free card. Catholics use them as mere reminders to stay close to God and to try to imitate the sanctity and holiness of the saints. They're just tangible symbols of the faith, such as a crucifix.

A Catholic can wear various medals, like the Miraculous Medal (first worn by St. Catherine Laboure in 1830), the St. Christopher (patron saint of travelers) Medal, the St. Michael the Archangel (patron saint of police officers) Medal, or the St. Luke (patron saint of physicians) Medal. A Catholic can also wear any one of several kinds of scapulars, the most famous being the Brown Scapular that's associated with the Carmelite Order of Priests and Nuns. It has a picture of Our Lady of Mount Carmel on one side and a picture of St. Simon Stock on the other. Other scapulars include the Black Scapular of the Servite Order, the Blue Scapular of the Immaculate Conception, the Red Scapular of the Precious Blood, and the Purple Scapular of St. Joseph, just to mention a few.

Praying the Rosary

Before Christianity, Hindus strung beads and used them to help count their prayers. Buddhists, Taoists, and Muslims have also used prayer beads to assist them in their private devotions. Hebrews used to tie 150 knots on a string to represent the 150 Psalms of the Bible.

According to pious Catholic tradition, in the 13th century, Mary, the Mother of God, appeared to St. Dominic de Guzman, gave him a rosary, and asked that instead of praying the Psalms on the beads or knots, the faithful pray the Hail Mary, Our Father, and the Glory Be. Fifteen decades made up the original Dominican Rosary, but it was later abbreviated. A *decade* refers to ten Hail Marys preceded by the Our Father and ending with a Glory Be. Today, most Catholics use the five-decade Rosary. (For more on St. Dominic, see Chapter 18.)

How to pray the Rosary

Want to know how to pray the Rosary? (Take a look at Figure 16-1 to help you follow along.)

1. **Start at the crucifix, and pray the Apostles' Creed.**

   I believe in God, the Father Almighty, Creator of Heaven and earth; and in Jesus Christ, His only Son, Our Lord, Who was conceived by the Holy

Spirit, born of the Virgin Mary, suffered under Pontius Pilate, was crucified, died, and was buried; He descended into hell; on the third day He
rose again from the dead; He ascended into heaven, and is seated at the
right hand of God, the Father Almighty; from there He will come to judge
the living and the dead. I believe in the Holy Spirit, the holy catholic
Church, the communion of saints, the forgiveness of sins, the resurrection of the body, and life everlasting. Amen.

2. **On the next large bead, say the Our Father (the Lord's Prayer).**

   Our Father, Who art in heaven, hallowed be Thy name; Thy kingdom
   come; Thy will be done on earth as it is in heaven. Give us this day our
   daily bread; and forgive us our trespasses as we forgive those who trespass against us; and lead us not into temptation, but deliver us from
   evil. Amen.

3. **On the following three small beads, pray three Hail Marys.**

   Hail Mary, full of grace. The Lord is with thee. Blessed art thou among
   women, and blessed is the fruit of thy womb, Jesus. Holy Mary, Mother
   of God, pray for us sinners, now and at the hour of our death. Amen.

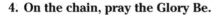

The first part of the Hail Mary is lifted from the Bible. The Archangel
Gabriel announces to Mary, "Hail, full of grace; the Lord is with you,"
(Luke 1:28), and St. Elizabeth said to her cousin Mary, "Blessed are you
among women and blessed is the fruit of your womb," (Luke 1:42).

4. **On the chain, pray the Glory Be.**

   Glory be to the Father, to the Son, and to the Holy Spirit, as it was in the
   beginning, is now, and ever shall be, world without end. Amen.

5. **Then announce the first mystery for that day of the week or season.**

   (See the next section, "Meditating on the mysteries," for an explanation
   of which mystery you should announce.)

6. **On the large bead, start the first decade and pray the Our Father.**

7. **On the ten beads after that, pray ten Hail Marys.**

8. **On the chain, pray a Glory Be.**

9. **Many Catholics add the Fatima Prayer after the Glory Be and before
   the next mystery.**

   O My Jesus, forgive us our sins, save us from the fires of hell and lead all
   souls to heaven, especially those in most need of Thy mercy. Amen.

   If you followed the preceding steps, you've just completed the first
   decade of the Rosary. Now, repeat Steps 5 through 9 four more times
   to finish the next four decades, continuing with the second mystery in
   the appropriate list (again, see "Meditating on the mysteries"), then the
   third, and so on.

10. **Then, at the end of your Rosary, say the Hail Holy Queen. (Saying this isn't obligatory, but it's customary.)**

Hail, Holy Queen, Mother of mercy, our life, our sweetness, and our hope. To thee do we cry, poor banished children of Eve, to thee do we send up our sighs, mourning and weeping in this valley of tears. Turn then, most gracious advocate, thine eyes of mercy toward us; and after this our exile show unto us the blessed fruit of thy womb Jesus, O clement, O loving, O sweet Virgin Mary.

Pray for us, O holy Mother of God. That we may be made worthy of the promises of Christ.

Let us Pray, O God, whose only-begotten Son, by His life, death, and resurrection, has purchased for us the rewards of eternal salvation; grant we beseech Thee, that meditating upon these mysteries of the most holy Rosary of the Blessed Virgin Mary, we may imitate what they contain and obtain what they promise. Through the same Christ our Lord. Amen.

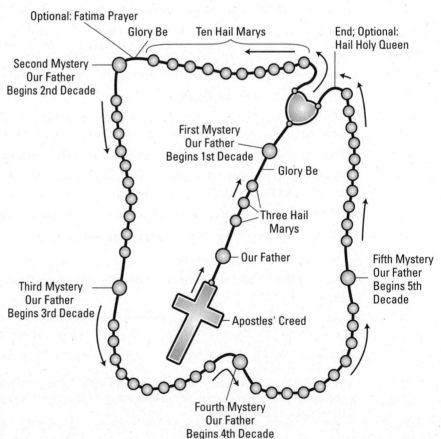

Figure 16-1:
How to pray
the Rosary.

Meditating on the mysteries

While saying the prayers of the Rosary, Catholics meditate on what are called the Joyful, Luminous, Sorrowful, and Glorious Mysteries of the Rosary. But saying the mysteries is really no mystery at all, because each so-called mystery refers to a different passage in the life of Christ or Mary, His mother. Each decade (an Our Father, ten Hail Marys, and a Glory Be) recalls a different mystery.

Joyful

The *Joyful Mysteries* are prayed on Mondays and Saturdays, and they remind the faithful of Christ's birth. Each decade corresponds with a different mystery. Starting with the Annunciation for the first decade, try meditating on these scenes sequentially with each decade that you say (they may also be said during the whole Christmas season):

1. The Annunciation (Luke 1:26–38)

2. The Visitation (Luke 1:39–56)

3. The Nativity (Luke 2:1–21)

4. The Presentation (Luke 2:22–38)

5. The Finding of the Child Jesus in the Temple (Luke 2:41–52)

Luminous

Pope John Paul II added on the *Mysteries of Light,* also known as the *Luminous Mysteries,* in 2002. Pray the Rosary and recall these Mysteries of Light on Thursdays (they may also be said during season of Advent):

1. The Baptism in the River Jordan (Matthew 3:13–17)

2. The Wedding Feast at Cana (John 2:1–11)

3. The Preaching of the Coming of the Kingdom of God (Mark 1:14–15)

4. The Transfiguration (Matthew 17:1–8)

5. The Institution of the Holy Eucharist (Matthew 26:17-29)

Sorrowful

The *Sorrowful Mysteries* are prayed on Tuesdays and Fridays, and they remind the faithful of His Passion and death (they may also be said during the entire season of Lent, the 40 days before Easter):

1. The Agony of Jesus in the Garden (Matthew 26:36–56)

2. The Scourging at the Pillar (Matthew 27:26)

3. The Crowning with Thorns (Matthew 27:27–31)

4. The Carrying of the Cross (Matthew 27:32)

5. The Crucifixion (Matthew 27:33–56)

Glorious

The *Glorious Mysteries* are prayed on Wednesdays and Sundays, and they remind the faithful of His Resurrection and the glories of heaven (they may also be said during all of Easter season):

1. The Resurrection (John 20:1–29)

2. The Ascension (Luke 24:36–53)

3. The Descent of the Holy Spirit (Acts 2:1–4)

4. The Assumption of Mary, the Mother of God, into heaven

5. The Coronation of Mary in heaven

These last two mysteries are inferred by Revelation (Apocalypse) 12:1; Jesus Christ was the source and center of these miraculous events in that He did them to His mother; she did not do them alone. What Christ did for His mom, He will later do for all true believers at the end of time.

Both the divinity and humanity of Jesus are presented in these mysteries. Only God could be born of a virgin, rise from the dead, and ascend into heaven, and yet only a man could be born, get lost, be found, suffer, and die. Meditating on the Joyful, Luminous, Sorrowful, and Glorious Mysteries helps Catholics confirm that Jesus is both divine and human. Contemplating the time when Jesus was crowned with thorns, scourged with whips, and nailed to the cross — meditating on Jesus's Passion — convinces the prayerful that those sufferings are real, and only a real man could feel such pain and agony. Yet reflecting on His Transfiguration, Resurrection, and Ascension reminds believers that only God can transfigure, rise from the dead, and ascend into heaven. By praying the Rosary, the faithful reaffirm that Jesus is true God and true man, one divine person with two natures — divine and human.

Just as Pope Paul VI did, Pope John Paul II reminded the faithful that the Rosary is *Christocentric* — it focuses on Christ and is more than a *Marian* (of Mary) devotion.

Saying the Divine Mercy Chaplet

The Rosary and the Divine Mercy Chaplet may be prayed at home, in church (as long as it's not during Mass), alone, or in a group. Our Lord presented the Divine Mercy Chaplet to St. Faustina Kowalska in a vision during the 1930s, but it didn't gain much notoriety until the late 20th century. The Divine Mercy Chaplet is said using rosary beads (see Figure 16-1), but it doesn't take as long as a Rosary, because the prayers are shorter. Make the Sign of the Cross and then:

1. **Optional: Begin the Divine Mercy Chaplet by saying this prayer on the first large bead after the crucifix:**

   You expired, Jesus, but the source of life gushed forth for souls, and the ocean of mercy opened up for the whole world. O Fount of Life, unfathomable Divine Mercy, envelop the whole world and empty Yourself out upon us.

   Then say the following three times in a row:

   O Blood and Water, which gushed forth from the heart of Jesus, I trust in You.

2. **Say an Our Father, a Hail Mary, and the Apostles' Creed on the three small beads.**

   (See Steps 1 through 3 in the "How to pray the Rosary" section, earlier in this chapter, to pray the Our Father, Hail Mary, and Apostles' Creed.)

3. **Then, on the large bead before each decade, say**

   Eternal Father, I offer you the Body and Blood, Soul and Divinity of Your Dearly Beloved Son, Our Lord, Jesus Christ, in atonement for our sins and those of the whole world.

4. **Then, on the ten small beads of each decade, say**

   For the sake of His sorrowful Passion, have mercy on us and on the whole world.

5. **Conclude the chaplet by saying the following three times:**

   Holy God, Holy Mighty One, Holy Immortal One, have mercy on us and on the whole world.

The Way of the Cross

Another popular devotion is the Way of the Cross. All Catholic parishes have what are called the *stations of the cross,* which are depictions of Christ's Passion and death. Often on Friday evenings during Lent, you can find a parish that's open with Catholics saying prayers in unison before each of the 14 stations that follow:

1. Jesus is condemned to death (Luke 23:24).

2. Jesus takes up His cross (John 19:17).

3. Jesus falls the first time (by inference from Stations 2 and 5).

4. Jesus meets His sorrowful mother (by inference from John 19:25–27).

5. Simon of Cyrene helps carry the cross (Matthew 27:32).

6. Veronica wipes the face of Jesus (not recorded in Scripture).

7. Jesus falls a second time (not recorded in Scripture).

8. Jesus meets the holy women of Jerusalem (Luke 23:27–31).

9. Jesus falls the third time (not recorded in Scripture).

10. Jesus is stripped of His garments (John 19:23).

11. Jesus is nailed to the cross (Mark 15:24).

12. Jesus dies on the cross (Mark 15:37).

13. Jesus's body is taken down from the cross and laid in the arms of His mother (Luke 23:53).

14. Jesus's body is laid in the tomb (Matthew 27:60).

Again, this devotion and all devotions we explain in this chapter aren't required like going to Mass every Sunday or obeying the Ten Commandments. But praying the Way of the Cross reminds Catholics of the supreme sacrifice Jesus made, offering His life to save us from our sins. This devotion helps promote appreciation for what Jesus did and encourages believers to carry their own crosses in life by enduring unavoidable suffering.

Chapter 17

Expressing Affection for Mary

. . . .

In This Chapter

▶ Honoring (but not worshipping) Mary

▶ Getting the facts straight on what Catholics believe about Mary

▶ Exploring a few Marian devotions

. . . .

You've heard about all those ladies — Our Lady of Lourdes, Our Lady of Fatima, Our Lady of Sorrows, Our Lady of Grace, Our Lady of Peace, Our Lady of Mount Carmel, and Our Lady of Guadalupe. Ever wonder who they are? They're one and the same person: Mary. Catholics refer to Mary in many ways, which can be confusing at times. They may also refer to her as the *Blessed Virgin Mary* (BVM for short), the *Virgin Mary, Our Lady,* and the plain and simple — Mary. No matter what the title, it refers to the Mother of Jesus, and she's what this chapter is all about.

No, Catholics Don't Worship Mary

Through the ages, more poems, hymns, statues (see Figure 17-1), icons, paintings, treatises, and sermons have been produced on this one woman than any other in all human history. Yet Catholics' devotion to Mary, known as *Marian devotion,* has been criticized by non-Catholics as unbiblical or even idolatry. In this section, we explain that Catholics definitely *don't* worship Mary, starting with some important facts about her life.

Born of two saintly parents — St. Joachim and St. Anne — Mary is mentioned in the Bible 47 times. Regarding Mary, the Bible says that

✔ She was engaged (Matthew 1:18 and Luke 1:27) to a carpenter (Matthew 13:55) named Joseph, whose ancestor was King David (Matthew 1:6–16).

✔ She came from Nazareth (Luke 1:26), and it was in Nazareth that the Archangel Gabriel appeared to her and *announced,* hence the term *Annunciation,* that she was to have a son and name Him Jesus (Luke 1:31).

Figure 17-1:
A statue of
the Virgin
Mary.

It is this second role, Mary as the mother of Jesus, that makes Catholics so devoted to Mary. People of other faiths are sometimes baffled by the attention Catholics pay to Mary. To understand why Catholics are so affectionate and attached to her, think about the most primal of all emotions: the strong, penetrating bond between a mother and her child. Nine months in the womb is just one part of it.

Mary was not just an incubator in which baby Jesus developed from embryo to infant. Like all mothers, she was a full and true mom in every sense of the word. A mother gives more to her child than her DNA and nine months in her womb; motherhood is emotional and intellectual as well as biological. A mother is intimately bonded and connected with her child; and in this case, the child was Jesus Christ.

Catholic theology teaches that Jesus Christ was human and divine — not 50/50, but true God and true Man. In other words, He was one divine person with two natures — human and divine. And His humanity wasn't overwhelmed or smothered by His divinity. So whatever He did or was in His human nature was as real and as much a part of Him as whatever He did or was in His divine nature. Whether He was performing miracles from His divinity or feeling and expressing emotions from His humanity, He was still one and the same person. That said, what can be more human than having strong feelings of affection and love for your own mother? So Catholics identify their own feelings for Mary with the feelings Jesus had for His mom, a logical extension of a child's personal affection for His mother. This feeling is nothing but devotion, without the slightest hint of worship or adoration in it.

Some people say that the word *Blessed* in the title *Blessed Virgin Mary* is idolatry (or Mariolatry, as some call it). But the term and concept is biblical. Mary tells her cousin Elizabeth, "All generations will call me blessed" (Luke 1:48). In the Bible's original Greek, the word for *blessed* is *markariousin.* For nearly 2,000 years, the adjective *blessed* has been used, and it has never taken away from the ultimate holiness of God — just as when Jesus Himself used the word in His Sermon on the Mount (Matthew 5:3–12): "Blessed are the poor in spirit, for theirs is the kingdom of heaven." *Blessed* isn't a word that's restricted to divinity, so using it with Mary is okay.

Another argument for discouraging devotion to Mary is the claim that Jesus Himself apparently rebuked His own mother and called Her *woman* rather than mom. This argument claims that if Jesus Himself had to put Mary in her place, Catholics shouldn't think so highly of her. Proponents of this opinion point to the Bible story of the wedding of Cana, when the guests ran out of wine and Mary told Jesus about it. In John 2:4 in the King James Bible, Jesus responds, "Woman, what have I to do with thee?" The International Standard Version reads, "How does that concern us, woman?" The Catholic response? Proper and accurate Scripture interpretation requires that we never take the text out of context, and that readers consider the original text. Indeed, in the King James version, Jesus says, "Woman, what have I to do with thee?" But the original Greek reads *Ti emoi kai soi gynai,* which literally translates to "What [is it] to me and you, woman?" This is exactly the same translation in Latin: *Quid mihi et tibi est mulier.*

Instead of a rebuke, Jesus's words can be interpreted as, "If you're concerned about it, then I am, too." In other words, if the fact that they ran out of wine is a concern to Mary, then it is a concern of Jesus, her son. This interpretation makes more sense than one of rebuke when we see what happens next. As soon as Jesus uttered the phrase, He changed the water into wine, performing His first public miracle at His mother's request. Had it been a rebuke, He probably would have ignored Mary's request altogether. By granting His mother's plea for help, He showed that He listened to her as a son, and as God He performed the miracle.

Calling His mother *woman* must also be seen in context with the whole of Scripture. For example, at the cross, as Jesus was dying, some of his last words were to Mary and then to John, His beloved disciple: "Woman, behold your son" and "Behold, your mother." (John 19:26-27) Using the term *woman* (*gynai* in Greek) was actually a compliment because Eve, the wife of Adam, is referred to as *the woman* (Genesis 2:23). There is a famous line between God and the serpent — "I will put enmity between you and the woman, between your seed and her seed" (Genesis 3:15) — that is considered a prophecy about Mary. We also see Mary associated with the word *gynai* in the last book of the Bible, Revelation (or Apocalypse) 12:1: "And a great portent appeared in heaven, a woman clothed with the sun, with the moon under her feet, and on her head a crown of twelve stars." In this passage — as in Genesis 3:15 — Catholics consider the woman referred to as being Mary, the mother of Jesus, because Revelation 12:2 says she was pregnant, and 12:5 says her son will rule all the nations.

In fact, Mary is the new Eve because her offspring was Jesus, the new Adam, and He conquered the devil by His death and Resurrection. So when seen in this light, the supposed insult turns out to be a term of endearment.

What Catholics Believe about Mary

Official Catholic doctrine on Mary is called *Mariology*, just as doctrine on God is called *Theology* (from the Greek word *theos* for *God*.) In this section, you get a peek at some significant aspects of Mariology. Much of Mariology is rooted in the many different titles the Church has given Mary over the centuries, so we explain some of her major titles to you here, as well as other facts Catholics believe about her life.

She's the Mother of God

Most titles for Mary are by way of metaphor (saying one thing to mean another, like, "It's raining cats and dogs"). But the title Mother of God is considered an analogy, which is a comparison considered deeper and more complex than a metaphor. Analogies imply that if two things are alike in one way, they are alike in others. Mary gave birth to the divine Jesus, so analogously, she is the Mother of God. Even though Mary isn't the mother of divinity, she did give birth to a divine person. Mary's son (Jesus) is the son of God, hence we can call her the *Mother of God* without making her a goddess, either.

The title *Mother of God* goes back to the year A.D. 431, when the Ecumenical Council of Ephesus determined that Mary could be called the Mother of God (*Theotokos* in Greek) instead of just the Mother of Christ (*Christotokos*) as the theologian and Archbishop of Constantinople Nestorius contended. (Nestorius was condemned by the Council of Ephesus for this heretical idea. For more on the Church councils, see Chapter 6.)

The thinking went like this: Granted, as a human being, Mary can't be the origin of a divine person. But Mary is the Mother of Jesus. He wasn't born in parts, like building blocks, needing to be put together after His birth. One divine person lived in Mary's womb for nine months, and one divine person came forth and was born. Even though Mary didn't give Jesus His divine nature and she was a creature and not the Creator, because she gave birth to the Son of God and because she is the Mother of the Son of God, she can be called analogously the Mother of God.

The Bible verifies this logic: Mary, pregnant with Jesus for only a few days, visited her cousin Elizabeth, who was six months pregnant with John the Baptist. Elizabeth greeted Mary, "And why is this granted me, that the mother of my Lord should come to me?" (Luke 1:43). Elizabeth used the word *Lord* (*Kyrios* in Greek and *Adonai* in Hebrew), which was also used to refer to God — the Lord God — *Adonai Elohim* in Hebrew. Elizabeth called Mary *the Mother of the Lord,* and the Lord is God. Mary is the Mother of God because she's the mother of the Lord. This title doesn't mean that Mary was divine or that she was a goddess or had any divine attributes.

Looking at your own mother is another way to see the concept: Your mother didn't give you your immortal soul. That came from God. She gave you 50 percent of your genetic makeup, but she needed your dad to give you the other half, and they needed God to give you a soul. However, on Mother's Day, do you send her a card titled, "To the woman who gave me half of my genetic code?" Or would you tell her that she didn't give you a soul — that she only gave you a body — so she's only half your mother? Of course not (that is, unless you want the wooden spoon across your hand). In your mind and your mother's mind, she may have only given you 50 percent of your DNA, but she gave birth to *you.* A whole and complete person was born — not two pieces. The body and soul were united at conception. A person grew and lived in the womb, and a whole and intact person was born from it.

She's the Mother of the Church

The title *Mother of the Church* is properly understood as a metaphor. Because the Church is called the "body of Christ" by Saint Paul (in his epistles to the Romans and to the Corinthians) and Mary is the mother of Christ, then one can say Mary is the mother of the Church. From the Catholic perspective, Mary becomes the Mother of the Church by adoption. This concept doesn't detract, diminish, or dilute the singular mediation of Christ because He's still the one mediator between God and humans. The only way that Christians can call themselves brothers and sisters in Christ is by way of adoption. In other words, Jesus is, was, and always will be the Eternal Son of the Father. Christians, however, are children of God and brothers and sisters in Christ by adoption (which takes place at Baptism). As brothers and sisters of Jesus by adoption, they also inherit the same mother. Mary is the Mother of Christ by nature, and she is the mother of Christians by adoption.

In another way, Mary is the Mother of the Church because she was at the foot of the cross on Calvary. The Bible says that as He was dying on the cross, Jesus turned toward his mother and said, "Woman, behold, your son." He then turned to the apostle John and said, "Behold, your mother" (John 19:26–27). The bestowal of Mary to John is symbolic insofar as John represents all disciples and all men and women.

Mary's presence at Pentecost, ten days after the Ascension of Christ into heaven and 50 days after his Resurrection, also establishes her role as Mother of the Church. Acts 1:14-2:4 says that Mary was with the apostles in the Upper Room — or probably, more accurately, they were with her. Until the Holy Spirit gave them strength and courage, they received encouragement from the Mother of Jesus as she and John were the only ones who did not abandon Christ while He died on the cross.

She's the Mother of the Mystical Body of Christ

Mary is the Mother of Christ. The Church is the Mystical Body of Christ. (Several passages from the Bible — I Corinthians 12:12–27, Romans 12:4–5, and Colossians 1:18 — refer to Christ's followers as His "body.") Hence, by extension, Mary can also be called the Mother of the Mystical Body of Christ because she is also called the Mother of the Church.

Catholics believe that Christ gave the Church the responsibility to safeguard and protect Revelation by authentically interpreting the biblical texts. The Church is a necessary and organic community, which St. Paul called the Body of Christ (Colossians 1:24) and Pope Pius XII later called the Mystical Body of Christ in his encyclical letter *Mystici Corporis* (1943).

This phrase — Mystical Body of Christ — means that the Church is more than an external organization, structure, and institution; it's a union of all the members forming one body. The human body has many parts, which are different and have different functions. Everybody has one head, and the Church has one visible head on earth: the pope. But a head with no body isn't alive. The Church is also a body made up of many members: laity and clergy. These individual members have different functions, just as your heart, lungs, kidneys, arms, legs, eyes, and ears have their respective functions, but they all work in harmony for the good of the whole body. Pope Pius added the adjective *mystical* just to accentuate the idea that the Church isn't a physical body with organs and limbs; it's mysteriously and spiritually organic.

She was conceived through Immaculate Conception

The Immaculate Conception is one of the most mysterious and most misunderstood Catholic dogmas. The Immaculate Conception (celebrated every year on December 8) is not the conceiving of Jesus within the womb of Mary — even though the Gospel reading at Mass on that day is the account of the Annunciation, when the Archangel Gabriel told Mary that she was to be the Mother of Jesus. At that moment, the Holy Spirit overshadowed her and she conceived of Christ. The feast and the dogma of the Immaculate Conception, however, is about the conception of Mary in her mother's womb. Long before the Annunciation took place, the parents of Mary (Saints Joachim and Anne) first brought their daughter into the world. Later, she grew up to become the mother of Jesus.

Catholics use the term *Incarnation* to refer to the conception of Jesus in His mother's (Mary's) womb. Catholics use the phrase *Immaculate Conception* to refer to the conception of Mary in her mother's womb.

In the eyes of the Church, Adam and Eve's sin, called *original sin* (see Chapter 8), is transmitted to every subsequent generation. So just as you inherit the color of your eyes and hair from your parents, you also spiritually inherit original sin from them. Yet, thanks to the grace of God, Mary didn't inherit original sin. You got that right . . . Mary was totally human, but she was not conceived nor was she born in sin like the rest of humanity.

Anyone can be baptized (see Chapter 8) and have their sins washed away and replaced with sanctifying grace. But God gave Mary the singular grace and privilege of the Immaculate Conception to prevent original sin from being transmitted to Jesus, so she was literally full of grace. A glass full of water has no room for anything else, and a soul full of grace has no room for sin.

When the Archangel Gabriel addressed Mary in the first chapter of Luke's Gospel, he said, "Hail Mary, *full of grace*" (*kecharitomene* in Greek, from the root word *charis,* meaning *grace; gratia plena* in Latin). She was full of grace because of the Immaculate Conception, a divine gift to her from God. She didn't earn or merit it. He freely gave it to her, so she could provide a worthy, spotless, and pure human nature for Jesus.

Because Jesus had no human father, His only human parent was Mary. She gave him His human nature, whereas He — as God — always possessed His divine nature. In order to give Jesus a completely untainted, spotless, and immaculate human nature so that He could be the Spotless Lamb of Sacrifice (Catholics have many titles for Jesus, too), Mary had to be kept free from original sin. She couldn't do so on her own because she was a mere mortal. She needed a Savior and Messiah like everyone else. But God isn't limited to time and space. Mary enjoyed an effect of salvation before Jesus actually did the work of salvation. She was given the gift of being preserved from original sin well before her son Jesus was born, let alone before He suffered and died, achieving salvation for the entire human race. Jesus, being divine and being

God, retroactively applied the fruits of His salvific suffering and death from Mary's future to her past. He extended the benefits backward in time just as you who live now can have the same fruits of redemption applied to you from the past into your present. If what Jesus did 2,000 years ago can be applied to a newly baptized person today, then what He did can go in the other direction and be applied to His mother as she was being conceived.

Aquinas and the Immaculate Conception

Some people try to use an old, archaic argument that even the great theologian St. Thomas Aquinas didn't fully endorse the doctrine of the Immaculate Conception. (For more on St. Thomas, see Chapters 2 and 21.) Well, we'd like to introduce those people to a little Renaissance history. First of all, the dogma wasn't solemnly defined until 1854 by Pope Pius IX, and Aquinas lived in the 13th century — almost 600 years before. Second, basic human anatomy and physiology that's now taken for granted wasn't understood until the Renaissance — 250 years after Aquinas. During the Renaissance, people like Leonardo Da Vinci began to paint and draw human bodies, often from cadavers and autopsies. But the biology known to Aquinas was primitive, and he relied heavily on Aristotle, not only for philosophy but for other disciplines as well.

The medieval concept of human reproduction was that a vegetative soul existed before a human being did and that the vegetative soul developed into an animal soul. Then God infused an immortal human soul, called *animation,* at which time the embryo was a human person. Sounds a little ridiculous to us nowadays, of course. But based on this medieval science, it didn't make sense to Aquinas that God would preserve Mary from original sin at the moment of conception, because the human soul (it was thought) didn't yet exist to benefit from the divine gift. But Aquinas believed that after the immortal soul was infused, Mary could and did receive the grace of being free from original sin. So Aquinas believed in the Catholic doctrine that Mary was *born* without original sin, but he had some reservations as to whether she was *conceived* without it.

If Aquinas had lived at the time of Leonardo Da Vinci, or if he could have seen a sonogram of an unborn fetus, or if he merely knew the common DNA science that grade-schoolers know today, then he would have realized that *at conception* a human being is created and *animation* (God infusing the immortal soul) occurs. The embryo may resemble something animal-like, but genetically, the DNA is human from the moment of conception and remains so throughout gestation, birth, and life. These blueprints tell the cells what to do and how to grow, and no animal or vegetable will ever become anything else but an animal or vegetable. Only humans beget other humans and nothing else.

So the bottom line is that St. Thomas Aquinas really didn't deny the Immaculate Conception. He merely had trouble reconciling it with the extremely primitive science of his time. His contemporary St. Bonaventure, on the other hand, did accept the Immaculate Conception, but back in the 13th century, it wasn't yet a defined dogma. It was taught, but no pope had given it the official nod. After Pius IX defined the dogma, however, the matter was no longer open for discussion.

It's like getting into a time travel machine (okay, we admit it — we're *Doctor Who* fans), going into the future, and finding that your son wants to become a physician but can't because neither you nor your son has the money for medical school. So you go back in time and leave a few hundred dollars in a bank account in your child's name, so when you return to the present, you can withdraw it and all the accumulated interest to send Junior to med school.

In all 2,000 years of Church history, only two papal *ex cathedra* statements have been made. When the pope, exercising his authority as Supreme Teacher, makes an *ex cathedra* statement, he's *infallible* — the Holy Spirit prevents him from teaching error. In 1854, Pope Pius IX made the first *ex cathedra* statement — the Immaculate Conception. The other *ex cathedra* statement was made in 1950; Pope Pius XII defined the dogma of the Assumption of Mary, body and soul, into heaven. (See the next section for details. See Chapter 6 for details about *ex cathedra* statements and the pope's infallibility.)

She went to heaven, body and soul

The Church professes that when Mary's time on earth came to an end, her body didn't decay on earth. Instead, her son, Jesus Christ, assumed her into heaven, body and soul.

We want to make something clear. Only God can rise from the dead of His own divine power, and only God can ascend into heaven of His own divine power. So Jesus Himself, being God, rose from the dead, but Lazarus was raised *by* Jesus. Likewise, Jesus Himself ascended into heaven, but He also assumed His mother (she didn't just up and go on her own).

So why would He do such a thing? For many reasons.

One is that having affection for your mom is as human as it gets. In His humanity, Jesus had all the emotions that any man or woman would have. If you were Jesus, wouldn't you want to prevent any decay from touching the body of your mother? Wouldn't you want her to be with you in heaven as soon as possible? To portray Jesus as an emotionless man (like some sort of Vulcan) who had no filial love for His mom is to deny His true humanity.

Also, the Immaculate Conception preserved Mary from original sin, so Mary would have also been free from the consequences of sin as well — namely, physical death, the separation of body and soul. That being the case, the Eastern Church uses the term *dormition* (falling asleep) rather than *death* to describe what happened to her before the Assumption. But because she voluntarily joined with her son's suffering on the cross, Pope John Paul II said that the logical conclusion is that she also willingly followed Him through her own death as well.

Sacred Tradition reigns on the Assumption

The Assumption of Mary isn't in the Bible. An apocryphal account of the Assumption is not of itself evidence of this miraculous event, but it does show that the early Church did believe in the Assumption. (*Apocryphal* means the account is not part of Sacred Scripture.)

Because divine revelation consists of both the written Word of God (the Bible) and the unwritten Word of God (Sacred Tradition), places where the Bible is silent or ambiguous can usually be ascertained by what was taught via Sacred Tradition. The Bible is silent on Mary's death, but Sacred Tradition says that she was taken up (by God) into Heaven. The Church maintains, however, that a biblical allusion to the Assumption does exist in Revelation (Apocalypse) 12:1: "A great portent appeared in heaven, a woman clothed with the sun, with the moon under her feet, and on her head a crown of twelve stars."

The more fundamental reason, however, that Jesus assumed His mother, body and soul, into heaven was to give people on earth encouragement. Sacred Tradition teaches that the Assumption was meant to give humans hope and consolation that Jesus will do for humanity at the end of time what He did for His mother in reward for her being a faithful disciple throughout her life. At his Second Coming, Jesus will raise the dead and take the righteous to heaven, and the reprobate will go to hell. So, in other words, Mary's Assumption was like a preview of coming attractions: She was the first human — but won't be the last — to be assumed by God into heaven. Someone had to be first, and why not the Mother of Christ?

Her never-ending virginity

Mary's virginity *before* the birth of Christ is a matter of Catholic dogma: No human father was associated with Jesus because He was the Son of God as well as the son of Mary. Having a human mother gave Him His humanity; having no human father but by the power of the Holy Spirit being conceived in His mother's womb gave Him His divinity.

But what about *after* the birth of Christ? Did Mary have other children besides Jesus? Some people say that she did because the New Testament speaks of the brothers and sisters of Jesus. Although it certainly wasn't necessary that Mary and Joseph not have any children of their own, Sacred Tradition says that they didn't. The way that Catholicism sees it, the doctrine of the Perpetual Virginity of Mary is no harder to believe than the miracle of the Virgin Birth, which most Christians accept. If Mary could remain a virgin before and during the birth of Christ her son, then it isn't any more difficult to believe that she could remain a virgin *after* His birth. (To find out more, see Chapter 4.)

Some people ask the Church to explain the reference to James as the brother of Jesus in the Bible (Matthew 13:55). But the word used to mean *brother* in the Bible's original Greek was *adelphos,* which can also mean *relative, cousin,* or *kinsman* as well as *sibling.* In the Bible, referencing the father indicates close relations. Jesus is referred to as the son of Joseph and the son of Mary, but no one else in the Bible is ever called the son or daughter of Joseph or Mary. So many possible scenarios exist for understanding the term *brother of Jesus* but only one for understanding *son* or *daughter.* Why doesn't the Bible call James the brother of Jesus and the son of Mary or just the son of Mary? The reason is that Mary had only one son. She was a virgin before, during, and after the birth of Jesus.

Mark 15:40 mentions Mary the mother of James, but the belief is that this reference is to another Mary — not the Mary who was the Mother of Jesus. The mother of James was in the distance looking on, while the Mother of Jesus was at the foot of the cross. (See Chapter 4 for more on the possibility that Jesus had siblings.)

Up Close and Personal with Mary

Devotions are traditional forms of prayer that aren't part of the Mass. They can be public or private, and they express love for God and for neighbor, as personified in Mary and the saints. This section discusses devotions to Mary. While we talk about the Rosary in this section, we don't get specific about how to say the Rosary. Don't get us wrong — we think it's a great devotion. It's just that we cover the Rosary in Chapter 16. No need to repeat ourselves, eh?

We must reiterate that Catholic Christians (and Eastern Orthodox Christians, too) do not *worship* Mary. The First Commandment forbids *adoring* anyone other than God. But the Fourth Commandment also commands us to *honor* our father and mother. Because Catholics regard Mary as their adopted mother, it only makes sense to give her proper honor and respect.

Devotion to Mary is not idolatry; it merely shows affection and respect to someone you honor and love. This next section deals with types of Marian devotion that help the faithful get close and personal with the Mother of Jesus and the Mother of the Church.

May crowning

May is the month of Mother's Day, and for Catholics it's the month for honoring two moms — their earthly one, who gave birth to them, and their spiritual mother, Mary.

Traditionally, Catholic parishes pick one day in May to host a devotion called a *May Crowning*. After the Ecumenical Council of Nicea II in 787, the public veneration of icons and images of Jesus, Mary, and the saints was no longer persecuted by some in the Church as though it were a form of idolatry. Consequently, the tradition of crowning a statue of Mary arose in recognition of her heavenly position as Queen of Heaven and Earth. This concept came from Revelation (Apocalypse) 12:1, where Mary is portrayed as the woman wearing a crown.

Mary's queenship comes from her relationship to her son, who is King. Jesus is the King of Kings, and Mary is His mother. Because her son is King, she is, *de facto,* Queen Mother. You can think of it like this: The Queen Mother of England was given the title, honor, and respect of queen because she's the mother of Queen Elizabeth II. So, too, the mother of the King of Kings is given the title and honor of being called *queen.*

Often for the occasion of the May crowning, roses and flowers galore adorn the Church. Typically, a young girl is chosen to place a crown of roses on a statue of Mary, which is sometimes carried in a *procession,* a dignified religious parade, around the inside or outside of the church or perhaps around the neighborhood. People march reverently to symbolize that they're fellow pilgrims — travelers who walk with the Lord and the saints, hopefully on the path to Heaven. All those in attendance sing hymns and pray the Rosary.

First Saturdays

Traditionally, Catholics honor Mary on the first Saturday of every month. Why that particular day? Well, the first Friday of the month is when Catholics give honor to Jesus with the Sacred Heart of Jesus devotion. Because Mary is secondary to Christ, the Church deemed that He would come first and then close by would be His mother with the Immaculate Heart of Mary devotion.

The focus on the heart is merely a romantic and metaphorical way of describing the love of Jesus and the love of Mary. It's just like sending hearts to loved ones on St. Valentine's Day even though you know that, biologically, the brain does the thinking and the heart merely does the pumping. Even in the 21st century, you hear the words "heartache" and winning someone's "heart," so the devotion to the Immaculate Heart of Mary is merely a recognition of her motherly heart because she loves her spiritual children.

The First Saturday devotion is relatively new compared with the First Friday devotion to the Sacred Heart of Jesus. The devotion came about because of the belief that Mary appeared to mere children, Lucia, Jacinta, and Francisco, in Fatima, Portugal, in 1917 (see Chapter 22) and then again to Sister Lucia in 1925, asking for the faithful to honor her on the first Saturday of the month. Saturday is also special; it was on the first Holy Saturday that Mary didn't lose faith, even though she'd just buried her son, Jesus. Her love and faith in Him got her through to His Resurrection on the next day.

Catholics believe that during her appearance in Fatima, Mary specifically asked that Catholics honor her Immaculate Heart on the five first Saturdays of five consecutive months by going to confession, receiving Holy Communion, praying five decades of the Rosary, and meditating for 15 minutes on the mysteries of the Rosary in reparation for sins. If done, she promised her maternal intercession and prayers at the hour of death when the devil has his last chance to get the soul.

Marian shrines and apparitions

Catholics believe that a *shrine* is a holy place, usually where an apparition or other miracle took place or where a saint lived, worked, or died. Shrines are often connected to or located inside of a chapel or church so the faithful can pray and worship God, especially through the Holy Sacrifice of the Mass, as a devotion. As another form of Marian devotion, Catholics can visit a holy place where an apparition of Mary has occurred.

An *apparition* is an appearance of Jesus, Mary, or one of the saints. It's not a physical presence of the holy person but an appearance — an image being imprinted on the senses. This is the reason that not everyone sees or hears the apparitions or *locutions* (speeches). Those who do are called *visionaries*. Catholics aren't obligated to believe in any particular apparition because apparitions aren't part of public revelation. The Church does, however, carefully investigate claims of alleged apparitions and then makes one of the following determinations:

✔ **It's a hoax.** Someone is pretending to see apparitions when, in reality, they're lies or staged illusions.

✔ **Natural causes can explain it.** Evidence of a supernatural occurrence is nonexistent. The visionaries may be prayerful and holy people without any intent to deceive, but upon investigation, evidence of a miraculous apparition can't be found. For example, maybe tears rolled down the cheeks of a statue of Mary, but when you look more closely, you see that some old steamy water pipes near the ceiling are slowly dripping right onto the statue's face.

✔ **The phenomenon can't be explained one way or the other.** Any evidence of a supernatural occurrence is inconclusive — too many unanswered questions exist and not enough, if any, evidence.

✔ **The devil is at work.** It's a supernatural event all right, but not of heavenly origin. Rather, it's an attempt by the devil to ridicule and mock the faith.

✔ **It's a supernatural event of heavenly origin.** The apparition or locution is credible and worthy of faithful pilgrims.

The Church condemns any and all hoaxes as well as any trick of the devil and repudiates any apparitions of natural explanation. It endorses only authentic apparitions of supernatural and heavenly origin. If the evidence that surrounds a particular apparition is inconclusive either way, then pilgrims are neither discouraged nor encouraged.

Even if the Church determines that an apparition is worthy of belief, Catholics aren't obligated to believe it as they're obligated to believe the words of the *Apostles' Creed* (see Chapter 2) or Sacred Tradition. Catholics are free to believe or disbelieve apparitions because they aren't considered revealed truth. But many saints and recent popes have given full support to all apparition places and shrines deemed legitimate and authentic.

Most accounts of apparitions are appearances of Mary to children and simple, humble people of faith. She asks them to pray to her son, pray for sinners, do penance, pray the Rosary daily for world peace, and live holy lives in obedience to God.

Anytime weird messages or secrets are supposedly released, particularly if someone claims to know when the world will end, the Church says you can be assured that it's not authentic. The reason, according to the Church, is that Jesus said, "But of that day and hour no one knows, not even the angels of heaven, nor the Son, but the Father only" (Matthew 24:36). So why would His mom know and why would she blab and spill the beans?

See the following listing of some famous Marian shrines and/or apparition sites that the Church has sanctioned:

- ✔ **Our Lady of the Snows, Rome, Italy:** In A.D. 352, several prayerful folks had the same dream: Mary told them that she would indicate the site on which to build a church in her honor by a miraculous snowfall. Now known as St. Mary Major (*Santa Maria Maggiore* in Italian), it's one of the churches where the pope says Mass.

- ✔ **Our Lady of Walsingham, England:** In gratitude for a favor received through the intercession of Our Lady, a wealthy woman built a small chapel to honor her in 1061. It inspired many pilgrims, the weak and the powerful, the poor and the wealthy, until Henry VIII outlawed the pilgrimages to this shrine.

- ✔ **The Black Madonna of Czestochowa, Poland:** Catholics popularly believe that St. Luke painted Mary's portrait, which eventually made its way to Czestochowa, Poland, where it has been enshrined since 1382. (See Chapter 22 for more on this icon.)

- ✔ **Our Lady of Guadalupe, Mexico:** Our Lady appeared to St. Juan Diego in 1531, leaving her image on his cloak. Today, a famous basilica in Mexico City now hosts her picture. (See Chapters 1 and 22 to find out more about this apparition.) The image is often depicted as shown in Figure 17-2.

Figure 17-2:
The traditional depiction of Our Lady of Guadalupe.

✔ **Our Lady of La Vang, Vietnam:** In 1798, a fierce persecution aimed at Catholics forced some to take refuge in the forest. Clustered together, praying the Rosary nightly, these Vietnamese faithful saw a consoling apparition of the Mother of God. A church was later built on the spot.

✔ **Our Lady of the Miraculous Medal, Paris, France:** Our Lady appeared to St. Catherine Laboure, a member of the order called the Sisters of Charity, in 1830. Communicating the exact design, Our Lady asked St. Catherine that a medal be struck in her honor.

✔ **Our Lady of La Salette, France:** In 1846, while tending their cows in a pasture, a young girl named Melanie and a young boy named Maximin, both born into poverty, saw a tall lady who never stopped weeping. Our Lady told them, in a nutshell, that folks needed to straighten up their acts and start praying or else. A beautiful Alpine shrine now marks the spot.

✔ **Our Lady of Lourdes, France:** In 1858, asking that a chapel be built and identifying herself as the Immaculate Conception, Our Lady appeared to another poverty-stricken child of God, St. Bernadette, on 18 different occasions. Today's pilgrims bring containers to fill with miraculous Lourdes water. In 1943, 20th Century Fox produced Hollywood's version of the event; *The Song of Bernadette* won four Academy Awards. (See Chapter 22 for more on Lourdes, and Chapter 18 for more on St. Bernadette.)

✔ **Our Lady of Knock, Ireland:** Our Lady, St. Joseph, and St. John the Evangelist appeared to 15 humble, hardworking Catholics of various ages in 1879. Many pilgrims experienced healings, and a shrine was built.

✔ **Our Lady of Fatima, Portugal:** In 1917, asking everybody to pray the Rosary daily for world peace, a beautiful lady clothed in white appeared to three young children. (For more on Fatima, see Chapter 22.)

Religious visions on toast?

Many people claim to have visions of Mary, Joseph, Jesus, saints, and angels, but local Church authorities determine that most of them aren't credible or lack conclusive evidence. The number of alleged apparitions and locutions in recent times is greater than ever, but most don't withstand the test of time. You may have heard of one alleged visionary who made bizarre statements about the pope being held hostage while an actor impersonated him! Or maybe you've heard of people seeing religious faces on their toast, and selling the buttered morsels online. Any messages such as these are sure to get the thumbs down from the local bishop and definitely from the Holy See in Rome.

Sensationalism, emotionalism, and the overly zealous can convince people of the veracity of an alleged apparition even though the Church has repudiated it or made no decision whatsoever. Anytime that Scripture or Sacred Tradition is contradicted, or anytime that disobedience to the pope is encouraged — or dissent from the Magisterium or disrespect for the hierarchy — you can be sure that the apparition isn't authentic. Real apparitions occur to help boost but never to replace the Christian faith. (See Chapter 6 for more on the Magisterium.) So we advise you to save your money and refrain from buying that sketchy toast.

Chapter 18

Honoring the Catholic Saints

In This Chapter

▶ Understanding the role of saints in Catholic life

▶ Examining the Church's process for recognizing a saint

▶ Celebrating on a saint's feast day

▶ Finding out what the communion of saints is

When you visit London, you may see larger-than-life likenesses of Sir Winston Churchill. In Washington, D.C., tourists flock to the Lincoln Memorial to see the 19-foot marble statue of the Great Emancipator. In fact, visit any city or town, and chances are good you can find a downtown monument of some national or local hero.

The same sense of pride and gratitude fills the hearts of Catholic Christians whenever they see a statue or picture of one of the saints. Catholicism honors and memorializes the saints as friends and faithful servants of God. They're considered heroes of the Church just as Ben Franklin and Susan B. Anthony are heroes to the United States.

In the case of visiting a statue or memorial, the honor given to the dead person is seen as appropriate, and no one's accused of idolatry. In the same way, Catholics aren't idolizing the saints, which is a common misconception among non-Catholic Christians. This chapter fills you in on the role that the saints play in Catholicism. To read about the lives of a few well-known saints, head to Chapter 21.

Having a Place in the Hearts of Catholics

Catholic devotion to the saints is nothing more than respect and admiration for the memory of the deceased heroes of the Church — the men and women who Catholics believe chose to surrender their will and in some cases their very lives to serve God and His Church. Just as a society honors the deceased who helped make the world a better place while they were alive, Catholics honor certain people who've gone on to heaven — the apostles, the martyrs, St. Peter (the first pope), St. Paul (the first missionary), St. Elizabeth (the mother of John the Baptist and cousin of Mary), and St. Anne (the mother of Mary and grandmother of Jesus), for example.

In the broader sense, everyone who's now in heaven is truly a saint. Human beings who lived holy lives in obedience to God's will and who are now in heaven for eternity are considered saints. When the Catholic Church *canonizes* a saint, however (see "Recognizing a Saint" for the whole process), it makes a spiritual pronouncement, and the faithful can be morally certain that this particular person is indeed in heaven. For this reason, prayers to and from the saint are considered *efficacious* (meaning they can produce their desired effect). For more on prayers and saints, read the section "It's All about Intercession."

Often, people consider the saints to be the exception to the norm. The Church, however, wants to portray them as the norm — or at least the norm that God would want. According to the Church, saints weren't born saints. Saints were born sinners in the state of original sin (see Chapter 8) and were sinners throughout their lives. They weren't perfect, sinless, and invulnerable. Unlike comic book superheroes, the saints didn't come from another planet like Krypton, and they didn't possess superhuman powers. Even though a few or more miracles took place in conjunction with any given saint, God was always the one doing the miracles *through* the saint because saints had no special powers of their own.

In other words, saints were ordinary people. They came from ordinary families with parents and siblings like any other human being. They grew up, got sick, got better, and attended school. Some got married, some remained single, and some entered religious life. Some were intelligent, some were average, and some were below average. Some were young and handsome, and some were old and not so pretty.

The bottom line is that all saints were human. They weren't born with halos around their heads, and they didn't glow in the dark. What separates these people from those who aren't given the title of saint is that the former group never gave up and never stopped trying to be and do better. The latter group did give up and literally stopped trying to be and do better. The saints persevered. Saints didn't have all the answers, nor were they spared pain and suffering simply because they were holy people. On the contrary, just because they possess more faith doesn't mean they suffer less. If a person has faith, he or she can persevere and endure much more for the sake of Christ, who suffered and died for all humankind.

Sins and imperfections of some famous saints

St. Peter, the first pope, wasn't perfect or sinless. The Bible says that he denied Christ three times (John 18:17, 25, and 27), and he should have sought out an oral podiatrist for treatment because he often opened his mouth and inserted his foot. He spoke before thinking, which is dangerous and foolish to do. Yet he became a saint.

One of the original 12 apostles, St. Thomas (nicknamed "doubting Thomas"), doubted that Jesus rose from the dead, but he became a saint. James and John fell asleep while Jesus prayed in the Garden of Olives, even though he asked them to stay awake and pray with Him. But they still became saints. St. Mary

Magdalene, an alleged prostitute, repented and became a saint.

St. Augustine (354–430) was a playboy. He got drunk, flirted, visited prostitutes, gambled — you name it, he did it, with the exception of murder. And for 20 long years, his saintly mother, St. Monica, prayed for him, until one day, he and his illegitimate son Adeodatus embraced the Christian faith, repented of their sins, were baptized, and even entered the religious life. He later became a bishop and finally a saint and *doctor* of the Church — a title given to a saint of significant knowledge and/or whose writings demonstrate outstanding faith.

Contemporary *hagiography,* the study of the lives of the saints, differs from older versions in that it seeks to tell the whole truth. Previous biographies of the saints tended to sanitize their histories and leave out imperfections. Occasionally, you may run into a book on saints depicting them as being almost divinelike in their holiness and intelligence, and as being almost sinless and perfect. But the Church says that those kinds of people never existed. Saints eventually wind up in heaven, but while alive on earth, they make mistakes. Instead of making excuses, though, they choose to admit their shortcomings and cooperate with God's grace to overcome them.

Instead of seeing or portraying saints as superheroes, Catholicism wants to present them as just heroes — ordinary people who made it to heaven. The idea is that if they could do it, so can you. Mother Angelica (see Chapter 20), the founder of the Eternal Word Television Network (EWTN), often says to her TV viewers, "God calls us all to become great saints. Don't miss the opportunity."

Honoring God's Good Friends

Some people think Catholics worship the dead because Catholics put statues of the saints in their churches and homes, address prayers to them, and name churches after the saints, too. Worshipping the dead, however, would be idolatry and a serious sin because the First Commandment forbids all worship of anyone or anything other than God. But Catholics don't worship the saints; they *honor* them. The images are like the public statues in national memorials — they're nothing but mere reminders of the special people who lived years and centuries ago.

Because the Fourth Commandment obligates the faithful to honor their parents, honoring the saints is considered the same type of respect. Catholics believe that worship can be given only to God, but honor can and should be given to certain human beings, such as parents and heroes of the faith. All the good guys and gals — the holy men and women — of the Bible are considered saints, which means that the Church regards them as being in heaven, honors their memory, and tries to encourage people to emulate their holiness.

The Church wants a saint's name to be used for Baptism or Confirmation. *Abraham, Sarah, Isaac, Noah, Rebecca, Mary, Elizabeth, Joseph, Matthew, Mark, Luke,* and *John,* for example, are all okay. These are all names of holy saints who are mentioned in the Bible and are living in heaven. But a name such as *Cain, Judas, Jezebel,* or *Herodias,* although biblical, isn't proper for Baptism or Confirmation because those people are villains, not heroes.

Why does a name matter so much? Catholics are encouraged to name their kids after saints so that when a child is old enough to find out about the saint he or she has been named after, the child will hopefully mimic that saint's behavior and lifestyle. Catholic moms and dads are delighted when their son or daughter tries to emulate a saint. Naming a child after a saint in Sacred Scripture or Church history used to be a hallmark of Christianity until the latter 20th century. Since then, strange and esoteric names have become prevalent.

It's All about Intercession

Praying to the saints is often misunderstood by non-Catholics; they want to know why Catholics pray to some folks who aren't even members of the Trinity. Traditionally, Catholicism has four kinds of prayer (you can read about these types of prayer in Chapter 15):

- ✔ **Adoration:** Praising God
- ✔ **Contrition:** Asking for God's forgiveness
- ✔ **Petition:** Asking God for a favor
- ✔ **Thanksgiving:** Showing God gratitude

This may surprise you, but only adoration is restricted for exclusive use for God. Think of it like this: Just as people can say they're sorry to God when they sin, they can also say that they're sorry to another person they've offended or hurt. Likewise, people can say, "Thank you!" to God or to another person. In the same way, making your petition known to a saint is asking the saint to pray for you. It isn't adoration, because the saint isn't worshipped. He's being asked for a favor: "Please pray for me!"

Often, the non-Catholic response is that Jesus Christ is the one and only mediator between God and humankind, so asking a saint for a favor is unnecessary. Plus no human being can duplicate, replace, or enhance what Christ the Mediator does. That's true from Catholicism's perspective, too. But the Church adds that when you read the Bible, you see people asking Jesus for favors on behalf of others. Whenever another person asks a favor on behalf of someone else, that's called *interceding* on behalf of someone else's petition.

For example, some parents came to Jesus and said that their little girl was sick. These parents were interceding before Jesus on behalf of their daughter (Matthew 15:22, Mark 5:23 and 7:26, and Luke 8:41–42). And when the Roman centurion approached Christ and interceded on behalf of his servant (Matthew 8:5–6), Jesus healed the servant. He didn't say to the centurion or to the parents of the sick daughter, "They have to come directly to me and ask me themselves to help them. They don't need your intercession." Instead, after those people made the request on behalf of another, the request was granted because they showed faith.

Similarly, if a saint asks God for a favor on your behalf, it's called an *intercession.* The word comes from the Latin *intercedere,* which means to plead on another's behalf — to act as an advocate, especially for a favor for someone else. The intercessors are still using the one and only mediator, Jesus Christ, because they're going directly to Him. Remember when you used to ask your mom to approach your dad about a request you had? That was using your mother as an intercessor.

So praying to Mary or a saint for their intercession is merely asking Mary or the saint to ask Jesus for help. Catholics believe that any response comes from God, but the saint brought the concern to Jesus Christ. The bottom line? Just because Catholics ask the saints for prayers doesn't mean that Catholics worship the saints.

Some non-Catholics ask, "Why even pray to Mary or a saint when you can go directly to God?" The answer is that Catholics never *have* to pray to any saint. They can always go directly to God. Catholicism doesn't say that saintly intercession is necessary or mandatory, but it's possible. Besides asking the saints to pray for them, the faithful can ask living people on earth to pray for them as well.

One way to honor a saint's memory and seek intercession is by venerating (not adoring) his or her *relics,* body parts or artifacts belonging to that saint, which have been kept by the Church as mementos of that holy person. (Body parts are first-class relics, artifacts are second-class, and items like holy cards or pieces of cloth touched to a first-class relic are third-class.) Relics aren't good luck charms and have no power on their own, but they're used to bless people, especially the sick, so that through the intercession of that saint, God's healing may occur. Some may think it's gruesome to have small bits of a saint's bone encased in glass and metal for public veneration, but it's not much different from keeping a lock of hair from a loved one after their death. The relic of a saint's body is only recognition that this same body was united to a soul who's now in heaven.

The Church believes that the only time prayers to and from the deceased have no effect is when the deceased are damned in hell. The Gospel parable of the rich man (traditionally known as *Dives,* which is Latin for *rich*) and the poor man, Lazarus, concludes with the former in hell and the latter in heaven (Luke 16:19–31). Dives asked "Father Abraham" if Lazarus could help him. Lazarus couldn't help, however, because the rich man was in hell. Catholicism teaches that the divide between heaven and hell can't be breached. The boundary between heaven and earth, however, is different, because you're still alive.

Recognizing a Saint

First of all, we want to make a clarification: The Catholic Church doesn't *make* saints like Hollywood makes movie stars. So, too, people can make chocolate chip cookies or Italian cannoli, but they can't make saints. However, the Church does formally *recognize* them.

Everyone in heaven is a saint, but knowing whether a particular person is in heaven is tricky. Evidence must be presented to persuade Church officials that the potential saint in fact lived a virtuous life, had faith, and had the support and help of God. The Church also looks at miracles as evidence that God is working through that person. (See the "St. Faustina's bona fide miracles" sidebar in this chapter.)

The pope decides who's in and who's out. By that, however, we don't mean that the pope decides who *is* a saint. Only God can make that judgment. We mean that the pope, as the supreme head of the Church, has the authority to decide who is publicly *recognized* as a saint in churches all over the world and gets his name on the calendar; that is, he gets a feast day. (For more on feast days, see Chapter 19.)

From the Catholic viewpoint, you don't have to be canonized a saint to be a saint. Billions and billions of people are saints in heaven, but they just aren't publicly recognized as saints. Canonized saints are merely those who are known, proven, recognized, and publicly honored for their holiness. Your grandma or grandpa in heaven, for example, may not be canonized, but they're saints just as much as St. Peter, St. Paul, St. James, and St. John. They have no feast day, no statues of themselves in church, no holy card with their face on it, and no church named after them, but they're still saints. They're in heaven and at peace, so they aren't bummed that St. Dominic and St. Francis of Assisi have churches, schools, and religious orders named after them. Catholicism teaches that in heaven, jealousy, regrets, and disappointments are nonexistent.

Looking at the process to becoming a saint

Why not imagine yourself becoming a saint? Maybe you already are and you just don't know it yet. (Saints are often very humble souls.) Just for now at least, imagine that you are a saint. Pretend that you passed away at least five years ago (there's a posthumous waiting period for canonization) and entered heaven after living an exemplary life on earth.

Looking down, you see that your relatives, friends, and even the people who barely knew you are all abuzz because they're convinced of your sanctity and recognize that you were especially virtuous during your lifetime, maybe even mystical. Now that you've passed away, they're nudging your pastor to present your cause to the bishop. Specific steps must be taken to declare that you're a saint in the Catholic Church. You have to be referred to as each of the following (in this order) to become a recognized saint:

1. **Servant of God:** As soon as your cause is opened for consideration, you're called a *Servant of God.*

2. **Venerable:** If the Vatican Congregation for the Causes of Saints determines that you did indeed live a life of heroic virtue, you're referred to as *venerable.* (Keep in mind that *heroic virtue* doesn't mean that you were perfect or sinless but that you worked aggressively to improve yourself spiritually and that you never gave up trying to be better and grow in holiness.)

3. **Blessed:** If the Church establishes that God performed one miracle through your intercession, your cause is presented to the pope to see whether he deems you worthy of being called *blessed.* This step is called *beatification.*

4. **Saint:** If the Church determines that you've performed a second miracle, your cause is presented to the pope again for his judgment. If he determines that the evidence for your miracles is clear and that contrary reports aren't credible, he may initiate the canonization procedure. If all goes well, you'll be publicly recognized as a saint.

We discuss each of the steps to sainthood in the following sections.

Everyone is called to holiness

Even if you don't think beatification or canonization are in your future, and you just think of yourself as an average Joe, the Church believes that all human beings are called to holiness because every man and woman on earth is made in the image and likeness of God, and by Baptism they become adopted children of God. St. Josemaría Escrivá, the founder of Opus Dei, taught that God wants all people, be they clergy or laity, male or female, children or adults, to live holy lives.

Escrivá often spoke of the sanctification of one's daily work, meaning that a person can transform his mundane and sometimes tedious chores into the Work of God (*Opus Dei* in Latin). Everyone can and should strive to become a saint by sanctifying their daily work. He pointed out (as did St. Francis de Sales, St. Thérèse of Lisieux, and other spiritual writers) that the holy family of Jesus, Mary, and Joseph spent most of their time doing ordinary work. St. Joseph worked as a carpenter, and it wasn't a cushy nine-to-five job. Mary spent 80 percent of her day cooking, shopping for groceries, cleaning, sewing, doing laundry, and other household chores. And until He turned 30, Jesus worked with Joseph so much that at one time in the Bible, He was called a carpenter (Mark 6:3). Escrivá taught that because Jesus, Mary, and Joseph didn't spend all their time in the Temple or on their knees in prayer, holiness isn't just doing holy things or going to holy places. Holiness is actually *being* holy and that means uniting yourself to God.

Going through the investigations for sainthood

Before being recognized as a saint you must go through several investigations. So you're only a candidate if your existence can be verified and your life examined. As a result, legendary figures don't make the cut if proof doesn't exist that they walked this earth. Also, the living can't be declared venerable, blessed, or saintly, because those titles are reserved for souls in heaven.

Only after death can someone be called a saint. Even Mother Teresa of Calcutta, for example, who was revered around the world by people of every religion, couldn't be given the title of saint until after her death and a thorough investigation of her life and miracles God performed through her. (You can read about Mother Teresa and her work in Chapter 20.)

In the following sections, we explain the background check and deep investigation the Church makes into the lives of those who are up for sainthood. We also include a discussion about the miracles needed for beatification and canonization.

The background check

Normally, from 5 to 50 years after death, a formal request is made to open your cause. This request is presented to the local bishop of the place where you died. The group making the request is called the *Actor Causae* and is usually composed of people from your former parish, diocese, religious community, or the organization you were associated with while you were alive.

Just being a nice guy or gal isn't enough. You must have demonstrated exemplary and heroic virtue. In other words, you must have gone beyond what was expected and necessary, and you must have done far more than the average person to serve God, the Church, and your neighbor. However, you didn't have to be perfect or totally sinless. Catholics believe that no one but God is perfect.

For example, the Bible tells of the good thief, St. Dismas, who hung on the cross next to Jesus on Good Friday. Jesus promised, "Today you will be with me in Paradise" (Luke 23:43). St. Dismas was a sinner, but he repented and sought the divine mercy and forgiveness of God. Despite his criminal past, Dismas's repentance and faith enabled him to become a saint.

Even though perfection isn't required, as a candidate for beatification (or, initially, a Servant of God or veneration) you must have lived an exemplary life. The purpose of the process isn't to get you into heaven but to recognize that you're already there and that you lived a life worthy to be imitated.

Usually, a number of people who lived and worked with you want to attest to your personal holiness and the effect that you had on many lives. One or two people aren't enough, however. The local bishop must decide whether enough initial interest and evidence exists and whether the possibility of completing the process exists before he asks Rome to open your cause. If the arguments from the group are persuasive and the evidence compelling, the bishop asks Rome and the Congregation for the Causes of Saints for permission. When permission is given, the bishop forms a special tribunal to investigate your cause.

During your initial background check, witnesses are called who can verify or refute your public life. Did you live a virtuous life or a scandalous one? Did you regularly practice your religion or were you lax? Did you treat others with love and respect or with contempt and disdain? Concrete examples of how you exhibited the theological virtues of faith, hope, and love — as well as the cardinal, or moral, virtues of prudence, justice, fortitude, and temperance — must be proven by oral testimony or written evidence. If sufficient witnesses and documentation are present, you're then called a Servant of God, and you're ready for deeper investigation.

The full-scale investigation

After you've become a Servant of God, those who remember you on earth likely want to continue pursuing your beatification. Three levels of deep investigation occur at this point:

- ✔ Informative inquiries into your reputation and activities
- ✔ Proof that no one has proclaimed or is already proclaiming and honoring you as a saint before it's been officially declared
- ✔ A thorough examination of your written and spoken works

Miracles aren't necessary at this point, but if the people nominating you believe that God worked a miracle through you during your life and/or after your death, that belief is noted in this stage of the investigation.

After the local diocesan investigation goes to Rome, the next step, called the *Apostolic Process,* is to translate the documentation into Italian because the cardinals and other theological experts live in Italy, not in the country where the case originated. After the documentation is translated, a summary called the *Positio* is presented to the Congregation for the Causes of Saints. Nine theologians scrutinize the evidence and documentation. If a majority of them agree, the cause then goes to a committee of cardinals and bishops who meet twice a month and work at the Congregation. If they approve, the Prefect of the Congregation gives permission for the title *venerable* to be associated with your name.

At this point, if you weren't *martyred* for the faith — killed because of your religion or because you refused to renounce Christ or the Church — and at least one posthumous miracle has been attributed to your intercession, the Prefect presents the case to the pope for his personal judgment. If you were martyred, no miracle is needed before beatification. The pope alone decides whether you're declared *blessed* (beatified). The pope or his representative makes this declaration at a Mass celebrated in your honor (see the section "Experiencing the beatification and canonization Mass"). If it can be proven that another miracle occurred after your beatification, the cause is presented to the pope again to consider canonization, at which time you're finally called a saint! Again, he makes this declaration at a special Mass. Canonizing a saint is considered a function of *papal infallibility* (see Chapter 2), because it's vital that the faithful give public veneration and honor only to those who truly are in heaven.

Miracles matter

Catholics take the miracles necessary for beatification and canonization very seriously. All miracles need to be documented and authenticated, so eyewitnesses alone are considered insufficient. Medical, scientific, psychiatric, and theological experts are consulted, and evidence is given to them for their professional opinion. If a scientific, medical, or psychological explanation exists for what had only appeared to be a miracle, it isn't considered an authentic miracle. Only immediate, spontaneous, and inexplicable phenomena are up for consideration as authentic miracles. A group of Italian doctors *(Consulta Medica)* examines the healing miracles. Some of the doctors aren't Catholic and some are, but all are qualified and renowned physicians. They don't declare a healing a miracle but instead say, "We can find no scientific or medical explanation for the cure."

Besides miraculous healings, the Church examines other phenomena:

- **Incorruptibility:** Long after the saint is dead, the body is found free of decay when exhumed from the grave. The Church considers St. Catherine of Siena to be an example. She died in 1380, and more than six centuries later without any embalming, her flesh hasn't decomposed.

- **Liquefaction:** The dried blood of the saint, long dead, miraculously liquefies on the feast day. The Church considers St. Januarius *(San Gennaro* in Italian; A.D. 275?–305), the patron saint of Naples, to be an example. According to the Church, a vial of his dried blood liquefies every year on the saint's feast day, September 19.

- **Odor of sanctity:** The body of the saint exudes a sweet aroma, like roses, rather than the usual pungent stench of decay. The Church considers St. Teresa of Avila (1515–82) to be just such an example. The Church believes her grave exuded a sweet odor for nine months after her death.

In addition, during the life of the saint, some miraculous things may have happened, including the following:

- **Levitation:** The saint floats in the air without the help of David Copperfield. An example is St. Joseph of Cupertino (1603–63), who, according to the Church, levitated often during prayer.

- **Bilocation:** The saint appears in two places at the same time. According to the Church, Padre Pio (1887–1968) was seen and heard in two places at the same time yet spanning great distances. (For more on Padre Pio, see Chapter 21.)

- **Stigmata:** The saint's body is marked with the five wounds of Christ on both hands, both feet, and on the side. These wounds often bleed during Mass and then stop. After death, the stigmata disappear. The Church believes that Padre Pio and St. Francis of Assisi (1181–1226) were blessed with the stigmata. (To find out more about St. Francis, flip ahead to Chapter 21.)

The Church believes that most saints don't have these rare experiences, but the experiences of those who did were proven to be authentic and inexplicable by modern science.

St. Faustina's bona fide miracles

In 1981, Maureen Digan of Roslindale, Massachusetts, traveled to Faustina's (1905–1938) grave outside of Krakow, Poland. From her early teens, Maureen suffered from an incurable illness known as Milroy's Disease, a form of lymphedema. It had already claimed one of her legs, and doctors recommended amputating the other. At Faustina's tomb, Maureen prayed for Faustina's intercession and immediately felt pain leave her and the swelling in her leg go down. Upon the doctors' examinations, they stated that Maureen's incurable ailment had disappeared. After exhaustive examination by medical professionals, the Church declared the healing a miracle through Faustina's intercession.

Fr. Ron Pytel of Baltimore, Maryland, knew that he had a problem. His doctors discovered a massive calcium build-up in his aortic valve. As a result, the left ventricle of his heart had become badly damaged, a condition that rarely heals, and if it does, it occurs over a span of many years. In June 1995, Fr. Ron had surgery to replace the valve with an artificial one, but the damage to his heart was another problem. Dr. Nicholas Fortuin, a world-renowned cardiologist from Johns Hopkins in Baltimore, said that Fr. Ron's heart would never be normal and that the 48-year-old priest would likely never be able to return to his priestly duties. On October 5, 1995, the 58th anniversary of Faustina's death, Fr. Ron prayed for Faustina's intercession (so she could be named a saint) at a healing service. After venerating her relic, he collapsed on the floor and felt unable to move for about 15 minutes. During his next regular check-up, Fr. Ron's doctor couldn't explain the condition of the priest's heart: It had returned to normal. On November 16, 1999, a panel of doctors declared the healing scientifically unexplainable. Theologians from the Church's Congregation for the Causes of Saints dubbed the healing a miracle on December 7. Then one week later, a panel of cardinals and bishops gave their unanimous approval. The pope then decided to go ahead with her canonization.

Experiencing the beatification and canonization Mass

The actual acts of *beatification,* in which a person is declared blessed, and of *canonization,* in which a person is declared a saint, usually take place in St. Peter's Square outside St. Peter's Basilica. It's a big event: In 2001, almost a half million people attended Padre Pio's outdoor canonization Mass. When Monsignor Josemaría Escrivá was canonized four months later, 300,000 were present

Sometimes, though, the pope beatifies and canonizes in the country where the person lived and/or died, as in the case of St. Juan Diego (canonized in 2002). He was an Aztec peasant, and the Church believes Mary, as Our Lady of Guadalupe, appeared to him in Mexico in 1531. In his case, 12,000 people were present in the Basilica in Mexico City, and 30,000 waited outside, watching on monitors.

Because the Mass is the highest form of worship for Catholics and the Holy Eucharist is the zenith of Catholicism, it makes perfect sense for the pope as supreme head of the universal Church to beatify or canonize a saint within the context of the Mass.

After the person's life history is read aloud, the pope chants Latin text.

At this point, a huge tapestry showing an image of the blessed or the saint is unfolded for the faithful to look at and admire.

Pope John Paul II chose to celebrate all beatification Masses himself, either in Rome or in the city where the newly beatified was buried. Pope Benedict XVI, however, has chosen to go back to the previous tradition of allowing the local bishop (archbishop or cardinal) to celebrate the beatification Mass and reserving just the canonization Masses for himself.

A Saint for Every Day of the Year

The Catholic Church assigns one date out of the year for each and every canonized saint — known as the saint's *feast day*. The saints are remembered on their individual feast days with special mention, prayers, and possibly a scripture reading. Usually, it's the day that the person died. That day is the day that the Church believes the person went to heaven, so it's the saint's heavenly birthday. The number of canonized saints, however, is greater than the number of days in a calendar year, so two or more saints often share the same feast day. Because overlap often occurs, and the Church isn't sure of the date of death of some saints, other calendar dates are sometimes chosen — such as the day that the saint was canonized.

Some saints' feasts are celebrated only in the particular saint's town or country. Others are internationally celebrated. For example, St. Patrick's Day, March 17, is celebrated in Ireland because St. Patrick is the patron saint of the entire nation. St. Patrick's Day is also celebrated in many areas of the United States due to the Irish immigrants who crossed the Atlantic. Another example is St. Joseph's Day, March 19, which is celebrated in Canada and Europe with more hoopla than in the United States. He's the patron of the universal Church and the head of the *holy family,* which refers to Jesus, Mary, and Joseph during the first 30 years of Jesus's life.

On some feast days — such as the Feasts of St. Patrick, St. Joseph, St. Januarius (September 19), and St. Gerard Majella (October 16) — Catholics process through the streets and host festivals with plenty of pomp and circumstance. And with other feasts — such as the Feasts of St. Anne (July 26); the Archangels St. Michael, St. Gabriel, and St. Raphael (September 29); and St. Thérèse of

Lisieux (October 1) — parishes have a special Mass and may even have a nine-day novena, which usually concludes on the day of the feast itself.

In addition, on the feast days of the founders of religious orders, such as August 8 (St. Dominic), October 4 (St. Francis of Assisi), July 11 (St. Benedict), and July 31 (St. Ignatius of Loyola), the religious orders that they founded — the Dominicans, Franciscans, Benedictines, and Jesuits, respectively — usually honor the feast of their founder with a healthy mix of praying and partying.

You can find saints for different places and saints for different occasions. The idea isn't to replace or diminish the role of Christ as the sole mediator but to show how the family of faith continues to remain a part of each member in different ways.

Discovering the Communion of Saints

Part of the Apostles' Creed says, "I believe in . . . the communion of saints." People sometimes ask us, "But what in the world does that mean? Is it holy people receiving Holy Communion?" Well, yes and no. The term *communion of saints* (*hagion koinonian* in Greek) is rich in meaning. It refers to the fellowship or community that exists among all the members of the Church. Three levels of union are traditionally identified:

- **The Church Triumphant:** Saints in heaven
- **The Church Militant:** Believers on earth
- **The Church Suffering:** Souls in purgatory

Catholicism teaches that death can't sever the ties that bind the members of the Church because the soul is immortal and only the body can die. So Catholics believe that the ties and connections that link them together in life continue in death. The beloved dead are still connected to the living and still love the living as much as the living still love the dead. Even though the body is dead, the immortal soul is very much still alive and in existence.

The Church believes that the communion of saints is most fully expressed and experienced during the Holy Sacrifice of the Mass — especially at the Consecration and at Holy Communion. The Church believes that heaven and earth are united at that time. The saints in heaven, the believers living on earth, and the souls in purgatory are all intimately connected and united at the Mass because the power of Jesus Christ binds them in the first place. We discuss each of the three levels in the upcoming sections.

Saints in heaven

The Catholic Church believes that the saints are ordinary and typical human beings — with faults and failures, talents and gifts, vices and virtues — who made it into heaven not by being perfect but by persevering (see the earlier section "Having a Place in the Hearts of Catholics"). In terms of the communion of saints, the *Church Triumphant* refers to all those saints who are now in heaven, reunited with other saints they knew on earth and with the great heroes of the faith.

Heaven is described in the Catechism as the communion of life and love with the Holy Trinity (God the Father, Son, and Holy Spirit), the Blessed Virgin Mary, and all the angels and saints. Salvation is not just getting to Paradise but much more. Heaven is your spiritual home, and home is where the family lives — in this case, the family of God.

Jesus said, "In my Father's house are many rooms; if it were not so, would I have told you that I go to prepare a place for you? And when I go and prepare a place for you, I will come again and will take you to myself, that where I am you may be also" (John 14:2-3).

Catholics believe that going to heaven is going home to your destiny because you were created to know, love, and serve God in this world so as to be happy with Him in the next. But heaven is also a great family reunion where you get to see all your deceased loved ones who went to heaven before you. Imagine seeing grandparents, parents, children, brothers and sisters, cousins, and in-laws, not to mention the famous people of history, such as Adam and Eve, Abraham and Moses, Mary and Joseph, and so on.

The joy and happiness of being with those you love and those who love you is nothing, however, in comparison with the bliss and ecstasy that the soul experiences just seeing God face to face (called the *beatific vision*) because he is all truth, goodness, and holiness. Heaven is so desirable that human beings should want to go there more than wanting anything else in the universe. Catholics believe that everybody should be willing to do anything to get there, which means that loving and obeying God while alive on earth is a must.

According to the Catholic Church, when a human being — even a baby or small child — dies, the person doesn't become an angel but, rather, may become a saint. The Church believes that angels are separate beings from humans. Anyone in heaven is called a saint, even the Archangels Saints Michael, Gabriel, and Raphael. But not all saints are angels; only those who were created as angels remain angels. Human souls remain human. Both are called "saint," just as both fallen angels and condemned human souls in hell can be called the "damned."

FROM THE BIBLE

Are angels among the living?

Whereas men and women have bodies and souls, angels are pure spirits. Angels were created before humankind, and some of them sinned and were cast into hell for all eternity. These fallen angels are known as *devils* and *demons*. Lucifer was an angel, but after his fall, he became known as Satan or the devil. Most of the angels remained obedient to God. St. Thomas Aquinas (see Chapter 21) described nine choirs or groupings of angels in his *Summa Theologica* based on Sacred Scripture (Colossians 1:16 and Romans 8:38) as well as Sacred Tradition. Here are the nine choirs in order from highest to lowest: *Seraphim* (Isaiah 6:2), *Cherubim* (Genesis 3:24), *Thrones* (Colossians 1:16), *Dominions* (Colossians 1:16), *Virtues* (Ephesians 1:21), *Powers* (1 Peter 3:22),

Principalities (Romans 8:38), *Archangels* (1 Thessalonians 4:16), and *Angels* (Romans 8:38).

Guardian angels are spirits God has commanded to watch over you and guard you. The belief in guardian angels is based on Matthew 18:10: "See that you do not despise one of these little ones; for I tell you that in heaven *their* angels always behold the face of my Father who is in heaven." Some angels, like the Archangels Michael, Gabriel, and Raphael, are mentioned in the Bible. Other angels like Uriel, Jophiel, Chamael, Zadkiel, and Jophkiel are listed only in what Catholicism calls the *Apocrypha* or what Protestantism calls the *Pseudepigrapha*. See Chapter 2 for more on the Apocrypha and the Pseudepigrapha.

Believers on earth

The second tier of the communion of saints is the *Church Militant,* the believers on earth. And they're always united in a mystical fashion to the Church Triumphant, the saints in heaven, and the Church Suffering, the souls in purgatory.

Vatican II described the faithful alive on earth as a Pilgrim People. The Church believes that those still living on earth are on a pilgrimage from this land to the promised land of heaven. St. Augustine (354–430) remarked that the faithful are citizens of the Heavenly Jerusalem while temporarily traveling through the earthly Babylon.

TIP

The word *militant* isn't used in the sense that Catholics are at war with Protestants, Jews, or Muslims. The term refers to a spiritual warfare against sin and the devil. Catholics believe that their fellow man is their ally, not their enemy. The devil and sin are the real enemies. Confirmation makes the faithful Soldiers of Christ, who battle against greed, envy, anger, lust, pride, laziness, and gluttony as well as prejudice, racism, anti-Semitism, hatred, violence, terrorism, abortion, euthanasia, pornography, physical/emotional/sexual abuse, child abuse, and so on. The Church believes that those sins are the enemies of God and of humankind, and therefore, the Church Militant does battle against vice and error through the weapons of grace and truth — not guns, tanks, and missiles. The spiritual battle is meant to rescue souls from sin and evil.

Souls in purgatory

Rounding out the third tier of the communion of saints is the Church Suffering, or those souls in purgatory. *Purgatory* is an often-misunderstood Catholic doctrine. It isn't considered a spiritual jail or hell with parole. Rather than a place, purgatory is a state of being in which the human soul is cleansed from attachments to sin. Catholicism doesn't teach that everyone goes to purgatory. On the contrary, the Church believes that many people are purified or purged, hence the term *purgatory,* in this life.

For example, the Church believes that many innocent persons who suffer from disease, poverty, or persecution are living their purgatory now, and when they die, they'll probably go straight to heaven. The same goes for people who live an exceptionally good and holy life — no need for purgatory. However, the Church believes that most people aren't bad enough to go to hell, but they also aren't good enough to skate into heaven without some introspection and purification.

Where is hell, anyway?

Ancient man believed that hell was underground, in the center of the earth, where it was hot. This belief was based on the erroneous notion that the earth was the center of the universe. When science proved that the sun was the center of the solar system, then what? Well, the Bible and Sacred Tradition never again tried to define the exact location of hell. Because God created hell as a place to incarcerate the devil and all the bad angels who rebelled with him, and because angels are pure spirits and have no bodies that take up space, hell isn't a physical place. It's as real as heaven or purgatory, but you can't travel to it anymore than a spaceship can reach heaven.

The essence of hell isn't a million degrees of heat from fire but from the heat that comes from hatred and bitterness. Hell is a lonely and self-ish place; no matter how many souls it contains, not one of them cares about anyone else. It's utter isolation as well as eternal torment, which is why everyone should want to avoid it at all cost. Heaven, on the other hand, is a place of happiness and joy because everyone there knows and loves each other. And, most of all, heaven is desirable because of what's called *beatific vision* — seeing God face to face for eternity. Being in the presence of the Supreme Being who is all truth and all goodness ought to be the desire of every person.

Upholding both mercy and justice

The real doctrine of purgatory consists of the conviction that God's mercy and justice must be kept intact and upheld. God's divine mercy refers to the fact that He forgives any sin as long as the sinner is truly repentant and sorry. God's justice, however, is that good is rewarded and evil punished. Catholics believe that purgatory evens the score and fulfills justice while accommodating mercy. They believe that purgatory isn't a place but a spiritual state of the soul in which it's purified before entering heaven. The souls in purgatory are definitely and absolutely going to heaven, just not yet.

Think of it this way: Joe and Max were both born on the same day and both died on the same day. Joe was a gambler, boozer, and womanizer, and he was dishonest, lazy, and undependable. Max, on the other hand, spent his life obeying the Ten Commandments, practicing virtue, and loving God and neighbor. Just before dying, Joe repented of his old ways and accepted the Lord into his heart. Should Joe and Max both go to heaven at the same time? Catholicism teaches no. The Church believes that Jesus's death allows everyone the possibility of heaven, and His mercy grants forgiveness, but His justice demands that good be rewarded and evil punished — in this life or the next. If one man struggles all his life to be good while another lives a life of selfishness, greed, and comfort, both can't walk through the pearly gates side by side.

Preparing the soul for heaven

Purgatory is more than the temporal punishment for sin. It's also the cleansing from the attachment to sin. Purgatory purifies the soul before the soul's grand entrance into heaven.

It may help to think of purgatory in terms of a major operation to save a life. Say a doctor performs surgery on someone's heart or brain and removes a cancerous tumor. The surgery achieves the main objective, but the wound needs to heal, and the incision needs to be cleaned and rebandaged. Purgatory is like the recovery stage — the healing, cleaning, and bandaging. The belief is that the evil of sin is revealed to the person so she can totally reject even the most venial and smallest of sins.

Often, after committing sin, people later regret it and are remorseful. Catholics confess their sins and believe that God forgives them in the Sacrament of Penance. However, many times people still have pleasant memories of those sins. They're sorry and regret doing them, but they have some enjoyable and pleasurable memories — some leftover attachment to the sins. Catholicism teaches that the souls in purgatory want to be in purgatory because they know that they have some leftover attachment to sin that they want to be removed.

Getting a close-up view of sin

You can think of purgatory like a spiritual electron microscope that shows all that nasty sin — mortal and venial — and reveals how dangerous and harmful any sin is to the soul. Purgatory allows people to recognize that even one small sin is repugnant and offensive to an all-loving and all-good God.

After you recognize the gravity of your sins, you don't just immediately hightail it into heaven. Purgatory lasts as long as it takes to render the soul undefiled and pure enough for heaven. Time, as mere mortals know it, doesn't exist in purgatory because departed souls have no bodies, so trying to specify how many minutes, days, months, or years souls spend in purgatory is merely analogous.

The word *purgatory* isn't in the Bible but neither is the word *Bible.* However, praying for the dead is mentioned in the Second Book of Maccabees (12:43–46):

> He also took up a collection, man by man, to the amount of two thousand drachmas of silver, and sent it to Jerusalem to provide for a sin offering. In doing this he acted very well and honorably, taking account of the resurrection. For if he were not expecting that those who had fallen would rise again, it would have been superfluous and foolish to pray for the dead. But if he was looking to the splendid reward that is laid up for those who fall asleep in godliness, it was a holy and pious thought. Therefore he made atonement for the dead, that they might be delivered from their sin.

The belief is that if the dead were in hell, no prayers could help them, and if they were in heaven, they wouldn't need any prayers. So a place must exist in between heaven and hell where the souls who aren't completely prepared or ready to enter heaven go after death.

Catholics don't see purgatory as a place of pain and torment. Instead, it's considered a place of expectant joy, although suffering occurs from the temporary distance. Imagine being in a room with a door that has no handle or knob on your side. You can hear the joy and merriment on the other side, smell the good food, and hear the music and laughter, but you can't see any faces or distinguish voices or aromas. You're close but yet far enough away to feel the pain of not being on the other side. Yet you know that you aren't quite a saint yet. Your clothes are dirty and wrinkled, your hair's a mess, and you need to shave and brush your teeth. Why all this preparation? Catholics believe that God and heaven are worth it.

Hankerin' for heaven

Dante Alighieri's (1265–1321) epic poem *La Divina Commedia* (The Divine Comedy) is made up of three parts: the *Inferno* (hell), *Purgatorio* (purgatory), and *Paradiso* (heaven). Dante described purgatory as a suburb of hell — close enough to smell the stench and feel the heat but still far enough away for hope.

Although not a theological work — and never meant as such — Dante's poem greatly influenced the Medieval and Renaissance mindset. Many people felt that Dante's literary spin on purgatory — hell with parole or a suburb of hell — was really true.

According to the Church, however, purgatory is more like a suburb of heaven. It's close enough to hear the laughter and singing, smell the sweetness in the air, and feel the warmth nearby, but it's far enough away to remind everyone that they haven't yet arrived.

Some people may think of purgatory as being stuck in traffic on the day before Thanksgiving. You know for certain that you're on your way home, but you just don't know when you'll arrive. And it's the not-knowing part that causes the anxiety and purgative pain.

Chapter 19

Practicing Catholic Traditions

In This Chapter

▶ Heading to church to adore the Blessed Sacrament

▶ Participating in religious processions

▶ Getting the hang of fasting and abstaining

▶ Understanding what a sacramental is

▶ Celebrating Catholic festivals and feasts

*Y*ou've probably seen Catholics wearing crucifixes around their necks, sporting ashes on their foreheads on Ash Wednesday, praying with rosary beads, and engaging in other Catholic traditions. They may have looked strange, but Catholic traditions are imperative to maintaining Catholic identity.

Still, Catholics don't practice their traditions simply for the sake of identity. Rather, these faith traditions all have religious significance and meaning. In this chapter, we help you understand the spiritual meaning behind various Catholic traditions so you can participate in them for the right reasons.

Adoring the Blessed Sacrament

It's no secret that the Holy Eucharist, or the bread and wine that become Jesus's body and blood, is central to Catholicism. Other terms for the Holy Eucharist are the *consecrated Host* and the *Blessed Sacrament.* To understand what *adoring* the Blessed Sacrament is all about, you first need to understand Catholicism's perspective on the Holy Eucharist. So we're going to take a roundabout way of getting to the tradition itself. Bear with us.

Catholicism has three perspectives on the Holy Eucharist (you can read even more about it in Chapters 8 and 10):

✔ **Sacrifice:** The same sacrifice of Jesus's death on the cross for the remission of sins occurs during Mass at the Consecration in the form of the Holy Eucharist. The *Consecration* is the moment during Mass when the bread and wine are changed into the real body and blood of Christ. This is called a *sacrifice* because Jesus, the Son of God, is being offered by the priest to God the Father.

✔ **Sacred banquet:** After the Consecration of the Mass, the faithful walk up to the altar to receive the Holy Eucharist. Entering a person's body, soul, mind, and heart all at once, Jesus — really, truly, and substantially — in the Holy Eucharist is placed on the tongue or in the hand. This is called a *sacred banquet* because the Holy Eucharist is food and nourishment for the soul.

✔ **Real Presence:** Catholics believe that the Holy Eucharist is Christ Himself — His real, true body and blood, soul and divinity, and substantial presence under the appearances of bread and wine. Some Christian religions regard it as a symbolic, spiritual, or moral presence, but Catholic Christianity and Eastern Orthodoxy staunchly hold to His Real Presence in the Eucharist. So the Holy Eucharist warrants the same adoration and worship given only to God. This sacrament is called the *Blessed Sacrament* because of all the seven sacraments, this one not only gives divine grace but is also God Himself.

When you're adoring the Blessed Sacrament, you have the opportunity to just worship the Real Presence and do nothing else. At Mass, the emphasis is on the sacrifice and the sacred meal (actually consuming the wine and bread), but simply adoring the Holy Eucharist outside of Mass is a time to just focus on Jesus. You can do this by celebrating Benediction (see the next section), or observing a holy hour.

The Eucharist should never be exposed at home. Adoration of the Blessed Sacrament can take place only in a church, a chapel, or an oratory, but adoration and Benediction can't take place during Mass.

Participating in Benediction

A formal service, Benediction takes place while adoring the Blessed Sacrament and can occur only if a priest or a deacon leads it. Many parishes have Benediction once a month, perhaps on the First Friday of the month, or maybe weekly on a Sunday afternoon or evening. There doesn't need to be a special occasion for Benediction, but it's never allowed during Mass or during other devotions, such as the Stations of the Cross (see Chapter 16).

Sacred Scripture is read, a homily may be preached, the Rosary may be said, and silent prayer is offered. At the end, the priest, his shoulders enveloped in a special stole called a *humeral veil,* blesses the faithful kneeling in attendance, making the sign of the cross, with Jesus exposed in the monstrance.

During Mass, a priest wears a *chasuble,* a colored outer garment, but during Benediction, the priest wears the humeral veil over a *cope,* the gold or white full-length liturgical cape worn for Eucharistic devotions. By covering his hands with the humeral veil, the priest or deacon symbolizes that the blessing being given isn't his own as a sacred and ordained minister (as at the end of Mass), but the blessing of Christ Himself present in the Holy Eucharist contained in the monstrance.

Bells are normally rung three times as the blessing is given with the Blessed Sacrament. Candles surround the monstrance that holds the Blessed Sacrament resting on the altar. That same Blessed Sacrament is *incensed:* As a sign that the people are now in the presence of divinity, incense is burned in a container and waved in front of the monstrance. Benediction also consists of the singing of certain hymns (often in Latin) and litanies, such as the *Divine Praises,* that follow:

> Blessed be God.
> Blessed be his holy name.
> Blessed be Jesus Christ, true God and true man.
> Blessed be the name of Jesus.
> Blessed be his most Sacred Heart.
> Blessed be his most Precious Blood.
> Blessed be Jesus in the most Holy Sacrament of the Altar.
> Blessed be the Holy Spirit, the Paraclete.
> Blessed be the great Mother of God, Mary most holy.
> Blessed be her holy and Immaculate Conception.
> Blessed be her glorious Assumption.
> Blessed be the name of Mary, Virgin and Mother.
> Blessed be Saint Joseph, her most chaste spouse.
> Blessed be God in his angels and in his saints.

Adoring at church during Perpetual Adoration or the 40-hour devotion

The Holy Eucharist is placed in an ornamental vessel called a *monstrance* (see Figure 19-1) and left on the altar for public adoration and worship. Catholics consider it a great privilege and blessing to be able to adore the Blessed Sacrament, and we recommend spending a holy hour in front of the Eucharist each week so you can privately and publicly pray and express your faith. Holy hour is the perfect chance to say prayers, such as the Rosary or the Divine Mercy Chaplet, silently in the company of Jesus.

The history of the 40-hour devotion in a nutshell

The 40-hour devotion originated in Europe and was known as *Quarant' Ore* in Italian, which simply means *40 hours.* St. Anthony Maria Zaccaria started the first 40 hours in Milan in 1527. He wanted to renew and reaffirm the belief in the Real Presence and the practice of giving adoration and worship to the Holy Eucharist, because it's no longer merely bread in the form of a wafer. It only looks and tastes like bread, but Jesus is now present in the Eucharist — the substantial body and blood, soul and divinity of Christ.

St. Philip Neri (1515–1595) brought the practice to Rome after Martin Luther initiated the Protestant Reformation. At the time, clergy and laity alike were getting confused about what the Church really taught. Even a few priests who celebrated Mass daily began to doubt that they had the power to actually change bread and wine into the body and blood of Christ.

St. John Neumann, Archbishop of Philadelphia (1811–1860), an immigrant from Bohemia, brought the tradition to the United States. Once a year, each and every Philadelphia parish had a 40-hour devotion on a regularly scheduled basis.

Figure 19-1:
The Blessed Sacrament exposed in the monstrance on the left and within the tabernacle on the right.

Courtesy of St. Louis de Montfort Church, Fishers, Indiana.

Some parishes offer adoration 24/7, which is called *Perpetual Adoration.* Some other churches offer 40-hour devotion. The 40 hours in the term *40-hour devotion* refer to the number of hours that the faithful believe Jesus was absent from the world. The period of time from his death on Good Friday at around 3 p.m. to his Resurrection on Easter morning at about 7 a.m. is 40 hours. These traditional three days — from Sunday afternoon to Tuesday evening — are when many Catholic parishes display the Blessed Sacrament in a gold monstrance on the altar. Displaying the Holy Eucharist is meant to promote adoration and worship of Jesus in his hidden but Real Presence in the Blessed Sacrament.

The 40-hour devotion usually begins after the last Mass on Sunday. Usually, a consecrated host from that Mass is placed in the monstrance and put in the center of the altar after the faithful have received Holy Communion. The priest says the final prayer, but no final blessing is given and no closing hymn is sung. The priest, deacon, and altar servers kneel down before the Blessed Sacrament, and incense is burned (as Psalm 141 says, "Let my prayer be counted as incense before thee"). Six candles, three on each side, are traditionally placed to the left and right of the monstrance. Parishioners come and go throughout the day to spend anywhere from 30 minutes to an hour or more, just praying before the Blessed Sacrament on the altar. This amount of time represents the request that Jesus made during his agony in the Garden of Olives: Before His Crucifixion and death on Good Friday, he asked, "Could you not watch with me one hour?" (Mark 26:40)

The goal is to have the church open all night and all day for 40 continuous hours to represent the time that Jesus spent in the grave. But this goal can be met only if safety and security needs are met to protect the church and any faithful making a visit (the same goes for Perpetual Adoration). Parishioners sign up to commit themselves for an hour or half-hour around the clock, never leaving Jesus unattended. Getting that many people to make such a commitment is easier in a large parish of a thousand families than in a small parish of, say, only 200 families. Some pastors ask different Catholic organizations within the parish, such as the Knights of Columbus, the Council of Catholic Women, the St. Vincent de Paul Society, and the Parish Council, to commit their members for time slots. And some have asked ushers, extraordinary ministers (laypersons who assist the priest with Holy Communion at Mass), altar servers, and so on, to take turns.

Today, many parishes are forced to repose the Blessed Sacrament (put the Holy Eucharist back into the tabernacle) each evening of the 40-hour devotion after a prayer service — usually a combination of *Vespers* (evening prayer that includes the Psalms and other Scripture readings) and a sermon from a visiting priest or deacon. Then the Blessed Sacrament is exposed again after morning Mass on the next day. It doesn't add up to 40 hours, but the traditional three days are still a part of the process.

On the final evening, after the prayers and sermon, the pastor, priests, deacons, religious sisters, and first communicants engage in a procession before the Blessed Sacrament around the church. They march in front of the monstrance in the Roman tradition of having the most important person at the end of the line — in this case, Jesus Himself. The act of processing reminds the faithful of the joyful procession of Jesus into Jerusalem on Palm Sunday, the Sunday before Easter. It also symbolizes the return entrance of the same Son of God at the end of time when the Second Coming of Christ will take place. Finally, the pomp and pageantry of processing with the singing of hymns, the burning of incense, and the solemnity of the moment also reaffirm the belief that this is no mere wafer of bread being paraded around. Rather, it is believed to be the actual and real body and blood, soul and divinity of Christ. When the Blessed Sacrament passes the faithful kneeling in the pews, they bless themselves with the sign of the cross. They kneel in adoration of their Lord and God present in the monstrance.

Following the elaborate procession outside around the church or inside around the four inner walls and through the aisles of the church, the priest or deacon places the Blessed Sacrament in the monstrance back on the altar and incenses it again. Benediction then follows. (See the "Participating in Benediction" section, earlier in this chapter.)

Representing Life's Journey: Other Religious Processions

The Catholic tradition of public processions is nothing new; they're as ancient as civilization itself. Kings, Caesars, and armies processed in triumphant victory after a battle or on the anniversary of the monarch's coronation. The Ark of the Covenant — believed to contain the tablets of the Ten Commandments (often called the *Debarim*, Hebrew for the *Ten Words*) — was often carried in procession by the Israelites to protect them in battle and to rejoice in victory.

In medieval times, the faithful had processions in which they prayed while moving from one church to the next, and they often asked God for rain during a drought, good weather during a storm, and safety in time of famine, plague, or war.

Church processions remind the faithful that they're pilgrims — people on a journey. The ultimate hope and goal is to get to heaven someday. A procession symbolizes that the faithful haven't arrived yet but, God willing, they're on the way and going the right way.

Besides the procession of the Blessed Sacrament at the end of a 40-hour devotion (see the section "Adoring at church during Perpetual Adoration or the 40-hour devotion," earlier in this chapter), some other processions are part of Catholic tradition:

- **Palm Sunday:** During this procession, the priest and people march around the church or from the outside of the church, through the doors, up the main aisle, and eventually, into the pews to represent the procession that they believe Jesus experienced on the first Palm Sunday.

- **Good Friday:** Processions occur in Rome and Jerusalem on this solemn day. The pope in Rome and the patriarch of Jerusalem in the Holy Land walk with a congregation to symbolize the walk that they believe Jesus was forced to endure while carrying the cross that He was then crucified on.

- **Corpus Christi:** On the Feast of the Body and Blood of Christ (called *Corpus Christi* in Latin for the *body of Christ*), a traditional procession takes place with the Blessed Sacrament in the monstrance. After Mass has just ended, the priest or deacon with all the faithful process from inside the church to outside and may stop at three different outdoor temporary and removable altars, pausing to read Scripture, pray silently, and offer Benediction with the Blessed Sacrament. Finally, they return to the church for more hymns, incense, and the last Benediction. In 1246, St. Juliana of Mont Cornillon (1192–1258) first promoted this feast, and in 1264, Pope Urban IV extended it to the universal Church, so as to bolster and reaffirm the belief in the Real Presence. (See Chapter 10 for more on the Real Presence.)

- **The Byzantine Divine Liturgy** has two small processions:

  - **The little entrance:** The Book of Gospels is carried around the altar by the priest or deacon. It symbolizes the entrance of Jesus (the Word) into the world by His holy birth.

  - **The great entrance:** The holy gifts of bread and wine are carried by the priest to the altar, while the choir sings the Cherubic Hymn. This procession symbolizes the entrance of Jesus on Palm Sunday into Jerusalem.

Meatless Fridays

Another Catholic tradition is abstaining from meat on Fridays during Lent. Practicing abstinence or abstaining, in the general sense, means voluntarily doing without food, drink, or some other pleasure. But for Catholics, it's a specified requirement: Catholics must abstain from meat on Ash Wednesday, every Friday of Lent, and Good Friday, and fast on Ash Wednesday and Good Friday. Here are the specifics:

- ✔ **Abstaining:** Abstaining from meat means refraining from eating all meat if you're at least 14 years old. Yep, chicken is *still* meat. You *can* eat fish and any non-meat product, such as fruits, vegetables, pasta, and so on. Only the flesh meat of warm-blooded animals is off limits on days of abstinence.

- ✔ **Fasting:** If you're required to fast, you can eat only one full meal for the whole day plus two small meals that cannot equal the main meal when combined. Snacking isn't allowed. Fasting applies only to Catholics who are 18 through 59 years old. (See Chapter 11 for more on the laws of fasting and abstinence.)

The tradition of abstaining

According to an urban legend, the pope, cardinals, and bishops initiated abstinence from meat on Friday to promote the pope's fishing business. Nah! That legend has no foundation in fact. St. Peter, the first pope, was a fisherman, and Jesus said to the apostles, "I will make you fishers of men." (Matthew 4:19) Yet subsequent popes have had no financial or economic interest in the fishing business despite this bizarre rumor.

The meatless Friday tradition goes back to the first century, when Christians abstained from eating meat on Fridays to honor Jesus's death on the cross on Good Friday. Because Jesus sacrificed His flesh for the salvation of humankind, the flesh of warm-blooded animals wasn't consumed on Friday.

The practice of abstaining from certain foods and fasting actually goes back to Old Testament times. The Bible says that God told the Hebrews through Moses how to prepare for celebrating *Yom Kippur,* the Day of Atonement. Although fasting isn't mentioned, the Bible does say for this day, "You shall afflict yourselves" (Leviticus 16:31; 23:27–32; Numbers 29:7), and from antiquity, rabbis have interpreted this to mean fasting. The New Testament also mentions the practice, saying "It has been seemed good to the Holy Spirit . . . to abstain from what has been sacrificed to idols and from blood and from what is strangled." (Acts 15:28–29)

Before Vatican II (see Chapter 10), Catholics weren't allowed to eat meat on any Friday of the year, and they also had to fast all the weekdays of Lent. But sick people, pregnant or nursing mothers, and those who worked in hard labor jobs, as well as those in the military during wartime, were dispensed. Going back even farther into Catholic history, Catholics weren't allowed to eat meat, eggs, cheese, or dairy products all during Lent. Since Vatican II, however, the obligation is to abstain from meat on Ash Wednesday, every Friday of Lent, and Good Friday, and to fast on Ash Wednesday and Good Friday.

Even though the U.S. bishops received a *dispensation* (relaxation of a rule for legitimate reasons) from Rome to refrain from abstinence on every Friday and not just during Lent, Catholics are strongly encouraged to do some form of penance, mortification, work of charity, or exercises of piety on all Fridays outside of Lent — to show respect and honor for the Lord. This isn't often mentioned when the revised rules are explained, but it's mentioned in canons 1252–1253 of the 1983 Code of Canon Law. Recently, many bishops and pastors have been suggesting that Catholics abstain from meat on every Friday of the year in reparation for the sin of abortion and to pray for the defense of the sanctity of human life in all its stages and conditions.

Substituting Corporal and Spiritual Works of Mercy for abstinence

One of the ways for Catholics to replace abstinence on every Friday outside of Lent is by performing one of the *Corporal* or *Spiritual Works of Mercy.*

The seven *Corporal Works of Mercy,* based on Christ's sermon on the Last Judgment (Matthew 25:35–36), are feeding the hungry, giving drink to the thirsty, clothing the naked, sheltering the homeless, visiting the sick, visiting the imprisoned, and burying the dead.

In contrast to the Corporal Works of Mercy, which attend to a person's physical needs, the seven *Spiritual Works of Mercy* respond to a person's spiritual needs: admonishing the sinner, instructing the ignorant, counseling the doubtful, comforting the sorrowful, bearing wrongs patiently, forgiving injuries, and praying for the living and the dead.

Using Sacramentals

Catholics love to have priests or deacons bless some of their personal belongings — their homes, cars, or pets. More often, however, Catholics ask priests to bless a personal and tangible religious item — their rosary, medal, statue, Bible, and so on. Any article of devotion or something integral to human life and activity can be blessed, but that doesn't mean it becomes a lucky charm. The priestly blessing is merely a way of showing gratitude to God for his divine grace and putting these blessed items under His watchful care.

For example, if you see an outdoor statue of Mary in the front or back yard of a Catholic home, chances are it has been blessed. It's not magic and does nothing to help the grass grow. It's just a gentle reminder of Mary, the Mother of God, and of Catholic affection for her.

Any time a priest or deacon blesses a religious article, such as a rosary, statue, or medal of one of the saints, he makes the sign of the cross with his right hand over the object(s) and sprinkles holy water on it after saying the prayers of blessing. After a priest, bishop, or deacon blesses such an object, it becomes a *sacramental,* which means that when it's used in conjunction with prayer, it invokes God's blessing. (By the way, holy water is a sacramental, too. Water that's been blessed by a priest, bishop, or deacon is then *holy* water, the most common sacramental, and it's used every day by Catholics around the world.)

Blessed objects — rosary beads, scapulars, medals, statues, icons, bibles, crosses, and crucifixes — are sacramentals. Almost anything can be blessed, but the Catholic who possesses the blessed item can't sell it or use it except in a holy manner.

Sacramentals aren't good luck charms, talismans, or magic objects. For Catholics, they're merely reminders of the supernatural gifts God gives — such as grace, which is invisible. These visible and tangible sacramentals remind Catholics of all that the senses can't perceive.

The word *sacramental* also refers to the blessing or ritual in which a sacramental object is used. For example, in an upcoming section, we note that an exorcism is a sacramental (as are the blessed objects — holy water and salt — used during the exorcism).

Don't confuse sacramentals with the seven sacraments. Sacramentals may be used in the course of administering and receiving a sacrament, but sacramentals do *not* refer to the seven sacraments: Baptism, Penance, Holy Eucharist, Confirmation, Holy Orders, Matrimony, and the Anointing of the Sick. We're talking apples and oranges. Christ instituted the seven sacraments (see Chapters 8 and 9) Himself, and they're unchangeable and permanent. Sacramentals, on the other hand, were created by the Church and can therefore be changed or revised. New ones can be made and old ones suppressed.

Signifying death with ashes

Marking the beginning of Lent, this tradition is a poignant reminder that our bodies will die someday and turn to dust. "Ashes to ashes, dust to dust" is said at the cemetery when the body is ready for burial, so ashes on Ash Wednesday, the first day of Lent, remind us of our mortality and the need for repentance. They're a physical religious reminder similar to holy water and palms on Palm Sunday. The words spoken as the ashes are imposed on the forehead are "Remember man that thou art dust and unto dust thou shalt return" (Genesis 3:19).

Commemorating with blessed palms

Blessed palm leaves, distributed to the congregation at Mass on Palm Sunday, the Sunday before Easter, commemorate the palms the crowd threw at the feet of Jesus as he processed through Jerusalem (Mark 11:1–11). Interestingly, in the Byzantine tradition, they use pussy willows rather than palms, merely because it was too difficult (if not impossible) to get palms in cold regions, such as Russia and Eastern Europe, in the old days before UPS and Federal Express.

Receiving the blessing of throats

On the Feast of St. Blaise (February 3), Catholics may walk up the aisle to have their throats blessed after Mass. The priest holds two blessed candles in criss-cross fashion around the throat of each individual, while praying, "Through the intercession of St. Blaise, Bishop and Martyr, may you be delivered from every ailment of the throat and from every other evil, in the name of the Father, and of the Son and of the Holy Spirit. Amen." Both the blessed candles *and* the blessing itself are sacramentals.

St. Blaise, a bishop and martyr of the fourth century, was a physician before becoming a priest and then a bishop. During a resurgence of Roman persecutions, a small boy, choking on a fish bone, was brought to St. Blaise, who was awaiting a martyr's death in prison. Because no one knew the Heimlich maneuver back then, praying was all that could be done. After St. Blaise blessed the boy, the fish bone popped out of his mouth miraculously, and the boy's life was saved.

Exorcising demons

Authentic demonic possession is quite rare. Demonic possession is mentioned several times in the New Testament, telling the story of how Jesus exorcised demons (Matthew 4:24). The Church maintains that demons are former heavenly angels who were cast into hell because they rebelled against God. The supernatural gifts that they had in heaven went with these devils into hell, so devils can manipulate people and things in supernatural ways. Demons may attack in one of several ways:

- **Possession:** Assaulting a person from within, the devil takes control of the individual in some ways.

- **Obsession (Oppression):** The devil attacks the individual from the outside.

- **Infestation:** A building or dwelling of some sort is taken over by Satan.

An *exorcist,* a priest with the faculty to drive out demons from a person, place or thing, may be called on to perform an *exorcism,* a prayer that asks God's blessing, using the sacramentals of holy water and blessed salt to ward off evil and to protect from diabolical assaults. But before the local bishop authorizes an exorcism, which is also a sacramental, competent psychiatrists and medical doctors are asked for their professional evaluation of the victim. If medical science can't explain or treat the person and the evidence of the diabolical is present, then an exorcism may be permitted. Diabolical phenomena may be any of the following:

- The possessed individual speaks in languages that he never knew

- Unnatural voices emanate from the possessed individual

- The body of the possessed *levitates* (rises up off the floor or ground)

- Objects or furniture levitates

- Foul odors are present

But exorcism is only a last resort because the majority of reported incidents are considered natural phenomenon.

The bottom line is that the devil can influence only the body and the physical world, and he has no power whatsoever over the soul, especially free will. The devil can't force someone to sin against his will. The best defense against most supernatural evil is faith in God and prayer. Whenever Catholics feel anxious that some form of evil is at work, they typically pray to St. Michael because he's the one who defeated Lucifer and cast him into hell for rebelling against God (Revelation or Apocalypse 12:7). The *Prayer to St. Michael the Archangel* follows:

> St. Michael the Archangel, defend us in battle, be our protection against the wickedness and snares of the devil; may God rebuke him, we humbly pray and do thou, O Prince of the heavenly host, by the power of God, thrust into hell Satan and all evil spirits who wander through the world for the ruin of souls. Amen.

Tolling bells

When a bell that's destined for the bell tower is blessed, it's sometimes called the *baptism* of the bell. Actually, only human beings are baptized through the

Sacrament of Baptism, but bells are sort of baptized in that the bishop may anoint the bell with Chrism Oil, and traditionally, a name is given to each bell just as a name is given to a baptized person.

Since the time of Charlemagne, churches, especially cathedrals, have been expected to have bells that ring out whenever Mass is being celebrated and at the hours of prayer — 6 a.m., 9 a.m., noon, 3 p.m., 6 p.m., 9 p.m., midnight, and 3 a.m. The hours of prayer coincide with the *Liturgy of the Hours* (also known as the *Breviary* or *Divine Office*), which is the official prayer of the Church after the Mass. It's basically a praying of the psalms with some other biblical readings that's done several times during the day. Customarily, bells rang so that the monks of the monastery could come in from the fields where they were working and enter the chapel for morning or evening prayer. Bells rung to announce the death or the election of a new pope, the death or ascension of a new king or queen, and so on. Traditionally, when the church bells ring at noon and at six o'clock, the *Angelus,* which originated in the 14th century, is prayed. One person may lead and the rest of the people respond saying the italicized words, and all say the *Hail Mary.* To say the *Angelus,* read the following:

> The Angel of the Lord declared unto Mary.
> *And she conceived by the Holy Spirit.*
>
> Hail Mary, full of grace. The Lord is with thee. Blessed art thou among women, and blessed is the fruit of thy womb, Jesus.
> *Holy Mary, Mother of God, pray for us sinners, now and at the hour of our death. Amen.*
>
> Behold the handmaid of the Lord.
> *Be it done unto me according to thy word.* (Say another Hail Mary here.)
>
> And the Word was made Flesh.
> *And dwelt among us.* (Repeat the Hail Mary here.)
>
> Pray for us, O holy Mother of God.
> *That we may be made worthy of the promises of Christ.*
>
> Let us pray: *Pour forth, we beseech Thee, O Lord, Thy grace into our hearts, that we to whom the Incarnation of Christ Thy Son was made known by the message of an angel, may by His Passion and Cross be brought to the glory of His Resurrection. Through the same Christ Our Lord. Amen.*

Celebrating Year-Round

Divine Worship has always been tied to the calendar in some way or another. The Catholic Church uses a liturgical calendar to determine what celebrations should take place in parishes around the world. This practice not only gives some uniformity and stability but also connects the religion to actual time and space as we experience it so as to make the faith less ethereal.

The Liturgical Year (the worship calendar) is divided into two distinct but simultaneous cycles:

- ✔ **The Sanctoral Cycle:** Also called the *Proper of Saints.* Every day in the calendar is assigned a feast day of one of the saints or of the Virgin Mary.

- ✔ **The Temporal cycle:** Also called the *Proper of Time.* This cycle is not controlled by the calendar day (with one exception: Christmas is always December 25) but by the seasons of the year. Winter is the time of Advent (four weeks of preparation for Christmas), and Spring is the time of Easter (preceded by 40 days of Lent).

  The Temporal Cycle is centered on two themes: *Christ Our Light* and *Christ Our Life.* The former is encapsulated in the feast of Christmas while the latter is in the feast of Easter. This organization makes sense when you consider that Christmas occurs shortly after the winter solstice (December 21, the shortest day of the year). From that day onward, the days slowly begin to become longer with more daylight until they reach their zenith at the summer solstice (June 21, the longest day of the year). Easter, on the other hand, takes place when the dead of winter is finally over and plant and animal life is renewed.

A feast day in the Church is a day of special liturgical remembrance, usually with some solemnity. Dinners and festivities were limited to a few feasts of national heritage, like Saint Patrick's Day for Ireland or Saint Joseph's Day in Sicily and Italy. Most feast days are the days a saint died and are considered their heavenly birthdays. Monks and nuns who follow a strict penitential diet year round would be dispensed on their patronal feast days and could eat meat or have a dessert, etc. Many major feasts were also secular holidays for Catholic countries in Europe so people would have the day off work. They would attend Mass and have a special dinner later in the day. Today, most feasts are just celebrated with a special Mass in Church.

Of course, calendar dates from the Sanctoral Cycle often coincide with seasonal dates of the Temporal Cycle. In such cases, the feasts of Christ the Lord outrank all else. For example, March 25 is the feast of the Annunciation (when the Archangel Gabriel told Mary she was to become the mother of Christ), but if Good Friday falls on that day in any particular year, Jesus trumps even his mother in this case, and the feast of the Annunciation is suppressed or moved to another date.

Part of the mystery of the Liturgical Year is that the Church uses the solar calendar to measure regular time, but the lunar calendar is still used to determine the date of Easter (the first Sunday after the first full moon after the vernal equinox). Hence, Easter is a movable feast every year. On the other hand, every December 6 is the feast of Saint Nicholas (also known as Santa Claus), every December 8 is the feast of the Immaculate Conception, and every March 19 is the feast of Saint Joseph.

Remember it this way: *Saints* are in the *Sanctoral* Cycle (from the Latin word for saint, *sancta*), and the feasts of the Lord are in the Temporal Cycle. The feast days of saints are assigned to calendar days (usually the day of their death, but not always). Feasts like Easter, Ascension, and Pentecost are movable from year to year, as are Ash Wednesday and the First Sunday of Advent.

The bottom line is that in Catholicism, many days of the calendar year are a cause for celebration. A date may be reserved to honor a saint or commemorate a special passage in the life of Christ, such as the Feast of the Transfiguration when Christ transfigured Himself before the apostles (Luke 9:28–36; Matthew 17:1–8; Mark 9:2–8). You may notice, as you continue reading, that many Catholic celebrations and customs involve their fair share of the priest blessing this and that. In the earlier section "Using Sacramentals," we explain how these blessings work.

Feast of the Epiphany

January 6 is the traditional and universal Feast of the Epiphany. Catholic parishes in the United States, however, which say the Mass in the Ordinary Form, celebrate this feast on the first Sunday after New Year's Day. Those parishes and chapels where the Mass is celebrated in the Extraordinary Form still follow January 6. Epiphany commemorates the visit of the Magi, the three kings bearing gifts for the newborn Christ in the stable at Bethlehem.

A Catholic custom among Polish, Slovak, Russian, and German families is to have their pastor bless chalk on this day. Then, with the blessed chalk, they write over their door the numerals for the current year and, in the middle of the numerals, the initials CMB for the three wise men: Casper, Melchior, and Balthasar. So on Epiphany Sunday 2014, for example, the custom is to write "20 + C + M + B + 14" over your door with your blessed chalk. This custom merely reminds all in the home to ask for the prayers of Casper, Melchior, and Balthasar during the calendar year 2014.

Besides being an abbreviation for the names of the three wise men, CMB is also the abbreviation for the Latin *Christus Mansionem Benedicat* (may Christ bless the home).

Feast of Candlemas

February 2 is the Feast of Candlemas, also known as the Presentation of the Lord (Luke 2:22–38). The Feast of St. Blaise (when Catholics get their throats blessed; see the section "Receiving the blessing of throats") is celebrated the day after Candlemas. For Candlemas, white beeswax candles are blessed during or after Mass on February 2, and people take a few home with them. Then when Catholics pray in their homes, asking for God's assistance (especially during a time of anxiety, distress, calamity, war, dangerous weather, or illness), they light the candles. When the priest is called to administer one of the seven sacraments, the Anointing of the Sick (formerly called *Extreme Unction*), these candles are lit before the priest enters the house.

St. Patrick's Day

March 17 is St. Patrick's Day. Who doesn't know about the wearing o' the green to commemorate the Emerald Isle on the Patron Feast Day of Ireland? Morning Mass, parades, Irish soda bread, potato soup, green beer — all great customs. Because many Irish immigrants came to the United States during Ireland's potato famine, it's no wonder that more people celebrate St. Patrick's Day in the United States than in Ireland.

St. Patrick was born in A.D. 387 at Kilpatrick, near Dumbarton, in Scotland and died on March 17 around the year 461. His father was an officer of the Roman Army. Irish pirates captured 16-year-old Patrick and sold him into slavery for six years in Ireland where he learned the Celtic language and combated the Druid religion. His *Confession* and his *Letter to Coroticus* are all that's officially known of St. Patrick. The *Confession* reveals his call by Pope St. Celestine I to convert the Irish, and Coroticus was a warlord with whom Patrick communicated. Pious tradition contends that he explained the Trinity — three persons in one God — by showing the converts a three-leaf shamrock.

St. Joseph's Day

March 19 marks the solemnity (feast) of St. Joseph, the husband of Mary and patron of the Universal Church.

Even though Lent is a time of penance and mortification, some feast days are so special that the Church wants us to celebrate them with gusto even if they happen to fall during the penitential days of Lent. (For more on the Lenten season, see Chapter 10.) This break from penance was extremely important in the old days when many Catholics refrained from eating any meat or dairy products all 40 days of Lent and also ate only one full meal a day. You can imagine how weak and frail that could make many people. So to ease up on the penance done in Lent, the faithful were dispensed from fasting on special feasts called *solemnities,* such as St. Joseph on March 19 and the Annunciation on March 25, when the Archangel Gabriel announced to Mary that she was to be the mother of Jesus.

Italians and Sicilians take full advantage of St. Joseph's Day being a solemnity and really whoop it up by eating foods normally given up for Lent, erecting tables with a statue of the saint, and asking a priest to bless breads and pastries. The breads are distributed to the poor, and family and friends consume the pastries. A favorite is *Zeppole,* a special cream puff made in honor of St. Joseph or, as he is called in Italian, *San Giuseppe.*

Marian Feasts in May

May is a month dedicated to Mary, the mother of Jesus. It's also the month of Mother's Day. Catholics traditionally have May Crownings, when crowns of roses adorn a statue of Mary, and boys and girls who just made their First Holy Communion wear the same outfits for the occasion. Catholics sing Marian hymns, and in some places, outdoor processions take place; a statue of Mary is carried through the streets. May 13 is the Feast of Our Lady of Fatima (when Mary appeared to three shepherd children in Portugal, 1917) and May 31 is the Feast of the Visitation (when Mary went to see her cousin Elizabeth, the mother of John the Baptist).

Feast of St. Anthony of Padua

June 13 is the Feast of St. Anthony of Padua. Many local Italian communities celebrate this feast with special Masses and processions. Ironically, Anthony himself wasn't Italian but Portuguese. Yet he did spend some time in Italy. St. Anthony, an eloquent preacher, came into this world in 1195, when St. Francis of Assisi was 13 years old. Although they were contemporaries who both lived in Italy, history didn't leave any records to confirm that these two great saints actually ever met. St. Anthony is the patron saint of lost items and marriages.

Feast of St. Thérèse of Lisieux

October 1 is the Feast of St. Thérèse of Lisieux (1873–1897), also known as the Little Flower. Roses are traditionally blessed and given to the sick, infirm, elderly, and other special-needs parishioners on this date. This tradition is undoubtedly the result of the saint's promise, made while she was on earth, to spend her time in heaven sending "a shower of roses" to the faithful still on earth. (See Chapter 20 for more on St. Thérèse.)

Feast of Our Lady of Guadalupe

December 12 is the Feast of Our Lady of Guadalupe. Catholics, especially those of Hispanic heritage, celebrate this feast about two weeks before Christmas every year. In Mexico City, the Basilica of Guadalupe stands on Tepeyac Hill, the site where a dark-skinned Virgin Mary appeared to St. Juan Diego, a poor Indian peasant, nearly 500 years ago. The Virgin of Guadalupe left her image on Juan Diego's cloak. Today, a picture of the Virgin of Guadalupe decorates just about everything Hispanic, from storefronts to T-shirts and from cars to shrines; many Hispanics identify with and devote themselves to her. (To read more about this basilica, see Chapter 22.)

Part V
The Part of Tens

In this part . . .

*I*n this short part, we look first at ten of the most famous Catholics and then at ten popular Catholic *saints* (Church heroes who have died and are deserving of Catholics' admiration). We also pop in on a few popular places that many Catholics try to visit sometime in their lives, both in the Old World and in the new.

Chapter 20

Ten Famous Catholics

In This Chapter

▶ Getting to know some famous Catholic leaders

▶ Finding out about the Catholic perspectives of celebrated authors

▶ Becoming familiar with the movers and shakers of the faith

*1*n this chapter, you get to see our picks for ten of the most famous Catholics, beginning with who we consider the most famous. But take heed: Just being *baptized* Catholic doesn't mean a person is a *good* Catholic.

The Catholic Church believes that a good Catholic is one who regularly and faithfully practices his faith every day of his life. A person who dissents from official Catholic teaching on faith and morals, who never or only irregularly attends Mass, or who has a scandalous, immoral lifestyle is *not* considered a practicing — or a good — Catholic.

For a thorough refresher on the kind of lifestyle that the Church encourages Catholics to live, flip to Part III.

Blessed Mother Teresa of Calcutta (1910–1997)

Agnes Gonxha Bojaxhiu was born August 26, 1910, of Albanian ancestry. She was baptized August 27, 1910, in Skopje, Macedonia, and was later known to the world as Mother Teresa of Calcutta.

She joined the Sisters of Loreto in 1928, was trained in Dublin, Ireland, and took her final vows in 1937. Known as Sister Teresa at the time of her final vows, she was named headmistress of a middle-class girls' school in Calcutta, India, after some years of teaching history and geography. Later, on a train ride to Darjeeling on September 10, 1946, she said that she had a strong intuition and message from the Lord to work among the poorest of the poor in the world. So contrary to myth, it wasn't an emotional reaction to seeing starving and dying people in the gutter that prompted her to leave the Sisters of Loreto and form the Missionaries of Charity. It was that train ride — where she said that Jesus spoke to her heart and called her to go and serve his poor brothers and sisters.

In 1950, Pope Pius XII gave Sister Theresa permission to form her own religious community as she asked to work among the poorest of the poor. Staunchly Catholic, she openly taught and defended Church doctrine on abortion, contraception, and euthanasia as well as on social justice and *preferential option for the poor* — Catholic social teaching that says believers and society have a special duty to help the poor because they lack the resources to help themselves.

She went on to found modest hospitals, clinics, schools, and centers to care for lepers in India and AIDS patients in the United States. She addressed the United Nations, the U.S. Congress, and the President of the United States, and she boldly defended the life of the unborn and promoted adoption and Natural Family Planning as the only moral alternatives to abortion.

The Missionaries of Charity grew into a community of 4,000 sisters in 123 countries around the world. Mother Teresa and her sisters spent an hour each day before the Blessed Sacrament. When asked why, she replied, "How else can we recognize Christ in the poor if we do not first see and know him in the Holy Eucharist?"

Probably the most famous Catholic of the 20th century, this nun, who earned the Nobel Peace Prize (1979) and who was only the fourth person in the world to be named honorary citizen of the United States (1996), traveled the world spreading the message of love for the poor — especially the poorest of the poor. Regarded as a modern-day St. Francis of Assisi, Mother Teresa is respected by peoples of all faiths, religions, cultures, and political persuasions. Whether a person was an "untouchable" leper in India or someone dying of AIDS in North America, she saw Christ in those who suffer. She was a true servant of charity to them.

Mother Teresa died on September 5, 1997, the same day as Princess Diana's funeral in England. Six years later, Pope John Paul II beatified Mother Teresa on October 19, 2003, with more than 300,000 pilgrims in attendance at Saint Peter's Square, Rome. For more on beatification, check out Chapter 18.

Blessed Pope John Paul II (1920–2005)

Pope John Paul II, a highly visible Catholic of the modern era, was the 264th pope and the first non-Italian pope in more than 450 years (see Figure 20-1).

He was born Karol Józef Wojtyla on May 18, 1920, in Wadowice, Poland, the son of Karol Wojtyla and Emilia Kaczorowska. His mother died nine years after his birth, followed by his brother, Edmund Wojtyla, a doctor, in 1932, and then his father, a noncommissioned army officer, in 1941.

The Nazi invasion and occupation of Poland in 1939 forced Karol to work in a stone quarry from 1940 to 1944 and then in a chemical factory to prevent his deportation to Germany. In 1942, he felt called to the priesthood and joined the clandestine underground seminary of Adam Stefan Cardinal Sapieha, Archbishop of Kraków. He was ordained a priest on November 1, 1946. He was sent to Rome, and he earned a doctorate in theology from the Dominican seminary of the Angelicum in 1948.

Figure 20-1:
Pope John
Paul II.

Dirck Halstead/Contributor/Getty Images

For the next ten years, Karol taught as a professor of theology at Catholic colleges and universities in Poland. On July 4, 1958, Pope Pius XII appointed him an Auxiliary Bishop of Kraków. In 1964, Pope Paul VI promoted him to Archbishop of Kraków and then made him a cardinal three years later. He was present at Rome for the Second Vatican Council, which met from 1962 to 1965.

Pope Paul VI died in August 1978, and Albino Cardinal Luciani was elected his successor and took the name John Paul to honor Paul VI and John XXIII, the two popes of Vatican II. But John Paul I lived only a month. So on October 16, 1978, Karol Cardinal Wojtyla was elected bishop of Rome and took the name John Paul II.

Blessed Pope John Paul II wrote 84 combined encyclicals, exhortations, letters, and instructions to the Catholic world; beatified 1,338 people; canonized 482 saints; and created 232 cardinals.

He traveled 721,052 miles (1,243,757 kilometers), the equivalent of 31 trips around the globe. During these journeys, he visited 129 countries and 876 cities. While home in Rome, he spoke to more than 17.6 million people at weekly Wednesday audiences.

At 5:19 p.m. on May 13, 1981, a would-be assassin, Mehmet Ali Agca, shot Pope John Paul II and nearly killed him. A five-hour operation and 77 days in the hospital saved his life, and the pope returned to his full duties a year later.

Fluent in several languages, Pope John Paul II took seriously the desires of the Second Vatican Council to revise the Code of Canon Law, which hadn't been done since 1917, and to revise the Universal Catechism, which hadn't been done since the Council of Trent in the 16th century. The 1983 Code of Canon Law and the 1992 Catechism of the Catholic Church stand along with his encyclicals as a lasting monument to his commitment to truth and justice.

A pope with a strong understanding of young people, Pope John Paul II held international World Youth Days. Despite his age and health, crowds of nearly 3 million attended the event in Rome in 2000, and 800,000 from 173 countries gathered in Toronto two years later.

When he died on April 2, 2005, Pope John Paul II had the third-longest reign as pope (26 years, 5 months, 17 days), behind only Pius IX (31 years) and Saint Peter himself (34+ years). John Paul II's funeral was attended by 4 kings, 5 queens, 70 presidents and prime ministers, 14 leaders of other religions, 157 cardinals, 700 bishops, 3,000 priests, and 3 *million* deacons, religious sisters and brothers, and laity.

His successor, Pope Benedict XVI, beatified Blessed John Paul II on May 1, 2011, the Feast of Divine Mercy Sunday. Between 1.5 and 2 million people attended the outdoor Mass.

Archbishop Fulton J. Sheen (1895–1979)

Born on May 8, 1895, in El Paso, Illinois, the son of Newton Morris and Delia (Fulton) Sheen was baptized Peter John (P.J.) Sheen. Later, he took the maiden name of his mother and was thereafter known as Fulton J. (John) Sheen (see Figure 20-2).

Figure 20-2: Archbishop Fulton J. Sheen.

Bachrach/Contributor/Getty Images

Ordained in Peoria on September 20, 1919, Fulton did graduate work at Catholic University of America and then post-graduate studies (PhD) at the University of Louvain, Belgium (1923). He also attended the Sorbonne in Paris and the Angelicum University in Rome, where he earned a doctorate in theology (1924).

He was made an assistant pastor for one year in Peoria at St. Patrick's Parish. Eight months later, Bishop Edmund M. Dunne of Peoria said he'd been testing the young priest to see whether his success had gone to his head. "I wanted to see if you were obedient," the bishop said. Fulton was then transferred to Catholic University to teach from 1926 to 1950.

His eloquent preaching and erudite speaking prompted the National Council of Catholic Men to sponsor an Sunday-evening radio broadcast called the Catholic Hour on NBC in 1930. When it aired, 118 NBC radio affiliates as well as short-wave transmitters ensured that 4 million people across America heard a Catholic preacher for the first time. Fulton believed this was his opportunity to intellectually show the errors and weaknesses of Communism.

Pope Pius XI made him a monsignor in 1934, and then he was ordained and consecrated an auxiliary bishop for the Archdiocese of New York in 1951. Later that same year, Fulton was asked to host a weekly television series, titled *Life is Worth Living*. The program ran for five seasons — from February 12, 1952, to April 8, 1957 — first on the Dumont Network and then on ABC. And at one point, it beat *The Milton Berle Show* as number one in the ratings. Fulton exhibited a classy, edified, yet also patriotic and pastoral approach, which helped to erode some deep-seated and hateful anti-Catholic bias prevalent since the days of colonial America.

In 1950, Fulton was named national director of the Society for the Propogation of the Faith, the Catholic Church's primary mission organization. Sixteen years later, he was promoted to Bishop of Rochester (1966–1969). But he remains most famous and influential for his radio and television programs and the numerous talks, lectures, retreats, and conferences he gave around the world.

Many famous celebrities, musicians, and politicians owe their conversion to Catholicism to Fulton J. Sheen. Actor Martin Sheen adopted his stage name because of this famous Catholic. He died at the age of 84 on December 9, 1979.

Mother Angelica (1923)

Rita Antoinette Rizzo was born in Canton, Ohio, on April 20, 1923, the daughter of John Rizzo and Mae Helen Gianfrancesco. Six years later, her parents divorced, and Rita and her mom were on their own. Rita entered the Franciscan Sisters (Poor Clares) of Perpetual Adoration in Cleveland, Ohio, on August 15, 1944, as Sister Mary Angelica of the Annunciation.

Sister Mary Angelica eventually ended up in Irondale, Alabama, the heart of the Baptist Bible Belt. Rome allowed her — despite her young age — to become an Abbess of a new monastery. Our Lady of the Holy Angels opened on May 20, 1962, just ten months from its groundbreaking. (Upon becoming Abbess, she received the title of respect of "Reverend Mother" or just "Mother" for short.) Her own mother entered the Our Lady of the Holy Angels community and took the name of Sister Mary David.

In 1973, Mother Angelica inaugurated a Catholic book and pamphlet apostolate to spread the faith. But the big stuff was yet to come; Mother Angelica decided to go into television, and on August 15, 1981, the Eternal Word Television Network (EWTN) was launched, broadcasting four hours a day to 60,000 homes. She reached 1 million homes in less than two years, and in 1987 the network was transmitting 24 hours a day. Today, through EWTN's own satellite, cable, radio, and short-wave broadcasting, 160 million people are reached across 140 countries. (EWTN is also online at www.ewtn.com.) EWTN has become the world's largest and most-watched Catholic network, and Mother Angelica is still very much a part of it.

In 1946, Mother Angelica suffered many injuries due to an accident with a floor-buffing machine when she was a *novice* (a new nun in training who hasn't yet made vows). On January 28, 1998, while she was praying the rosary with an Italian lady she didn't know, she was miraculously cured — her legs and back no longer needed braces or crutches.

One year later, on December 19, 1999, Mother Angelica had her new monastery and temple consecrated: The Shrine of the Most Blessed Sacrament in Hanceville, Alabama, which is one hour north of Irondale (home of the television studio and Internet services). Built by the generosity of a handful of millionaires, this house of God rivals any in Europe. The 7-foot monstrance is the jewel of the crown containing the Holy Eucharist, which is exposed for public adoration outside of Mass. See Chapter 22 for further description of this shrine.

John F. Kennedy (1917–1963)

John Fitzgerald Kennedy, the 35th President of the United States of America, was the first Roman Catholic to hold the highest office in the land.

Born in Brookline, Massachusetts, on May 29, 1917, to Joseph P. Kennedy and Rose Fitzgerald Kennedy, he was one of nine children in this affluent and influential family. His father was the head of the Securities and Exchange Commission (SEC) and later became the Ambassador to Great Britain.

John graduated from Harvard in 1940 and a year later enlisted in the U.S. Navy before the attack on Pearl Harbor and the declaration of war. The boat he commanded (PT-109) in the Pacific theater was attacked and sunk by the Japanese. He saved his crew but seriously injured his back. He was discharged in 1945 and ran as a Democrat for the U.S. Congress in 1946. He was re-elected twice.

On September 12, 1953, he married Jacqueline Bouvier, who gave him three children (Caroline, 1957; John, Jr., 1960; and a son who died in infancy). He became a U.S. Senator from Massachusetts in 1953. Seven years later, he ran against Vice President Richard M. Nixon and won the presidency.

During the campaign, his Catholicism was thrown into his face as a possible impediment to being an effective president — as though he'd have dual or torn loyalties between the U.S. Constitution and the pope as supreme head of the Catholic Church. Cartoons ran in the papers depicting John in a boat with Jesuit sailors coming from Rome to invade America. Anti-Catholic prejudice reared its ugly head in editorials and articles across the nation. But he dispelled the irrational anxieties by assuring the public of his commitment to upholding and defending the Constitution. He maintained that defending the Constitution didn't, couldn't, and wouldn't conflict with his personal religious beliefs. The public finally accepted the fact that Catholics could be patriotic Americans and good Catholics at the same time.

Historians still debate whether John was a devout or practicing Catholic. What's known is that he was the first Catholic to be elected president and that his Catholicism received positive press coverage during his term in office: He, Jackie, and the kids went to Sunday Mass, bishops and cardinals frequented the White House, and an elaborate, solemn, and sad Catholic requiem Mass was said for his funeral following his assassination in November 1963.

Alfred E. Smith (1873–1944)

Born on the East Side of New York City in 1873 to poor parents and Irish immigrant grandparents, Alfred Emanuel Smith was the first Catholic politician to be nominated as a major-party presidential candidate. He was the Democratic Governor of New York four times and worked hard for political reforms. His Catholicism, however, and his opposition to Prohibition cost him the election to Herbert Hoover in 1928. Each year, the Archdiocese of New York sponsors the Alfred E. Smith Memorial Foundation Dinner where ecclesiastics and politicians from both sides of the aisle get together.

Father Edward Flanagan (1886–1948)

Born in Roscommon, Ireland, in 1886, Edward Flanagan came to America in 1904. He was ordained a priest in 1912 after attending Mount St. Mary's University in Emmitsburg, Maryland, and St. Joseph's Seminary in Dunwoodie, New York, and finally finishing his studies in Rome and Innsbruck, Austria.

When he was sent to Omaha, Nebraska, as a newly ordained priest, he found the extreme poverty among the orphans in Omaha heart-wrenching. The situation motivated him to found Boys' Town in 1917 for homeless boys, which today takes care of both boys and girls who are underprivileged. In 1938, Spencer Tracy won an Academy Award for portraying Father Flanagan in MGM's *Boys Town.*

John Ronald Reuel Tolkien (1892–1973)

J.R.R. Tolkien, author of *The Lord of the Rings* and *The Hobbit,* was born in South Africa in 1892, but after his father died four years later, he and his mother and younger brother, Hilary, moved to England. There, his aunt and mother converted to Catholicism, which annoyed both sides of the family. Ronald (as he was known then) and his brother, however, embraced the Roman Catholic religion.

A contemporary and close friend of C.S. Lewis, the author of the *Chronicles of Narnia* and the *Screwtape Letters,* Tolkien learned to use fantasy writing to strategically but subtly convey Catholic values while retaining imagination and excitement in his works.

Gilbert Keith Chesterton (1874–1936)

Born in London in 1874, G. K. Chesterton was baptized in the Church of England. Surprisingly, he wrote many of his famous Father Brown mysteries before joining the Roman Catholic Church in 1922.

Those mysteries tell of a quiet, unassuming priest who solves mysteries like Sherlock Holmes, Lord Peter Wimsey, or Hercule Poirot. Ironically, this author didn't learn to read until he was 8 years old, but he would eventually be a prolific and scholarly author of 17 nonfiction books, 9 fiction books, and numerous essays and poems. His book *Orthodoxy* remains a classic for Catholic *apologists* — people who defend Catholicism through the use of logic, reason, and debate — and for literary critics alike.

Christopher Columbus (1451–1506)

The famed 1492 European explorer of the American continents may be the bane of politically correct historians' existences, but no one can deny that his insistence on bringing Franciscan and Dominican missionaries with him to the New World was pivotal to the spread of Catholicism among the natives in North, Central, and South America.

Born in Genoa in 1451, Cristoforo Columbo (his name in Italian) became a superior sailor in his youth. He always dreamed of making a voyage to find a shortcut to the Far East, because Marco Polo's land route to China was becoming more and more dangerous and expensive. He knew the world wasn't flat, and so did most educated, literate people of his time. King Ferdinand and Queen Isabella of Spain eventually funded the expedition to secure Spain's wealth (Ferdinand's goal) and to evangelize and spread the Catholic faith (Isabella's dream).

Before setting sail on the Nina, Pinta, and Santa Maria, Columbus went to confession and Mass, and he received Holy Communion. His flagship had a chapel, where Mass was offered daily. Today, the chapel's altar is in Boalsburg, Pennsylvania, at the Columbus Chapel.

Before making its way to Pennsylvania, the altar had become part of the Columbus (*Colón* in Spanish) Castle in Spain. But Mathilde de Lagarde Boal, the wife of Colonel Theodore Boal, inherited it from her aunt, Victoria Columbus, a descendant of Columbus, in 1908. A year later, the altar was shipped to Pennsylvania, where it remains today on display just a stone's throw away from Penn State University. (David Boal, the great-great grandfather of Theodore Boal, founded Boalsburg, Pennsylvania.) For more on amazing places to visit that relate to the Catholic faith, head to Chapter 22.

Keep in mind that 1492 was still the Middle Ages. The Reformation didn't occur for another 15 years. And the sociological dimension to exploration and colonization wasn't comprehensible to that mindset. Unlike some other European explorers, Columbus didn't see Native Americans as slaves or enemies but as potential converts to and allies of Catholic Spain.

Chapter 21

Ten (Plus One) Popular Catholic Saints

In This Chapter

▶ Discovering the stories behind beloved Catholic heroes

▶ Getting inspired by their faith

Catholics do not worship saints, but the saints are near and dear to Catholic hearts. Catholics respect and honor the saints and consider them to be the heroes of the Church. The Church emphasizes that they were ordinary people from ordinary families, and they were totally human. They weren't born with halos around their heads, and they didn't always wear a smile, either. What separated them from those who weren't given the title of *saint* was that they didn't despair; they kept right on honing their souls for heaven come hell or high water. Get the full Catholic perspective on saints in Chapter 18.

In this chapter, we share some tidbits about the lives of 11 such ordinary people who became popular saints. We've listed them in chronological order.

St. Peter (Died around A.D. 64)

The brother of Andrew and the son of Jona, St. Peter was originally called Simon. He was a fisherman by trade. Biblical scholars believe that Peter was married because the Gospel speaks of the cure of his mother-in-law (Matthew 8:14; Luke 4:38). But whether he was a widower at the time he met Jesus, no one knows for sure. Scholars believe it's likely that his wife was no longer alive because after the Crucifixion, Resurrection, and Ascension of Christ, Peter became head of the Church (the first pope) and had a busy schedule and itinerary. He also never mentioned his wife in his epistle. (An *epistle* is a pastoral letter written by one of the apostles and found in the New Testament, immediately after the Four Gospels and the Book of Acts and just before the Apocalypse or Book of Revelation. These letters were composed to give the early Christian communities encouragement and/or instruction.)

According to the Bible, Andrew introduced Peter to Jesus and told his brother, "We have found the Messiah!" (John 1:41). When Peter hesitated to follow Jesus full time, Jesus came after him and said, "I will make you fishers of men" (Matthew 4:19).

The faithful believe that Peter's confession of faith made him stand out in the crowd, even among the 12 apostles. Matthew 16:13–16 tells the story: Jesus posed the question, "Who do men say that the Son of man is?" The other 11 merely reiterated what they'd heard others say: "Some say John the Baptist, others say Elijah, and others say Jeremiah or one of the Prophets." Jesus then asked directly, "But who do you say that I am?" Only Peter responded, "You are the Christ, the Son of the living God." His answer received the full approval of Jesus, which is why Peter was made the chief shepherd of the Church and head of the Apostles. Matthew 16:17–19 says:

"Blessed are you, Simon Bar-Jona! For flesh and blood has not revealed this to you, but my Father who is in heaven. And I tell you, you are Peter *(Petros),* and on this rock *(petra)* I will build my church, and the powers of death shall not prevail against it. And I will give you the keys of the kingdom of heaven, and whatever you bind on earth shall be bound in heaven, and whatsoever you loose on earth shall be loosed in heaven."

The Greek language, in which the Gospel was first written, uses the word *Petros* as the proper first name of a man and the word *petra* to refer to a rock. *Peter* means *rock,* but in Greek, as in most other languages except English, nouns have gender. *Petra* is the word for rock, and it's feminine, so you wouldn't call a man *petra* no matter how "strong as a rock" he may be. We believe that had Jesus used *petra* instead of *petros* for Peter, the other apostles and disciples would never have let Peter live it down because using a feminine ending would have been inappropriate. (These were sailors and fishermen, after all.)

St. Jude (Died during the first century A.D.)

St. Jude, not to be confused with Judas, was believed to be a relative of Jesus and was the brother of St. James the Less (as opposed to St. James the Greater, the brother of St. John the Evangelist. *The Greater* and *the Less* were simply indications of which James was called to be a disciple before the other: James the Greater was a disciple first.)

Jude is also known as Jude Thaddaeus, Patron Saint of Hopeless Cases. One reason is that the effort to find information about him is almost hopeless. In fact, we like to call him St. Jude the Obscure. But another reason he is invoked for hopeless cases could be that his name is so close to Judas, who betrayed Christ.

It's conjectured that Jude's father was Clopas, who was murdered for his support of Jesus, and that his mother was Mary Clopas, who was mentioned in the Gospel as being at the cross (John 19:25). Jude was allegedly martyred by being clubbed to death. (See Chapter 16 to read a popular novena to St. Jude.)

Famous American actor Danny Thomas, who was a Lebanese-American Catholic, visited a church in Detroit named after Saint Jude during the beginning of his career in the 1950s. He left his last seven dollars in the collection basket and prayed that Saint Jude would intercede for him. He needed more work to support his new bride and their new child. Very soon afterward, he got many steady and lucrative gigs. In appreciation, Thomas helped establish a fund to build a children's hospital under the protection of Saint Jude. The Saint Jude Children's Research Hospital was built in 1955 thanks to Thomas and with the support of many of his fellow Arab-Americans.

St. Benedict (480–circa 543)

Benedict of Nursia, the founder of Western monasticism, was the son of a Roman nobleman and the twin brother of St. Scholastica, foundress of the Benedictine nuns. He grew up and studied in Rome until the age of 14, when he decided to leave the city for a quieter life of prayer and work.

He developed a structure for monastic life called a *Rule,* which is a set of laws, customs, and practices for all members of a religious community that continues to this day and is the basis for many religious communities. Living a simple life of poverty, chastity, and obedience in community with others and devoting oneself to sanctity and holiness is the main objective of Benedictine life. Known for their hard work and their love of the Sacred Liturgy and Sacred Scripture and dedicated to study and learning, the Benedictines were role models for many religious communities that came later, such as the Dominicans. The Benedictine monks fled the morally decaying cities of the disintegrating Roman Empire and preserved culture, language, heritage, art, and learning.

The famous Benedictine monasteries of Monte Cassino and Subiaco, Italy, date back to the time of Benedict and still house members to this day. A hallmark of Benedictine life, besides work and prayer, is the vow of stability: Unlike diocesan priests who get transferred frequently, after a man joins a Benedictine monastery, he usually stays on-site for the rest of his life unless special circumstances require him to join another abbey.

St. Dominic de Guzman (1170–1221)

St. Dominic was a contemporary of St. Francis of Assisi, whom we discuss next. The faithful believe that when St. Dominic's mother, Joanna of Aza (the wife of Felix de Guzman) was pregnant, she had a vision of a dog carrying a torch in his mouth, which symbolized her unborn son who would grow up to become a *hound of the Lord.* The name Dominic was thus given to him, because in Latin *Dominicanis* can be *Domini + canis* (*dog* or *hound of the Lord*).

Dominic lived at a time when some followers of Christ believed only in his divine nature; they denied his human nature. These believers couldn't accept a god who would suffer and die for humankind's sins. Their beliefs were called the *Albigensian heresy.* Catholics believe that Mary gave the rosary to Dominic to help him conquer Albigensianism. Dominic promoted devotion to Mary and the practice of praying the rosary (see Chapter 16) around Western Europe.

Dominic also established the Order of Friars Preachers (shortened to Order of Preachers), called the *Dominicans.* Along with their brother Franciscans (whom we discuss in the next section), the Dominicans re-energized the Church in the 13th century and brought clarity of thought and substantial learning to more people than ever before. The motto of St. Dominic was *veritas,* which is Latin for *truth.*

St. Francis of Assisi (1181–1226)

The son of a wealthy cloth merchant, Pietro Bernadone, Francis was one of seven children. Today, people would say that he grew up with a silver spoon in his mouth.

Even though he was baptized Giovanni, his father later changed his name to Francesco (Italian for *Francis* or *Frank*). He was handsome, courteous, witty, strong, and intelligent, but very zealous. He liked to play hard and fight hard like most of his contemporaries. Local squabbles between towns, principalities, dukedoms, and so on were rampant in Italy in the 12th century. Francis was a playboy of sorts but wasn't a nasty or immoral one. After spending a year in captivity with the rival Perugians, who fought their neighbors the Assisians, Francis decided to cool his jets for a while. One day, he met a poor leper on the road whose stench and ugliness repulsed him at first. Remorseful, Francis turned around, got off his horse, embraced the beggar and gave him clothes and money. The man immediately disappeared, and Francis believed it was Christ visiting him as a beggar. He then went to visit the tomb of St. Peter in Rome, where he gave all his worldly possessions — money, clothes, and belongings — to the poor and put on the rags of a poor man himself. Lady Poverty was to be his bride.

His dad wasn't happy about the embarrassment Francis caused, so he dragged, beat, and locked up Francis in attempts to make him come to his senses. His mother helped Francis escape to a bishop friend of his, but his father soon found him. Because he was on church property, however, Signor Bernadone couldn't violate the sanctuary and force his son home. Francis took what little clothing he had from home still on his person and threw it at his father and said: "Hitherto I have called you my father on earth; henceforth I desire to say only 'Our Father who art in Heaven.'"

Sometime around 1210 he started his own religious community called the Order of Friars Minor (OFM), which today is known as the Franciscans. They took vows of poverty, chastity, and obedience, but unlike the Augustinian and Benedictine monks who lived in monasteries outside the villages and towns, St. Francis and his friars were not monks but *mendicants,* which means that they begged for their food, clothes, and shelter. What they collected they shared among themselves and the poor. They worked among the poor in the urban areas.

Catholics believe that in 1224, St. Francis of Assisi was blessed with the extraordinary gift of the *stigmata,* the five wounds of Christ imprinted on his own body.

St. Francis of Assisi loved the poor and animals, but most of all he loved God and his Church. He wanted everyone to know and experience the deep love of Jesus that he felt in his own heart. He is credited with the creation of two Catholic devotions: the Stations of the Cross (see Chapter 16) and the Christmas crèche.

St. Anthony of Padua (1195-1231)

St. Anthony was born as Ferdinand, son of Martin Bouillon and Theresa Tavejra. At the age of 15 he joined an order of priests called the Canons Regular of St. Augustine. Later he transferred to the newly formed Order of Friars Minor (OFM), or Franciscans, where he took the religious name of Anthony.

He is famous for being an effective orator. Anthony's sermons were so powerful that many Catholics who strayed from the faith and embraced false doctrines of other religions would repent after hearing him. This skill led to his nickname, "Hammer of Heretics." Anthony got so disgusted one day with the locals who obstinately refused to listen to his preaching that he went to the river and started preaching to the fish. So many fish gathered at the bank that the townsfolk got the message and began to heed his instructions.

St. Anthony is invoked as the patron saint of lost items. On one occasion, a little boy appeared in the town square, apparently lost. Anthony picked him up and carried him around town looking for the boy's family. They went to house after house, but no one claimed him. At the end of the day, Anthony approached the friary chapel. The boy said, "I live there." Once in the oratory, the child disappeared. It was later discerned that the child was in fact Jesus. Since then, Catholics invoke St. Anthony whenever they lose something, even car keys or eyeglasses.

St. Thomas Aquinas (1225–1274)

The greatest intellect the Catholic Church has ever known was born of a wealthy aristocratic family, the son of Landulph, Count of Aquino, and Theodora, Countess of Teano. Thomas's parents sent him at the age of five, which was customary, to the Benedictine Abbey of Monte Cassino. It was hoped that if he didn't show talents suited for becoming a knight or nobleman, he could at least rise to the rank of abbot or bishop and thus add to his family's prestige and influence.

However, ten years later, Thomas wanted to join a new mendicant order, which was similar to the Franciscans in that it didn't go to distant monasteries but worked in urban areas instead. The new order was the Order of Preachers (O.P.), known as Dominicans.

His family had other ideas, putting him under house arrest for two years in an effort to dissuade his Dominican vocation. He didn't budge. While captive, he read and studied assiduously and learned metaphysics, Sacred Scripture, and the *Sentences of Peter Lombard.* (Lombard was the premier theologian of the 12th century, and his "sentences" comprised a theology primer.) His parents finally relented, and at the age of 17 he was put under the tutelage of St. Albert the Great, the pride of the Dominican intelligentsia. Albert was the first to bridge the gap between alchemy and chemistry, from superstition to science. Thomas learned much from his academic master.

Thomas Aquinas is best known for two things:

✔ His monumental theological and philosophical work, the *Summa Theologica,* covers almost every principal doctrine and dogma of his era. What St. Augustine and St. Bonaventure were able to do with the philosophy of Plato regarding Catholic Theology, St. Thomas Aquinas was able to do with Aristotle. (Philosophy has been called the handmaiden of theology because you need a solid philosophical foundation in order to understand the theological teachings connected to it.) The *Catechism of the Catholic Church* has numerous references to the Summa some 800 years later.

> ✔ He composed hymns and prayers for Corpus Christi at the request of the pope, and he wrote *Pange Lingua, Adoro te Devote, O Salutaris Hostia,* and *Tantum Ergo,* which is often sung at Benediction. (See Chapter 16 for more on Benediction.)

He died while on the way to the Second Council of Lyons, where he was to appear as a *peritus* (expert). For more on St. Thomas Aquinas, see Chapters 3, 8, 9, 14, and Appendix A.

St. Ignatius of Loyola (1491–1556)

Son of Don Beltrán Yañez de Oñez y Loyola and Marina Saenz de Lieona y Balda, Ignatius was born in 1491 and grew up to become a soldier. Military life suited him. He liked the regimen and discipline, and it gave him a sense of accomplishment because he was serving and defending the homeland and his monarch.

When a cannon ball injury to his leg compelled him to a long recuperation, he asked for reading materials to pass the time. The only thing available was a book on the lives of the saints. One day, he realized that instead of fighting for earthly kings and princes, he should become a Soldier of Christ and win souls away from the real enemy, the devil, and bring them back to the true King of Kings, Almighty God. He saw how the military discipline could be used to discipline the soul rather than just the body.

Ignatius developed a method of spirituality, *Ignatian Spiritual Exercises,* which focused on using the fullest amount of imagination during meditation. People were asked to pick a scene from the Bible and imagine they weren't spectators, like in the audience of a play, but actual bystanders or participants in the biblical scene being contemplated.

For example, say you're at the wedding feast of Cana (John 2:1–11). You feel a cool breeze blow across the left side of your face. You can smell the aroma of lamb being roasted in an open pit. The sun is out, and people are laughing and talking as they often do at wedding receptions. Then you hear the words being whispered around the table, "They have no wine," just as you take a sip from your goblet and realize that it's almost empty. Now, try to imagine the rest of the story on your own.

This use of the imagination helped the faithful appreciate the reality of the scriptural text. It also enabled them to transcend what they merely knew cognitively from memory and to use previous sense experiences not only to pretend but also to learn and experience the event.

Ignatius was ordained a priest at the age of 46, so he's often invoked as the Patron Saint of Delayed or Second Career Vocations. In 1534, he formed the Society of Jesus, which would later be known as the Jesuits. Feared, admired, scorned, and often misunderstood, the Jesuits became a powerful and influential religious community for two reasons:

- ✔ **Their fourth vow of total obedience to the Roman pontiff:** Other orders took the vow of obedience, but sometimes loyalty to the order came before obedience to the hierarchy. Ignatius preferred that his priests be at the total disposal of the pope to go wherever he sent them and to do whatever task he gave them.

- ✔ **Their professional expertise and background:** Most Jesuits have one or more doctorates or the equivalent and study more before ordination as opposed to their diocesan or other religious community colleagues.

St. Bernadette Soubirous (1844–1879)

Bernadette was born on January 7, 1844, in Lourdes, France. Her parents, Francis and Louise Soubirous, were extremely poor but loved their daughter very much. She suffered from severe asthma, which kept her behind a few years in school.

The faithful believe that on February 11, 1858, she saw an apparition of Mary in a cave on the banks of the Gave River near Lourdes. The woman didn't identify herself but asked Bernadette to faithfully come to the grotto and pray the rosary for the conversion of sinners so that they might turn away from their evil ways and come back to God.

Initially, the townsfolk thought Bernadette was insane. But on February 25, the woman asked Bernadette to dig in the soil until a spring of water would appear. She did as the woman asked, and the spring did appear. It's believed that the water had immediate miraculous properties, and the skeptic populace of Lourdes flocked to the grotto to get some of this healing water. The blind could see, the lame could walk, the deaf could hear, the sick regained their health, and so on.

The faithful believe that on March 25, 1858, the woman announced to Bernadette that she was the *Immaculate Conception*. Interestingly, the dogma of the Immaculate Conception had been defined by Pope Pius IX only four years earlier (1854), and scholars maintain that an intellectually challenged peasant girl from the rinky-dink town of Lourdes couldn't have heard about such a term, let alone have understood it.

The public authorities, which were anti-Catholic and anti-clerical, closed the grotto only to have the Emperor Louis Napoleon III order it reopened. His son had taken ill and his wife, the Empress Eugenie of France, obtained some Lourdes water, which the faithful believe cured his imperial royal highness.

Bernadette didn't live a normal life after that, and in 1866 she entered the convent of the Sisters of Notre Dame in Nevers where she spent the rest of her short life. Thirteen years later, she was found to have an illness similar to tuberculosis, which produced excruciating and chronic pain, but she said the healing waters of Lourdes were not for her.

She died in 1879, but today, her body remains *incorrupt* (free of decay despite the lack of embalming or mummification treatments). The Shrine at Lourdes is an international place of prayer, and some miraculous healings are still being attributed to those waters from the grotto where Catholics believe Mary appeared to Bernadette.

St. Thérèse of Lisieux (1873–1897)

Francoise-Marie Thérèse, the youngest of five daughters, was born on January 2, 1873. When she was four, her mother died and left her father with five girls to raise on his own. Two of her older sisters joined the Carmelite order of nuns, and Thérèse wanted to join them when she was just 14 years old. The order normally made girls wait until they were 16 before entering the convent or monastery, but Thérèse was adamant. She accompanied her father to a general papal audience of His Holiness Pope Leo XIII and surprised everyone by throwing herself before the pontiff, begging to become a Carmelite. The wise pope replied, "If the good God wills, you will enter." When she returned home, the local bishop allowed her to enter early. On April 9, 1888, at the age of 15, Thérèse entered the Carmelite monastery of Lisieux and joined her two sisters. On September 8, 1890, she took her final vows. She showed remarkable spiritual insights for someone so young, but it was due to her childlike (not childish) relationship with Jesus. Her superiors asked her to keep memoirs of her thoughts and experiences.

At the age of 23, she coughed up blood and was diagnosed with tuberculosis. She lived only one more year, and it was filled with intense physical suffering. Yet it's said that she did so lovingly, to join Jesus Christ on the cross. She offered up her pain and suffering for souls that might be lost, so they could come back to God. Her *little way* consisted of, in her own words, "doing little things often, doing them well, and doing them with love." She died on September 30, 1897.

Despite the fact that she lived such a short and cloistered life, having never left her monastery after she took her vows, she was later named Patroness of the Foreign Missions. The reason was that during World War I, many soldiers who were wounded in battle and recuperating in hospitals — as well as those who were in the trenches awaiting their possible death — read her autobiography, and it changed their hearts. Many who had grown cold or lukewarm in their Catholic faith wanted to imitate St. Thérèse of Lisieux, who was also known as the *Little Flower,* and become a little child of God.

St. Pio of Pietrelcina (1887–1968)

Padre Pio was born on May 25, 1887, in Pietrelcina, Italy. Because he showed evidence of having a priestly vocation early in his youth, his father went to the United States to make enough money so Francesco (his baptismal name) could attend school and seminary. At the age of 15, he took the vows and habit of the Friars Minor Capuchin and assumed the name of Pio in honor of Pope St. Pius V, patron of his hometown. On August 10, 1910, he was ordained a priest. Catholics believe that less than a month later, on September 7, he received the stigmata, just like St. Francis of Assisi.

During World War I, he served as a chaplain in the Italian Medical Corps. After the war, news spread about his stigmata, which stirred up some jealous enemies. Because of false accusations that were sent to Rome, he was suspended in 1931 from saying public Mass or from hearing confessions. Two years later, Pope Pius XI reversed the suspension and said, "I have not been badly disposed toward Padre Pio, but I have been badly informed."

In 1940, he convinced three physicians to come to San Giovanni Rotundo to help him erect a hospital, *Casa Sollievo della Sofferenza* (House for the Relief of Suffering). It took until 1956 to finally build the hospital due to World War II and slow donations, but it eventually came to pass.

Catholics believe that he was able to read souls, meaning that when people came to him for confession, he could immediately tell if they were lying, holding back sins, or truly repentant. One man reportedly came in and confessed only that he was unkind from time to time, and Padre Pio interjected, "Don't forget when you were unkind to Jesus by missing Mass three times this month, either."

He became so well loved all over the region and indeed all over the world that three days after his death on September 23, 1968, more than 100,000 people gathered at San Giovanni Rotundo to pray for his departed soul.

Chapter 22

Ten Popular Catholic Places

In This Chapter

▶ Seeing some miraculous shrines near and far

▶ Discovering Catholic history, art, and architecture

Although some religions require their members to visit their holy and sacred places, the Catholic Church doesn't. Catholics are simply encouraged to make *pilgrimages* — religious journeys to holy places. This chapter covers our picks for the top ten most popular places that Catholics like to visit sometime in their lives. Bon voyage!

Rome

Just as Jews want to visit Jerusalem and Muslims want to visit Mecca, many Catholics have a passion and desire to see Rome at some point in their lives. Since the conversion of the Roman Empire in the mid fourth century, the Eternal City, as it's often been called since it was founded in 753 B.C., has been the center of Catholicism. The first pope, St. Peter, and the great missionary and apostle St. Paul were both martyred in this city between A.D. 64 and 67.

During early Church history (see Appendix A for details), Christian men, women, and children suffered 300 years of violent and aggressive persecution; many martyrs are buried in Rome. The city is a place of remembrance and memorial for those who died for being Christian.

The Roman tradition was to burn dead bodies. But the Christians buried their dead, especially the remains of martyrs, in underground cemeteries called *catacombs* because they believed in the resurrection of the body at the end of the world. Five catacombs are open to the public in Rome:

- St. Agnes on Via Nomentana
- St. Priscilla on Via Salaria
- St. Domitilla on Via Delle Sette Chiese
- St. Sebastian on Via Appia Antica
- St. Callixtus on Via Appia Antica

Rome is also predominantly a city of churches — at least 900 of them. Of these, four are called *papal basilicas* or *major basilicas:*

- St. Peter (*San Pietro in Vaticano*), shown in Figure 22-1.
- St. John Lateran (*San Giovanni in Laterano*)
- St. Mary Major (*Santa Maria Maggiore*)
- St. Paul Outside the Walls (*San Paolo fuori le mura*)

Figure 22-1:
The Basilica
of St. Peter
in the
Vatican.

Alinari / Art Resource, NY

All basilicas have a special chair or throne for the pope to sit on whenever he celebrates Mass in that church, and only the pope may use it — no one else, not even a bishop or cardinal. A set of holy doors in each basilica is opened only during the Holy Year, which occurs every 25 years, and pilgrims pass through. Basilicas are considered either major or minor:

- **Major basilicas** are often large churches that were imperial or aristocratic palaces during the pagan era of Rome. The emperor gave the palaces to the Catholic Church in compensation for all the lives, land, property, and money confiscated from the Christians during the Roman persecutions. These comprise only the four papal basilicas, listed earlier.

✔ **Minor basilicas** are those in Rome not considered a major basilica, or those outside of Rome that are specially designated by the pope, such as the basilicas in Lourdes and Czestochowa.

The Basilica de Guadalupe

The Basilica de Guadalupe in Mexico City, Mexico, is the number two pilgrimage site for Catholics, after Rome. This basilica contains the miraculous image of Our Lady of Guadalupe that Catholics believe was imprinted by Mary on the cloak of an Aztec Indian, 57-year-old St. Juan Diego, on December 12, 1531.

Walking north of Mexico City in the Tepayac hill country, Juan Diego saw the Virgin Mary, but she had the appearance of an Aztec woman, not a European, and she was pregnant. She directed St. Juan Diego to go to the local bishop and tell him that she wanted a church built in her honor.

After waiting several hours to see the noble Spanish-born Bishop Fray Juan de Zumarraga, St. Juan Diego was granted an audience. The respectful yet incredulous bishop told St. Juan Diego that he needed a sign from heaven that this was indeed God's will to build a church in that location. St. Juan Diego went back and told Mary what the bishop had requested, and she told him to gather roses from a bush that appeared out of nowhere. These Castilian roses weren't indigenous to Mexico, and certainly not in cold December, but they were popular in Spain. It just so happened that the bishop's hobby was gardening, and he'd been an official rose expert back in Spain before being sent to Mexico.

Juan Diego carried the roses in his *tilma* (cloak) to the bishop, opened his garment, and the bishop fell to his knees. Not only were the roses beautiful and rare, but also, a gorgeous image of Our Lady of Guadalupe was on the tilma. She was like the scriptural passage that describes a woman who is "clothed with the sun, with the moon under her feet, and on her head a crown of twelve stars; she was with child." (Revelation 12:1–2)

The tilma remains on display in the Basilica Church in Mexico City. To this day, science can't explain how that image got onto the tilma. It's not painted, dyed, sewn, printed, or the product of any man-made process. Blessed Pope John Paul II canonized Juan Diego in 2002. Millions of people from around the world visit this holy place.

San Giovanni Rotondo, Italy

San Giovanni Rotondo is the resting place of St. Pio of Pietrelcina, affectionately known as Padre Pio. (Pietrelcina is the town where Padre Pio was born.) He was a humble, simple but holy Capuchin monk, a type of Franciscan. (We provide a brief bio of his life in Chapter 21, if you're interested.)

While he was alive, thousands came to him for confession and his priestly blessing. Since his death, hundreds of thousands have made pilgrimages to this town to see where Padre Pio celebrated Mass and heard confessions, and to see the church where he's buried. Most of all, they want to see the Church of Our Lady of Grace, where they believe he received the *stigmata* — the five wounds of Christ. *Casa Sollievo della Sofferenza* (House for the Relief of Suffering) is the hospital founded by him in the same town and visited by many pilgrims as well. In nearly every store, restaurant, and home in San Giovanni, you can see pictures and statues of local saint Padre Pio.

At the *National Padre Pio Center* in Barto, Pennsylvania, not far from Reading, Pennsylvania, you can see a replica of the chapel in San Giovanni. One of the bloodstained gloves that Padre Pio wore while he had the stigmata is on display in the chapel.

The Basilica of Czestochowa, Poland

Pious tradition maintains that St. Luke the Evangelist painted an icon of the Virgin Mary (see Figure 22-2) sometime after Christ's crucifixion on the cross. Scholars believe Luke used the mother of Jesus as a primary source for the beginning of his gospel where the infancy of Christ is told. And pious tradition also has it that St. Helena, the founder of the True Cross (see Appendix A) in the fourth century and the mother of Emperor Constantine, was the one who discovered this painting.

No matter where the icon originally came from or who painted it, the fact remains that it has been one of the great spiritual treasures of Poland. Somehow during the Muslim invasions, the image made its way to Poland through Russia. Polish Prince St. Ladislaus, in the 15th century, kept it safe in his castle until the Tartar invaders threatened to overrun Poland. Intending to move it to his hometown of Opala, Prince Ladislaus stopped overnight in Jasna Gora near Czestochowa.

According to the tradition, the next morning, the horses refused to move while the image was in the carriage. The Prince took this as a sign from God that the icon should stay there. So he entrusted the icon, thereafter known as the "Black Madonna of Czestochowa," to the Pauline Fathers who cared for the spiritual needs of Czestochowa and Jasna Gora.

Figure 22-2:
Many believe that St. Luke created this painting of Mary and baby Jesus, called the "Black Madonna of Czesto-chowa."

Nicolas Sapieha/Art Resource, NY

Today, the Black Madonna resides in a magnificent basilica in Czestochowa. Some say her face is black from attempts to destroy her, claiming that the heretical Hussites set it on fire but it would not burn. Others maintain that it is from the pigmentation in the paint, which was affected by the dark smoke from the hundreds of candles burning in front of it for centuries.

On one occasion, it's said that a Tartar soldier drew his sword and struck it twice, hence the two gashes to this day on her right cheek. The story continues that when he made a third attempt to strike the icon with his sword, before he could complete the swing of his arm, he yelled in pain and dropped dead of a massive heart attack.

Millions of pilgrims visit the town and Basilica of Czestochowa where the icon remains on display. Providentially, the painting survived the diabolical Nazi invasion and occupation and then the Communist takeover until Poland became independent again.

A replica of the icon adorns the National Shrine of Our Lady of Czestochowa in Doylestown, Pennsylvania, not far from Philadelphia.

The Basilica of Lourdes, France

St. Bernadette (see Chapter 21) was a young girl in Lourdes, France, and Catholics believe that Mary appeared to her in 1858 — from February 11 to July 16. Mary instructed St. Bernadette to dig with her hands in the soil and uncover a miraculous spring of water. To this day, the spring has been the catalyst for hundreds of thousands of inexplicable, immediate, and total cures. The water from the grotto is freely available to the faithful to take home with them. Many use it to bless the sick and dying in the hopes a miraculous cure may be granted from God by the intercession of Our Lady of Lourdes.

The original basilica, built above the grotto in 1876, eventually became overcrowded, and in 1958, a concrete church accommodating 20,000 was built. Today, 4 to 6 million pilgrims visit each year, and approximately 200 million have come since 1860. You can see hundreds of canes, crutches, and other artifacts used by the sick and disabled that were left at Lourdes following a miraculous cure. If you visit, you may participate in the praying of the Rosary in all languages, which occurs on-site each night, complete with a candlelight procession.

Fatima, Portugal

Catholics believe that Mary appeared to three small shepherd children, Lucia, Jacinta, and Francisco, in Fatima, Portugal, in 1917. She visited the children six times on the 13th of the month from May to October, asking them to pray the Rosary and to do so for the conversion of sinners so that they might repent of their sins and seek God's mercy and forgiveness. She said many souls were lost because no one prayed for them, and they lived evil lives.

The faithful believe that during her apparitions to the children in Fatima, she also predicted World War II and the expansion of Communism, especially the Soviet Union's evil empire, which enslaved most of Eastern Europe throughout the Cold War. She asked that the pope and bishops of the world consecrate Russia to her Immaculate Heart and that the faithful receive Holy Communion on the First Saturday of the month.

In May 1982, one year after an assassination attempt nearly killed him, Pope John Paul II asked the world's bishops to join him in consecrating Russia to the Immaculate Heart of Mary in thanksgiving for saving his life on May 13, 1981. Seven years after the consecration, the Berlin Wall fell, and in 1991, the Soviet Union collapsed and ceased to exist. Russia survived. Many attribute the end of the Cold War to political forces like Ronald Reagan and Mikhail Gorbachev. Some Catholics attribute it to the spiritual influence of Blessed Pope John Paul II and the intercession of Our Lady of Fatima.

On the last day of the apparitions in Fatima, October 13, 1917, what's known as *the Miracle of the Sun* occurred. It had rained earlier, and the ground was wet, as was the clothing of the crowd. The sun began to shrink and expand and then rotate and spin as if it were going to impact the earth. Most of the crowd thought that it was the end of the world. It wasn't. And when it was over, their clothes were dry. Astronomers to this day can't explain what happened.

Jacinta and Francisco died shortly afterward, but the oldest of the three children entered a cloistered convent of the Carmelite order. Sr. Lucia died in 2005. Blessed Pope John Paul II beatified Jacinta and Francisco on May 13, 2000.

Jacinta, Francisco, and Lucia are all buried at the Shrine of Our Lady of Fatima. Weather permitting, today's pilgrims pray the Rosary every evening where Our Lady of Fatima appeared. Pilgrims may also attend one of the outdoor Masses that are held on-site.

The Cathedral of Notre Dame

Not the home of the Fighting Irish in South Bend, Indiana, but the original Notre Dame (see Figure 22-3) in Paris, France, is another popular Catholic place to visit. King Louis VII of France wanted a gorgeous cathedral for the eldest daughter of the Church (what France is often called), and he asked Bishop Maurice de Sully to oversee the project. The cornerstone was laid in 1163, and it took until 1250 to finally complete the magnificent cathedral.

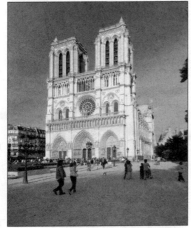

Figure 22-3:
The
Cathedral of
Notre Dame.

Chris Hill/National Geographic/Getty Images

Kings and queens have had their coronations in this cathedral; heads of state, such as General de Gaulle, have had their funeral Mass on-site; and several popes have celebrated Mass in this building over the centuries. It has become the prototype of Gothic cathedrals.

Notre Dame is so large that its enormity can be appreciated only by looking at it from across the bridge that covers the Seine. This famous cathedral
became the focus of Victor Hugo's novel *The Hunchback of Notre Dame*.

The National Shrine of the Immaculate Conception

You don't need to go to Europe to see large and beautiful churches. Many
Catholics visit the National Shrine of the Immaculate Conception every day in
Washington, D.C. (Take a look at Figure 22-4.)

Since 1847, the Patroness of the United States of America has been Our
Lady of the Immaculate Conception. On August 15, 1913, the Feast of the
Assumption of Mary, Bishop Thomas J. Shahan, Rector of the Catholic
University of America in Washington, D.C., had a papal audience with Pope
St. Pius X and asked for permission to build a national shrine in the United
States in honor of Mary. The pope not only gave his permission and blessing
but also a personal check for $400 to start the contribution campaign. James
Cardinal Gibbons, Archbishop of Baltimore, blessed the cornerstone on
September 23, 1920, but the Depression and World War II slowed progress.

Figure 22-4:
The
National
Shrine
of the
Immaculate
Conception.

SAUL LOEB/Stringer/Getty Images

In 1953, the nation's bishops pledged their support to finish the Great Upper
Church, which is the main body of the shrine. (It's called the Upper Church

to distinguish it from the basement or lower church, which is much smaller.) The largest Roman Catholic Church in the United States and the eighth largest in the world, the shrine was completed on November 20, 1959.

The Minor Basilica of Saint Anne de Beaupré

The oldest pilgrimage site in North America is the Minor Basilica of St. Anne de Beaupré in Quebec, Canada. The original church was built in 1658, followed by two more. The first basilica was erected in 1876, but a fire destroyed it in 1922. A second basilica and the fourth church were consecrated in 1976.

The church is built in honor of St. Anne, the mother of Mary and grandmother of Jesus Christ. The French settlers who came to Canada had a strong devotion to St. Anne, so it was natural for them to name it after her. It's the pride and joy of French Canadians and English Canadians alike. Numerous miraculous healings have been associated with pilgrimages to this fantastic shrine. Every year, more than 1 million people visit this holy place.

The Shrine of the Most Blessed Sacrament

Mother Angelica (see Chapter 20), who founded the Eternal Word Television Network (EWTN) in Irondale, Alabama, also built the Shrine of the Most Blessed Sacrament in Hanceville, Alabama.

Mother Angelica says that while on a pilgrimage in Bogota, Columbia, she saw a statue of the Child Jesus come alive and speak to her: "Build me a temple, and I will help those who help you." She says that she was puzzled because Catholics aren't accustomed to using the word *temple.* The words *church, cathedral, basilica,* and *shrine* are familiar and used often, but not *temple.* Later, Mother Angelica, visiting St. Peter's Basilica in Rome, saw the word *temple* chiseled in the marble. She says that she knew then that it had to be impressive.

It took 200 workers — 99 percent of them non-Catholic — to build the temple in five years with donations from five millionaire families who demanded anonymity. Not one penny of the contributions collected from viewers for the

EWTN network went to the project, which is calculated to have cost somewhere between $25 and $30 million.

"Nothing but the best for Jesus," was Mother Angelica's motto. "If the President of the United States has the White House and the Queen of England has Buckingham Palace, then Our Lord and Savior, Jesus Christ, present in the Blessed Sacrament, deserves the very best for His house." The Shrine of the Most Blessed Sacrament may be in Hanceville, Alabama, but the materials used to build it came from all over the world. The ceramic tile came from South America, the stones from Canada, and the bronze from Madrid, Spain. The floors, columns, and pillars are made of marble from Italy. And a rare red Jasper marble came from Turkey that was used for the red crosses in the floor. The wood for the pews, doors, and confessionals is cedar imported from Paraguay. The stained glass windows were imported from Munich, Germany. The most striking and moving feature, however, is the seven-foot *monstrance* (ornamental vessel) containing the Blessed Sacrament (see Chapter 19).

Part VI
Appendixes

EARLY CATHEDRAL WALL MOSAICS

"We'd like some scenes from Genesis over here, followed by David composing the Psalms over there, and at the end, let's have Abraham pointing the way to the coat room."

In this part . . .

Appendix A is a *very* abridged and condensed history of the Catholic Church that touches on 2,000 years of development, life and death, joy and sorrow, intrigue and inspiration, vice and virtue, and sin and grace.

To make sure we included the kitchen sink, Appendix B features some familiar prayers that most Catholics know and use regularly.

Appendix A

A Brief History of Catholicism

A h, history lessons. To some, they're as exciting as a Stephen King novel (and often as gruesome). To others, they're as boring as a tax form. We're of the former variety. If you are too, you're definitely in the right spot.

Ancient Times (A.D. 33–741)

This section looks at the history of the Catholic Church from the time of Jesus through the fall of the Roman Empire.

Non-Christian Rome (A.D. 33–312)

Present-day Israel was known as Palestine at the time of Jesus, and even though it had a king (Herod), it was a puppet monarchy because the real civil power ruling the Holy Land was the Roman Empire. Caesar Tiberius, the emperor from A.D. 14 to 37, appointed Pontius Pilate the procurator (governor) of Judea, and he was the real political power in Jerusalem.

Yet Palestine wasn't considered a conquered territory of Rome — rather, it was an unwilling and impotent ally. And the Jews were initially exempt from the normal Roman requirement of worshipping the Imperial gods, even though divine attributes were ascribed to Caesar himself, beginning with Augustus. As long as the Christians were seen as a fringe group of the Jews, they enjoyed the same protection and tolerance under Roman rule.

The early Christians

The faithful believed that after Jesus was crucified and died, he rose from the dead. His followers became known as Christians. Mostly Jews who had come to accept Jesus as the Messiah, they wanted to maintain their Jewish traditions and keep practicing the Hebrew faith. They went to Temple and Synagogue, observed Sabbath and Passover, obeyed the dietary laws (kosher), and yet gathered every Sunday, the day of the Resurrection, to hear what Jesus preached and to celebrate the Mass (see Chapter 10).

The Roman persecutions

The Roman persecutions of the Christians were almost as fierce and as geno-cidal as the Nazi Holocaust was against the Jews during World War II, but the Roman persecutions lasted almost 300 years. The persecutions lasted as long as each particular Caesar promoted them. Historians designate three periods of persecution: The first period lasted from A.D. 64 to 112, the second period from A.D. 112 to 186, and the third from A.D. 189 to 312.

The first period

The first period of Roman persecutions began in A.D. 64 during the reign of Nero (A.D. 54–68), who blamed the Christians for the burning of Rome. (Many historians believe *he* initiated the burning of Rome to rebuild the city against the opposition of the local Roman aristocracy.) The period continued through the reign of Domitian (81–96) and finished with the reign of Emperor Trajan (98–117). During this period, falsehoods spread about Christians making human sacrifices and promoting cannibalism (based on a misunderstanding of the Holy Eucharist; see Chapter 8). People became so superstitious that they linked any calamity to the Christian presence in the empire. The response was to feed Christians to the lions to try to eliminate their presence.

The second period

The second period of Roman persecutions continued with Trajan through the reign of Philosopher Emperor Marcus Aurelius (161–180) and ended with Commodus (180–192) — the emperor alluded to in the movie *Gladiator* (2000; Universal Pictures). This period had less tyrannical and despotic emperors than the first period, but the persecutions were still promoted. Most of the animosity toward Christians during this time was of a mob mentality. When a large group of Romans got together and had too much wine, they went out Christian-bashing.

The third period

The final period of persecutions was the most virulent, violent, and atrocious. The successor to Commodus, Septimus Severus (193–211), changed the tone from letting local yokels beat up the Christians to reinstating full-fledged, across-the-board imperial persecutions. Four emperors later, Maximus Thrax (235–238) had it out for the bishops and started a campaign to arrest and execute popes and bishops, hoping to destroy Christianity by hitting its lead-ers. Three emperors later, Decius (249–251) inaugurated the bloodiest of per-secutions. Not just baptized Christians but anyone even suspected of being a Christian was treated as a traitor and potential terrorist, even though no threats whatsoever came from Christians against the emperor, the Empire, or anything Roman. They merely wanted to worship their own god. And under Diocletian (284–305), Emperor of the Eastern Empire (the Roman Empire split in half in 286), the most pervasive and intense persecution took place. Entire families were tortured and put to death. He literally hated all Christians and Christianity and swore he'd rid the world of this cancer.

Famous martyrs of the Roman persecutions

Many were martyred during the Roman persecutions. *Martyr* is actually a Greek word for *witness.* These faithful Christians tried to avoid persecution, but if hours of torture and a horrible death resulted from witnessing to the faith, they accepted it.

St. Stephen was the first deacon of the Church and the first Christian martyr (also called the Proto-martyr). He was stoned to death for being a Christian (Acts 7:58). Saul of Tarsus was present at the event and later became St. Paul the Apostle. Emperor Nero had him beheaded. (Because St. Paul was a Roman citizen, unlike St. Peter and the other apostles, Paul couldn't be crucified, but he could be beheaded.) Peter was crucified upside down at his own request, because he felt unworthy to die in the same manner as Jesus.

All the apostles were martyred except St. John, known as the beloved disciple. His persecutors tried to burn him alive in boiling oil, but he survived. So he was exiled to the island of Patmos, where he wrote the Book of Revelation. He died of old age in A.D. 100. If you're interested in the martyrs, be sure to check out the stories of St. Agnes, St. Agatha, St. Lucy, St. Sebastian, St. Lawrence, and St. Cecilia. These saints endured swords, arrows, being burned alive, and more in the name of their faith.

Christian Rome (A.D. 313–475)

"The blood of martyrs became the seed of Christians," said Tertullian, a Christian apologist who lived from 160-220. Three hundred years of relentless and violent persecutions ended when the Roman Emperor Constantine issued his famous Edict of Milan in A.D. 313, which legalized Christianity. Being that it was no longer a capital crime, Christians were able to come out in the open for the first time.

Although Constantine's edict allowed Christians to freely practice their faith, it wasn't until A.D. 380 that Christianity became the official state religion by the Emperor Theodosius. At that point, the tables were turned: Paganism was outlawed, and the once-outlawed Christianity became the official religion of the Roman Empire.

The consequences of this new alliance of church and state were many. The Church obtained financial, material, and legal advantages from the state. Buildings (particularly the former pagan temples), land, estates, and properties, as well as money, were donated in compensation for the losses incurred during the 300 years of Roman persecutions.

To this day, some of the ancient basilicas in Rome and throughout Italy resemble pagan temples in their architecture because that's what they were before being transformed into Christian houses of worship. Altars that sacrificed animals to the pagan gods of Rome became altars for the Holy Sacrifice of the Mass.

Barbarian invasions and the fall of Rome (A.D. 476–570)

One of the important developments in this period of time was an establishment of religious life, especially monasticism. *Monks* were men of prayer who left the secular world to commit themselves to a life of *ora et labora* (Latin for *prayer and work*), the motto of St. Benedict, the father of Western monasticism.

Monasteries were large houses that held anywhere from 10 to 50 or more residents with individual austere rooms called *cells* connected to several community rooms with the chapel as the focal point. Everything was done and shared in common, from food to work to leisure and even prayer. The only private things were sleep and sanitary habits.

Monks took solemn vows of poverty, chastity, and obedience. They had no wives or children, and their material wealth went to the monastery to be shared by all under the stewardship of the abbot, who was in charge and had the rank of bishop. This pooling of resources, when aristocrats and middle-class Romans entered monastic life, enabled poor men to join as well and truly be considered and treated as equal and full members of the community.

The monks chose to leave the hectic and worldly cities of Imperial Rome, which saved them during the barbarian invasions. The cities were plundered, but the countryside was basically left untouched. The Goths, Huns, Franks, and many more groups invaded the frontier of the Roman Empire, which had grown too vast, too thin, and too undermanned. (More Germanic and Gallic tribes filled the ranks of the Roman Army than tribes of Roman blood from the Italian Peninsula.)

The most famous and ruthless barbarian, Attila the Hun, made his way right up to the city gates of Rome in A.D. 452, accompanied by thousands of troops. Emperor Valentinian III asked Pope St. Leo the Great to do something, and he did: He went out to meet Attila with 100 priests, monks, and bishops, chanting in Latin, burning incense, and carrying crosses, crucifixes, and holy images of Jesus and Mary.

Attila became afraid for the first time in his career. He knew that everyone else feared him and trembled at his name, and he knew that he had superior troops. Yet seeing this saintly man and hearing that he was called the Vicar of Christ on earth and that even angels were under his authority, Attila feared the unseen power of God. Attila agreed not to sack Rome, and he turned back. But Atilla wasn't the last threat to Rome. Odoacer sacked Rome in A.D. 476, deposing the last Western emperor, Romulus Augustulus.

After the collapse of the Roman Empire, the Teutonic kings and overlords realized that governing all the people and all the territory would be extremely difficult. No more Roman Senate, no more legal system, and no more local authorities — just the authority of the conquering king. Yet the bishops survived the fall. The pagan kings dealt with the Christian bishops, and that contact with them gradually introduced the faith to the barbarian invaders.

The bishops depended on the monks to help. During the invasions, the cities were destroyed, but the monasteries survived. The monks went out and preached about Jesus and the Catholic Church, and many converts were made — especially after a successful conversion of a king or tribal chief.

The invaders got urbanized and suburbanized, as well as civilized. They stopped pillaging and abandoned a nomadic life for a more stable one. This was the genesis of the European nations of Spain, France, Germany, and England. The Church had adopted the Roman Imperial model for governing by creating parishes, dioceses, archdioceses, and metropolitan areas, and that same structure helped the tribes form the civil boundaries and cultures of the Franks, the Lombards, the Saxons, and so on. And guess who taught those newly civilized people to read and write? For that matter, guess who preserved Latin and Greek as a spoken and written language — who protected the books and writings of philosophy and law, poetry and literature, geometry and grammar to allow culture to flourish again? The monks.

The monks not only preserved Greco-Roman literature, law, philosophy, and art, but also agriculture. Nomadic barbarians weren't natural farmers. They knew nothing of raising livestock, planting, harvesting, and such, but the monks did these things as part of their life, so they taught the barbarians how to live off the land.

Pope St. Gregory the Great to Charles Martel (590–741)

St. Benedict of Nursia (A.D. 480–547) is known as the Father of Western monasticism because he established the first monastery in Europe at Subiaco, Italy. He also founded the famous monastery of Monte Cassino, Italy, where a crucial battle took place during World War II in 1944. His religious order of monks is the Order of St. Benedict, more commonly known as the Benedictines.

Pope St. Gregory the Great (A.D. 540–604) was a Roman-born nobleman, the son of a senator, who became a Benedictine monk in A.D. 575. The people and clergy of Rome were so impressed with his personal holiness, wisdom, and knowledge that when Pope Pelagius II died in A.D. 590, Gregory was elected to succeed him by *acclamation* — unanimous consent. Before becoming a monk, he had been Prefect of Rome (A.D. 572–574), and that experience helped him later on as pope when the political and military leadership of Rome disintegrated and left the city abandoned. He rallied the citizens by coordinating and personally participating in a monumental project to care for victims of the plague and the starving who literally overran the city of Rome, which more or less had no civil government left. Gregory's position as the only visible leader in Rome further enhanced the power, prestige, and influence of the papacy.

Gregorian Chant, religious chants sung in Latin, gets its name from Pope St. Gregory due to his love of music and the Sacred Liturgy. In A.D. 596, he sent St. Augustine of Canterbury with 40 other missionaries to England to convert the Angles, Jutes, and Saxons, who were the Teutonic invaders of Britain, which had been a Roman outpost from A.D. 43–410.

Muhammad, born in Mecca, A.D. 570, became the founder and prophet of Islam at the age of 40 (A.D. 610) and died in Medina in A.D. 632. By A.D. 711, Muslim forces occupied Spain after they had successfully conquered the Visigoths who had controlled it since A.D. 419.

Charles Martel (A.D. 688–741) is another key person in Catholic Church history. He was the illegitimate son of Pepin II and also the grandfather of Charlemagne. Charles won a decisive and pivotal victory over Abd-er-Rahman and the Moors (Spanish Muslims of this period) at the Battle of Poitiers in 732. This was the most crucial victory for all Christendom because it determined whether Islam or Christianity would be the predominant religion in Europe for centuries to come.

The Middle Ages (A.D. 800–1500)

This section looks at the history of the Catholic Church from the time of Charlemagne to the dawn of the Protestant Reformation.

Christendom: One big, mighty kingdom

The strength of the ancient Roman Empire was its unification of many different peoples of various languages and cultures — unity within diversity. One emperor ruled many citizens from many places, and one law was enforced, applied, and interpreted all over the vast empire. But when Rome fell after different groups of barbarians invaded and occupied the empire, the unity dissolved, and only diversity remained, bringing chaos. After the barbarians settled down, settled in, and became truly civilized, thanks to the monks, the local barbarian chiefs, princes, and kings fought among themselves instead of unifying.

Yet one single vestige of unity survived both the moral and military decline of the Roman Empire, and that was the Catholic Church, which had one head (the pope in Rome), one set of laws (canon law), and the same seven sacraments all over the world. And unity existed between the pope and the bishops, between the priests/deacons and their respective bishop, and between the people of the parish and their pastor.

The rise of the Holy Roman Empire

On Christmas Day A.D. 800, Pope Leo crowned Charlemagne (King of the Franks) the Holy Roman Emperor. Pope Leo's intent was that one ruler, the Holy Roman Emperor, would be the secular ruler over the known world. But by having the emperor crowned by the pope in Rome, the Church achieved the superiority it needed: The one who installed could also depose. So later, in the 11th century, when the Holy Roman Emperor Henry IV tried to control who was made bishop in his realm, he was deposed and excommunicated by Pope Gregory VII, also known as Hildebrand.

Under Charlemagne, one standard liturgical language also united the people of the Holy Roman Empire. Latin was the *lingua franca* (common language) for the Catholic Church and the government as well. This made sense because the other languages spoken at the time were still primitive (they didn't have an extensive vocabulary), and many of them were never written — only spoken. Making Latin the language of worship solidified the empire because people could travel anywhere and still experience the same exact Mass.

Splitsville: The east/west schism

The Eastern Roman Empire, known as Byzantium, didn't take too kindly to having a Holy Roman Emperor or empire arise because it was clear that the pope wanted to make the *Carolingians* (the dynasty that included Charlemagne) the sole rulers of the entire old Roman Empire — East and West. This would make the emperor of Byzantium and the Patriarch of Constantinople, who was always closely aligned with him, virtually redundant. Ever since the old Roman Empire was divided in A.D. 286 and the imperial town of Constantinople was established by the Emperor Constantine (A.D. 306–337), the Eastern part of the Roman Empire survived despite the barbarian invasions in the West. After Rome fell in A.D. 476, Byzantium was the only vestige of the Empire.

The Byzantines saw the crowning of Charlemagne as Holy Roman Emperor as a slap to the Eastern emperor and empire itself. From then on, relations between the East and the West deteriorated until a formal split occurred in 1054, called the *schism*. The Eastern Church became the Greek Orthodox Church by severing all ties with Rome and the Roman Catholic Church. In the end, Pope Leo and the Patriarch of Constantinople excommunicated each other and their respective churches. (More than 900 years later, in 1965, Pope Paul VI and Patriarch Athenagoras I of Constantinople removed the mutual excommunications.)

The Crusades

The intention of the Crusades was initially honorable: It was a response to a plea for help from the Byzantine Empire, still a sister church at the time. In 1095, the Byzantine Emperor, Alexius Comnenus, sent ambassadors to Pope Urban II in Rome, asking for help to defend Christianity from an imminent attack. The Saracens (Arab Muslims during the time of the Crusades) had overrun the Holy Land, and Christians were no longer free to move about and visit their holy pilgrimage sites. A crusade to free the Holy Land was under way before you knew it.

The pope also saw the Crusades as a way to diffuse and dissolve internal fighting and battles being waged by the Christian monarchs for territory and power. (Clear and defined nation states didn't exist as of yet.) He wanted to unite them under one banner, Christianity, for one purpose, to free the Holy Land for pilgrims, against one common enemy, Islamic extremism and expansionism.

Between 1095 and 1270, eight Crusades took place. In addition, the infamous Children's Crusade occurred in 1212: On their own, thousands of children wanted to free the Holy Land, but ruthless and evil men took advantage of them and sold many into slavery to some *Moors* (Muslims that inhabited Spain). Many of the children died of hunger and exhaustion on the way.

Deemed a total failure, the Crusades didn't free the Holy Land from Islamic rule, and injustice, debauchery, greed, envy, animosity, petty infighting, and prejudice erupted on both sides during these holy wars. For example, Latin Christians were invited by their Eastern brethren to free the Holy Land, and yet Crusaders attacked Byzantine territory, seizing it for themselves. Christian kings and princes often fought on the way to a crusade; jealousy and envy prevented them from working together successfully. In addition, brutality and the absence of mercy — or even human decency — crossed over religious boundaries. Christians and Muslims alike slaughtered helpless, innocent women and children. Both sides acted atrociously. It wasn't that the religions of Christianity and Islam were at war; rather, some members of those religions abused faith as a catalyst for territorial, economic, and political purposes on both sides.

That said, had the Crusades not occurred, many historians believe that the Islamic military forces would've taken the opportunity to prepare for a massive assault on Europe, and no unified leadership or defense would have prevented it. The Crusades did contain the expansion. They also reopened trade routes to the Far East, which had been closed for several centuries due to the strength and spread of Islam in Arabia and the Middle East.

To Catholics, the Crusades are a poignant reminder that the ends never justify the means. The Catholic belief is that no matter how lofty the goal or noble the purpose, only moral means can be used.

The Golden Age

During the late Middle Ages, the Catholic Church flourished — especially under Pope Innocent III. The Church was at its zenith both spiritually *and* politically. In fact, never again would these two spheres be united so strongly in the Church.

Two new orders developed at this time: the Dominicans and Franciscans. They were known as *mendicant* orders because they didn't own any property and relied on alms. They weren't cloistered; rather, they became itinerant preachers, going from town to town preaching the Gospel. So instead of people going to the monastery for religion, the monastery now came to them. See Chapter 21 for profiles of the founders of these orders, St. Dominic and St. Francis of Assisi.

The building of the great cathedrals occurred during this period in history. The architecture was gothic, and the new style allowed for high vaulted ceilings and large, stained-glass windows.

Books were rare during this time because the printing press hadn't been invented yet. Manuscripts were penned by hand and were very expensive, so the general public was predominantly illiterate. Stained-glass windows became picture-bibles for the peasants.

Every important city wanted a bigger cathedral than the others. Building these houses of God took centuries and kept people employed when a war or insurrection wasn't taking place. Today, travelers to France and Germany can still visit these awesome testimonies of faith. This period also saw a rise of towns, guilds, and societies. Great artists also flourished during this period. Giotto di Bondone (1266?–1337) painted with perspective and drew realistic scenes of men, women, and nature.

This was also a time of great literature: Dante Alighieri of Florence (1265–1321) wrote the greatest of all Christian poems, the *Divine Comedy*, which is a story of an imaginary journey through hell, purgatory, and heaven; Geoffrey Chaucer of England (1343–1400) wrote the *Canterbury Tales*, which are vignettes of pilgrims on their way to a shrine.

Universities developed in the Middle Ages. First, they were attached to the cathedrals and staffed for the education of clergy. Later, they branched out into the secular sciences. Bologna developed a school of law; Paris, philosophy, rhetoric, and theology; and Salerno, a school of medicine. Oxford, Cambridge, St. Andrews, Glasgow, Prague, and Dublin universities all began at this time, too. With great schools came great teachers, such as Peter Lombard, St. Albert the Great, Hugh of Saint Victor, Alexander of Hales, and John Duns Scotus — just to name a few. The two most notable and influential intellects and scholars were St. Thomas Aquinas (a member of the Dominican order) and St. Bonaventure (a Franciscan). In Chapter 21, we provide a brief profile of Aquinas.

The downward spiral

If the 13th century was a golden one for the Church, the 14th and 15th centuries were tarnished ones.

The unstable and dangerous climate of Rome

Whereas Pope Innocent III (1198–1216) epitomized the zenith of papal power and influence, Pope Boniface VIII (1294–1303) personified one of the most complicated, mysterious, and at times contradictory pontificates of the Church.

King Philip IV of France and Boniface became bitter enemies early on. Their relationship worsened over time, and in 1303, Philip sent mercenaries to arrest and bully Boniface into resigning. He was beaten and humiliated at Anagni but refused to quit. The local citizens arose to his defense and rescued him. He intended to excommunicate Philip but died before the excommunication could be enacted.

After his death, Pope Benedict XI was elected, but he proved too weak and conciliatory to tangle with Philip. His nine-month reign evenly split the College of Cardinals between those who hated the French for what Philip did to Boniface and French sympathizers who wanted to reconcile and move on. (For more on the College of Cardinals, see Chapter 6.)

Pope Clement V (1305–1314) followed Benedict. The papal coronation took place in Lyons, and Clement never set foot in Rome. Four years into his pontificate, Clement moved to his French palace at Avignon, allegedly to escape the dangerous mobs in Rome, because he was French and easily influenced by King Philip who offered to protect him.

After Pope Clement arrived in Avignon, the popes remained there for 70 years — the same amount of time that the Jews were held captive in Babylon; hence the term *Babylonian Captivity of the Popes.*

Philip ensured his prestige by pressuring Clement to appoint more French cardinals than Italian ones. This way, when he died, the majority (two-thirds) would elect another Frenchman, which they did again and again.

Seventy years passed with seven popes in Avignon, while the people in Rome endured having no resident bishop. Enough was enough, said St. Catherine of Siena (1347–1380), who made her way to France and pleaded with Pope Gregory XI (1370–1378) to return to Rome where the pope, as bishop of Rome, belongs. He listened and moved the papacy back to the Eternal City.

Two popes at the same time means double trouble

Pope Gregory XI died in 1378, and the conclave (see Chapter 6) that met to choose his successor was ready to pick another Frenchman so that he could move back to France. But Italian mobs in Rome had other ideas. The Italians became so animated about the non-Italian pope thing that they pried the roof off the conclave at the Vatican and shouted at the cardinals, many of whom were French, "Give us a Roman pope, or at any rate, an Italian." The conclave quickly elected the oldest, most feeble Italian cardinal — 60-year-old Urban VI. The plan was to choose someone with one foot in the grave, return to France, and then, after the pope died, hold another conclave in France. But as soon as he was elected, Urban perked up and showed his real mettle. After he was made pope, his health improved, and he began the necessary reforms of the hierarchy to curb abuse and corruption.

You can imagine how the French felt when they realized that the pope would not return to France and that he intended to make reforms. Instead of going back to France, the French cardinals fled to Fondi in the Kingdom of Naples to decide their next move. They realized Urban would be around for a while *and* would also clean house. The French cardinals cried foul and said that the election of Urban VI was invalid. They claimed they were under pressure and duress to elect an Italian or suffer the angry mob. So with King Philip's blessing, five months after the election of Urban VI in Rome, the *Avignon conclave* (all the French cardinals) met in 1378 at the Cathedral of Fondi and elected the *antipope* (the term used for an invalidly elected pope) Clement VII in Naples. Born in Geneva, Clement was neither French nor Italian (so he seemed like a good compromise) but spent most of his priesthood in France anyway. Eight months later he fled to Avignon.

At that point, a full-blown *schism* (division in the church) existed. Some Catholics obeyed and followed the Roman Pope Urban, and other Catholics followed the Avignon Pope Clement instead. When Urban died in 1389, the cardinals elected Boniface XI to succeed him. Five years later, Clement died, and the schism could have ended, but the French cardinals elected another antipope — Benedict XIII. So two men still claimed to be pope at the same time.

Better make that three

Having two men claiming to be pope simultaneously got so frustrating that scholars and secular rulers got in on the act and called for a General Council of the Church. The problem was that only a pope could call a council and only a pope could approve or reject its decrees. And neither the Avignon Pope Benedict nor the Roman Pope Boniface wanted to resign or step down.

In 1409, an illicit Council did meet in Pisa with neither pope present and without either's sanction. The cardinals who attended deposed both popes and elected a third one, Alexander V. Talk about going from the frying pan into the fire. Suddenly, three different popes claimed the throne of St. Peter: The

Roman pope, the Avignon pope, and the Pisan pope. Each one denounced the other, and most of the faithful were genuinely confused as to who the real pope was.

The Pisan Pope Alexander V survived only 11 months, and his successor was John XXIII. (Because he's not recognized as a legitimate pope, when Angelo Roncalli was elected pope in 1958, he took the name and number John XXIII.)

A solution to the too-many-popes issue

The Holy Roman Emperor Sigismund demanded a General Council at Constance. The 16th Council of the Church met from 1414–1418. All cardinals and bishops had to attend, and 18,000 clerics took part as well. The agenda included finding a solution to the Great Schism, and one was found. Martin V was chosen to be the one and only pope, and the others were asked to resign or else. The Council also denounced and condemned the writings of John Wyclif (English) and Jan Hus (Bohemian) as heretical. Hus was turned over to secular authorities and burned at the stake in 1415. Wyclif had died in 1384.

Roman Pope Gregory XII, the true pope, voluntarily resigned after formally approving of the Council of Constance. (Without papal approval, this council would've become as lame as the Council of Pisa.) But Avignon's Benedict XIII refused to resign and was deposed publicly. Pisan's John XXIII tried to escape, but he was caught and deposed. Martin V (1417–1431) was then the only claimant and only recognized pope — the Bishop of Rome and Supreme Roman Pontiff.

The Church survived, but the wounds and scars ran deep and came back to haunt it later. The crisis of the Great Schism greatly weakened the political power of the papacy and sowed the seeds for anti-papal arguments during the Reformation.

The Black Death

As if the Babylonian Captivity (Avignon papacy) and the Great Schism (three popes at once) weren't enough, another fly in the ointment was the Black Death — the bubonic plague — killing 25 million people in five years. That's more than one-third of all Europe.

The Black Death lasted from 1347 to 1352. The largest percentage of casualties came from the lower clergy because parish priests were needed to give the Sacrament of the Anointing of the Sick (then known as Extreme Unction), and they became infected. So many priests died from the plague that an extreme vocations crisis arose. In desperation, many bishops and religious superiors accepted unworthy, incompetent, or inadequately trained candidates for Holy Orders. This led to the introduction of many ignorant, superstitious, unstable, untrustworthy clerics running around Europe.

In the aftermath of the plague, amid immense devastation in Europe, abuses proliferated in the Church due to the poorly trained, immoral, and unreliable clergy filling in for all the good and holy ones who died from the plague. And the upper clergy (bishops, cardinals, and popes) fared no better. Their plague didn't come from a flea hiding on a rat but from their own hearts. Nepotism, greed, lust, avarice, envy, sloth — you name it, they did it. Not all the hierarchy, of course — not even the majority. But even one case was too many.

The Reformation to the Modern Era (1517–Today)

This section looks at the history of the Catholic Church from the time of the Reformation through the modern era.

The growing need for reform

During the Middle Ages, Greek philosophy (as epitomized by Plato and Aristotle) was used to help develop a Christian one, which became partner with sacred theology. The Latin language was known and used — mostly in religious and legal contexts. The liberal arts and religious sciences were the main staples of university education, and *Christendom* was the term given to a unified Christian culture, religion, and empire that predominated Medieval Western and Central Europe.

At the end of the 15th century, however, people witnessed the gradual disintegration of that unity. They saw the appearance of modern nations and languages; the discovery of the New World by Columbus in 1492; and a revival of classical art, architecture, and literature. Greek and Roman classics from Homer, Sophocles, Virgil, Ovid, Horace, and Cicero eclipsed the former staples of Plato and Aristotle. Humanism arose as a system of thought that bridged the sacred world of heavenly faith and the secular world of earthly wisdom (at least that was its original intent). This classical resurgence became the impetus of what we call the Renaissance.

Witnessing the Renaissance

The Renaissance was born in Florence, Italy, which gave the world poets Dante Alighieri and Francesco Petrarch, artists Michelangelo Buonarroti and Leonardo da Vinci, and thinkers Vittorino da Feltre and Giovanni Boccaccio. And that city is also associated with such famous names as Medici, Machiavelli, and Borgia.

From Italy, the ideals of the Renaissance flowed, crossing the Alps into France, Germany, and finally, England.

The Church encouraged the Renaissance and became a great patron of the sciences, literature, and art. However, a great deal of *secularism* (worldliness) crept in, and people lost much of their respect for their spiritual leaders. Many abuses in the Church weren't dealt with in a timely manner. Ignorant clergy and a greedy episcopacy eventually gave rise to *reformers,* people determined to bring about reform. Unfortunately, some of it wasn't really reform (change made within the Church structure) but revolt, which led to division.

St. Francis of Assisi was a reformer in his time — the Middle Ages. The key difference between him and Martin Luther is that Francis reformed *within* the Church structure and Luther, as well as others such as John Calvin (see the upcoming section on Calvin), and Hus (see the earlier section "A solution to the too-many-popes issue"), sought to reform *outside* the Church structure, which eventually led to a division within and break from the Catholic Church.

Corruption in the Church

Pope Julius II (1503–13) decided to rebuild St. Peter's Basilica, which was in desperate need of repair. He communicated to the faithful that anyone who went to confession and Holy Communion and then donated according to their means (called *almsgiving*) toward the restoration of the historic Church could receive a plenary indulgence if all the conditions were met. Thus began a descent into corruption that would ultimately lead to the Reformation.

Some background: A *plenary indulgence* is a total remission of the temporal punishment due to sins already forgiven in confession. Simply put, it's an application of God's divine mercy to remove the effects of past sin. An indulgence isn't forgiveness itself nor is it absolution; it presupposes both before it can happen. Sin can have two consequences, *eternal* punishment (hell) and *temporal* punishment (purgatory). Unrepentant and un-forgiven mortal sins result in eternal punishment. Forgiven sins are free from eternal punishment, but they retain a temporal punishment. God's mercy forgives sin, and God's justice rewards good and punishes evil.

Of course, no one can *buy* an indulgence. To gain an indulgence, the person has to be in the state of grace — not conscious of any mortal sins — and *free of all attachment to sin,* even venial ones. By attachment, we mean any fond memories of past but forgiven sins. So no amount of money could automatically guarantee someone an indulgence. Only someone who had sorrow for his sins, confessed them, was absolved of them, and then performed a charitable work, such as giving alms or some other act of mercy, could be eligible for an indulgence.

The problem was that after Pope Julius's statement, a few avaricious and greedy bishops and priests, along with some like-minded princes, literally sold indulgences, which was a violation of canon law then and now and is also a mortal sin called *simony*. Telling people, "If you donate some silver pieces for this project, you can use the indulgence to get grandma out of purgatory," is a mortal sin. Indulgences don't work that way, but some unscrupulous people saw an opportunity to exploit others. Pope Julius's successor, Leo X (son of Lorenzo de Medici), was just such an unscrupulous man. In Germany as well, this practice was encouraged, and preachers went from town to town to encourage the rebuilding of St. Peter's. Pope Julius II's original message became distorted, and it began to look like the Church was indeed selling spiritual favors for money.

The rise of the middle class

After the fall of the Roman Empire, people belonged to one of three groups — the peasants, the nobility, or the Church — for most if not all of their lives. The Church (especially bishops, abbots, and cardinals) along with the nobility (kings, queens, lords, dukes, barons, counts, and so on) were the educated members of society and held power and authority. Things changed, however, when a middle class emerged and moderate wealth was achieved not by noble birth or by entrance into religious life or by ordination. Merchants became a middle ground between the poverty of peasants and the affluence of the aristocracy.

Before the Reformation, the last three significant events of the Middle Ages were The Black Death, The Babylonian Captivity, and The Great Schism. (See the earlier section "The downward spiral" for the lowdown on each of these.) All of these events contributed to the need for reform.

The reformers

The corruption of some of the clergy and hierarchy was inexcusable, which aroused the righteous anger of the reformers.

Martin Luther

Martin Luther (1483–1546), a Catholic Augustinian priest, challenged John Tetzel, another Catholic priest, for selling indulgences. On October 31, 1517, Luther nailed a document he wrote, "The Ninety-Five Theses," to the door of a Wittenberg church, a kind of university bulletin board. (Posting on the church door in and of itself was no revolutionary act because all announcements and news items — be they public debates or requests for bake sale items — were tacked to the door of the church where people could look at them every day when they entered.) Those 95 theses became the cornerstone of the Reformation.

Luther had many valid points and good intentions, but his famous doctrine that "Only by faith alone can man be saved. Good works are useless" (a reinterpretation of St. Paul's citation in Romans 3:28) put him directly at odds with the Catholic Church.

St. Augustine (354–430), whose religious order Luther joined, was a foe of Pelagius, a heretic who claimed that humans could earn their way to heaven and that humans were in no need of God's assistance. This heresy was condemned, and the Church solemnly taught that every good work depended on divine grace; alone, humans could do nothing but sin, but with grace, they could do great things. Augustine rightly condemned Pelagius's idea that good works alone, without faith, could make a person holy. Luther, an Augustinian, went to the other end of the spectrum, however, saying that faith alone without works was all a person needed. The phrase "faith alone" is never used by St. Paul in the Bible but is used by St. James when he says "man is justified by works and not by faith alone" (James 2:24).

Gutenberg's invention of the moveable type printing press earlier in the 15th century revolutionized religious and political debate, and Luther was keenly adept at using this technological innovation. With mass printings, pamphlets could be disseminated to more people quickly and thus influence public opinion greatly.

Luther found an ally in Elector Frederick (who founded the University of Wittenberg, where Luther taught). For Frederick, Luther and the Reformation were catalysts to separate from the empire and begin an autonomous German kingdom. For Luther, Frederick offered protection (like being a bodyguard) and a guarantee that he could dissent from papal teaching and authority. Luther's followers and subsequent Reformers became known as Protestants because they were *protesting* against the Church of Rome. After the formal split from Catholicism, adherents of Luther's theology became known as Lutherans.

Sharing the Bible with all

The Catholic Church was not against the printing of the Bible in the native (vernacular) tongue or in large quantities for public use. On the contrary, in the fourth century, the pope asked St. Jerome to translate the Hebrew, Greek, and Aramaic manuscripts of Sacred Scripture into the common language of the day (Latin) and for the first time ever combine all the books of the Bible into one large volume. This made the use and spread of the Word of God much easier.

Venerable Bede was the first to translate the Latin Bible into English at the end of the seventh century, and St. Cyril translated the Latin into Old Slavonic in the ninth century, proving that there was no Church prohibition against Bibles in the native language. Yes, most Bibles were chained in the churches — not to keep them *from* the people but to keep them *for* the people, just like banks chain pens and the phone company used to chain directories in their phone booths.

Henry VIII

At first, Henry VIII, King of England, opposed Luther and the Protestant Reformation. But when his wife, Catherine of Aragon, couldn't give him a male heir, Henry wanted an annulment so he could marry Anne Boleyn. (Catherine did give him a daughter, Mary I, who would later be Queen after Edward VI succeeded Henry.)

The pope refused to grant the annulment, no matter how much money or how many threats were sent. So in 1533, Henry declared himself Supreme Head of the Church in England and dissolved the allegiance that the clergy in England had to Rome. He broke from Rome, starting the Anglican Church, and divorced Catherine to marry Anne. As it happens, she couldn't give him a son either, but she did give him a daughter, Elizabeth I, the half-sister of Mary. The king had Anne executed.

The English hierarchy and aristocracy went along with Henry's split from Rome except for a few loyal Catholics, such as St. John Fisher, the Bishop of Rochester, and St. Thomas More, the Chancellor of England. The movie *A Man For All Seasons* (1966; Columbia Pictures), based on the play by Robert Bolt, depicts the life and martyrdom of St. Thomas More, who sacrificed his life rather than compromise his Catholic faith and accept Henry as the Supreme Head of the Church in England.

Henry VIII went through a total of six wives and fathered just one sickly son, Edward VI. Edward finally took his father's throne, but his reign was short due to his bad health. Mary Tudor, the daughter of Henry VIII and his first wife Catherine, a staunch Catholic, took the throne after her half-brother Edward died as a young man. Her Catholicism and marriage to Spanish royalty made her unpopular with the nobility. After Henry had broken from Rome, he'd seized all the lands owned by the Church, dissolved the monasteries, and sold their property or given it away to his court and other aristocrats. It's no wonder that the nobility didn't want a restoration of Catholicism under Queen Mary. Mary's half-sister, Elizabeth, followed Mary to the throne, re-impressing her dominion with the Anglican faith during her long reign from 1558 to 1603.

John Calvin

John Calvin, an austere Catholic layman of Switzerland, followed the ideals of Luther and established a new Calvinist church in Geneva in 1541. Calvinism frowned on most forms of entertainment and pleasure because they were presumed sinful. Calvin believed in an absolute *predestination* — that is, that a soul was damned for eternity in hell or was saved for heaven solely by an act of God's will. Being successful in business and having good health were signs of being one of the Elect or Predestined.

These ideas disseminated into parts of France, where followers were called *Huguenots*. Scotland also took a form of Calvin's new religion, with the aid of John Knox, which developed into the Presbyterian Church.

The good and bad effects of the Reformation

Martin Luther taught that Scripture alone *(sola scriptura)* and faith alone *(sola fide)* were the cornerstones of Christian religion and that the Church wasn't a necessary institution for the believer's salvation. This teaching had a domino effect, with others dissenting from Catholic doctrine and starting their own religions.

But Luther and the Protestant Reformation did compel the Catholic Church to spell out its teachings on grace, salvation, and the sacraments more clearly. It also prompted internal reforms, such as the establishment of seminaries to give unified and thorough priestly training. The Reformation instigated an internal reevaluation, not of doctrine or worship, but of how to rid the Church of abuse and to delineate exactly and precisely what differentiated Catholic Christianity from Protestant Christianity.

The Catholic Church's response: The Counter Reformation

In 1545, the Church called the general Council of Trent, which lasted more than 18 years due to wars and other interruptions, such as the death of a pope. During this age, known as the Counter Reformation, men and women who were considered outstanding in their holiness combated the attacks.

Using the printing press now to its own advantage, the Church was able to counterattack its opponents, mass-producing its catechisms, canon law, the Catholic Bible, and the lives of the saints so that many new religious communities could evangelize through their schools and parishes. Parts of Germany, Switzerland, and France that had become Protestant then returned back to the Catholic religion. The Catholic monarchs of Spain, Ferdinand and Isabella, colonized the New World, and religious orders, such as the Franciscans, Dominicans, and Jesuits, went to that vast new area, evangelizing native peoples and establishing churches, missions, and schools.

The Society of Jesus (the Jesuits) gave rise to some of the best colleges and universities in the world. A Jesuit priest often received a doctoral degree in a secular science, such as math, chemistry, biology, or law, along with his religious background of philosophy and theology. Jesuits were considered the best answer to the Reformation by using positive means to show the advantages, logical rationale, beauty, and history of Catholicism without having to resort to bitter or personal attacks against their Protestant counterparts. Jesuit missionaries preached and taught where no European had gone before: Japan, China, India, and the New World.

The Counter Reformation also gave rise to a new style of art and architecture, known as Baroque. And whereas the new Protestant faith emphasized the written Word of Scripture, Catholicism continued its ancient tradition of appealing to the symbolism used by the sacraments: tangible signs to the physical body (via the human senses) of the invisible work and presence of divine grace.

The Age of Reason

The latter half of the 16th century through the middle of the 18th century brought even more changes to the world's way of thinking — and to the Catholic Church.

Science and religion

Some people believe that Galileo Galilei (1564–1642) was ahead of his time and that the Catholic Church held back science for centuries. Actually, quite the opposite is true. Modern science and the scientific method of experimentation and observation came from Catholic monks, such as St. Albert the Great and Gregor Mendel. Albert, for example, bridged the gap between alchemy and chemistry; otherwise, science wouldn't have been taught in the medieval universities. The science being taught may have been primitive, but it was still science.

Galileo wasn't the first person to propose a *heliocentric solar system:* the idea that the sun is the center of the solar system and the earth is just one of many planets in orbit around it. The Polish monk and astronomer Nicolaus Copernicus (1473–1543) had already disproved the erroneous *Ptolemaic system:* the idea that the earth is the center of the universe and the sun and other planets revolve in orbit around it.

Galileo wasn't arrested, excommunicated, or mistreated for his scientific theory. He *was* ridiculed, however, because back then his theories lacked overwhelming and conclusive evidence. Only later did advances in astronomy and telescopes bring the needed proof.

To say that Galileo was imprisoned to keep him quiet on his heliocentric ideas is false. He was under house arrest (comfortable, mind you) only because he crossed a line by asserting that the Bible was in error when it said that the sun rose and set. He maintained that the sun was stationary and that the earth moved. His science was correct, but the Church believes his biblical theology was wrong. Those figures of speech — *the sun sets* and *the sun rises* or even just *sunrise* and *sunset* — are still used today even though everyone believes in a heliocentric, not a geocentric, universe. The Bible contains many types of literature, genres, and forms of speech, such as analogy, metaphor, and simile. Had Galileo stuck to science, he would have been okay, but he chose to publicly attack what the Church believes is the inerrancy of Sacred Scripture. That's what got him into hot water.

Faith and reason

During the middle of the 18th century, lukewarm attitudes became evident in the French Church. Religious practices and morals were in decline. Then came the view that the Church wasn't necessary and that the human mind didn't need any guidance from divine grace. Reason alone was sufficient, and faith was nonsensical. This way of thinking was called *rationalism*.

Philosophy and empirical science sought truths that the human mind could attain. Theology wasn't treated as a science but as superstition. The rationalists saw religion as a myth, and they had no respect for divine revelation. The Church taught that revelation was the divine communication of truths that human minds could never achieve — or at least not everyone in the same way. And only faith could embrace revelation.

Yet the Church believed that faith and reason could coexist — because the Church believed that God created both. Catholic theologians didn't see philosophers or scientists as the enemy. Theologians believed that theological truths known by revelation and accepted on faith didn't contradict philosophical truths known by reason or scientific truths known by observation and experimentation. Instead, they saw it all as looking at the same universe from different perspectives.

The rationalists were confident in the world, human nature, and its power. Voltaire was the famous philosopher who incorporated rationalist ideas. Through the development of his philosophy, the Enlightenment movement became an anti-Christian war machine. Jean-Baptiste Rousseau, another philosopher of the period, claimed that the world could be saved through education instead of Jesus Christ.

The Age of Revolution

The 18th century witnessed the dawn of the Industrial Revolution in England. The American and French Revolutions also occurred during this time. Many new ideas and concepts were being introduced into philosophy, religion, and society, and these ideals were embodied in a movement called the Enlightenment. The age of revolution had begun.

The French Revolution's effect on the Church

Freemasons, rationalists, and philosophers supported the extremes of the Enlightenment, laying the cornerstone for the French Revolution. In addition, many of the French aristocracy and some corrupt monarchs had oppressed the common people for too long. Unfortunately, the Church in France had become too closely bound with the state. A pronounced division existed between the upper clergy (bishops and cardinals) and the lower clergy (priests).

In 1789, the atmosphere began to change in France. Church land was taken over by the government with the understanding that the state would take care of the clergy. The following year, all monasteries and convents were suppressed. The Civil Constitution of the Clergy was enacted, and one-third of the dioceses were done away with.

In 1793, the Reign of Terror began, resulting in the execution of many (often innocent) people during the French Revolution. King Louis XVI was deposed and put to death. Hatred for the Church reached the point of insanity. Poulenc's *Dialogues of the Carmelites* (1957), a famous opera, highlights the ill effects of the French Revolution. Based on a true story, the opera portrays cloistered Carmelite nuns who refused to take the new oath and submit to the laws of suppression. It finally led them to the guillotine. This was all too common in France during that time. The Cathedral of Notre Dame in Paris, a bastion of French Catholicism, was reduced to a barracks for animals, and a statue of the goddess of reason replaced the one of the Virgin Mary.

Napoleon came to power in France and saw that the French people were basically Catholic at heart. He tried to win them to his side by making pseudo and bogus overtures to the Catholic Church. In 1801, he signed a *concordat* (Vatican treaty) with Pope Pius VII giving back Church property seized during the French Revolution and the infamous Reign of Terror. He went so far as to have the pope come to Paris and crown him emperor in the Cathedral of Notre Dame. With audacious pride, he grabbed the crown from the aged pope and literally crowned himself and then his Empress Josephine.

The Revolution drastically changed Catholicism forever — not only in France but also throughout Europe. The people of France were able to declare themselves non-Catholic or non-Christian. By the creation of a civil state, divorce became acceptable. Anti-clericalism and atheism later flourished in a country that was once called the Eldest Daughter of the Church.

The restoration of the monarchy and Church to France

The 19th century saw the restoration of the monarchy to France after the fall of the Emperor Napoleon and the chaos of the Reign of Terror. Absolute monarchies in Europe were being replaced with Constitutional ones that preserved tradition while maintaining some form of representative government, like Parliament.

Catholic schools, convents, monasteries, and seminaries were reopened. Great attention was given to clerical formation. As a result of the new freedom, the Church enjoyed a sense of renewed optimism. New religious communities were established, and new parishes and new dioceses were created. A revival in devotion commenced, and the Church believes that two great spiritual events occurred:

- ✔ In 1858, the Blessed Virgin Mary appeared 18 times to a poor peasant girl named Bernadette Soubirous in Lourdes. Even now, hundreds of thousands of people flock to Lourdes for spiritual renewal or a miracle. (See Chapters 21 and 22 for more on St. Bernadette and Lourdes, respectively.)

- ✔ The little town of Ars, France, became the home of one the holiest parish priests, St. John Vianney (1786–1859). He didn't belong to any religious order, like the Dominicans or Franciscans. Rather, he was a diocesan priest (see Chapter 6), the first diocesan priest to be canonized. Today, he's the patron saint of all parish priests. His work and evangelization became a hallmark to be studied and copied by every priest.

The Oxford Movement in England

In England, with the Act of Emancipation in 1829, the Catholic Church was allowed freedom of worship — something that had been denied since the Reign of Henry VIII. As a result, a great renaissance in the faith occurred. Religious communities were able to come from Italy and preach, teach, and commence devotions.

At this time, a great revival also occurred in the Anglican Church, the official Church of England. It was known as the Oxford Movement (1833–1845), and it attempted to recapture many Catholic doctrines and to introduce many of the customs, traditions, rituals, pageantry, and color of the Catholic Church. Up until then, the Anglican Church had leaned toward the Puritan style: few vestments and little use of liturgical colors, statues, candles, and so on. In other words, the Oxford Movement attempted to Romanize belief and worship while retaining the Anglican identity.

One of the great supporters of this movement was Blessed John Henry Newman. An Anglican minister and professor at Oxford, he became influenced by the Catholic Church and later converted to Catholicism. He then became a cardinal and joined the Oratory of St. Philip Neri.

A revival of Catholicism was beginning in England.

Catholicism in the New World

In the New World, the Catholic Church was firmly planted in French Canada and Spanish Central and South America, but in the Protestant colonies of

England that would eventually become the United States, the Catholic Church grew slowly in the face of anti-Catholic prejudice and bias.

In 1792, Fr. John Carroll became the first bishop of the United States in Baltimore, Maryland, which had been colonized by Lord Calvert, a Catholic. From this colony, the Catholic faith spread by a priest who celebrated Mass secretly in Catholic homes during this time of persecution. Fr. Ferdinand Farmer provided for the spiritual and sacramental needs of Catholics already living in the colonies up to New York. By his hard work and effort, many converts were made, and by 1808, a new diocese was established in New York, Philadelphia, Bardstown (KY), and Boston.

The conversion of St. Elizabeth Ann Bailey Seton, a wealthy Episcopalian, to Catholicism saw the establishment of a new religious community devoted to education: the Sisters of Charity. The Episcopalian Church is the American — post revolution — version of the Anglican Church in England. In 1791, the first American seminary and Catholic college were established: St. Mary's Seminary in Baltimore, and Georgetown University in Washington, D.C. The early 19th century saw an increase in many orders dedicated to education, such as the Christian Brothers, Brothers of the Holy Cross, the Religious Sisters of Mercy, Sisters of St. Joseph of Chestnut Hill), Sisters of St. Francis, and the Xaverian Brothers.

Nuns and brothers of the immigrants' own nationality followed the different waves of immigration. These nuns and brothers were able to speak the immigrants' own language, making it possible for their children to enter into the life of the New World without losing their faith. The New World was a new continent on which to reestablish the Catholic Church.

But during the 19th century, with the increase of immigration from Catholic countries of eastern, southern, and central Europe, as well as Ireland, bigotry against Catholics increased. In New York, the Know Nothing party was established, and it provoked riots and the burning of Catholic churches. In Boston, convents were burned down. The Ku Klux Klan, which became very powerful in the 1920s, included Catholics and Catholic churches on its list of targets, along with Jews and blacks.

However, by the end of the 19th century, the Church was firmly planted and rooted in the American soil. And in the early part of the 20th century, the United States wasn't considered missionary territory anymore.

The Modern Era

Roughly at the same time as the First Vatican Council (1869–1870), which defined the doctrine of Papal Infallibility (see Chapter 6), the Italian unification process took shape under Victor Emmanuel, threatening the Papal States. Back in the 8th century, the Carolingian Frankish King Pepin the Short, who was the father of Charlemagne, had given the Papal States (*Patrimonium Petri*) to the pope for his secular rule. The temporal powers of the pope were threatened by the unification of Italy, especially because Rome was the center of the Papal States and the future capital of a unified Italy. Indeed, the pope lost his temporal power in 1870. However, he would later be recognized as the head of state of the smallest independent nation of the world: 0.44 square miles. (To accomplish this, Vatican City and the Republic of Italy signed the Lateran Treaty in 1929.)

In the late 19th century, Europe was undergoing many changes. Areas that were parts of empires became separate countries. This era defined France, Germany, and Italy as countries. Germany formed a nation and saw the pope as a threat to its unification. Chancellor Otto von Bismarck (1815–1898) passed laws that persecuted the Catholic Church in Germany. This conflict between the Catholic and German government was called the *kulturkampf* (literally, "conflict of cultures"). This environment led to a vast emigration of German Catholics fleeing persecution in the fatherland to the United States.

In this setting, Leo XIII (1878–1903) became pope. The Industrial Revolution was also in full swing in England, Germany, and the United States at this time. The common rights of workers were threatened and denied. As a result, Pope Leo wrote the magnificent papal encyclical *Rerum Novarum* on the sanctity of human work, dignity of workers, and the justice that's owed to them. He condemned all sorts of radical stances, such as extreme capitalism and atheistic communism, while defending the rights of private property and the right to form guilds or trade unions. This social encyclical gave the impetus for Catholic unions in the United States.

Pope St. Pius X (1903–1914) followed the reign of Leo XIII. He was known as the pope of the children. He extended the right to receive Holy Communion to all Catholic children who had reached the age of reason — 7 years old. Also, he composed a syllabus of errors. In it he condemned certain tenets of *modernism,* a heresy that denied aspects of the faith and accepted all sorts of progressivism to the point that it damaged the integrity of the faith. To be a modernist didn't mean that you were a modern thinker and able to communicate to your contemporaries. Rather, to get its message across, modernism used falsehoods to prove its point. If anything, modernism was nothing more than elaborate academic skepticism run rampant.

World wars, communism, and fascism

World War I (1914–18), the war that was supposed to end all wars, was truly bloody. Many lives were lost on both sides, and in the end, the Austrian Hungarian Empire was divided up. People in the old empire who hated

Austria saw that the Church was in line with the old regime; therefore, the Church was persecuted in these areas. Otto von Bismarck and his Germany were defeated, going into deep economic depression.

When a worldwide depression hit in 1929, fascism gained power. Europe was in turmoil. In Spain, anti-Catholic communists combated royalists in a terrible civil war. As in the French Revolution, many Catholic priests and sisters were martyred. However, under General Francisco Franco (1892–1975), the communists were defeated in 1939. Though the Church was able to flourish, Spain remained under Franco's dictatorship until the 1970s.

Italy, ruled by the House of Savoy after its unification in 1870, came under the influence of the fascist dictator Benito Mussolini (1883–1945) in 1928. Later, he teamed up with Adolf Hitler (1889–1945) during World War II (1939–1945). It was in Nazi Germany that fascism reached the depth of depravity and evil.

The Church was unanimously against the evils of communism on the one hand and fascism on the other. With the onslaught of World War II, Pope Pius XII (1939–1958) diplomatically tried to help those affected by the diabolical evil of Adolf Hitler. Though maligned terribly by some in the secular press today, Pius XII actively worked for the safety of the Jewish people. Shortly after his election as pope (March 2, 1939), the Nazi newspaper *Berliner Morganpost* blasted the news that his papal election wasn't popular in Germany because he was well known as a Nazi opponent.

At one point during the war, the Vatican, considered neutral territory by the Geneva Conference, hid and cared for up to 3,500 Jews. Through its *nuncios* (ambassadors), the Church falsified documents to aid Jews by providing fictitious baptismal certificates that identified them as Catholic Christians. Many priests, nuns, and Catholic laymen lost their lives rescuing and sheltering their brother and sister Jews. Recently released Vatican records indicate that the Catholic Church operated an underground railroad that rescued 800,000 European Jews from the Holocaust.

Pope Pius XII accomplished a lot to help the Jews during World War II, but the most eloquent testimony to his efforts is the conversion of the chief Rabbi of Rome, Israele Anton Zolli, to Roman Catholicism in 1945 in appreciation. He even took the baptismal name Eugenio because it was Pius XII's baptismal name. When Pius XII died, Prime Minister Golda Meir sent a eulogy praising him for his efforts during the war to help Jews.

The Church's rocky road in Eastern Europe

Czarist Russia fell to the Communists in 1917 during World War I. As a result, a godless government came into being that later proved to be a nemesis for the Orthodox Church, as well as the Catholic Church in Eastern Europe. After

World War II, many of the Eastern countries were occupied by the U.S.S.R. This godless state actively persecuted the Church and anyone who belonged to it. Bishops couldn't be appointed to their diocese. Seminaries were illegal. The Catholic faith stayed alive in Eastern Europe because of the underground Church.

Let the sun shine in

Not all was gloom and doom after World War II. The Catholic Church greatly expanded in the United States. From 1910 to 1930, the population of the United States grew tremendously as a result of a vast emigration from Southern and Eastern Europe, which were mainly Catholic countries. By the 1950s, these emigrant groups grew financially, politically, and socially. The 1950s saw a rise in vocations to the priesthood and religious life. Churches, seminaries, schools, colleges, universities, hospitals, and other institutions grew tremendously.

With the death of Pius XII, a new era in the Church began with the reign of Pope John XXIII (1958–1963). Some of the man-made customs that had crept into the Church since the Council of Trent were archaic and needed reform. John XXIII called for a new council, the Second Vatican Council (1962–1965), also known as Vatican II. One year into the Council, John XXIII died. Paul VI (1963–1978) was elected after him and concluded the council. The council didn't define any new doctrines, nor did it substantially alter any. It didn't abolish any Catholic traditions or devotions but asked that they be kept in proper perspective to the revealed truths of the faith and subservient to the Sacred Liturgy of the Church. Vatican II didn't create new teaching but explained the ancient faith in new ways to address new issues and concerns. (See Chapter 10 for more on Vatican II.)

Paul VI wrote many *encyclicals* (letters from the pope addressed to the world), his most famous one being titled *Humanae Vitae* or *On Human Life*. It challenged modern-day society, which had given in to the contraceptive men- tality. He predicted in 1968 that if people didn't respect human life from the beginning, they wouldn't respect it in the end. He claimed that artificial con- traception would lead to an increase in abortions, divorce, broken families, and other social troubles. Twenty-five years later on the anniversary of the encyclical, Pope John Paul II wrote another encyclical, titled *Gospel of Life*. In it, he stated that the warnings of Paul VI had come true. (See Chapter 14 for more on the controversial issues addressed by the Church.)

Paul VI died on August 6, 1978, and John Paul I was elected his successor 20 days later. He chose to take the names of his two most immediate predecessors, John XXIII and Paul VI, the two popes of the Second Vatican Council. Unfortu- nately, he lived only one month as pope and died mysteriously in his sleep on September 28, 1978. Rumors abound about the circumstances of his untimely demise, but nothing credible has ever been established or demonstrated.

John Paul II

On October 16, 1978, Karol Cardinal Wojtyla was elected pope and became Pope John Paul II. (See Chapter 20 for details on his life.) During his pontificate, the Berlin Wall fell, the Soviet Union collapsed, and much of the world went to war in the Persian Gulf. Though the Church faces new problems at the beginning of the 21st century, the encouraging words of John Paul II as he began his reign re-echo: "Be not afraid."

The Polish Pope reigned for 26 years until his death on April 2, 2005. John Paul II was the first pope to visit a Jewish Synagogue since St. Peter and the first pope ever to visit an Islamic Mosque. Prior to the papacy of John Paul II, most people had to go to Rome to see the Pope. His papal visits to other countries and World Youth Day (a bi-annual international gathering of young people in different countries each time) made the Bishop of Rome a familiar face even to non-Catholics in many parts of the world. Accessibility via the travels and modern media made the papacy itself a more international player in world affairs.

Back home in Rome, Pope John Paul II accomplished two historic milestones. First was the revision of the Code of Canon Law in 1983. Second was the implementation of the Catechism of the Catholic Church in 1992. Canon Law is the set of rules and regulations that govern the Catholic Church around the world, at the Vatican, in the local diocese, and even in the neighborhood parish. It affects cardinals, bishops, priests, deacons, religious men and women, and the largest group in the church, the lay faithful. Canon Law had not been revised since 1917 and desperately needed an overhaul to keep up with the changes in the modern world.

The previous universal Catechism was from the Council of Trent in the 16th century. A *Catechism* is a collection of official church dogmas and doctrines that all Catholics are obliged to know and believe. They are based on teachings rooted in Sacred Scripture and/or Sacred Tradition. All religion books for children and adults are to be based on the doctrines contained in the Catechism.

Pope John Paul II was credited with a significant role in the demise of the Soviet Union, along with U.S. President Ronald Reagan and Great Britain's Prime Minister Margaret Thatcher. His frequent visits and communications with Polish Solidarity leader Lech Walesa helped promote hope and encouragement that human rights, especially religious freedom, could be achieved even behind the Iron Curtain. John Paul II was diagnosed with Parkinson's Disease in 1993 at the age of 73. Although plagued with health problems, he stayed active until his death in 2005.

Pope Benedict XVI

Josef Cardinal Ratzinger was elected to succeed John Paul II at the papal conclave that took place on April 18 and 19, 2005. Pope John Paul II had named him the Prefect of the Sacred Congregation for the Doctrine of the Faith (CDF) in 1981. He held this post until his election as pope. During his tenure in the CDF, Cardinal Ratzinger was known for his staunch orthodoxy and for being totally loyal and obedient to the Magisterium and the pope.

In April 2008, Pope Benedict XVI (or *B16,* as he's sometimes called) made his first visit to the United States since becoming pope. Two years later, he made the first state visit of the Vatican to Great Britain and was officially received by Her Majesty Queen Elizabeth II.

Benedict XVI issued the motu proprio *Summorum Pontificum* on July 7, 2007, which granted universal usage of the Extraordinary Form of the Roman Rite (formerly known as the Traditional Latin Mass, TLM, or the Tridentine Mass). It had been replaced with the Novus Ordo Mass of Pope Paul VI, which was issued in 1969 in response to the Second Vatican Council. The Ordinary Form of the Roman Rite remains the Mass of Paul VI used in most parishes around the world in the Latin Rite.

Appendix B

Popular Catholic Prayers

The following are some of the most ancient and most beloved prayers of Catholic Christianity. Most are learned from mom and dad and reiterated by religion teachers and pastors alike. All of these prayers are rooted in Sacred Scripture, Sacred Tradition, and/or popular piety. While never mandatory, these formal prayers theologically and spiritually express what the Church officially teaches and believes.

Catholics can go to either Eastern or Latin Catholic Churches, receive Holy Communion in either one, and pray any prayer said in either the East or West (check out Chapter 1 for more explanation of these two main lungs of the Church).

Latin Rite (Western Catholic) Prayers

The prayers in this section are traditionally learned by Catholics in the West; check them out in both English and Latin.

Our Father (Pater Noster)

Our Father
Who art in heaven
Hallowed be thy name.
Thy kingdom come,
Thy will be done,
On earth, as it is in heaven.
Give us this day
our daily bread,
And forgive us our trespasses,
as we forgive those
who trespass against us.
And lead us not into
temptation,
But deliver us from evil.
Amen.

Pater Noster
qui es in caelis,
sanctificetur nomen tuum.
Adveniat regnum tuum.
Fiat voluntas tua,
sicut in caelo et in terra.
Panem nostrum quotidianum
da nobis hodie,
et dimitte nobis debita nostra,
sicut et nos
dimittimus debitoribus nostris.
Et ne nos inducas in
tentationem:
sed libera nos a malo.
Amen.

Hail Mary (Ave Maria)

Hail Mary, full of grace
The Lord is with thee
Blessed art thou among
women
and blessed is the fruit of thy
womb, Jesus
Holy Mary, mother of God
Pray for us sinners
Now and at the hour of our
death.
Amen.

Ave Maria, gratia plena,
Dominus tecum
Benedicta tu in mulieribus,
et benedictus fructus ventris
tui, Iesus
Sancta Maria, Mater Dei
ora pro nobis peccatoribus,
nunc, et in hora mortis
nostrae.
Amen.

Glory Be

Glory be to the Father
and to the Son
and to the Holy Spirit
as it was in the beginning
is now and ever shall be
world without end.
Amen.

Gloria Patri
et Filii
et Spiritui Sancto.
Sicut erat in principio
et nunc et semper
et in saecula saeculorum.
Amen.

Salve Regina

Hail, holy Queen, Mother of
Mercy;
our life, our sweetness,
and our hope.
To thee do we cry, poor
banished children of Eve;
to thee do we send up our
sighs,
mourning and weeping
in this valley of tears.
Turn, then, most gracious
advocate,
thine eyes of mercy towards
us;
and after this our exile,
show unto us the blessed fruit
of thy womb, Jesus. O
clement, O loving, O sweet
Virgin Mary

Salve Regina,
Mater misericordiae.
Vita, dulcedo, et spes nostra,
salve.
Ad te clamamus exsules filii
Hevae.
Ad te Suspiramus,
gementes et flentes
in hac lacrimarum valle.
Eia ergo, Advocata nostra,
illos tuos
misericordes oculos
ad nos converte.
Et Iesum, benedictum fructum
ventris tui,
nobis post hoc exsilium
ostende.
O clemens, o pia, o dulcis
Virgo Maria.

Memorare

Remember,
O most gracious Virgin
Mary,
that never was it known
that anyone who fled to thy
protection,
implored thy help,
or sought thine intercession,
was left unaided.

Inspired by this confidence,
I fly unto thee,
O Virgin of virgins, my
mother;
to thee do I come,
before thee I stand, sinful
and sorrowful.
O Mother of the Word
Incarnate,
despise not my petitions,
but in thy mercy hear and
answer me.
Amen.

Memorare,
O piissima Virgo Maria,
non esse auditum a saeculo,
quemquam ad tua currentem
praesidia,
tua implorantem auxilia,
tua petentem suffragia,
esse derelictum.

Ego tali animatus confidentia,
ad te,
Virgo Virginum, Mater,
curro,
ad te venio,
coram te gemens peccator
assisto.
Noli, Mater Verbi,
verba mea despicere;
sed audi propitia et exaudi.
Amen.

Act of Contrition

O, my God,
I am heartily sorry
for having offended you.
I detest all my sins
because of your just
punishment,
but most of all
because they offend you,
my God, who are all-good
and deserving of all my love.
I firmly resolve,
with the help of Your grace,
to sin no more
and to avoid the near
occasions of sin.
Amen.

Deus meus,
ex toto corde paenitet me
omnium meorum peccatorum,
eaque detestor, quia
peccando,
non solum poenas a Te iuste
statutas promeritus sum,
sed praesertim quia offendi
Te,
summum bonum, ac dignum
qui super omnia diligaris.
Ideo firmiter propono,
adiuvante gratia Tua,
de cetero me non peccaturum
peccandique occasiones
proximas fugiturum.
Amen.

Alternative Translation

O, my God, I am heartily sorry
for having offended Thee,
and I detest all my sins
because I dread the loss of Heaven and the pains of Hell.
But most of all,
because I have offended Thee
Who art all good
and deserving of all my love.
I firmly resolve,
with the help of Thy grace
To confess my sins, to do penance,
and to amend my life.
Amen.

Prayer to Guardian Angel

Angel of God,
my guardian dear,
to whom God's love
commits me here,
ever this day be at my side,
to light and guard,
to rule and guide.
Amen.

Angele Dei,
qui custos es mei,
me, tibi commissum pietate
superna,
illumina, custodi,
rege et gubérna.
Amen.

Grace Before/After Meals

Before

Bless us O Lord,
and these Thy gifts
which we are about to receive
from Thy bounty.
Through Christ Our Lord.
Amen.

Benedic Domine,
nos et haec tua dona
quae de tua largitate
sumus sumpturi
per Christum Dominum
Nostrum.
Amen.

After

We give Thee thanks
for all Thy benefits,
O Almighty God,
Who livest and reignest
forever.
And may the souls of the
faithful departed,
through the mercy of God,
rest in peace.
Amen.

Agimus tibi gratias,
omnipotens Deus,
pro universis beneficiis tuis,
qui vivis et regnas in saecula
saeculorum.
Fidelium animae,
per misericordiam Dei,
requiescant in pace.
Amen.

Prayer to St. Michael the Archangel

Saint Michael the Archangel,
defend us in battle;
be our defense against
the wickedness and snares
of the devil.
May God rebuke him, we
humbly pray.
And do thou,
O prince of the heavenly host,
by the power of God
cast into hell Satan
and all the evil spirits
who prowl about the world
seeking the ruin of souls.
Amen.

Sancte Michael Archangele,
defende nos in proelio,
contra nequitiamet
et insidias diaboli esto
praesidium.
Imperet illi Deus, supplices
deprecamur:
tuque, Princeps militia
coelestis,
Satanam aliosque spiritus
malignos,
qui ad perditionem animarum
pervagantur in mundo, divina
virtute,
in infernum detrude.
Amen.

Act of Faith

O my God, I firmly believe that Thou art one God in Three Divine Persons, Father, Son and Holy Spirit. I believe that Thy Divine Son became Man, and died for our sins, and that He will come to judge the living and the dead. I believe these and all the truths which the Holy Catholic Church teaches, because Thou hast revealed them, Who canst neither deceive nor be deceived.

Act of Hope

O my God, relying on Thy almighty power and infinite mercy and promises, I hope to obtain pardon of my sins, the help of Thy grace, and Life everlasting, through the merits of Jesus Christ, my Lord and Redeemer.

Act of Love (Charity)

O my God, I love Thee above all things, with my whole heart and soul, because Thou art all-good and worthy of all love. I love my neighbor as myself for the love of Thee. I forgive all who have injured me, and ask pardon of all whom I have injured.

Byzantine and Eastern Catholic Prayers

The following prayers originated in the East but can be prayed by anyone. Wherever you see a plus sign (+) within a prayer, make the Sign of the Cross.

Prayer before meals

O Christ God, bless + the food and drink of Your servants for You are holy always, now and ever, and forever. Amen.

Prayer after meals

We thank You, Christ our God, for You have satisfied us with the good things of Your earth. Do not deprive us of Your heavenly kingdom, but as You appeared to Your disciples, O Savior, granting them peace, come also to us and save us.

Lord have mercy, Lord have mercy, Lord have mercy.

Give the blessing. Blessed is our God who, through His grace and loving kindness, is merciful to us and nourishes us from the abundance of His gifts, always, now and ever, and forever. Amen.

Prayer of the Publican

God, have mercy on me, a sinner + (Bow)

God, cleanse me of my sins and have mercy on me + (Bow)

I have sinned without number, forgive me, O Lord + (Bow)

Prayer of St. Ephraim of Syria

O Lord, Master of my life, grant that I may not be infected with the spirit of slothfulness and inquisitiveness, with the spirit of ambition and vain talking.

Grant instead to me, your servant, the spirit of purity and humility, the spirit of patience and neighborly love.

O Lord and King, bestow upon me the grace of being aware of my sins and not thinking evil of those of my brethren.

Prayer to St. Maron

O Lord, accept the prayers we offer in memory of our Father, St. Maron. Bless and protect the people who bear your name. Make us worthy of his holy legacy that we may carry the message of your Gospel throughout the world. Grant faithfulness to his people and courage to his inheritance.

Index

• A •

abortion
  canon law and, 182
  Catholic teachings about, 19, 219, 228–231
  living the Commandments and, 195
  receiving communion and, 120
Abraham (prophet), 1, 50, 57, 101
absolution, 136–137, 141–142
abstinence. *See* fasting and abstaining; Natural Family Planning
accessories. *See* sacramental accessories
accidents, 106, 159
Act of Contrition. *See* Catholic prayers
Adam and Eve. *See* Garden of Eden
adoption, 241
adoration and veneration, 189–190, 248, 294–296
Adoration of the Blessed Sacrament, 311–312
adultery, 196–199, 215
Advent, season of, 171–172
Agca, Mehmet Ali (assassin), 206, 334
Age of Reason, 30, 381–382
Age of Revolution, 382–385
Agnus Dei (Lamb of God), 162
Albert the Great (Saint), 346, 381
Albigensian heresy, 344
alcohol/alcohol abuse, 196, 205, 209, 216
Alexander V (Pope), 374
Alexander VI (Pope), 83
Alexandrian Rite, 98
almsgiving, 257
Ambrose (Saint), 55
Angelicum University (Rome), 333, 335
angels/angelic life, 36, 40–41, 305–306
anger, sin of, 215–216

Anglican Church, 238, 379
animals/animal life
  God as Creator, 30, 35
  instinct and reason, 178–179, 198, 215
  intelligent design, 39
  mistreatment of, 196
  reproduction and, 282
Anne (Saint), 275, 292, 303, 359
annulments, 127–128, 132
Annunciation, 231, 275
Anointing of the Sick, 12, 15–16, 88, 143–144
Anthony Maria Zaccari (Saint), 314
Anthony of Padua (Saint), 327, 345–346
anti-Catholic prejudice, 336, 338, 385
Antichrist (Evil One), 44–46
Antiochian Rite, 98
anti-Semitism, 31, 62
Apocalypse. *See* Book of Revelation
apostasy, 136
apostles, 59, 69, 71, 135. *See also apostles by name*
Apostles' Creed. *See* Catholic prayers
apostolic nuncio, 85
apostolic succession, 66, 68, 71
apparitions and visions, 287–290
archbishops/archdiocese, 85–87
architecture and art, 55, 103. *See also* sacramental accessories; sacred art
Arianism, 62–63, 156
Aristotle (philosopher), 59
artificial conception, 197–198, 238, 241–242
artificial contraception, 238–239
artificial insemination, 193, 241
Ascension of Christ to heaven, 31, 172, 263
Ash Wednesday, 104, 172, 184, 317
ashes at Lent, 20, 320–321

Assumption of Mary, 29, 80, 169–170
astrology (horoscopes), 188
attendance at Mass
  full participation, 147
  holy days, 169–170
  moral obligation, 16, 192
  precept of the Church, 17
  televised Mass, 154
  weekday, 169
Augustine (Saint), 116, 201, 234, 293, 306, 368
Augustinian order, 91–92
auxiliary bishops, 88–89

• B •

Babylonian Captivity (Avignon papacy), 372–374
bad habits. *See* seven deadly sins
Baptism
  about, 107–108
  beliefs, 11–12, 108–110
  by blood, 115–116
  ceremony, 112–114
  creating unity, 66–67
  by desire, 116–117
  forgiveness from sin, 32
  godparents, 111–112
  grace of, 12, 15–16, 70
  holy water as symbol, 100
  profession of faith, 30
  RCIA program, 72
  use of Chrism Oil, 88, 105
  by water, 110–111
Baptism of the Lord, 171–172
baptismal names, 294
basilicas. *See* churches
Beatific Vision, 40
beatification, 297, 299
Beatitudes, 27–28, 57–58, 277
Benedict IX (Pope), 75, 83
Benedict of Nursia (Saint), 304, 343, 366, 368
Benedict XI (Pope), 372
Benedict XIII (Pope), 374

Benedict XVI (Pope), 68, 74, 77, 82–83, 166, 252, 303, 334, 390

Benedictine order, 91–92, 366–367

Benediction, 312–313, 347

Bernadette Soubirous (Saint), 12, 289, 348–349

Bible. *See also* New Testament; Old Testament; Gospels
about the history, 2, 24
basic Catholic beliefs, 11
combining Old and New Testaments, 56
inspiration from Holy Spirit, 78
interpretation, 24–25
oral tradition, 25–27
as oral tradition, 55
reading as prayer, 248
readings at Mass, 152–154
references to Mary, 275, 277
revealed Word of God, 23–24
translation to Latin, 45, 56, 194

The Bible For Dummies (Geoghegan and Homan), 25

Big Bang theory, 37

birth control. *See also* Natural Family Planning
about, 19, 219
contraceptives, 230, 238–239
premarital instruction, 127
rhythm method, 240

birth control pills, 238, 240

birth rate, 239

Bishop of Rome, 9, 14–15

bishops
appointment of, 86
authority, 71, 86–87
celebration of the sacraments, 133
celibacy, 221, 223
eligibility to be Pope, 75
episcopal conferences, 87
successor of Apostles, 15

bishop's chair (*cathedra*), 80, 87

"Black Madonna of Czestochowa," 288, 354–355

Blaise (Saint), 104, 321, 326

blasphemy, 184, 190

Blessed Sacrament. *See also* consecration of bread and wine; Holy Eucharist
Adoration, 311–312
Benediction, 312–313

Blessed Virgin. *See* Virgin Mary

blessing of palms. *See* Palm Sunday

blessing of throats, 104, 321, 326

Body of Christ. *See* Mystical Body of Christ

Bojaxhiu, Agnes Gonxha. *See* Mother Teresa of Calcutta

Bonaventure (Saint), 372

Boniface VIII (Pope), 372

Book of Revelation, 46, 55, 277–278, 341, 365

Borgia, Cesare and Lucrezia, 83

"born again," baptism as being, 108–109

Boy's Town (Omaha, Neb.), 338–339

Breviary. *See* Liturgy of the Hours

brothers/friars. *See* religious communities

Buddhism and Taoism, 252, 268

Bulls and Briefs, 80–81. *See also* papal documents

Byzantine Rite, 13, 98

• C •

Calvin, John (theologian), 379–380

Canon law (Ecclesiastical law). *See also* Code of Canon Law
authority and categories, 175–176, 180
defined, 14, 180–181
interpretation, 85
Latin as language of, 166
papal authority and, 182
punishments, 181–182
relation to civil law, 182
vacations for priests, 91
women's role in, 228

Canonical Books, 26–27

canonization of the saints, 296–303

Canterbury Tales (Chaucer), 211, 371

capital punishment, 195–196, 219, 233–234

Capuchin order, 350

cardinal virtues
about, 258–259
Catholic teachings, 204
fortitude, 209–210
justice, 206–208
prudence, 204–206
temperance, 208–209

cardinals. *See* Catholic hierarchy; College of Cardinals

Carroll, John (priest), 385

catechumens, 115–116

catacombs, 61, 351

Catechism of the Catholic Church
authority of, 1, 11
baptism by blood, 116
baptism by desire, 117
The Creed, 29
definition of faith, 22
John Paul II revision, 334
marriage and family, 243
references to *Summa Theologica*, 346

cathedral, 80, 87. *See also* churches

Catherine Laboure (Saint), 268, 289

Catherine of Siena (Saint), 213, 301, 372

catholic (universality), 68

Catholic Bible, 25–27

Catholic Church. *See also* Church/church
about the history, 2
basic beliefs, 9–10
four marks of, 67–68
implementation of *Roman Missal*, 149
interpretation of Scripture, 24–27
Jesus as founder, 13
membership, 72
non-Catholics, 120
universal church, 13, 68
Vatican II and, 180

Catholic hierarchy. *See also* clergy; Magisterium; pope/papal authority
authority and role, 14–15
cardinals, 15, 74–76, 84–85

Christ as creator, 71–72
clergy titles and roles, 73,
84–92, 88–89
consecrated religious, 92–94
Catholic Hour (NBC radio
program), 335
Catholic Mass For Dummies
(Trigilio, Brighenti, and
Cafone), 145
Catholic prayers. *See also*
prayer
Act of Contrition, 137,
140–141, 393–394
Act of Faith, 395
Act of Hope, 396
Act of Love, 396
Angelus, 323
Apostles' Creed, 11, 29,
30–33, 113
Confiteor, 150
Gloria, 151
Glory Be, 392
Grace at meals, 394–395
Hail Mary, 392
Kyrie, 150
Memorare, 393
Nicene Creed, 155–156
Orthodox, 396–397
Our Father, 3, 11, 161–162,
254–256, 391
Prayer to Guardian
Angel, 394
Prayer to St. Michael,
322, 395
Salve Regina, 392
Catholic schools, 90
Catholic traditions. *See also*
Sacred Tradition
about the practice of, 20, 311
adoration of the Blessed
Sacrament, 311–312
beatification and
canonization, 303
Benediction, 312–313, 347
blessing of throats, 321
blessing religious items,
319–320
celibacy, 220–225
exorcism, 321–322
fasting and abstinence, 317–319
40-hour devotion, 313–316
palms and ashes, 320–321
preservation of Latin, 166

processions, 316–317
tolling of bells, 322–323
wedding etiquette, 131
Catholic University, 335
Catholic worship. *See*
sacramental accessories;
symbols and gestures;
vestments and clothing
Catholicism
Abrahamic origins, 1
Apostolic Church, 28–29
basic beliefs, 3, 9–10, 17
controversial issues, 219
heresies, 61–64
as one true religion, 117
practicing the faith, 15–20, 30
Catholicism, history (in
chronological order)
non-Christian Rome (A.D.
33-312), 363–365
Christian Rome (A.D. 313-475),
363–365
fall of Rome (A.D. 475-570),
366–367
Gregory the Great to Charles
Martel (A.D. 590-741),
367–368
early Middle Ages
(A.D. 800-1000s), 368–370
mid-Middle Ages
(A.D. 1000s-1300s),
371–372
late Middle Ages
(A.D. 1300s-1500s),
372–375
early Reformation
(A.D.1515-1545), 375–380
Counter-Reformation
(A.D. 1545-1650), 380–381
Age of Reason
(A.D. 1650-1700s), 381–382
Age of Revolution
(A.D. 1700s-1800s),
382–385
Modern Era (A.D.
1800s-present), 385–390
celibacy
biblical background, 222
Catholic teaching, 19, 219–221
Church tradition, 28, 93,
221–222
dispensation to marry, 134
Eastern Orthodox, 220–221
of Jesus Christ, 49

priest shortages, 220, 223
pros and cons of, 223–225
sexual abuse, 225–226
Chair of St. Peter. *See* pope/
papal authority
chalice. *See* sacramental
accessories
Charlemagne (emperor),
221, 368, 369
chastity
virtue of, 215
vow of, 67, 91, 94, 343, 348, 366
Chaucer, Geoffrey (author),
211, 371
Chesterton, Gilbert Keith
(author), 339
Chrism Mass, 87–88, 105
Chrism Oil (Sacred Chrism),
88, 113, 123
Chrismation (Orthodox
Confirmation), 114
Christianity
Abrahamic origins, 1
Apostolic Church, 28–29
belief in Triune God, 51
Catholicism as true
religion, 117
creationism and evolution,
38–39
early persecution, 12, 60–61,
83, 115–116
evangelical and
fundamentalist, 45, 108,
182, 238
split from Judaism, 26
Christmas, 170–172
Christological heresies, 61–64
Christopher (Saint), 268
Church calendar.
See liturgical year
Church law. *See also* Canon
law; precepts of the
Church
about the authority of, 175
categories of, 175–176
divine positive law, 176–177
natural moral law, 177–179
right to appeal, 182
Church of Scientology
(Dianetics), 62, 188
Church/church. *See also*
Catholic Church
about the meaning of, 13–14
Body of Christ, 66–67

Church/church *(continued)*
  Bride of Christ, 225
  communion of the saints, 67,
    304–310
  continuing Christ's mission,
    69–72
  defined, 2, 32, 65
  founding by Christ, 65–66
  home as Church, 100
  Mary as Mother, 279–280
  Second Coming of Christ,
    44–46
  societas perfects (perfect
    society), 72
churches
  Basilica de Guadalupe
    (Mexico), 353
  Basilica of Czestochowa
    (Poland), 354–355
  Basilica of Lourdes (France),
    289, 348–349, 355–356
  Basilica of St. John Lateran
    (Rome), 71, 87
  Basilica of St. Peter (Rome),
    71, 87
  Cathedral of Notre Dame
    (Paris), 102, 357–358
  Minor Basilica of Saint Anne
    de Beaupré (Quebec), 359
  National Shrine of the
    Immaculate Conception
    (Washington, DC),
    358–359
  Rome as city of, 351–353
  San Giovanni Rotondo (Italy),
    354
Cicero (philosopher), 178
civil law
  authority of, 179–180
  canon law relation to, 182
  capital punishment, 195–196,
    219, 233–234
  commutative justice, 206–207
  distributive justice, 207
  Just War Doctrine, 234–237
  natural moral law, 178–179
  property rights, 199
  social justice, 208
Clare (Saint), 93
Clement (Pope), 66
Clement V (Pope), 372–373

clergy. *See also* Catholic
    hierarchy; consecrated
    religious
  authority of, 133
  bishops, 86–87
  cardinals, 84–86
  deacons, 92
  laicization, 134
  ordination, 132–133
  parish priests, 89–92
  pastoral formation, 133–134
  priests, 89–92
  role in Body of Christ, 66–67
  role in Mass, 16–17
  sexual abuse, 225–226
  vicars general, 88–89
  women as, 19, 226–228
Cletus (Pope), 66
cloistered communities, 93–94
cloning, 198, 242
clothing. *See* vestments and
    clothing
Code of Canon Law, 166, 180,
    182–183, 319, 334, 389. *See
    also* Canon law
College of Bishops, 74
College of Cardinals
  appointment to, 71, 85
  papal election, 74–77
Columbus, Christopher
    (explorer), 339–340
Commandments. *See* Ten
    Commandments
Communion. *See* Holy
    Eucharist
communion of the saints
  about the levels of, 304
  Church Militant, 306–307
  Church Suffering, 307–310
  Church Triumphant, 305–306
  defined in The Creed, 32
  Mass as, 147
  seeing Church as, 66–67
conception
  creation of life, 229
  Natural Family Planning, 240
  outside of sex, 197–198, 238,
    241–242
conclave, 76, 86
concupiscence, 43, 215
condoms, 239

Conferences of Catholic
    Bishops, 87
Confession. *See* Penance
confessional, 138
Confirmation
  about, 107, 121
  RCIA program, 72
  religious education, 122
  source of grace, 12, 15–16
  sponsors, 123
  understanding, 123
  use of Chrism Oil, 88, 105
Confirmation name, 123, 294
Confraternity of Christian
    Doctrine (CCD), 121–122,
    185–186
Congregation for the Causes of
    Saints, 302
Congregations, Vatican, 85
consecrated religious. *See*
    religious communities
consecration of bread and
    wine. *See also* Holy
    Eucharist
  Catholic beliefs, 118–119
  Christ as Real Presence, 148
  Eucharistic prayer, 158–159
  transubstantiation, 79, 106,
    159, 160
consistory, 85
Constantine (emperor), 61, 62,
    83, 115
Constantinopolitan Rite, 98
consubstantiation, 63, 156
contraception. *See* birth
    control
contraceptive, 230, 238
contrition (sorrow for sin),
    140–141, 248–249, 294
convents. *See* religious
    communities
conversion, 93, 108, 123, 256
Corporal Works of Mercy. *See*
    works of mercy
Corpus Christi, Feast of, 170,
    317, 347
councils. *See* Ecumenical
    Councils
Couple-to-Couple League, 240
creation, 30–38, 44–46

creationism and evolution, 38–39
Creed, The, 3, 29. *See also* Catholic prayers, Apostles' Creed; Nicene Creed
crucifix, 99, 143
Crucifixion of Jesus, 30–31, 52–53
Crusades (A.D. 1095-1270), 266, 370
cursing. *See* blasphemy

• D •

daily Mass, 169
Dante (poet), 310, 371
Dark Ages, 221
Day of Reckoning, 31
days of recollection, 267
deacons
  authority and role, 92
  celebration of the sacraments, 133
  election as Pope, 75
  role in the church, 15, 71
death penalty. *See* capital punishment
"defrocking," 134
devil worship, 188
devil/devils
  exorcism, 100, 321–322
  Lucifer (Satan), 41, 213, 306
  man's fall from grace, 41–42
  origin of, 40–41
devotions. *See also* prayer; symbols and gestures
  about, 19–20, 261–262
  differences from Sacred Liturgy, 262
  Divine Mercy Chaplet, 272–273
  medals and scapulars, 267–268
  novenas and litanies, 263–265, 313
  pilgrimages and retreats, 266
  praying the Rosary, 268–272
  Saints, 291–294
  statues and icons, 265–266
  Way of the Cross, 262, 266, 273–274

Dianetics (Church of Scientology), 62, 188
diligence, virtue of, 218
diocese
  defined, 71
  as a faith community, 109
  as the local church, 15
  role of bishops in, 86–87
  role of cardinals in, 85
  vicars general, 88–89
  women's role in, 228
disciples. *See* apostles
Dismas (Saint), 299
dispensations, 134, 186, 319
distributive justice, 207
divine law, 176
Divine Liturgy (Orthodox), 148–149, 317
Divine Mercy Chaplet, 272–273
Divine Office. *See* Liturgy of the Hours
divine positive law, 176–177
Divine Revelation. *See* Bible; Sacred Tradition
divine worship. *See* Holy Sacrifice of the Mass
divorce, 120, 127–128, 132, 164
Docetism, 61–62
doctrine/dogma
  Assumption of Mary, 29
  celibacy as, 221, 222
  defining, 79–80
  deposit of faith, 22
  Immaculate Conception, 282
  Jesus as God-Man, 47–54
  Just War theory, 234–237
  marriage and family, 243
  papal infallibility, 77–78
  purgatory, 33, 307–309
  Universal Salvific Will of God, 116–117
  Word of God, 22–23
domestic church, 100, 242
Dominic de Guzman (Saint), 268, 304, 344
Dominican order (Order of Friars Preachers), 91–92, 344, 346, 371
donor, egg/sperm, 198, 242
drug abuse, 196
Dunne, Edmund M. (bishop), 333

• E •

Easter, 170–172, 184
Easter Vigil, 100, 121
Eastern (Oriental) Catholicism, 9, 13, 220–221
Eastern mysticism, 252, 268
Eastern Orthodox Church
  Abrahamic origins, 1
  burning of incense, 105
  celibacy, 220–221
  Code of Canon Law, 180
  communion, 119
  defined, 2
  Divine Liturgy, 148–149
  married clergy, 93
  ordination of women, 226–228
  prayers, 396–397
  public processions, 317
  sexual abuse issue, 225
  union with Rome, 9
eating meat. *See* fasting and abstaining
Ecumenical Councils
  Council of Carthage, 56
  Council of Chalcedon, 64, 79
  Council of Elvira, 221
  Council of Ephesus, 63, 79, 278
  Council of Lateran II, 221
  Council of Lateran IV, 79
  Council of Nicea, 29, 62–63, 79, 156
  Council of Nicea II, 286
  Council of Trent, 79, 166, 334, 380
  defining doctrine, 29
  papal infallibility, 79
  Vatican I, 33
Edict of Milan, 83, 115
Elizabeth (Saint, mother of John the Baptist), 231, 292
Encyclicals. *See* papal documents
envy, sin of, 213–214
Epiphany, 171–172
Episcopal conferences, 15
episcopal ordination and consecration, 86
error of faith or morals, 78
Eternal Law of God, 175–176

Eternal Word Television Network (EWTN), 263, 293, 336–337, 359–360
Eucharist. *See* Blessed Sacrament; Holy Eucharist
Eucharistic Liturgy. *See* Holy Sacrifice of the Mass
euthanasia, 19, 195, 219, 231–233
Evangelical Christians, 45, 108, 182, 185, 238
evil, 43, 48
Evil One (Antichrist), 44–46
evolution, theory of, 38–39
ex cathedra/ex nihilo announcements, 38, 79–80
excommunication, 138, 181–182
exorcism, 100, 321–322
Extraordinary Form of the Roman Rite. *See* Traditional Latin Mass
extraordinary ministers of communion, 119, 149, 228
Extreme Unction. *See* Anointing of the Sick

• F •

faith
about, 21–23
Bible as Word of God, 23–27
denial of (apostasy), 136
Nicene Creed and, 47
papal infallibility, 77–78
RCIA program, 72
theological virtue of, 204
unwritten Word of God, 27–33
using reason, 33–36
families/family life
Catholic doctrine on, 243
domestic church, 100, 242
marriage and, 242–243
parental responsibility, 193–194
role of the Church in, 244
Fastina Kowalska (Saint), 272
fasting and abstaining
Church precept, 17, 185
communion, 164, 184
spiritual growth, 257
substituting works of mercy for, 319

tradition of, 28, 317–319
virtue of, 217
Fatima, Portugal, 286–287, 289, 356–357
Faustina (Saint), 302
Feast days. *See* liturgical year
fertility drugs, 241–242
Fides et Ratio (John Paul II, 1998), 82
finances/financial support
almsgiving, 257
Church precept, 185–186
missionary work, 186
taxes/taxation, 207
tithing, 17, 185–196
five senses, worship and, 101–106
Flanagan, Edward (Father), 338–339
forgiveness of sin
absolution, 136–137, 141
Anointing of the Sick, 142
commutative justice, 206–207
defined in The Creed, 32
John Paul II and, 206
fornication, 196–199, 215
fortitude, virtue of, 209–210, 259
fortune telling, 188
40-hour devotion, 313–316
Francis (Saint), 93
Francis de Sales (Saint), 298
Francis of Assisi (Saint), 266, 301, 304, 344–345
Franciscan order, 91–92, 345, 371
Francisco (Saint), 357
free will
basic beliefs, 10, 36
exorcism, 100
grace and, 116
making choices, 40, 48
mortal sin and, 210–211
power of evil, 41–43, 322
sexuality and, 198
sin as result of, 210–211
free will offerings, 91
friars/brothers. *See* religious communities
fruits of the Holy Spirit, 122
Fundamentalist Christians, 185, 238
furnishings. *See* sacramental accessories

• G •

Gabriel the Archangel (Saint), 231, 275, 281, 303, 305–306
Galilei, Galileo (scientist), 381
Garden of Eden, 37, 40–43, 277–278
general confession and absolution, 139
General Intercessions, 152, 157, 249. *See also* intercessory prayer
generosity, virtue of, 217
genetics and creationism, 39
genocide, 178–179, 196
Gentiles, 26, 45, 57–59, 178
genuflection, 99
Gerard Majella (Saint), 303
Gibbons, James (cardinal), 358
gifts of the Holy Spirit, 122
gluttony, sin of, 216–217
Gnosticism, 61–62, 188
God
as Creator, 37–38
Mary as Mother, 278–279
nature of Holy Trinity, 51
proofs of, 33–36
relationship to Jesus, 53
revelations, 176–177
visualizing, 101–102
Good Friday
Catholic beliefs, 16, 44, 69, 112, 169, 315
fasting, 17, 185
public processions, 317
good habits. *See* cardinal virtues
The Gospel According to John, 54–55, 60
The Gospel According to Luke, 54–55, 57–59
The Gospel According to Mark, 54–55, 59
The Gospel According to Matthew, 54–55
Gospels
about, 27–28, 55–56
basic beliefs, 54–55
comparisons of, 56–60
concept of church, 65
as inspiration, 77–78
interpretation, 56
readings at Mass, 105–106, 152–154

grace/divine grace
  Catholic beliefs, 10
  defined, 12
  Original Sin and man's fall
    from, 41–42
  preparation for communion,
    164
  promise of redemption, 43–44
  received in state of sin,
    99–100
  sacraments as a source of,
    12, 15–16, 70, 109–110
Great Fast (Orthodox), 185
Great Schism, 369–374
greed (avarice), sin of, 217
Greek Orthodox Church, 2, 13
Gregorian chant, 106, 368
Gregory the Great (Pope), 80,
    106, 211, 367–368
Gregory VII (Pope), 221, 369
Gregory XI (Pope), 372–373
Gregory XII (Pope), 82, 374
guardian angels, 306, 394
Gutenberg Bible, 2

• *H* •

habits, good/bad. *See* cardinal
    virtues; seven deadly sins
hagiography, 293
heaven
  about, 40–41
  Catholic beliefs, 296, 297,
    304–305
  judgment at death, 44
  man's fall from grace, 41–42
  promise of redemption, 43–44
Hebrews/Hebrew people. *See*
    Judaism
Helena (Saint), 354
hell
  Catholic beliefs, 296, 307
  descent of Christ to, 31
  punishment for evil, 44
  punishment of fallen
    angels, 41
Henry VIII (king), 379
heresy. *See* Christological
    heresies
Herod Antipas (tetrarch of
    Galilee), 116, 363
Hinduism, 268

history. *See* Catholicism,
    history
Holy Days of Obligation. *See
    also* liturgical year
  burning of incense, 105
  Mass attendance, 17, 29,
    183–184
  Mass forms for, 169–170
Holy Eucharist. *See also*
    Liturgy of the Eucharist
  about, 107, 118
  consecration, 118–119, 158–159
  eligibility to receive,
    119–120, 164
  fasting, 164, 184
  First Communion, 121, 137
  genuflection, 99
  Holy Hour devotion, 251
  preparation of gifts, 157–158
  punishment for pretended
    celebration, 182
  receiving the body and
    blood, 17, 162–163
  receiving in state of sin, 137
  role in the Mass, 106
  source of grace, 12, 15–16
Holy Grail, 49
Holy Hour (devotion), 251
Holy Innocents, 116
Holy Land, 266
Holy Orders
  about, 132–133
  abuse of authority, 134
  academic and pastoral
    preparation, 133
  ordination and consecration,
    86
  ordination of women, 19,
    226–228
  removal of clergy, 134
  source of grace, 12, 15–16
  use of Chrism Oil, 88
Holy Roman Empire, 221,
    368–370
Holy Sacrifice of the Mass
  about, 145–146
  attendance, 16, 17, 147, 154,
    169, 192
  communion of saints, 147
  divine worship, 16–17
  Introductory Rites, 149–152
  Liturgy of the Eucharist,
    157–165
  Liturgy of the Word, 152–157

  rubrics, liturgical, 99
  Scripture, 105–106
  Sunday worship, 147
  unifying ritual, 148
  women's role in, 228
Holy Saturday, 100
Holy See. *See* Vatican
    (Holy See)
holy sites, 266
Holy Spirit
  defined in The Creed, 32
  Feast of Pentecost, 122, 172
  Immaculate Conception, 231
  inspiration as gift, 54, 78
  seven gifts, 122
  twelve fruits, 122
  visualizing, 101–102
Holy Thursday, 16, 88
Holy Trinity, 11, 32, 51, 99,
    101–102
holy water, 99–100, 104, 144
Holy Week, 88
home. *See* families/family life
Homily, 106, 154
homosexuality, 19, 197, 243
hope, virtue of, 204
horoscopes (astrology), 188
human cloning, 242
human life, origins, 38–40
human positive law, 178–182
human sexuality
  contraception, 238–239
  artificial insemination, 193
  lust, sin of, 214–215
  marriage and, 196–197
  Natural Family Planning
    (NFP), 127, 197–198
  same-sex marriage, 194
  sex outside of marriage,
    198–199
  sexual abuse, 225–226
humility, virtue of, 213
The Hunchback of Notre Dame
    (Hugo), 358

• *I* •

icons. *See* statues and icons
idolatry, 20, 159, 188, 189, 202,
    213, 265, 277, 293–294
Ignatius of Loyola (Saint), 304,
    347–348

Immaculate Conception. *See also* Virgin Mary
    appearance of, 289
    conception of Jesus, 231
    free from sin, 280–284
    Holy Day, 169–170
    infallibity of, 80, 348
Immaculate Heart of Mary, 286–287
immortal/immortality
    angelic life, 36
    creation of soul, 229–230, 241
    creationism and evolution, 38–39
    man's fall from grace, 41–42
    resurrection, 46
    soul as, 279, 282, 304
imperfect contrition, 140
Incarnation of Christ, 30, 156, 281
indulgences, 251, 376–377
infallibility. *See* pope/papal authority
infant baptism, 110–111
Innocent III (Pope), 372
INRI (*Jesus Nazarenus Rex Iudaeorum*), 53
intelligent design, 38–39
International Commission on English in the Liturgy (ICEL), 168
intercessory prayer, 189, 254, 263, 264, 265–266, 294–296. *See also* General Intercessions
involuntary laicization, 134
Irenaeus (Saint), 56
Islam
    Abrahamic origins, 1
    Battle of Poitiers, 368
    birth of Muhammad, 368
    monotheism, 11, 51
    pilgrimages, 266
    prayer beads, 268
    sexual abuse issue, 225

• J •

Jacinta (Saint), 357
James (apostle), 293
Januarius (Saint), 301, 303
jealousy, sin of, 214
Jerome (Saint), 45, 56, 194

Jesuits, 91–92, 304, 347–348, 380
Jesus Christ
    baptism of, 171–172
    basic beliefs, 47–48
    brothers and sisters, 50–51, 284–285
    celibacy of, 222
    founder of the Church, 13, 65–66
    Gospel record of, 27–28
    heresies, 60–64
    human/divine nature, 30, 48–54, 79, 276
    Lamb of God, 56, 162
    marriage of, 28, 49–50
    Messiah, 14, 32, 52
    mission on earth, 69
    power to forgive sins, 135
    relationship to God, 53
    symbolism, 103
    visualizing, 101–102
Jews. *See* Judaism
Joachim (Saint, father of Mary), 275
Joan (Pope), 83
John (apostle, Saint), 28, 50–51, 54–55, 60, 103, 293, 365
John II (Pope), 77
John Nepomucene (Saint), 138
John Neumann (Saint), 314
John of the Cross (Saint), 213
John Paul I (Pope), 77, 334, 388
John Paul II (Pope, Saint), 74, 77, 81, 82, 84, 168, 192, 225, 227, 233, 244, 271, 283, 303, 332, 333–334, 356–357, 389
John the Baptist (prophet), 56, 162, 172, 231
John Vianney (Saint), 139
John XXIII (Pope), 77, 165, 334, 374, 388
Josemaría Escrivá (Saint), 298, 302
Joseph (Saint, husband of Virgin Mary), 50, 82, 231, 241, 275, 298, 326
Joseph of Cupertino (Saint), 301
Juan Diego (Saint), 302
Judaism
    Abrahamic origin, 1, 50, 57
    books of Bible, 26–27
    burning of incense, 105
    death of Jesus, 31

fasting, 318
monotheism, 11, 51, 101
Sabbath day, 147
Second Coming of Christ, 45
sexual abuse issue, 225
Ten Commandments, 176, 187
Judas (apostle), 82
Jude (Saint), 263, 342–343
judgment. *See* Last Judgment
Judgment Day, 31
Julius II (Pope), 376–377
Just War Doctrine, 234–237
justice, virtue of, 206–208, 259

• K •

Kennedy, John F. (politician), 337–338
kindness and meekness, virtue of, 214
King James Bible, 24, 27, 50
Knights Templar, 49
knowledge and choices, 40–43, 48, 64

• L •

La Divina Commedia (Dante), 310, 371
laicization, 134
laity
    Body of Christ, 66–67
    communion minister, 119
    election as Pope, 75
    opportunities to serve, 75
    pastoral associate, 89
Lamb of God, 56
Last Judgment, 31, 44–46
Last Rites. *See* Anointing of the Sick
Last Supper
    folklore/legend, 49, 263
    Mass as reenactment, 148
    transubstantiation, 160
Latin (language)
    official language, 2, 166, 369
    translation of Bible, 45, 56, 194
    translation of Roman Missal, 167–168
    Tridentine Mass, 81, 166

Latin (Western) Catholicism, 9, 13, 98
  burning of incense, 105
  communion, 119
  Vatican II, 165–167
Latin For Dummies (Hull, Perkins, and Barr), 2
Latin Vulgate Bible, 45, 56, 194
law. *See* Canon law; Church law; precepts of the Church; Ten Commandments
Lazarus (friend of Jesus), 48, 49, 51, 296
Lectio Divina (Holy Reading), 252
Lectionary, 153–154
Lent
  ashes and palms, 20, 319–320
  fasting and abstaining, 17, 185, 317–319
  liturgical year, 172
  special Lenten rites, 256
  stations of the cross, 273–274
Leo (Pope), 369
Leo the Great (Saint), 366
Leo X (Pope), 377
Leo XIII (Pope), 81, 349
Lewis, C. S. (author), 339
Life is Worth Living (TV program), 336
Limbo (for unbaptized babies), 111
Linus (Pope), 66
liturgical year (Church calendar). *See also* Holy Days of Obligation
cycles, 171–172, 323–325
  Feast of Candlemas, 326
  Feast of Christ the King, 171
  Feast of Corpus Christi, 170, 317, 347
  Feast of Our Lady of Guadalupe, 328
  Feast of Pentecost, 122, 172, 263, 280
  Feast of St. Anthony of Padua, 327
  Feast of St. Blaise, 104, 321, 326
  Feast of St. Joseph, 326–327
  Feast of St. Patrick, 326
  Feast of St. Thérèse of Lisieux, 327–328
  Feast of the Epiphany, 325
  Marian Feasts, 327

Sanctoral cycle, 303–304, 324
  special solemnities, 151, 156, 170–171
  Temporal cycle, 171–172, 324
Liturgy of the Catechumens (Eastern Orthodox), 149
Liturgy of the Eucharist (Mass), 157–165. *See also* Holy Eucharist
Liturgy of the Faithful (Orthodox), 149
Liturgy of the Hours, 253–254, 323
Liturgy of the Word (Mass), 149–157
Lord's Prayer. *See* Catholic prayers
Lost Books of the Bible, 27
Louis VII (king), 357
Lourdes. *See* churches
love (charity), virtue of, 204
Luciani, Albino. *See* John Paul I
Lucifer (Satan). *See* devil/ devils
Lucy Filippini (Saint), 93
Luke (disciple of Jesus, Saint), 28, 54–55, 57–59, 268, 354
Lumen Gentium (Dogmatic Constitution on the Church), 180
lust, sin of, 214–215
Luther, Martin (theologian), 27, 201, 377–378
Lutheran Church, 201–202
lying and false oaths, 191, 199–201

• *M* •

magic, white/black, 188
Magisterium. *See also* pope/ papal authority
authority, 68, 70–71
  Creed as summation, 156
defined, 3
Extraordinary Magisterium, 78–80
interpretation of Scripture, 25
Ordinary Magisterium, 80–82
role of the Church, 32
Margaret Clitherow (Saint), 224
Marian devotions, 275, 285–287, 327

Marian shrines and apparitions, 12, 287–290
Mariolatry, 277
Mark (disciple of Jesus), 28, 54–55, 59
marks of the Church, 67–68
marriage. *See also* Matrimony
  Church as Bride of Christ, 225
  compared to Matrimony, 126
  contraception, 238–239
  dispensions, 134
  divorce/remarriage, 120
  marriage of Jesus, 28, 49–50
  to a non-Catholic outside the church, 186
  priests and deacons, 92–93, 225
  same-sex marriage, 194, 243
  sex outside of, 197
  voluntary laicization, 134
  wedding etiquette and planning, 128, 131
  wedding followed by convalidation, 131–132
  wedding with Mass, 129–130
  wedding without Mass, 130
Martel, Charles (politician), 368
Martin V (Pope), 374
martyrs/martyrdom
  baptism by blood, 115–116
  beatification, 300
  grace as inspiration, 12
  priests as, 224
  Roman persecutions, 365
Mary (mother of James), 285
Mary (mother of Jesus). *See* Virgin Mary
Mary and Martha (friends of Jesus), 49
Mary Magdalene (Saint, disciple of Jesus), 49, 293
Mass. *See also* Holy Sacrifice of the Mass; Ordinary Form of the Roman Rite; Traditional Latin Mass
communal prayer, 253–254
  Feast days, 171
  holy days, 169–170
  simple celebrations, 170
  solemn celebrations, 171
  weekday, 169
Mass of Anointing, 143
Mass of the Oils (Chrism Mass), 87–88, 105

masturbation, 197
Matrimony. *See also* marriage
    about the sacrament, 125
    annulments, 127, 132
    Church precept, 18, 186
    covenant with God, 198
    Pre-Cana preparation,
        127, 186
    source of grace, 12, 15–16
    validity of the union, 126–129,
        131–132
    as vocation, 126–127
    woman's role in, 228
Matthew (apostle), 28, 54–55,
    57–59
May Crowning (Marian
    devotion), 285–286, 327
meat, abstaining, 20, 185
medals and scapulars,
    267–268, 289
meditation and contemplation,
    252–253, 271–272
Messiah. *See* Jesus Christ
Michael the Archangel (Saint),
    41, 213, 268, 303, 305–306,
    322
miracles
    apparitions, 287–290
    Assumption of Mary, 284
    Fatima, 356
    healings, 302
    by Jesus, 51, 346
    Lourdes, 348–349
    through the saints, 292,
        300–301
    water into wine, 49, 130, 264
Missal of John XXIII (1962), 166
*Missale Romanum. See Roman
    Missals*
missionary activities
    Church precept, 18, 186
    clergy commitment, 224
    immigration to America, 385
    Society for Propagation of
        Faith, 336
Monica (Saint), 293
monks/monasteries. *See*
    religious communities
Monophysitism, 63–64
monotheism, 11, 188
Montini, Giovanni. *See* Paul VI
morality. *See* cardinal virtues;
    seven deadly sins

mortal sin. *See also* Penance;
    seven deadly sins
    avoiding, 18
    confession of, 184–185
    missing Mass, 183–184, 192
Moses (prophet), 101, 105, 176
Mother Angelica (Our Lady
    of the Holy Angels), 293,
    336–337, 359–360
Mother of Jesus. *See*
    Virgin Mary
Mother Teresa of Calcutta
    (Saint), 32, 93, 298,
    331–332
Muhammad (prophet), 368
Muslims. *See* Islam
Mysteries of the Rosary,
    271–272
Mystery of Faith, 161
Mystical Body of Christ
    benefits of belonging, 72
    Church as, 13–14, 66–68
    Mary as Mother of, 280
    role of sacraments, 70

• N •

National Council of Catholic
    Men, 335
National Padre Pio Center, 354
National Shrine of Our Lady of
    Czestochowa, 355
nationalism, 194
Natural Family Planning (NFP)
    about, 237
    artificial contraception,
        238–239
    human sexuality, 197–198
    infertility issues, 241–242
    practice of, 239–240
    premarital instruction, 127
natural moral law
    abortion and, 228
    basic Catholic beliefs, 10
    civil law and, 178–179
    Just War Doctrine, 234–237
    rules for behavior, 18
    story of Cain and Abel,
        177–178, 196
    as unwritten law, 178
Nazi Germany, violation of
    moral law, 178–179
neo-Gnosticism, 62

Nestorianism, 63
New Age spirituality, 62, 188
new Mass. *See* Ordinary Form
    of the Roman Rite
New Testament
    affirmation of celibacy, 222
    Books of Bible, 27, 56
    fasting, 318
    Jesus Christ as Lord, 48
    readings at Mass, 105–106,
        152–154
Nicene Creed. *See also*
    Catholic prayers
    about, 29, 62–63
    pillar of Catholic faith, 11
    as profession of faith, 47
    Roman Missal, 156
    use at Mass, 154–156
non-Catholics and the Church
    Catholics at non-Catholic
        services, 184, 192
    conversions, 256
    Lord's Prayer, 162
    marrying a Catholic,
        126–127, 186
    RCIA program, 186
    receiving communion,
        120, 164
    veneration of Mary and the
        Saints, 275, 291, 295
    wedding etiquette, 131
novenas and litanies,
    263–265, 313
Novus Ordo (Vatican II Mass),
    166, 390
nuclear weapons, 236–237
numerology, 188
nuns and religious sisters. *See*
    religious communities
Nuptial Mass (wedding Mass),
    129–130

• O •

obedience
    Jesuit loyalty to Pope, 343
    vows, 67, 91, 94, 348, 366
    vox populi/vox Dei, 219
occult, 188
Oil of Catechumens, 88, 105,
    113
Oil of the Sick, 88, 105, 143

old Mass. *See* Traditional Latin Mass
Old Testament. *See also* Bible
burning of incense, 105
fasting, 318
identifying God, 48
as oral history, 25–26
readings at Mass, 105–106, 152–154
Septuagint, 26–27
story of Cain and Abel, 177–178
Ten Commandments, 176–177
Opus Dei, 298
Ordinary Form of the Roman Rite (*Novus Ordo*, Vatican II Mass), 166, 390
ordination. *See also* Holy Orders
bishops, 86
married clergy, 93
permanent deacons, 92
priests and deacons, 86
transitional deacons, 92
use of Chrism Oil, 105
of women, 19, 81
Oriental (Eastern) Catholicism, 9, 13
Original Sin. *See also* Immaculate Conception; sin
baptism as washing away, 109–110
basic Catholic beliefs, 37
concupiscence, 43, 215
man's fall from grace, 41–42
Mary, free from, 280–284
orthodox Christianity, 62. *See also* Eastern Orthodox Church
Orthodoxy (Chesterton), 339

● *p* ●

Pacelli, Eugenio. *See* Pius XII
Padre Pio. *See* Pio of Pietrelcina
paganism, 101, 188
Palm Sunday, 104, 316, 317, 320–321

papal documents
authority of, 80–81
Deus Caritas Est (Benedict XVI), 82
encyclicals, 81–82
Evangelium Vitae (John Paul II, 1995), 82
Fides et Ratio (John Paul II), 82
Gospel of Life (John Paul II), 388
Humanae Vitae (Paul VI), 81, 238, 388
Laborem Exercens (John Paul II), 82
Marialis Cultus (Paul VI), 262
Ordinatio Sacerdotalis (John Paul II), 227
Pastores Dabo Vobis (John Paul II), 225
Rerum Novarum (Leo XIII), 81
Summorum Pontificum (Benedict XVI), 390
Veritatis Splendor (John Paul II), 82
Papal offices, 88
Papal States, 83–84. *See also* Vatican City
parents/parenthood. *See* families/family life
parish priests (pastors). *See* clergy; priests
parishes
cemeteries, 90
defined, 71
as a faith community, 109
Mass and penance services, 139, 169
role as local church, 16
women's role in, 228
parochial schools, 90
parochial vicar, 15, 89
Passion of Christ (crucifixion)
Mass as link to, 148
Sorrowful Mysteries, 271–272
vestment colors, 104
Way of the Cross, 273–274
pastoral associates, 228
patience, virtue of, 216
Patrick (Saint), 303, 326
patriotism, 194
Paul the Apostle (Saint), 13, 48, 66–67, 178, 292, 365

Paul VI (Pope), 77, 81, 165, 167, 238, 262, 333–334
pedophilia, 197, 225
Pelagius (Pope), 367
Penance (Confession)
about, 135–136
absolution, 136–137, 141
annual requirement, 184–185
assigned penance, 141
First Communion, 121, 137
forgiveness from sin, 32
precept of the Church, 17
Seal of Confession, 137–138, 200
source of grace, 12, 15–16
spiritual growth, 257
true contrition, 140–141
types of, 138–139
Pentecost, Feast of, 122, 172, 263, 280
Peregrine (Saint), 263
perfect act of contrition, 137
perfect contrition, 140, 248–249
permanent deacons, 89, 92
Perpetual Adoration, 313–316
personal/private property
living the Commandments, 199
restitution for stealing, 207
social justice, 208
Peter (Saint)
about the life of, 341–342
crucifixion, 365
first pope, 12, 13, 68, 82–83, 334
foundation of the Church, 65–66, 71
as sinful man, 293
source of the Gospels, 28
symbolism, 103
Peter Celestine V (Pope), 82
petition, prayer as, 249, 294. *See also* General Intercessions
Philip Neri (Saint), 314
physical abuse, 195–196
Pilate, Pontius (Roman governor), 30–31, 53
pilgrimages and retreats, 266
pillars of Catholic faith, 3
Pio of Pietrelcina (Saint), 301, 302, 350, 354
Pius V (Saint), 350
Pius IX (Pope), 282, 334, 348

Pius X (Pope), 184, 358
Pius XI (Pope), 84, 336, 350
Pius XII (Pope), 29, 77, 332, 333, 387
Plato (philosopher), 59
political correctness, 205
politics
  birth rate, 239
  celibacy, 221–222
  collapse of the Soviet Union, 356
  election of Catholics to presidency, 337–338
  patriotism and nationalism, 194
polytheism, 188
Pontian (Pope), 82
pope/papal authority. *See also individual popes by name;* Vatican (Holy See)
  about the titles for, 74
  apostolic succession, 66, 68, 82–83
  appointment of cardinals, 74
  authority, 68, 71–72, 182
  Avignon papacy, 372–374
  bishop of Rome, 9, 86
  coronation ceremony, 80
  election procedure, 75–77
  infallibility, 70–71, 300, 385–386
  symbols of, 75, 80
  teaching authority, 71
  Vicar of Christ, 14–15, 66
pornography, 197
poverty, vow of, 67, 91, 94, 343, 348, 366
practicing Catholic, 183–186
prayer. *See also* Catholic prayers; devotions
  about, 152, 248–249, 294
  communal prayer, 253–254
  formal prayer, 250
  intercessory prayer, 189–190
  private prayer, 251–253
  relationship with God, 247–248
  spontaneous prayer, 249–250
prayer beads, 268
prayer books, 250
Prayers of the Faithful, 157
Pre-Cana preparation, 127, 186

precepts of the Church
  about, 17–18
  confession, 184–185
  fasting and abstinence, 185
  marriage laws, 186
  Mass attendance, 183–184
  missionary works, 186
  receiving Eucharist, 184
  supporting the Church, 185–186
pregnancy. *See* abortion; birth control; conception; Natural Family Planning
pride, sin of, 212–213
priests (presbyters)
  authority and role, 70–71
  celebration of the sacraments, 133
  as confessors, 138–139
  election as Pope, 75
  martyrdom, 224
  meaning of "Father," 224
  ordination of women, 19, 226–228
  pastoral preparation, 133
  role in local church, 15
  sexual abuse, 225–226
  vocation crisis, 220, 223
private confession, 138–139
private sin, 136
Profession of Faith. *See* Nicene Creed
prostitution, 196–199
Protestant Reformation
  causes of, 375–377
  Counter Reformation, 380–381
  key figures of, 377–380
  persecution of priests, 224
Protestantism
  Abrahamic origins, 1
  Bible as revelation, 24–25
  Books of the Bible, 27
  contraception, 238
  open communion, 120
  Ten Commandments, 201–202
  tithing, 185
  validity of baptism, 108
  women as ministers, 226
prudence, virtue of, 204–206, 258
Pseudepigrapha, 27
psychic readings, 188

public procession, 316–317
punishment, Canon law violations, 181–182
purgatory
  beliefs, 33, 307–309
  defined, 31
  indulgences, 251
  purification from sin, 44
  Second Coming of Christ, 46

quid pro quo, 206–207

Raccolta (prayer book), 251
racial segregation, 178–179
radio programs. *See* television and radio
rape and incest, 197, 228, 230
Raphael the Archangel (Saint), 303, 305–306
rapture ("being taken up"), 44–46
Ratzinger, Josef. *See* Benedict XVI
reason, faith through, 33–36
Reconciliation, 138. *See also* Penance
Redeemer, Jesus Christ as, 52–53
reincarnation, 33
religious communities
  Benedictines, 91–92, 366–367
  Carmelite Order, 92, 253, 268, 349–350, 357, 383
  communal prayer, 253–254
  consecrated religious, 91–94
  contemplatives, 253
  feast days, 304
  Franciscans, 91–92, 345, 371
  Friars Minor Capuchin, 350
  immigration to America, 384–385
  Missionaries of Charity, 93, 94, 332
  monasticism, 366–367

Order of Friars Minor, 91–92, 345, 371
Order of Friars Preachers, 344, 346, 371
pastoral associates, 228
Poor Clares, 93, 253, 336
role in Body of Christ, 66–67
Sisters of Loreto, 331–332
Sisters of Notre Dame, 349
Society of Jesus, 347–348
religious education (CCD), 121–122, 185–186
religious objects. *See* sacramental accessories
religious processions, 316–317
remarriage, 120
resurrection
    as Catholic belief, 33, 46
    of Christ, 135, 148, 161, 171, 280, 315
    Glorious Mysteries, 272
    Second Coming of Christ, 46
revelation. *See* Book of Revelation
revenge, sin of, 215–216
rhythm method, 239–240
Rite of Christian Initiation for Adults (RCIA), 72, 185–186
Rite of Marriage Outside of Mass, 130
rites and rituals, 98
Rizzo, Rita Antoinette. *See* Mother Angelica
Roman Catholic Church (Roman Rite). *See* Latin (Western) Catholicism
Roman Curia, 84–85
Roman Missal (Missal of John XXIII), 166
Roman Missal of the Second Vatican Council, 167
Roman Missal, Second Edition, 167–168
Roman Missal, Third Edition
    about changes, 145, 167
    background, 167–168
    ite missa est, 165
    Mystery of Faith, 161
    Nicene Creed, 156
    summary of changes, 168
    translations, 166
    use at Mass, 149
Roman Ritual, 98

Rome. *See also* Catholicism, history; Vatican
    about churches, 351–353
    Angelicum University, 333, 335
    Basilica of St. John Lateran, 71, 87
    Basilica of St. Peter, 71, 87, 352
    fall of Roman Empire, 221
    persecution of Christians, 12, 60–61, 115–116
    pope as bishop, 71, 87
Roncalli, Angelo. *See* John XXIII
Rosary, praying the, 104, 262, 268–272
rubrics (liturgical laws), 99
The Rule (*regula*), 91
Russian Orthodox Church, 2, 13

• S •

Sabbath (day of worship), 147, 191
Sacrament of Reconciliation. *See* Penance
sacramental accessories.
    See also symbols and gestures; vestments and clothing
    altar/altar rail, 103, 163
    baptismal font, 109
    chalice, 76, 100, 119, 157–158
    holy water font, 100
    monstrance, 99, 313, 337
    paintings and images, 101–102
    relics, 296
    stained glass windows, 102
    statues and icons, 16, 265–266, 293–294
    tabernacle, 99, 159
    thurible (censor), 153
Sacramentary (Mass book), 167
Sacraments, The. *See also* *specific sacraments*
    authority of clergy, 133
    elements of, 226–227
    physical symbols, 16
    pillar of faith, 3, 11
    rites and rituals, 98
    as source of grace, 10, 70

spiritual development, 15
using the senses, 103–104
women's role in, 228
Sacraments of Initiation. *See* Baptism; Confirmation; Holy Eucharist
sacred art. *See* architecture and art; sacramental accessories
sacred authors, 54
Sacred Chrism (Chrism Oil), 88
sacred literature. *See* Bible; Gospels
sacred liturgy. *See* Holy Sacrifice of the Mass
sacred music, 16, 106, 368
Sacred Scripture. *See* Bible; Gospels; Lectionary
Sacred Tradition. *See also* Catholic traditions
    Assumption of Mary, 12, 284
    Creed in, 29–33
    defined, 28–29
    Gospels, 27–28
    human nature of Jesus, 48–51
    life of Christ, 28
    location of hell, 307
    ordination of women, 226–228
    unwritten word, 27
Sacrifice of the Mass. *See* Holy Eucharist; Holy Sacrifice of the Mass
sacrilege, 137, 164, 184–185, 189, 190–191
saints of the Church. *See also* *specific saints by name*
    about the lives of, 341
    beatification and canonization, 292, 296–303
    communion of saints, 304–310
    devotions to, 291–294
    feast days, 303–304
    intercessions, 294–296
    veneration, 20, 189–190, 291
salvation
    Bible as history, 25
    Christ as Redeemer, 14
    grace and, 12, 116–117
    Protestantism and, 380
    sacraments as path to, 70
    sign of the cross as reaffirmation, 99

same-sex marriage, 194, 243
sanctifying grace. *See* grace/
   divine grace
Sapieha, Adam Stefan
   (cardinal), 333
Saturday, Mass attendance,
   192
Savior. *See* Messiah
schisms, 369, 373–374
Scripture (written Word of
   God). *See* Bible
Seal of Confession, 136,
   137–138, 200
Second Coming of Christ, 31,
   44–46
Second Vatican Council. *See*
   Vatican II
self-control. *See* cardinal
   virtues
seminary/seminarians
   celibacy and marriage, 223
   early history, 380, 383–384
   establishment in U.S., 385
   pastoral and academic
      preparation, 89, 133
   post-WWII growth, 388
   transitional deacons, 92
Septuagint (Old Testament),
   26–27, 50
Serbian Orthodox Church, 2
Sergius IV (Pope), 77
sermon. *See* Homily
Sermon on the Mount, 27–28,
   57–58, 277
Seton, Elizabeth Ann Bailey
   (Saint), 385
seven conquering virtues, 211
   chastity, 215
   diligence, 218
   fasting and abstinence, 217
   generosity, 217
   humility, 213
   kindness/meekness, 214
   patience, 216
seven deadly sins
   about, 210–211
   anger, 215–216
   envy, 213–214
   gluttony, 216–217
   greed, 217
   lust, 214–215

pride, 212–213
sloth, 217–218
Seven Sacraments, 4, 70. *See
   also* Sacraments, The;
   specific sacraments
sexual abuse, 225–226
sexuality. *See* human sexuality
Shahan, Thomas J. (bishop),
   358
Sheen, Fulton J. (bishop), 117,
   335–336
Sheen, Martin (actor), 336
shrines and apparitions
   Marian shrines and
      apparitions, 287–289
   National Shrine of Our Lady
      of Czestochowa, 355
   Shrine of Our Lady of Fatima,
      356–357
   Shrine of the Most Blessed
      Sacrament, 103, 337,
      359–360
"sick call set" crucifix, 143
sign of peace, 161–162
sign of the cross, 98–99
Simon Stock (Saint), 268
sin. *See also* Original Sin;
   Penance; sacrilege; Ten
   Commandments
   about, 10
   atonement for, 52–53
   communion preparation, 164
   confession of, 184–185
   forgiveness, 32
   grace in state of, 99–100
   human nature of Jesus, 48–49
   judgment at death, 44
   missing Mass as, 16
   purgatory, 307–309
   redemption, 43–44
   separation from God, 42
   seven deadly sins, 210–218
   spiritual health and, 18
sloth, sin of, 217–218
Smith, Alfred E. (politician), 338
social justice, 208
Social Security, 239
societas perfects (perfect
   society), 72
Society for the Propagation of
   Faith, 336

Society of Jesus. *See* Jesuits
Socrates (philosopher), 59
Solemnities. *See* Holy Days of
   Obligation; liturgical year
Sorrowful Mysteries, 271–272
spiritism, 188
spiritual growth/development
   about the stages, 12, 256
   avoiding sin, 258–259
   self-denial, 256–258
   unity with God, 259–260
spiritual healing. *See* Anointing
   of the Sick; Penance
Spiritual Works of Mercy. *See*
   works of mercy
St. Patrick's' Cathedral (New
   York City), 102
stations of the cross. *See* Way
   of the Cross
statues and icons. *See*
   sacramental accessories
stealing, 199, 207
Stephen (Saint), 365
stigmata, 301, 345, 350, 354
suicide, 195
Sully, Maurice de (bishop), 357
Summa Theologica (Aquinas),
   33–36, 306, 346
Sunday ("Day of the Lord")
   attendance at non-Catholic
      services, 184
   day of worship, 147
   honoring God, 191–192
   Mass attendance, 16, 17,
      183–184, 192
   televised Mass, 154
   weekday Mass, 169
symbols and gestures. *See also*
   devotions; sacramental
   accessories
   blessing religious items,
      319–320
   crucifix, 99, 143
   genuflection, 99
   holy water, 99–100
   incense, 104–105, 153
   kneeling, 266
   sign of the cross, 98–99
Synoptic Gospels, 60

• T •

taxes/taxation. *See* finances/financial support
television and radio
  Catholic Hour (NBC radio program), 335
  Eternal Word Television Network, 263, 293, 336–337, 359–360
  Life is Worth Living (TV program), 336
  televised Mass, 154
temperance, virtue of, 208–209, 259
Ten Commandments
  first, 188–190
  second, 190–191
  third, 191–192
  fourth, 193–194
  fifth, 194–196
  sixth, 196–199
  seventh, 199
  eighth, 199–201
  ninth, 196–199
  tenth, 199
  comparison to Protestant version, 201–202
  Judaism and, 316
  love of God, 188–192
  love of neighbor, 193–201
  natural moral law and, 177–179
  pillar of faith, 187
  revelation by God, 176–177
Teresa of Avila (Saint), 213, 301
terrorism, 195, 234
thanksgiving, prayer as, 249, 294
theological virtues, 204
Thérèse of Lisieux (Saint, the Little Flower), 298, 303–304, 327–328, 349–350
Thomas (apostle), 293
Thomas Aquinas (Saint), 21, 33–36, 53, 148, 175, 233, 234, 255, 282, 346–347, 371
tithing. *See* finances/financial support
Tolkien, John R. R. (author), 339
Traditional Latin Mass (Tridentine Mass), 81, 166, 390
transmutation, 38
transubstantiation, 79, 106, 159, 160
truth, using reason, 33–36

• U •

Universal Catechism. *See Catechism of the Catholic Church*
Universal Church, 13, 68, 71, 166
Universal Salvific Will of God, 116–117
unwritten law. *See* natural moral law
unwritten Word of God. *See* Sacred Tradition
Urban VI (Pope), 373
U.S. Conference of Catholic Bishops, 154, 168

• V •

Vatican (Holy See), 15, 75, 84–85. *See also* College of Cardinals; Magisterium; pope/papal authority
Vatican City, 12, 71, 83–84, 87
Vatican I (1869-1879), 33, 79, 385–386
Vatican II (1962-1965)
  about the goals of, 165
  Dogmatic Constitution on the Church, 180
  reception of both bread and wine, 167
  sacred traditions, 29
  vernacular languages, 166
Vatican Radio, 84
venial sin, 18, 135, 140, 211
vernacular languages, 166
vestments and clothing.
  See also sacramental accessories
  Advent, 171–172
  cassock, 88–89
  chasuble, cope, humeral veil, 313
  ferraiolone (silk cape), 89
  habits, 91, 94
  papal crown, 80
  symbols/colors, 102, 104
Viaticum, 144
vicars general, 88–89
vices. *See* seven deadly sins
Vigil Mass (Saturday), 192
Virgin Mary. *See also* Immaculate Conception; Rosary, praying the
  Assumption into heaven, 29, 284
  "Black Madonna of Czestochowa," 288, 354–355
  blessing of marriage, 130
  Catholic beliefs, 278–285
  devotions to, 285–287
  holy days, 169–170
  marriage and children, 50–51
  Mother of God, 79
  Our Lady of Fatima, 356–357
  role in redemption, 44
  shrines and apparitions, 12, 287–290
  source of the Gospels, 28
  various names for, 275
  veneration of, 20, 189–190, 275–278
virtue. *See* cardinal virtues; seven conquering virtues
visions/visionaries. *See* apparitions and visions
in vitro fertilization (IVF), 198, 241–242
vocations, 91–94, 126, 186, 220, 223
voluntary laicization, 134
vow of celibacy, 19, 28, 93, 134, 220–226
vow of poverty, chastity, and obedience, 67, 91, 94, 343, 348, 366
vox populi and *vox Dei*, 219
Vulgate Bible, 45, 56, 194

• W •

war. *See* Just War Doctrine
war crimes, 177–178, 179, 196, 234
Way of the Cross, 262, 266, 273–274
weapons of mass destruction (WMD), 236–237

websites
  Couple-to-Couple League, 240
  Eternal Word Television
    Network, 263, 337
  U.S. Conference of Catholic
    Bishops, 154
weddings. *See* marriage;
  Matrimony
weekday/daily Mass, 169
Wenceslaus IV (king), 138
Western (Latin) Catholicism,
  9, 13
Whore of Babylon (accomplice
  of Antichrist), 46
Wiley & Sons, Inc.
  The Bible For Dummies
    (Geoghegan and
    Homan), 25

Catholic Mass For Dummies
  (Trigilio, Brighenti and
  Cafone), 145
Latin For Dummies (Hull,
  Perkins, and Barr), 2
witchcraft and sorcery, 188
Wojtyla, Karol Józef. *See* John
  Paul II
women
  myth of Pope Joan, 83
  ordination of, 19, 81, 226–228
  religious communities, 91–94
Word of God. *See also* Bible
  about use of the term, 24
  Church teachings, 69
  Gospels as, 56–60
  Homily as reflection, 154
  interpretation of, 25

Jesus Christ as, 60
readings at Mass, 105–106
relationship with, 247–250
role in Holy Mass, 16,
  105–106, 154, 165
translations, 378
written and unwritten, 23
Work of God (*Opus Dei*), 298
works of mercy, 69, 141, 172,
  185, 258, 319
World Youth Days, 334